JOURNAL FOR THE STUDY OF THE OLD TESTAMENT
SUPPLEMENT SERIES

74

Editors
David J A Clines
Philip R Davies

JSOT Press
Sheffield

The Structural Analysis of Biblical and Canaanite Poetry

edited by
**Willem van der Meer
& Johannes C. de Moor**

Journal for the Study of the Old Testament
Supplement Series 74

Copyright © 1988 Sheffield Academic Press

Published by JSOT Press
JSOT Press is an imprint of
Sheffield Academic Press Ltd
The University of Sheffield
343 Fulwood Road
Sheffield S10 3BP
England

Printed in Great Britain
by Billing & Sons Ltd
Worcester

British Library Cataloguing in Publication Data

The structural analysis of biblical and
    canaanite poetry.—(Journal for
the study of the Old Testament supplement series)
1. Poetry in Hebrew, to 700 - Critical Studies
I. Meer, Willem van der   II. Moor,
Johannes C. de
892.4′11′09

ISSN 0309-0787
ISBN 1-85075-194-3

Contents

Preface

This volume is intended as an introduction to a new method of structural analysis of biblical and Canaanite poetry. In its initial form the method was developed by Pieter van der Lugt in his Dutch dissertation *Strofische structuren in de bijbels-hebreeuwse poëzie*, written under the guidance of Johannes de Moor who himself contributed a number of widely scattered articles on the subject. A growing number of enthusiastic supporters, most of them alumni of the Kampen School of Theology, demonstrated the usefulness of the method in various studies published in Dutch. Because we realize that this way of presenting a new approach might not succeed in eliciting the international discussion we believe it deserves, we decided to present our method to a wider audience in the form of a collection of studies ranging from Ugarit to the New Testament, although the main emphasis is on the Old Testament.

Our approach involves ten relatively simple steps:

1. Provisional delimitation of the passage to be analysed on the basis of the $p^e t \bar{u} h \bar{o} t$ and $s^e t \bar{u} m \bar{o} t$ (very ancient divisions of the text) as well as the content.

2. Translation and textual criticism.

3. Provisional division of the text into poetical verses. Here we make use of the Massoretic accents which often, though by no means always, prove to be a more reliable guide than is generally assumed. Of course the internal parallelism between cola belonging to the same verse also helps us to establish the most likely colometry. Usually we check, with the help of a computer, whether a parallel pair is attested elsewhere. Some of us supplement this with an analysis of the rhythmical balance between cola and verse.

4. Provisional description of the content of larger portions of text within the passage. In the past this was the customary procedure to delimit 'strophes' or 'stanzas'. Comparison of a number of commentaries and translations soon reveals an astonishing lack of agreement between the various divisions proposed on this basis. Apparently delimitation on the basis of content alone is a highly subjective approach which did

viii

not help to inspire much confidence in strophic division as such. Nevertheless, content analysis is useful because it provides us with a first, be it provisional, idea of the literary structure of the unit.

5. Production of a concordance of all words, including suffixes, used in the passage.

6. Detection of markers of separation. Larger units appear to be delimited by formal separators such as vocatives, imperatives, deictic particles, syntactic constructions attracting the attention of the audience, long verses (tricola for example).

7. Just as internal parallelism binds the cola of verses together, so *external* parallelism forms the connection between the higher structural units of a North—West Semitic poem. First we try to establish which verses are bonded by this kind of parallelism to form a strophe.

8. Identification of the strophes that appear to form the next higher structural unit, which we call stanza or canticle. Again, external parallelism, often amounting to a kind of refrain, is our most important guide.

9. Identification of external parallelistic bonds between canticles forming a larger whole (sub—canto or canto).

10. Determination of the definitive form of the poem on the basis of the results attained during the preceding stages. If several possibilities seem to present themselves, the outcome of our previous work warrants the conclusion that the structure which is most regular and offers the lowest number of counter—indications (e.g. markers of separation within the body of a strophe) is probably the correct one. If no satisfactory structural division emerges, the causes may be manifold of course, but the researcher should check first of all whether the delimitation of the passage (step 1) was correct and/or whether the passage might contain redactional glosses.

The results of the work hitherto undertaken are encouraging, but much remains to be done and no doubt the method can be improved in many respects. Even at the present, fledgling stage differences of opinion do occur, as the reader of this volume will not fail to note. However, we feel that it is a considerable advance on current methods that henceforth one has a relatively objective basis for discussion.

Many people have helped us in the production of this book. To all of them we owe thanks, but we single out William Koopmans who translated or corrected most of the contributions with amazing speed.

The Editors.

FUNDAMENTALS OF UGARITIC AND HEBREW POETRY*

Marjo C.A. Korpel − Johannes C. de Moor

1. Introduction

In this study we want to elaborate a number of principles members of our research team formulated in earlier publications dealing with the structure of early North−West Semitic poetry.[1] We do not aim at giving a full overview of all phenomena that have been studied or might be studied in this connection. That would require nothing less than a series of monographs. We only want to state a few basic rules which in our opinion should be part and parcel of any serious theory on the poetry of Canaan and Israel. Since essentially the same laws appear to govern both the poetry of Ugarit and the poetry of ancient Israel, our study will lend support to the view that there existed an unbroken poetic tradition between Canaan and Israel.

2. The Foot

2.1. General

The smallest building block is the foot. *The foot is a word*

---

* Reprinted, with the publisher's permission and with minor corrections, from: *Ugarit−Forschungen*, Bd.18: Jahresband 1986, Internationales Jahrbuch für die Altertumskunde Syrien−Palästinas. Hrsg. v. Kurt Bergerhof, Manfried Dietrich, Oswald Loretz. Koproduktion mit dem Vlg. Butzon & Berker, Kevelaer, Neukirchener Verlag, Neukirchen−Vluyn 1986.
1 J.C. de Moor, 'The Art of Versification in Ugarit and Israel', I, in: Y. Avishur−J. Blau (eds.), *Studies in Bible and the Ancient Near East Presented to S.E. Loewenstamm* (Jerusalem, 1978) 119−139; II, *UF* 10 (1978) 187−217; III, *UF* 12 (1980) 311−315; 'The Poetry of the Book of Ruth', I, *Or* 53 (1984) 262−283; II, *Or* 55 (1986) 2−32. Furthermore P. van der Lugt, *Strofische structuren in de bijbels−hebreeuwse poëzie* (Kampen, 1980); studies by W. van der Meer, J. Renkema and K. Spronk appearing in the near future. We are happy to note that in many respects we find ourselves in agreement with W.G.E. Watson, *Classical Hebrew Poetry. A Guide to its Techniques* (Sheffield, 1984).

containing at least one stressed syllable. In Ugaritic poetry words
are usually defined as separate units by the word–divider which
is a small wedge, stroke or point. In Hebrew manuscripts words
are separated by spaces, just as we are accustomed to.

2.2. The smallest foot

The smallest elements identified in the ways described in the
preceding paragraph are *one–syllable words* like Ugaritic *p* =
Hebrew *ph* 'mouth', Ugaritic *l* = Hebrew *l'* 'not', Ugaritic *'al* =
Hebrew *'l* 'not' (prohibitive), Ugaritic *k* = Hebrew *ky* 'surely'.

2.3. Expansion and contraction

Already on the level of the foot we meet what appears to be a
fundamental law of ancient North–West Semitic poetry: *Within
certain limits every structural unit could be expanded or
contracted, as the singers saw fit*[2]. This law lended an enormous
flexability to this kind of poetry. Every song was a breathing
universe, adapting itself to the occasion. Simple Ugaritic
examples of this phenomenon on the level of the foot are *ln* for
l, *wn* for *w*, *km* for *k*.

All ancient Oriental poetry was meant to be sung or recited
to the accompaniment of music. This music was of a type
characterized by a so–called free rhythm.[3] This means that
stressed syllables could be combined with a considerable number
of unstressed syllables or could be drawn out at will to make
one word sound as long as a whole phrase.

Normally a foot in Ugaritic or Hebrew poetry counted one to
five syllables. However, the number was never rigidly fixed[4]
and therefore any kind of real metre is sought in vain in
ancient North–West Semitic poetry.[5] For this reason the
counting of syllables or even characters is a meaningless

---

2   In its general form this law was formulated by De Moor in FS
Loewenstamm: 1978:139.
3   Cf. De Moor, FS Loewenstamm: 1978:129–132; *UF* 10 (1978) 217.
4   De Moor, FS Loewenstamm: 1978:133ff.
5   Cf. D. Pardee, in: G.D. Young (ed.), *Ugarit in Retrospect* (Winona Lake,
1981) 113–130; J.C.de Moor, *Or* 53 (1984) 263f. (with further references).

occupation.

Nevertheless a tendency to keep the number of stressed syllables per colon approximately the same throughout fairly large portions of text can be observed. If the number of stressed syllables had to be reduced to achieve this, two or three feet could be combined to form one stressed unit. This was especially the case with particles and with genitive constructions.[6] What we have here is a kind of *enjambement* on the level of the feet, an expansion of one foot beyond its own 'territory' into that of a neighbouring foot. In medieval Hebrew manuscripts the joining of feet into one stressed unit has often been indicated by the *maqqeph*. In the tablets of Ugarit no such device has been employed. However, it may be significant that in a frequent and rather lengthy combination like *rbt 'atrt ym* 'Lady Athiratu of the Sea' the word–divider is more often than not omitted between the genitive construction.[7] This might be an indication that there too the singers were accustomed to read the two words as one stressed unit.

2.4. The largest foot

In the general law we formulated at the beginning of 2.3 we spoke of 'certain limits'. To what extent could a foot be expanded? On the basis of the evidence we collected thus far we feel confident that the foot, whether as a combination or not, *never exceeded a total of eight syllables*. As an Ugaritic example we cite *lbn 'ilm mt* (*KTU* 1.4:VI.45f. — 8 syllables) which judging from the context was probably read as one foot. For Hebrew we refer to the seven syllables in Ps. 20:6 *wbšm–'lyhnw* and the eight syllables in Ps. 69:15 *wmm'mqy–mym*.

---

6 It has long been known that this was possible in Hebrew. For Ugaritic poetry the principle was demonstrated by S.B. Parker, *UF* 6 (1974) 289; B. Margalit, *UF* 7 (1975) 294f.; De Moor, FS Loewenstamm: 1978:133ff.
7 With word–divider: *KTU* 1.4:I.14; III.29,34,38; IV.4,53. Without: 1.4: III.25,27; IV.40; V.2; 1.6:I.44,45,47,53.

3. The Colon

3.1. General

One to five feet form the next higher structural unit: the colon.[8]
Because of its average length of three words it is likely that the
colon is the unit that could be recited or sung in one breath.[9]
As with the foot it is easy to demonstrate that the Ancients
themselves regarded the colon as an important structural
element of their poetry. Several tablets from Ugarit have been
written in such a way that every physical line of text coincided
with a colon of 3 to 5 words.[10] In other cases large portions of
text have been written in colometrical form indicating that the
scribes were inclined to identify cola with lines.[11] In these cases
the length of the cola varies between 2 and 6 words.[12]
With regard to Hebrew, acrostical poems like Ps. 111 and
112 testify to the relative independence of the colon. In this
case too the cola count 2 to 5 words.[13] Medieval manuscripts
and ancient testimonies prove that the poetry of the Hebrew

---

8   In earlier publications members of our team used the term 'stichos' in
accordance with the prevailing European tradition. It is preferable, however,
to reserve this term, if it is used at all, for the verse.
Some scholars adopt the term 'hemistich' for a unit about half the length of
a colon. Cf. Watson: 1984:12. However, this so−called hemistich is evidently
not an indispensable building−block because many cola cannot be divided
into two whereas others should clearly be divided into three if we are to
adopt this principle.

9   De Moor, FS Loewenstamm: 1978:130.

10   *KTU* 1.10−11, cf. A. Herdner, *CTA*, 48,52. Lines of five words are 1.10:
II.9, 12.

11   E.g. *KTU* 1.4: IV.8−22; V.49−65; VI.1−12, 18−23; 1.6: II.21−25;
III.1−21; IV.4−12; 1.14: I.10−17, 24−32; II.29−43; III.38−42, 45−54;
IV.16−21, 44−52; 1.161: I.1−17.

12   Two words: *KTU* 1.4: VI.23; 1.14: I.13,17,28,32; III.52; IV.48,49,50,52;
1.16: I.49; VI.12, 26.
Five words: *KTU* 1.6: II.23; III.3; IV.12; 1.14: I.15. Six words: *KTU* 1.4:
VIII.15−17; 1.6: II.25.

13   Two words: Ps. 111:1a; 112:1a. If feet are counted and words connected
by the *maqqeph* are also taken as one feet 111:3a, 7b, 9b; 112:3a, 6a can be
added. Five words (disregarding the *maqqeph*): 112:1b.

Bible was often written in colometrical form.[14] A fragmentary Psalm scroll from the fourth cave of Qumran exhibits the same writing convention.[15]

Nevertheless the colometrical form of ancient tradition cannot always be trusted. Because in *KTU* 1.4: IV.7— 22 the cola coincide with the physical lines on the tablet it would seem natural to read *KTU* 1.4: IV.9 as one colon:

mdl . ʿr . ṣmd . pḥl   He saddled a he—ass, harnessed a male.

However, a slightly expanded parallel in *KTU* 1.19: II.8f. argues strongly against this:

bkm . tmdln . ʿr   Thereupon she saddled a he—ass,
  bkm . tṣmd . pḥl   thereupon she harnessed a male.

Because in this case too the physical disposition is colometrical it cannot be doubted that *two* cola are involved. For this reason we are forced to conclude that the bicolon in *KTU* 1.4: IV was written on one line only to save space.

This example may serve to demonstrate that even under exceptionally favourable conditions it is not always easy to establish the correct colometry. Usually, however, the conditions are much worse, the scribes having cramped as many characters on a line as they could, totally ignoring the colometry they knew by heart. In order to recover the original division into cola scholars have tried different approaches:

A) The internal parallelism within the verse can be used to create a more or less symmetrical arrangement of cola. This method is certainly helpful, but it has its limitations. In case of the so—called synthetical parallelism[16] we are unable to balance

---

14   R. Kittel, *Über die Notwendigkeit und Möglichkeit einer neuen Ausgabe der hebräischen Bibel* (Leipzig, 1901) 71ff.; J.L. Kugel, *The Idea of Biblical Poetry. Parallelism and Its History* (New Haven/London, 1981) 119ff.

15   P.W. Skehan, 'A Psalm Manuscript from Qumran (4QPs^b)', *CBQ* 26 (1964) 313—322.

16   Cf. Van der Lugt: 1980:180ff. The terminology was rightly criticized by S.A. Geller, *Parallelism in Early Biblical Poetry* (Missoula, 1979) 375ff.

the cola on a purely semantical and/or morphological basis. Moreover, if the existence of enjambement has to be recognized (see below), the value of parallelism becomes even more questionable.

B)   The Massoretic cantillation is a venerable witness to the traditional colometry of the Hebrew verses. It should be taken more seriously than has been the case hitherto. Nevertheless modern scholarship has often proved the Massoretic division to be unreliable.

C)   The rhythmical balance between cola of the same verse has frequently been invoked to defend a certain colometrical division. As we saw above (2.3) there does exist a remarkable tendency to balance the number of feet per colon. However, since cola could be expanded or contracted at will (see 2.3 and 3.3) and because unbalanced verses do occur (4.1), this method too fails to produce reliable results.

D)   As in the example quoted above comparison of parallel passages may sometimes help to decide difficult cases. However, due to the limited number of attested parallels and the considerable labour involved in documenting all kinds of similar constructions, this method too has only a limited effect.

Summing up, the re—establishment of the colometric division intended by the ancient poets is often a hazardous undertaking. Even the most conscientious researcher would do well to recognize this in all fairness. Yet the systematic combination of the approaches described above can help us to make more responsible choices. We want to illustrate this with an example from Ugarit.

The phrase *ḥšk ʿšk ʿbṣk* occurs in *KTU* 1.1: II.21f.; III.10; 1.3: III.18; IV.11. Although its interpretation is somewhat uncertain, it is mostly translated as 'Hurry up! Press on! Make haste!'.[17] Because a colon could consists of only one word (3.2), the question is whether we should read this sequence as one colon or as three ultra—short cola. The synonymous parallelism renders the latter a real possibility (approach A). Since it is impossible to try approach (B) in this case we pass on to (C): the rhythmical balance of the context. In all cases the colon is

---

17   Cf. J.C. de Moor, *The Seasonal Pattern in the Ugaritic Myth of Baʿlu.* According to the Version of Ilimilku (AOAT 16; Neukirchen–Vluyn, 1971) 106. For a possible Akkadian parallel see W.G.E. Watson, *UF* 9 (1977) 274.

followed by two apparently parallel cola of three feet (words) each:

'my p'nk tlsmn	Let your feet run towards me,
'my twth 'išdk	let your legs rush towards me !

So approach (C) decidedly argues in favour of *one* colon. Finally we try (D). Here Ugaritic does not help us because as far as we know no exactly similar construction occurs in the tablets published to date.[18] Hebrew, however, may help us out. In Isa. 55:1 we have three parallel imperatives in what is clearly the second colon of a bicolon:

hwy kl ṣm'	Ho, all who are thirsty,
lkw lmym	come to the water,
w'šr 'yn lw ksp	and who has no silver,
lkw šbrw w'klw	come, buy and eat !

Because grammatically the Ugaritic forms are infinitives it also apt to cite Hos. 4:2 where we have the colon *'lh wkhš wrṣh* 'swearing and lying and murdering'. See furthermore e.g. Isa. 24:17; 52:11; Jer. 4:2; Joel 2:19. Thus the approaches (C) and (D) both advocate the reading of the sequence *hšk 'ṣk 'bṣk* as one colon, and not as a tricolon. In this particular case we are fortunate enough to find our tentative conclusion confirmed by the sole place where the formula has been written on a single physical line, like the two cola preceding it: *KTU* 1.3: III.18, cf. 16—17.

3.2 *The smallest colon*

The smallest possible colon consists of only one foot. First we give some Ugaritic examples:

KTU 1.3: IV.5

[y]'n . ǵlmm .	The lads answered,
y'nyn .	they answered her:

---

18 See, however, the three parallel verbs in *KTU* 1.3: I.5f. and 8f., as well as the three parallel nouns in *KTU* 1.5: V.7f.

KTU 1.24: 30f.

wyᶜn yrḫ nyr šmm	But Yarikhu, the illuminator of heaven, answered,
wn ᶜn	yea, he answered:

KTU 1.6: I.45f.

tn 'aḥd . b . bnk .	Give one of your sons,
'amlkn	that I make him king !

KTU 1.19: II.19

ydnh .	He urged it on,
ysb . 'aklth .	went around his fissured field.

KTU 1.19: II.40

tmġyn .	They arrived.
tš'a . ghm . w[tṣḥn]	They lifted up their voices and cried:

Because of the very frequent cases of *mġy* being used in a fully developed colon and because *nš' g* invariably heads a new line we have no choice but to assume a strongly contracted colon here, probably as an expression of grief. We continue with some Hebrew examples:

Num. 6:24f.

ybrkk yhwh	May YHWH bless you,
wyšmrk	and keep you,
y'r yhwh pnyw 'lyk	May YHWH make his face shine upon you,
wyhnk	and show you grace !

Jer. 2:5

mh−mṣ'w 'bwtykm by ᶜwl	What wrong did your fathers find in me,
ky rhqw mᶜly	that they went far from me,
wylkw 'hry hhbl	and went after what is worthless,
wyhblw	and became worthless ?

Isa. 49:6a

wy'mr	And He said:
nql mhywtk ly ᶜbd	It is too light for you to be a servant for me.

Compare Isa. 49:3 where the first colon is slightly expanded whereas the second is contracted:

wy'mr ly	And He said to me:
'bdy 'th	You are my servant.

Ps. 78:19
wydbrw b'lhym	And they spoke against God,
'mrw	they said:

Cant. 3:1f.
'l—mškby blylwt	Upon my bed by night
bqšty 't š'hbh npšy	I sought him whom my soul loves.
bqštyw	I sought him,
wl' mṣ'tyw	but I did not find him.

'qwmh n'	I will rise now,
w'swbbh b'yr	and go round in the city,
bšwqym wbrhbwt	in the streets and in the squares.
'bqšh 't š'hbh npšy	I will seek him whom my soul loves.
bqštyw	I sought him,
wl' mṣ'tyw	but I did not find him.

3.3. *Expansion / contraction of the colon*

In previous studies one of us has discussed numerous Ugaritic and Hebrew examples of expansion and contraction on the level of the colon.[19] On the basis of textual evidence derived from parallel transmission it was demonstrated that several feet could be added to or omitted from a colon without disturbing the

---

19 De Moor, FS Loewenstamm: 1978:123–126; *UF* 12 (1980) 311–314; *Or* 53 (1984) 268,273. Other scholars soon followed suit with a host of totally convincing examples of the same phenomena: S.E. Loewenstamm, 'The Adress "Listen" in the Ugaritic Epic and the Bible', in: *The Bible World. Essays in Honor of C.H. Gordon* (New York, 1980) 123–131; W.G.E. Watson, 'Introductions to Discourse in Ugaritic Narrative Verse', *Aula Orientalis* 1 (1983) 253–261.

framework of a poem. Suffice it to cite a few additional
examples now.

KTU 1.23: 24
ynqm . b'ap zd . 'aṯrt   who suck the nipple of the breast
                                of Athiratu.

KTU 1.23: 61
ynqm . b'ap . dd . št   who suck the nipple of the breast
                                of the Lady.

KTU 1.23: 59
ynqm . b'ap . dd   who suck the nipple of the Breast.

The reduction was possible because 'Breast' was an epithet of
'Anatu.[20] In this case one might argue, however, that the
number of feet remained the same if both *zd 'aṯrt* and *dd št*
were read as one foot. Such an easy explanation is not possible
in the next examples.

KTU 1.18: IV.25f.
tṣ'i . km rḫ . npšh   Let his soul go out like wind.

KTU 1.18: IV.35
yṣ'at . km . rḫ . npš[ḥ]   His soul went out like wind.

KTU 1.19: II.38bis (edge)
[š]ṣ'at krḫ . npšhm   She made his soul go out like wind.

Although the expanded form *km* would seem to indicate that
the first two examples were read with *four* feet, we are willing
to concede that three feet might be possible. This is not the
case, however, in

KTU 1.19: II.42f.
[šṣ'at] bṯlt . 'nt . kr[ḫ . npšḥ] The virgin 'Anatu made
                                his soul go out like wind.

---

20   Cf. *UF* 12 (1980) 308.

Here the colon has been expanded with two words representing
at least one extra foot. The reverse is true in the next example:

KTU 1.19: III.4f.
hm . 'iṯ . šmt   If there is fat,
  hm . 'i[ṯ] 'ẓm   if there is bone ...

KTU 1.19: III.33f.
hm . 'iṯ . šmt .   If there is fat,
  'iṯ 'ẓm .   (if) there is bone ...

KTU 1.19: III.39
'iṯ . šmt   There was fat,
  'iṯ . 'ẓm   there was bone.

The ellipsis of *hm*, first from the second colon, then also from
the first, clearly creates a climactic tension. No metrical theory
is able to explain such unequivocal cases of expansion and
contraction on the level of the colon. See also 2.3.

Just as the expansion of the foot could lead to the
appropriation of the 'territory' of another foot, so the colon can
at times spill over in the room intended for the next colon. A
convincing example of this kind of enjambement is found in

KTU 1.16: I.44f.
'adnk . šqrb . k[sp]   Bring your Lord silver
  bmgnk . wḫrṣ lkl   as your personal gift, and gold
                            for all.

Because from line 42 onwards the beginning of every colon
coincides with the beginning of a new line, there is hardly room
for doubt in this case.[21] One might ask here whether the
numerous instances of unbalanced verses consisting of a long
and a short colon (e.g. four feet followed by two)[22] should not
be regarded as examples of this kind of enjambement. This is
unlikely. In *KTU* 1.4: V.6—9 all cola coincide with the physical

---

21 For other cases of enjambement in Ugaritic and Hebrew see Watson:
1984:333f.
22 De Moor, FS Loewenstamm: 1978:138f.

lines on the tablet. Yet line 7 counts 5 words representing at
least 4 feet, none of which can be carried over to the next
colon:

wn 'ap . 'dn . mṭrh (2—4 feet)
  b'l . y'dn . 'dn . ṯkt . bglṯ (4—5 feet)
    wtn . qlh . b'rpt (2—3 feet)
      šrh . l'arṣ . brqm (3 feet)

Also it is the prime time for his rains,
  Ba'lu should appoint the time of the barque with snow,
    and of the giving forth of his voice in the clouds,
      of his letting loose the lightnings to the earth.

The same is the case in Hebrew, e.g. in Ps. 62:2,4 where we
have clear examples of the sequence 4 + 2 feet.

3.4. The largest colon

Not only in texts written in colometric form (3.1.) but in all
material we analysed at Kampen the maximum length of a
colon appears to be six words.

KTU 1.6: I.50—52
dq . 'anm . l yrẓ 'm . b'l . (5 or 6 words)
  l y'db . mrh 'm . bn . dgn . ktmsm (6 or 7 words)

One of feeble strength cannot run like Ba'lu,
  one who knuckles under cannot poise the lance like the son of
  Daganu.

The question here is whether *l* 'not' should be counted as a
separate word. Usually the Ugaritic scribes omit the
word—divider after *l*. Does that mean they always combined it
with the next word to form one accentuated foot (cf. 2.3)? This
is unlikely. In the Book of Psalms Hebrew *l'* is written 110
times with *maqqeph*, 120 times without. The combination *wl'* is
written 30 times with, 45 times without *maqqeph*. This would
seem to indicate that the singers were free to choose whether or
not to take *l'* as an independent unit. Because in texts of
Ugarit the negation *l* is sometimes followed by the
word—divider, the same would seem to apply in Ugaritic

poetry.[23]
 In the case cited above all cola surrounding the very long
lines count 3 or 4 feet. In the Massoretic tradition cola of six
words are invariably read as cola with a lesser number of feet:

Ps. 3:8
ky—hkyt 't—kl—'yby lḥy (6 words, 3 feet)
 šny rš'ym šbrt (3 words, 3 feet)
For you do smite all my enemies on the cheek,
 you do break the teeth of the wicked.

Ps. 34:11
kpyrym ršw wr'bw (3 words, 3 feet)
 wdršw yhwh l'—yhsrw kl—ṭwb (6 words, 4 feet)
Young lions are wanting and hungry,
 but those who seek YHWH lack no good thing.

Ps. 74:22
qwmh 'lhym rybh rybk (4 words, 4 feet)
 zkr ḥrptk mny—nbl kl—hywm (6 words, 4 feet)
Arise, o God, plead your cause,
 remember how the fool mocks at you all day.

Ps. 146:6
'šh šmym w'rṣ (3 words, 2 or 3 feet)
 't—hym w't—kl—'šr—bm (6 words, 2 feet)
 hšmr 'mt l'wlm (3 words, 2 or 3 feet)
Who made heaven and earth,
 the sea and all that is in them,
 who keeps faith for ever.

For this reason we are entitled to read the Ugaritic example

KTU 1.6: I.50—52
dq—'anm l—yrẓ 'm(—)b'l (3 or 4 feet)
l—y'db mrḥ 'm—bn—dgn ktmsm (4 feet).

---

23 *KTU* 1.1: IV.7; 1.3: II.19; III.26; V.3; 1.5: I.9,22; II.13; 1.6: VI.27; 1.10:
I.3; 1.19: II.39; Ps. 123:2c.

However, a colon of four feet is not the longest possible colon with regard to the number of feet.

Ps. 63:6
kmw ḥlb wdšn tśbˁ npšy (5 words, 5 feet)
  wśpty rnnwt yhll—py (4 words, 3 feet)

As with fat and ointment my soul is sated,
  and with joyful lips my mouth praises you.

Because *kmw* could have been connected with the following *ḥlb* by means of the *maqqeph*[24] it is certain that the Massoretes read this colon as a colon of five feet.
  A comparable Ugaritic example may be found in

KTU 1.17: I.20f.
bl . ʾiṯ . bn . lh km ʾaḫḫ (probably 5 feet)
  wšrš km . ʾaryh . (2 or 3 feet)

He has no son like his brothers,
  nor a root like his kinsmen.

It is highly probable that both *km ʾaḫḫ* and *km ʾaryh* were read as combinations with one main accent.
  We did not find unequivocal examples of cola of more than five feet in the material we analysed, so we draw the tentative conclusion that *the largest possible colon counted six words or five feet.*

4. The Verse

4.1. General

The colon cannot be the sole or even the most important building block of North—West Semitic poetry simply because very often the colon is an incomplete sentence, either running on in the next colon[25] or truncated by ellipsis (the omitting of self—evident elements). Although in Ugarit no tablets exhibiting

---

24   As in Ex. 15:5,8; Isa. 41:25; 51:6; Ps. 78:13,69; Prov. 23:7; Job 12:3; 41:16; Cant. 6:10.
25   So—called synthetical parallelism, cf. note 16.

a verse—form in the physical disposition of the lines have come to light, the parallelistic structure of sequential cola proves the poets to be acquainted with the same form of verse we know from the Bible. Acrostics like those of Ps. 34, Ps. 119 and Lam. 3 prove beyond any doubt that verses of more than one colon were known in Israel. In ancient Hebrew manuscripts the scribes sometimes appear to have written the poems in the form of bicola.[26]

In the Ugaritic poetry we analysed we were able to identify a total number of 1889 verses. For the sake of comparison we took a random sample of the same proportion from the poetry of the Hebrew Bible. It appeared that both in Ugarit and in Israel *the normal verse consists of two cola.* Other numbers of cola are possible however:

	Ugaritic[27]		Hebrew	
Unicola	320	(17%)	49	(3%)
Bicola	1.198	(63%)	1.442	(76%)
Tricola	341	(18%)	361	(19%)
Multicola	30	(2%)	37	(2%)

In view of the limited size of the sample the differences can hardly be called spectacular. The larger number of unicola in Ugaritic is easily explained by the difference in genre. The major part of the Ugaritic sample consisted of epic literature in which unicola, e.g. those introducing direct oration, are more frequent than in hymns, prayers and prophetic texts.[28] The maximum number of cola per verse we encountered was nine (see 4.4. below).

So we can now define the verse in close harmony with the

---

26 Van der Lugt: 1980:171ff.

27 Our findings sharply differ from the last comprehensive assessment by G.D. Young, 'Ugaritic Prosody', *JNES* 9 (1950) 124—133, especially 125. The reason for this is that Young included higher structural units which we call strophes, canticles and cantos in his discussion of verse—forms so that he could even state: 'Combinations up to 22 stichs (text 51: I.20ff.) may be found'.

28 In Hebrew narrative poetry the proportion of unicola is equally high, cf. *Or* 53 (1984) 262ff; 55 (1986) 2ff.

definitions we found for its constituting parts: *one to nine cola form the verse.*

In accordance with the tendency towards symmetry in this kind of poetry the number of feet of the cola forming a verse is usually the same. However, unbalanced verses are quite common. A well–known example is the so–called *qinah*–verse (3 + 2 feet, or, less frequently, 2 + 3) where the lack of symmetry is an expression of strong emotion, usually grief.[29] However, other unbalanced combinations do occur:

KTU 1.6: VI.10f.
phn . 'aḥym . ytn . bʿl sᵢp'uy
 bnm . 'umy . klyy

Look here ! Baʿlu has given me my own brothers to eat,
 the sons of my own mother to consume !

The interesting aspect of this verse is that the number of feet per colon can be established with absolute certainty. The first colon does not contain very short words or genitive constructions allowing the singers to compress several words into one foot. In the second colon the expanded foot *bnm* (instead of *bn*) renders it practically certain that this colon counted three feet. Another plausible example of the pattern of 5 + 3 feet is

KTU 1.3: V.38f. (par.)
wn . 'in . bt [.] lbʿl . km . 'ilm (5 or 6 feet)
 ḥẓr . kb[n .] 'aṯrt (2 or 3 feet)

And there is no house for Baʿlu like the gods,
 nor a residence like the sons of Athiratu !

It is certainly noteworthy that both examples of a 5 + 3 pattern happen to be complaints. Apparently grief was expressed in the form of 'untidy', unbalanced verses. It is impossible, however, to reverse this thesis. See the examples quoted under 3.2 − 3.4.

---

29 K. Budde, 'Das hebräische Klagelied', *ZAW* 2 (1882) 1–52; G.W. Randalf, 'The Qinah: A Study of Poetic Meter, Syntax and Style', *ZAW* 95 (1983) 54−75. With regard to Ugaritic: De Moor, FS Loewenstamm: 1978:136f.

Ever since the classical study of Lowth[30] it has been recognized that usually the cola forming a Hebrew verse are connected by semantical and/or formal parallelism. Today we know many of these pairs to have been part of a kind of standard stock of fixed parallel terms upon which the poets and singers of Canaan and Israel could draw in composing or expanding their verses.[31] However, the existence of unicola (see 4.2) and the so—called synthetic parallelism[32] prove parallelism to be a non—vital element in this kind of poetry.

Because as we shall see the verse was not the only plane on which parallelism was operative we follow Van der Lugt[33] in speaking of *internal parallelism* to denote parallelism on the level of the verse whereas *external parallelism* denotes parallelism on a higher level (strophe, canticle, canto). *The main function of parallelism is to bind structural elements of a poem together.* With regard to the verse there is no need to prove this all over again. Parallelism is our most precious help in establishing which cola should be joined to form a verse. However, as with the colon (3.1) it has to be recognized that often an absolutely certain delimitation of verses is impossible. Most disturbing in this respect are the unicola and the 'synthetical' parallelism. To illustrate this problem we adduce an Ugaritic example in which it would seem logical to treat the sequences of cola as cases of 'synthetical' parallelism.

KTU 1.14: V.12—14 (non—stichometrical arrangement)
['apn]k [p]bl[. mlk .]   Thereupon king Pubala
[g]m . l'att[h . k]y[sh .]   cried aloud to his wife:

---

30 R. Lowth, *Lectures on the Sacred Poetry of the Hebrews*, Vol. 2, transl. G. Gregory (London, 1787; reprinted Hildesheim, 1969, New York, 1971). See also, to cite only a few modern authors, Geller: 1979; Van der Lugt: 1980:176ff.; Kugel: 1981:1ff.; Watson: 1984:114ff.
31 See e.g. M. Dahood, 'Ugaritic—Hebrew Parallel Pairs', in L.R. Fisher (ed.), *Ras Shamra Parallels*, Vol. 1 (Roma, 1972) 71—382; Vol. 2 (Roma, 1975) 1—39; Y. Avishur, *Stylistic Studies of Word-Pairs in Biblical and Ancient Semitic Literatures* (Neukirchen—Vluyn, 1984).
32 See note 16.
33 Van der Lugt: 1980:176ff., 189ff.

KTU 1.6: I.56—59 (non—stichometrical arrangement)

'apnk . 'ttr . 'rz	Thereupon 'Athtaru the Rich
y'l . bṣrrt . ṣpn	went up into the highlands of Sapanu,
ytb . lkht . 'al'iyn b'l .	he sat down on the throne of Ba'lu the Almighty.[34]

Even a quadrocolon would be attested:

KTU 1.17: V.28 (non—stichometrical arrangement)

'apnk . mtt . dnty	Thereupon lady Danatiya
tšlhm . tššqy 'ilm	gave the god to eat, gave (him) to drink,
ts'ad . tkbd . hmt .	she regaled, honoured him,
b'l hkpt 'il . klh	the lord of all the divine Egypt.[35]

Yet this most natural conclusion would be utterly wrong because in a number of other cases the *'apnk*–phrase is only the first colon of a *bicolon* proving that the *'apnk*–cola in the examples we quoted are *unicola* followed by another unicolon, a bicolon or even a tricolon.

KTU 1.17: V.13—15

'apnk . dn'il mt . rp'i .	Thereupon Dani'ilu, the man of the Saviour,
'aphn . ǵzr . mt hrnmy .	thereat the hero, the Harnamite man,
gm . l'atth . kyṣh	surely cried aloud to his wife:

The bicolon may be followed by another bicolon:

KTU 1.17: V.33—36

'apnk . dn'il . m[t] rp'i	Thereupon Dani'ilu, the man of the Saviour,
'aphn . ǵzr . mt hrnmy .	thereat the hero, the Harnamite man,

---

34 See also *KTU* 1.16: I.46—48; 1.19: I.38—40.
35 See also *KTU* 1.5: VI.11—14

qšt . yqb . [yb]rk .	named, blessed the bow,
ʿl . ʾaqht . kyq[bh]	for Aqhatu surely he named it.[36]

Or it may even be followed by a tricolon:

KTU 1.17: II.27—31

ʾapnk . dnʾil mt .rpʾi .	Thereupon Daniʾilu, the man of the Saviour,
ʾap . hn . ġzr . mt hrnmy	thereat the Hero, the Harnamite man,
ʾalp . ytbḫ . lkṯrt .	slaughtered an ox for the Kathiratu,
yšlḥm . kṯrt .	gave the Kathiratu to eat,
wyššq . bnt . hll . snnt	and gave the daughters of Hilalu, the swallows, to drink.

Therefore both the sequences [unicolon − unicolon, unicolon − bicolon, unicolon − tricolon] and [bicolon − unicolon, bicolon − bicolon, bicolon − tricolon] are fully attested. Had we not been lucky enough to have so many examples of this standard formula in parallel and contemporaneous transmission our stichometry would almost certainly have been inadequate. For the time being scholars would do well to recognize the tentative nature of their stichometric division in all cases where a unicolon might be involved and conclusive evidence settling the matter is still lacking.

4.2 The smallest verse

The smallest possible verse consists of only one colon. Nowadays the existence of such so−called unicola[37] is accepted by almost every scholar in the field.[38] Very often a unicolon is used to introduce a larger structural unit, e.g. a speech in the direct oration, as in

KTU 1.16: VI.40—41

yšʾu gh wyṣh	He lifted up his voice and cried:

---

36   See also *KTU* 1.17: I.1–3; V.4–7; 1.19: I.19–23.
37   Next to 'bicolon' the term 'unicolon' is preferable to 'monocolon'.
38   Cf. Van der Lugt: 1980:206ff.; Watson: 1984:168ff.

The admonition to hear is very often a unicolon, although it can be expanded to become a verse of more cola:[39]

KTU 1.16: VI.29–30

'ištm['] *wtqġ* [*.'udnk* .]   Listen and let your ear be
                               attentive !

KTU 1.4: VI.4
šm' . *m'* . *l'a*[*l'i*]*yn b'l*   Now hear, o Ba'lu the Almighty !

but also

KTU 1.4: V.59–60
šm' . *l'al'iyn* . *b'l*   Hear, o Ba'lu the Almighty,
  bn . *lrkb* . *'rpt*   pay attention,
                       o Rider on the Clouds !

proving that the unicolon does not stand outside the poetical framework.

The use of unicola is by no means confined to introductory phrases. A few examples:

KTU 1.101: 8
[*y*]*š'il* . *ṭr*<*m*> . *'iṯ*   It was asked: 'Is there a meal?'.

KTU 1.3: III.8f.
km ġlmm w . *'rbn*   Then, o lads, enter !

KTU 1.3: III.36
'ik . *mġy* . *gpn* . *w'ugr*   Why did Gupanu–and–Ugaru
                       arrive ?

KTU 1.3: IV.40
šrhq . *'aṯt* . *lpnnh* .   He removed the women
                       from his presence.

---

39 De Moor, *UF* 10 (1978) 187ff.; 12 (1980) 311ff.; Loewenstamm, FS Gordon: 1980:123ff.

KTU 1.2: I.21
b'l . qm . 'l . 'il   Ba'lu was standing by Ilu.

Ps. 16:11
twdy'ny 'rḥ ḥyym   You do show me the path of life.

1.Sam. 2:10
yhwh yḥtw mrybw   YHWH—those who oppose him
                      are crushed.

In the Septuaginta this colon has been expanded to a bicolon. This and the circumstance that vs. 10b is clearly a bicolon too (*bšmym // 'psy 'rṣ*) establish the status of vs. 10a ·(MT) as a unicolon.

It is often difficult to decide whether we are dealing with a unicolon or with an asymmetrical verse of more than one colon. This is especially the case when several unicola follow each other, lending a peculiar prosaic flavour to the poem. Many Hebrew examples of this so—called 'Kurzvers' were collected by G.Fohrer.[40] Again we have to stress the importance of careful study of texts preserved in parallel transmission as a means to decide such matters. In this connection we want to discuss the Ugaritic *'ny*—formulae. Short *'ny*—formulae are found in

KTU 1.2: IV.7
w'n . kṯr . wḫss   But Kotharu—and—Khasisu said:

KTU 1.4: III.27
wt'n . rbt . 'aṯrt ym   And Lady Athiratu of the Sea said:

One might be inclined to join such introductions of direct oration to the following bicola. As a result we would have asymmetrical tricola. However, other examples contradict this hypothesis:

---

40 G. Fohrer, 'Uber den Kurzvers', *ZAW* 66 (1954) 199—236. See now also W.A.M. Beuken — H.W.M. van Grol, in: P.—M. Bogaert (ed.), *Le livre de Jérémie* (Louvain, 1981) 327ff.
Sequences of four unicola are attested in the following Ugaritic passages: *KTU* 1.4: VI.1—4; 1.6: II.11—14.

KTU 1.3: IV.5
[*y*]'*n* . *ǵlmm* .   The lads answered,
  y'*nyn*   they answered her:

KTU 1.24: 30f.
wy'*n yrḫ nyr šmm* .   But Yarikhu, the Illuminator of
                                 heaven, answered,
  wn '*n*   yea, he answered:

KTU 1.2: III.15
[*t*'*ny*]*nn nrt*[.]'*ilm* . *špš* .   Shapsu, the lamp of the gods,
                                 answered him,
  tš'*u* . *gh* . *wt*[*šḫ*]   she lifted up her voice
                                 and cried:

KTU 1.17: VI.52f.
wt'*n* [*btlt* . '*nt* .]   And the Virgin 'Anatu answered,
  [*tš*'*u*]*gh* . *wtšḫ* .   she lifted up her voice
                                 and cried:

KTU 1.3: IV.21f.
wt['*n*] . *btlt* .[']*nt* .   And the Virgin 'Anatu answered,
  ttb [*ybmt* .]*l*'*imm* .   the Wanton Widow of the
                                 Nations replied:

In *KTU* 1.19: IV.17–20 the '*ny*–formula is even part of a quadrocolon:

[*m*]*k* . *bšb*' *šnt* .
  wy'*n* [.*dn*'*il* . *mt* .]*rp*'*i*
    ytb . *ǵzr* . *m*[*t* . *hrnmy* .]
      [*y*]*š*'*u gh* . *wysḫ* .

Then, in the seventh year,
  Dani'ilu, the man of the Saviour, answered,
    the hero, the Harnamite man, replied,
      he lifted up his voice and cried:

All these examples of various expansions of the shorter '*ny*–
formula would seem to prove that the latter should indeed be
taken as a unicolon, a verse in its own right consisting of only
one colon and characterized as poetry only by the style of
delivery.

At this point it must be asked whether something like 'synthetical' parallelism really did exist. We believe it did, but find it very hard to prove this point of view in any conclusive way.[41] Because sentences running on through more than one verse do occur (see 5.1 below), there is no reason whatsoever why we should not write a 'synthetical' bicolon as two independent unicola. This question has to be resolved by further research.

4.3. Expansion / contraction of the verse

Just like the foot and the colon *the verse could be expanded or contracted* according to the mood of the singers. To the numerous examples collected in earlier studies[42] we add a few quotations showing that a unicolon could develop into a bicolon, tricolon or multicolon, and backwards of course.

KTU 1.4: V.48
ʿd . lḥm . šty [. 'ilm]   Again they ate, the gods drank.

KTU 1.4: VI.55−58 (par.)
ʿd . lḥm . šty . 'ilm	Again they ate, the gods drank,
wpq . mrġtm . ṯd	and they were provided with a suckling,
bḥrb . mlḥt . qṣ[. m]rʾi .	with a salted knife they carved a fatling.

Tricolon − bicolon:

KTU 1.2: I.8f.
[trd m]mt . mṭ .   May you descend into the place of death below,[43]

---

41 Of course it is an important, though not decisive factor that the Massoretic tradition recognized the 'synthesis' as a legitimate form of parallelism.

42 Cf. note 1.

43 Cf. Deut. 28:43; Prov. 15:24 and with regard to *mmt* as a designation of the realm of death Job 33:22 with De Moor: 1971: 186.
Of course the question whether or not our restoration is correct is irrelevant to the argument developed above, for it is certain that an extra colon precedes the colon we know from *KTU* 1.16: VI.57f. here.

tpln . bg[*bl . šntk .*]	may you fall down at the height of your years,
[*bḥpnk . wtᶜn .*]	in the prime of your strength, and yet be humbled !

KTU 1.16: VI.57f.

tqln . bgbl šntk .	May you fall down at the height of your years,
bḥpnk . wtᶜn	in the prime of your strength, and yet be humbled !

Apart from offering some interesting examples of expansion and contraction the following two passages demonstrate the relative freedom of the poets in choosing their wording:

KTU 1.4: IV.2−15

[*šmᶜ . lqdš*] *w'amr*[*r .*]	'Hear, o Qidshu−and−Amruru,
[*ldgy . rbt*] *'atrt . ym*	o fisherman of Lady Athiratu of the Sea !

[*mdl . ᶜr*]	Saddle a he−ass,
ṣmd . pḥl .	harness a male.
š[*t . gpnm . dt*] *ksp .*	Put on the reins of silver,
dt . yrq[*. nqbnm*]	the straps of gold,
ᶜdb . gpn . 'atnt[*y*]	prepare the reins of my donkey !'.
yšmᶜ . qd<*š*> *. w'amr*[*r*]	Qidshu−and−Amruru obeyed.

mdl . ᶜr .	He saddled a he−ass,
ṣmd . pḥl	harnessed a male.
št . gpnm . dt . ksp	He put on the reins of silver,
dt . yrq . nqbnm	the straps of gold,
ᶜdb . gpn . 'atnth	he prepared the reins of her donkey.
yḥbq . qdš . w'amrr	Qidshu−and−Amruru embraced (her),
yštn . 'atrt . lbmt . ᶜr	he put Athiratu on the back of the he−ass,
lysmsmt . bmt . pḥl	on the most comfortable part of the back of the male.

KTU 1.19: II.1−11

šm' . pġt . ṯkmt . my	'Hear, Pughatu, (you) who carry water on your shoulder,
ḥspt . lš'r . ṯl .	who scoop up dew from the wool,
yd'[ṯ]hlk . kbkbm .	who know the course of the stars !
mdl . 'r	Saddle a he−ass,
ṣmd . pḥl .	harness a male.
št . gpny . dt ksp	Put on my reins of silver,
dt . yrq . nqbny .	my straps of gold !'.
tš[m'] pġt . ṯkmt . my .	Pughatu obeyed, (she) who carried water on her shoulder,
ḥspt . l[š']r . ṯl	who scooped up dew from the wool,
yd't . hlk . kbkbm	who knew the course of the stars.
bkm . tmdln . 'r	Thereupon she saddled a he−ass,
bkm . tṣmd . pḥl .	thereupon she harnessed the male.
bkm tš'u . 'abh .	Thereupon she lifted up her father,
tštnn . lbmt 'r	put him on the back of the he−ass,
lysmsm . bmt . pḥl	on the most comfortable part of the back of the male.

It appears that contraction could go as far as the reduction to zero of a full−fledged tricolon.

A comparable case is that of the well−known Ugaritic *'idk*−formula. It exhibits the following variations:
1) The verse is attested as a bicolon,[44] tricolon[45] and quadrocolon.[46]
2) The verb *ytn* with emphasizing negation may either precede or follow the object *pnm*.[47]

---

44   *KTU* 1.1: II.13f.; 1.3: IV.37f.; VI.12−14; 1.4: V.22f.; VIII.9−11; 1.5: I.9f.; V.6−8; 1.6: IV.7f.; 1.10: II.8f.; 1.14: V.29−31; VI.1ff.; 1.18: I.20−21.
45   *KTU* 1.1: III.21f.; 1.2: I.19f.; 1.3: V.5−7; 1.4: IV.20−22; 1.5: II.13−15; 1.6: I.32−34; 1.17: VI.46−48; 1.100: 63a−64a.
46   *KTU* 1.4: VIII.1−4.
47   The anomalous order *pnm ('a)l ytn* is attested in *KTU* 1.2: I.19f.; 1.5:

3) The negation may either be *l* or *'al*.

4) The colon following the *'idk*–colon may count from two to five words,[48] a circumstance defeating once again any attempt at restoring 'metrical order', whatever that may be.

5) The same colon may either begin with *'m* or with *tk*.[49]

We may conclude that the phenomena of expansion and contraction are also operative on the level of the verse. The poets and singers enjoyed a considerable amount of freedom. Any theory on the poetry of Canaan and Israel unable to account for the discrepancies we found in the texts themselves must be considered a failure.

Finally we have to observe that also on the level of the verse enjambement may take place, *i.e.* expansion at the expense of the preceding or following verse. Some particularly convincing examples of this phenomenon were collected by Van der Lugt.[50]

On the basis of the internal parallelism one might feel inclined to read Ps. 145:15f. as a unicolon followed by a tricolon:

'yny–kl 'lyk yṣbrw
w'th nwtn–lhm 't–'klm b'tw
   pwth 't–ydk
   wmṣby' lkl–ḥy rṣwn

However, all other verses of the Psalm are bicola and the acrostic renders it absolutely certain that the participle–construction of vs. 16 has encroached upon the 'territory' of vs. 15:

V.6–8; 1.14: V.29–31; 1.100: 63a–64a.

48   Two words: *KTU* 1.1: II.14 [*'m* .]*'inbb*. Three words: *KTU* 1.2: I.20 *tk* . *ġr* . *ll*; 1.4: VIII.2 *'m* . *ġr* . *trġzz*; 1.4: VIII.10f. *tk* . *qrth hmry*; 1.5: V.7f. *tk* . *ġr knkny*; 1.14: V.31 *'m* . *k[rt* . *msw]n*; 1.100: 63a *tk 'aršḫ* . *rbt*. Four words: *KTU* 1.1: III.21f. [*'m* . *ltpn*] *'il dp'id*; 1.3: IV.37f. *'m* . *b'l mrym* . *ṣpn* (see also 1.4: V.22f.; 1.5: I.9f.); 1.3: V.6 [*'m* . *'il*] . *mbk nhr[m]* (see also 1.4: IV.20f.; 1.6: I.32–34; 1.17: VI.47); 1.3: VI.13f. *tk* . *ḥ{q}kpt 'il* . *klh*; 1.5: II.14 *'m* . *bn* . *'ilm* . *mt*; 1.6: IV.8 *'m* . *nrt* . *'ilm* . *špš*. Five words: *KTU* 1.10: II.9 *tk* . *'aḫ* . *šmk* . *ml'a[t* . *r]'umm*.

49   See the preceding note.

50   Van der Lugt: 1980:192ff.

Ps. 145:15f.

'yny—kl 'lyk yśbrw	The eyes of all look to you
w'th nwtn—lhm 't—'klm	and you are giving them
b'tw	their food in time,
pwth 't—ydk	opening your hand,
wmśby' lkl—ḥy rṣwn	and satisfying the wish of
	every living creature.

Ps. 98:5f. might be read as a tricolon followed by a unicolon but the overall structure of the Psalm advocates adherence to the Massoretic tradition of two bicola:

zmrw lyhwh bknwr	Make music to YHWH with the lyre,
bknwr wqwl zmrh	with the lyre and the sound of music,
bḥṣṣrwt wqwl šwpr	with trumpets and the sound of the horn,
hry'w lpny hmlk yhwh	make joyful noise before the King, YHWH !

Clearly it is not always easy to distinguish such bicola exhibiting an A1 — B1 — B2 — A2 — pattern from a sequence like unicolon followed by tricolon, or even a quadrocolon.

4.4 The largest verse

Many scholars doubt that verses of more than three cola do occur. In their opinion all purported examples of such multicola have to be regrouped into combinations of unicola, bicola and tricola. We intend to prove, however, that *multicola did occur, some of them counting as many as 9 cola*.

With regard to the A1 — B1 — B2 — A2 — pattern of a passage like *KTU* 1.19: IV.43—46 one might hesitate between a quadrocolon and two bicola with enjambement, as in the preceding paragraph. Such doubts are unfounded, however, in the following cases.

KTU 1.3: IV.50—53, cf. V.41—44
mṯb . pdr[y . bt . 'ar .]
  [mẓll] ṯly . bt . r[b .]
    [mṯb . 'arṣy] bt . y'bdr [.]
      [mṯb . klt] knyt

...is the dwelling of Pidrayu, the girl of the honey–dew,
the shelter of Tallayu, the girl of the mist,
the dwelling of Arsayu, the girl of the ample flowing,
the dwelling of the respectable brides.

Because in *KTU* 1.4: I.14–18 and IV.54–57 the last colon of this
passage has become the first colon, it is absolutely certain that
the four cola belong together. This is corroborated by another
quadrocolon of the same type in

KTU 1.3: III.5–8

t!šr . l . dd . 'al'iyn b'l .	She will sing of the love of Ba'lu, the Almighty,
yd . pdry . bt . 'ar	the affection of Pidrayu, the girl of the honey–dew,
'ahbt [.]tly . bt .rb .	the passion of Tallayu, the girl of the mist,
dd . 'arṣy bt . y'bdr	the love of Arsayu, the girl of the ample flowing.

In 4.2 and 4.3 we discussed the *'ny–* and *'idk*–formulae which
apparently could be expanded to quadrocola. An equally
convincing example is found in

KTU 1.4: I.41–43

ṣ' . 'il .	a tremendous bowl,
dqt . k'amr	delicate as in Amurru,
sknt . khwt . ym'an	shaped as in the region of Yam'anu,
dbh . r'umm . lrbbt	in which there were wild oxen by the myriads.

Because in the preceding lines every piece of furniture is
followed by *'il* 'tremendous' and one or two cola describing the
object, there is no choice but to take the passage we quoted as
a concluding quadrocolon.

In other cases the parallelism is so uniform as to make any
break–up into smaller verses unlikely, e.g.

KTU 1.100: 65–67

'r'rm . yn'rn!h	The tamarisk – he shook it out,
ssnm . ysynh.	the date–cluster – he did away with it,
'dtm . y'dynh	the scab – he took it off,
ybltm . yblnh	the wart – he carried it off.

The translation will be defended in a different context but actually a translation is superfluous as far as the argument is concerned. The four nouns ending in −*m* and the four *yqtl*−verbs ending in −*nh* speak for themselves. A particularly convincing Hebrew example of a quadrocolon occurs in

Lam. 2:19

š'y 'lyw kpyk	Lift your hands to him
'l−npš 'wllyk	for the life of your children
h'twpym br'b	who faint for hunger
br'š kl−ḥwṣwt	at the head of every street.

The whole chapter consists of strophes of three bicola each, marked by the acrostic. Therefore in verse 19 we have the choice either to delete a complete bicolon or to regard the final part of the strophe as a quadrocolon. Because the former would be highly arbitrary and is unfounded if we accept the principle of occasional expansion as a perfectly normal phenomenon, we definitely prefer the latter alternative.

Verses longer than four cola are relatively rare. Verses of five cola would seem to occur in *KTU* 1.6: II.31−35 and in *KTU* 1.17: VI.20−23, whereas *KTU* 1.6: V.11−19 has seven parallel cola. Both in Ugaritic and Hebrew the longest verses we encountered comprised nine cola: *KTU* 1.107: 13−19 and Isa. 3:18−24. In all these cases of multicola we are dealing with long enumerations, so it seems that verses longer than four cola were restricted to this particular genre.

5 The Strophe

5.1 General

The verse cannot be the largest building block of the poetry of the Canaanites and Israelites because in too many cases a sentence runs on from one verse into another. We are still unable to give a complete review of all these cases. Such a survey should prove to be extremely helpful because it may be assumed that as a rule these uninterrupted sentences form higher structural units. Therefore they provide us with a means to establish what kind of strophes and larger units are possible. The following incomplete survey gives an impression of the rich variety of attested forms.

The bicolon

KTU 1.19: III.14f. (cf. 28–29)

bnš'i . 'nh . wyp<h>n	When he lifted up his eyes
	he sighted,
yhd . hrgb . 'ab . nšrm	he saw Hargubu, the father of the
	eagles.

indicates that the following two lines of poetry do not constitute a bicolon but are a sentence running on from one unicolon into the other (1 + 1):

KTU 1.19: II.27f.

bnš'i 'nh . wtphn .	When she lifted up her eyes
	she sighted:
'in . š[lm] bhlk . ǵlmm .	there was no peace
	in the walking of the two lads.

This conclusion is confirmed by the fact that the formula occurs in an expanded form as a unicolon plus a tricolon (1 + 3):

KTU 1.4: II.12–16

bnš'i . 'nh . wtphn	When she lifted up her eyes,
	she sighted,
hlk . b'l . 'at{t}rt kt'n .	surely Athiratu saw
	Ba'lu coming,
hlk . btlt 'nt[.]	the Virgin 'Anatu coming,
tdrq . ybmt [l'imm]	The Wanton Widow of the
	Nations marching on.

However, a sequence of 1 + 2 + 2 cola was also an option:

KTU 1.17: V.9–11

bnš'i . 'nh . wyphn .	When he lifted up his eyes,
	he sighted
b'alp šd .	over a thousand acres,
rbt . kmn .	ten thousand miles,
hlk . ktr ky'n .	surely he saw Kotharu coming,
wy'n . tdrq . hss	and he saw Khasisu marching on.

This in turn could be contracted by omitting the introductory unicolon (2 + 2, see below 5.3).

In order to present the material at our disposal in a more

orderly fashion we drew up the following inventory.

Sentences running on through two verses :

1 + 1   colon: See above.

1 + 2   cola: *KTU* 1.6: I.56−59; 1.14: III.26−29; 1.17: II.32−34, 34−36, 36−38, 39f.; V.28−31; 1.19: I.32f.; 1.23: 63f.; Job 31:35.

1 + 3   cola: *KTU* 1.5: VI.11−14; 1.16: VI.21−24; 1.17: I.5−8, 8−11 (etc), V.28−31.

2 + 1   cola: *KTU* 1.15: V.18−21; 1.17: V.13−15.

2 + 2   cola: The most frequent pattern. See e.g. *KTU* 1.1: II.14−17; III.2f.; 1.2: IV.6f.; 1.3: III.28−31; IV.38−40; VI.17−20; 1.5: I.5−8, 14−17; 1.6: III.10−13; Isa. 41:13, 20; 42:1; Ps. 17:8f.; 48:3; 58:5f.

2 + 3   cola: *KTU* 1.1: III.27−29; 1.3: III.20−25 (par.); 1.4: III.17−21; 1.5: I.18−22; 1.10: I.1−5; 1.17: II.27−32; 1.19: II.44−47; IV.13−16; 1.22: IV.12−14; 1.23: 61−63; 1.161: 4−8; Isa. 40:12; 51:19; Ps. 49:2f.; 72:16; 78:30f.; Job 34:18f.

2 + 4   cola: *KTU* 1.3: IV.48−53; 1.4: I.11−18; IV.52−57.

3 + 1   cola: *KTU* 1.100: 1f.

3 + 2   cola: *KTU* 1.3: V.1−4; 1.5: I.1−5; II.5−7; 1.15: II.21−25; 1.108: 24−27; Isa. 40:24; 41:5; 42:5; 51:20; Ps. 144:7f.

3 + 3   cola: *KTU* 1.3: II.38−41; 1.23: 1−5; 1.108: 20−24; Isa. 42:6b−7a; Job 24:16f.

4 + 1   cola: *KTU* 1.1: II.1−3, 21−24.

4 + 2   cola: *KTU* 1.1: III.10−13, expansion of the preceding.

Sentences running on through three verses:

1 + 2 + cola: *KTU* 1.17: V.3−7, 9−11; 1.19: III.3−6 (par.); 1.23: 23−25, 39−41 (par.); Ps. 95:7b−9.

2 + 2 + 2 cola: The most frequent pattern, see e.g. *KTU* 1.1: III.17−21; 1.3: III.46−IV.3; IV.32−36 (par.); 1.5: V.6−11; 1.6: III.2−7; 1.14: I.21−25; V.6−12; 1.15: II.1−6; III.6−11; 1.22: IV.17−20; 1.82: 15−17, 23−25, 40−42; Isa. 40:2; 51:17; Ps. 8:7−9; 18:33−35; 27:4; 104:14f.; 123:2.

2 + 2 + 3 cola: Ps. 7:4−6; 17:13f.; 78:3f.; 129:6−8; Job 10:20−22; 13:25−27.

2 + 3 + 2 cola: *KTU* 1.1: III.12−15; 1.3: IV.13−17; 1.22: IV.21−25;

1.114: 22—28; 1.119: 29—34.

2 + 3 + 3 cola: Ps. 146:5—7.

3 + 2 + 2 cola: KTU 1.3: I.9—15; 1.24: 40—45; RIH 78/20: 1—4;
Isa. 41:8f.

Sentences running on through four verses:

2 + 2 + 1 + 2   cola: KTU 1.5: I.22—27.

2 + 2 + 2 + 2   cola: The most frequent pattern in this category,
see e.g. *KTU* 1.161: 27—30; Ps. 83:6—9; 149:6—9; Job 33:19—22;
38:8—11.

2 + 2 + 2 + 3   cola: Isa. 31:4.

2 + 2 + 3 + 2   cola: KTU 1.108: 1—5; 1.161: 20—26.

3 + 2 + 2 + 2   cola: KTU 1.108: 6—10.

Sentences running on through five or more verses:

KTU 1.4: I.29—43; 1.14: III.38—49; 1.17: I.25—33, 42—52 (par.);
Ps. 148:7—12; Job 29:2—6, 7—11; 31:16—22, 24—28, 29—34;
33:15—18; 39:23—25.

In some cases we find convoluted sentences embodying fairly
large parentheses, e.g. *KTU* 1.17: VI.30—34 (2 + 2 + 2 cola)
and Isa. 55:10—11 (2 + 2 + 3 + 3 + 2 cola).

Even on the basis of this very provisional survey of sentences
running on through more than one verse, a few conclusions are
possible:
1) Not all the cases cited can be strophes, so sentences can also
spill over into the next strophe(s). An example of this is Ps.
148:7—12. Van der Lugt has argued convincingly that we are
dealing there with three strophes of two verses each.[51]
2) Even if only part of the collection consists of real strophes, it
is clear that a rich variety of strophical patterns is theoretically
possible.
3) As with the cola per verse a certain preference for balanced
sequences can be observed.
     The on—running sentences alone do not prove the existence of
strophes.   However, we may further point to acrostics of the

---

51   Van der Lugt: 1980:467ff.

type used in the Book of Lamentations. Other poems, like Ps. 107, have been divided into strophes by means of easily identifiable refrains. And again this kind of evidence confronts us with a variety of forms, 2 + 2 cola (Lam. 4) or 2 + 2 + 2 cola (Lam. 1–3; Ps. 107:4–9, 17–22; 115:9–11) or 3 + 2 + 2 cola (Ps. 107:10–16).

Mostly, however, we have to look for other means to recover the strophical structure of a poem. In his brilliant thesis of 1980 Pieter van der Lugt has shown that usually *the verses forming a strophe are connected by external parallelism*. The outer borders of the strophe are indicated by *markers securing the renewed interest of the audience*, for example deictic particles, imperatives, vocatives, tautological parallelism, extra long verses, and so on.[52] The strophic patterns Van der Lugt found show the same wide variety we observed earlier.

We give a few illustrations of the method developed by Van der Lugt and further refined by our team at Kampen. The following standard verses doubtlessly form a separate strophe because they are surrounded by other standard phrases:

KTU 1.4: II.16–20

bh . p'nm [ttt .]	With her the feet began to totter,
[b']dn . ksl [ttbr .]	at her back the spine loosened,
['ln . p]nh . td[']	her face above began to sweat,
tġṣ [.pn]t [.]k[s]lh	the joints of her spine shook,
'anš . dt . ẓr[h]	the small of her back too.

First we try to identify *the markers of separation*. The preceding tricolon *KTU* 1.4: II.13–16a as well as the tricolon 16b–18 are long verses indicating a break. The syntactic order puts special emphasis on the adverbial expressions *bh*, *b'dn* and *'ln*. It is our impression that in many cases the sole reason for this kind of emphasis by means of the syntax is the indication of a separation between strophes. In this particular case the separation downwards is not indicated within the final verse, but there was no need to do so because there followed a unicolon introducing direct oration.

Next we establish *the external parallelism* binding the verses

---

52 Van der Lugt: 1980:508ff.; see also De Moor, *Or* 55 (1986) 31f.

of the strophe together. In this case we find:

ttṭ — tṭbr // tǵs
pnh // pnt (assonance)
ksl // kslh
suffixes −*h*

It is also noteworthy that the limbs are enumerated first from
the feet via the back to the face, and then down again via the
back to the region of the hips, beautifully imitating the coursing
of a shiver.

Our next example is *KTU* 1.5: V.6−11:

w'at . qh 'rptk .	And you, take your clouds,
rhk . mdlk mṭrtk .	your winds, your thunderbolts,
	your rains,
'mk . šb't ǵlmk .	(take) with you your seven lads,
ṭmn . ḫnzrk	your eight 'boars',
'mk . pdry . bt . 'ar	(take) with you Pidrayu, the girl
	of the honey−dew,
'mk . {ṭ}ṭly . bt . rb .	with you Tallayu,
	the girl of the mist.

Separation upwards: Independent pers.pronoun *'at* − imperative
qh.
Separation downwards: Tautological parallelism *'mk // 'mk, bt
// bt* −*'idk*−formula following.
External parallelism: Suffixes −*k* in all cola − meteorological
phenomena − *'mk // 'mk.*

Ps. 33:16f.

'yn hmlk nwš' brb hyl	The king is not saved by the greatness of the force,
gbwr l'ynṣl brb kh	the hero is not delivered by the greatness of strength,
šqr hsws ltšw'h	a lie is the horse for saving,
wbrb hylw l'ymlṭ	and by the greatness of its force it does not help out.

Separation upwards: Emphasized position of *'yn hmlk* and *gbwr*
− tautological *brb // brb.*
Separation downwards: Emphasized *šqr.*

External parallelism: nwš' // tšw'h — brb — brb // brb — hyl // hylw.

Ps. 126:5f.

hzr'ym bdm'h	Those who sow with tears
brnh yqṣrw	will reap with cries of joy.
hlwk ylk wbkh	Surely he goes out and weeps,
nś' mšk hzr'	carrying the sack with seed.
b' ybw' brnh	Surely he comes in with cries of joy,
nś' 'lmtyw	carrying his sheaves.

Separation upwards: Emphasized position of hzr'ym.
Separation downwards: End of Psalm — paronomasia.

In this case the paronomasia *hlwk ylk* is a contra–indication against taking the three verses together. However, such a contra–indication may be neutralized by a strong external parallelism, as is the case here.

External parallelism: hzr'ym // nś' mšk hzr' — bdm'h // wbkh — brnh // brnh (inclusion) — yqṣrw // nś' 'lmtyw (inclusion) — hlwk ylk // b' ybw' — nś' // nś'.

This approach promises to make the discussions about the strophical division of the North–West Semitic poetry much more objective. However, a lot of work still has to be done before the results can be termed absolutely reliable.

5.2 The smallest strophe

The shortest possible strophe consists of only one verse which according to the rule established in paragraph 4.2 may turn out to be a unicolon. Van der Lugt has found convincing examples of this type of strophe in the Psalms, e.g. Ps. 15:5b; 125:5b.[53] Strophes of one bicolon or tricolon are quite common.

In Ugaritic the number of unicola forming an independent strophe is much higher (cf. 4.1). One example may suffice. The standard–phrase *'ap mṯn rgmm 'argm(n/k)* 'And I have yet another thing to say (to you)' occurs three times in a

---

53 Van der Lugt: 1980:501, 508.

completely different context.[54] It must be regarded as an independent, very much contracted strophe.

5.3 *Expansion / contraction of the strophe*

Like the smaller constituent parts of a poem the verse could be expanded in such a way that other verses had to be added. As a consequence the strophe grew. The Ugaritic seven–day formula, the Hebrew *n'm*– and *šm'w*–formulae and Ps. 107 are among the examples we discussed in earlier publications.[55] Two further illustrations of this point come from Ugarit.

Under 5.1 we discussed the unicolon *bnš'i 'nh wy/tphn*. We saw that it could be followed by two bicola:

KTU 1.17: V.9–11

bnš'i . 'nh . wyphn .	When he lifted up his eyes, he sighted,
b'alp šd .	over a thousand acres,
rbt . kmn .	ten thousand miles,
hlk . ktr k y'n .	surely he saw Kotharu coming,
wy'n . tdrq . hss	and saw Khasisu marching on.

In the following parallel the introductory unicolon has been reduced to zero:

KTU 1.3: IV.38–40

b'alp . šd .	Over a thousand acres,
rbt . kmn	ten thousand miles,
hlk . 'ahth . b'l . y'n .	Ba'lu saw his sister coming,
tdrq ybnt . 'abh	(saw) the Wanton Widow of his father marching on.

A well–known strophe describing how gods do enter the holy precinct of Ilu has been expanded with an extra bicolon in only one instance:

---

54   *KTU* 1.3: IV.31f.; 1.4: I.20f.; 1.17: VI.39.
55   *UF* 10 (1978) 187; 12 (1980) 311–315.

KTU 1.3: V.5−9
'*idk* [.] *l*[*ttn* . *p*]nm
[*'m* . *'il*] . *mbk nhr*[*m* .]
[*qr*]*b* . *'a*[*p*]*q* [*thm*]*tm* .
tgl . *ḏd* '*il* [.]
wtb'u [*qr*]*š* . *m*[*l*]*k* . '*ab* [. *šnm* .]
mṣr [*t*]*b'u* .
ḏdm . *qny* [. *w*]'*adn* . ['*i*]*lm*

Thereupon she headed straight
   for Ilu at the fountain−head of the two Rivers,
      in the middle of the bedding of the two Floods.
She appeared in the encampment of Ilu,
   and entered the camp of the King, the Father of Years,
she entered the stronghold,
   the encampment of the Creator and Lord of the gods.

The last two cola are a unique addition for which no reasonable explanation can be given. It is purely the mood of the poet that appears to be decisive here. No strophical theory requiring a fixed number of verses per strophe can do justice to the flexibility that is characteristic of all North−West Semitic poetry.

5.4 The largest strophe

In the material we analysed we found *no convincing instances of strophes longer than four verses*. A particular clear case of the latter is

KTU 1.6: VI.16−20

yt'n . *kgmrm*	They eyed each other like fighting−cocks,
mt . '*z* . *b'l* . '*z* .	Motu was strong, Ba'lu was strong.
ynghn kr'umm .	They gored like wild oxen,
mt . '*z* . *b'l* . '*z* .	Motu was strong, Ba'lu was strong.
ynṯkn . *kbṯnm* .	They bit like serpents,
mt . '*z* . *b'l* . '*z* .	Motu was strong, Ba'lu was strong.
ymṣhn klsmm .	They pulled like sporting−dogs,
mt . *ql b'l* . *ql* .	Motu fell, Ba'lu fell.

The passage is surrounded by direct speech so its delimitation is not at all problematical. The strong internal parallelism and the total absence of markers of separation render any subdivision artificial. It is a strophe of four verses. Under 5.1 we discussed a number of sentences running on through four and more verses. Careful analysis of all these cases invariably showed four verses to be the maximum, so we can safely assume that any on–running sentence involving more than four verses is composed of more than one strophe. We intend to discuss a few of these cases in paragraph 6. Of the sentences running on through four verses *KTU* 1.161: 27–30; Ps. 83:6–9; 149:6–9; Job 33:19–22; 38:8–11 exhibit the same pattern of four cola constituting one strophe we found for *KTU* 1.6: VI.16–20.

At first sight an acrostic like that of Ps. 119 would seem to suggest that strophes of up to 8 verses are possible. This is not true however. All sequences of 8 verses in this Psalm must be divided into strophes of 3 + 3 + 2 or (a few times) 2 + 2 + 2 + 2.[56]

6. The Canticle

6.1 General

The strophe is not the highest structural unit in North–West Semitic poetry because fairly often a sentence runs on through several strophes. Some simple examples of sentences covering two strophes are:

Ps. 64: 2–5[57]

šmʿ–'lhym qwly bśyhy	Hear my voice, o God, in my complaint,
mphd 'wyb tṣr hyy	preserve my life from the threat of the enemy.
tstyrny mswd mrʿym	Hide me from the conspiracy of the wicked,
mrgšt pʿly 'wn	from the roaring of the evildoers,

---

56   Van der Lugt: 1980:477.
57   Cf. Van der Lugt: 1980:292ff.

'šr šnnw kḥrb lšwnm	who whet their tongues like swords,
drkw ḥṣm dbr mr	aim bitter words like arrows,
lyrwt bmstrym tm	to shoot the pious from ambush,
pt'm yrhw wl' yyr'w	suddenly they shoot at him
	and do not fear.

The external parallelism between these four verses renders it
absolutely certain that in spite of the on—running sentence they
have to be grouped into two strophes of two verses each.

A similar case, involving strophes of two and three verses
respectively, is found in

Ps. 103: 1—5[58]

brky npšy 't—yhwh	Bless YHWH, my soul,
wkl—qrby 't—šm qdšw	and all my inmost
	being, (bless) his holy name !
brky npšy 't—yhwh	Bless YHWH, my soul,
w'l—tškhy kl—gmwlyw	and forget not all
	the benefits of Him,
hslḥ lkl—'wnky	who forgives all your iniquity,
hrp' lkl—tḥl'yky	who heals all your
	diseases,
hgw'l mšḥt ḥyyky	who redeems your life from the Pit,
hm'ṭrky ḥsd wrḥmym	who crowns you with faith and
	mercy,
hmšby' bṭwb 'dky!	who satisfies you with the best of
	your time,
tthdš knšr n'wryky	so that your youth is renewed
	like an eagle.

The reverse order, three plus two verses, is also attested: Ps.
102:19—23.[59] An on—running sentence covering three strophes
occurs in Ps. 148:7—12.[60]

An Ugaritic example of the same category is the following:

---

58   Van der Lugt: 1980:374ff.
59   Van der Lugt: 1980:367ff.
60   Van der Lugt: 1980:467ff.

KTU 1.17: I.25–33 (par.)

wykn . bnh . bbt .	And let there be a son for him in (his) house,
šrš . bqrb hklh .	a root within his palace,
nṣb . skn . 'il'ibh .	one who sets up the stelae of his ancestral gods,
bqdš ztr . ʿmh .	in the sanctuary the marjoram of his clan,
l'arṣ . mšṣ'u . qṭrh	one who makes his smoke come out from the earth,
lʿpr . ḏmr . 'aṭrh	from the dust the Protectors of his place,
ṭbq . lḥt n'iṣh .	one who puts the lid on the abuse of his revilers,
grš . d . ʿšy . lnh	one who chases away those who do something to him,
'aḫd . ydh . bškrn .	one who grasps his hand when he is drunk,
mʿmsh [k]šbʿ yn .	one who supports him when he is sated with wine,
sp'u . ksmh . bt . bʿl	one who serves his emmer–corn in the house of Baʿlu,
[w]mnth . bt . 'il .	and his portion in the house of Ilu,
ṭḫ . ggh . bym [ṭ'i]ṭ .	one who plasters his roof on a day when it is muddy,
rḥṣ . npṣh . bym . rṭ	one who washes his equipment on a foul day.

At first sight one might be inclined to regard the whole episode as one connected strophe. However, the last verse of the first strophe is marked by a slight syntactical deviation from the otherwise uniform pattern. Moreover, the external parallelism reveals strong bonds between the first three verses: *bbt* — *bqrb hklh* // *bqdš* // *'aṭrh*, and the ancestral cult of course. The bonds between the next four verses are much looser. Nevertheless the formal parallelism between the participles heading every verse is strong enough to defend the unity of the piece. Because the singers felt free to switch the position of the two middle verses (see *KTU* 1.17: II.4–6) it is impossible to divide the passage into two strophes of two verses each.

We call *a unit consisting of one or more strophes a canticle.*[61]
Usually the strophes belonging to the same canticle are held
together by external parallelism, sometimes a very clear and
repetitive type of parallelism, more often only a few words here
and there. A few examples from Ugarit:

KTU 1.4: VI.47—54

špq 'ilm . krm . y[n]	He supplied the ram gods with wine,
špq . 'ilht . ḥprt [. yn]	he supplied the ewe goddesses with wine.
špq . 'ilm . 'alpm . y[n]	He supplied the ox gods with wine,
špq . 'ilht . 'arḫt [. yn]	he supplied the cow goddesses with wine.
špq . 'ilm . kḫṯm . yn	He supplied the throne gods with wine,
špq . 'ilht . ks'at [. yn]	he supplied the chair goddesses with wine.
špq . 'ilm . rḥbt yn	He supplied the vase gods with wine,
špq . 'ilht . dkrt < . yn>	he supplied the bowl goddesses with wine.

In spite of the repetitious parallelism the piece should be
divided into two strophes the first of which concerns the divine
cattle, the second the divine furniture. The strophical pattern of
2 + 2 bicola is common both in Hebrew and Ugaritic. The
canticle consists of two symmetrical strophes.

KTU 1.6: I.18—29

ttbḫ . šb'm r'umm .	She slaughtered seventy wild oxen,
k gmn . 'al'iyn b'l .	because Ba'lu the Almighty had been defiled.[63]
ttbḫ . šb'm . 'alpm	She slaughtered seventy oxen,
[k g]mn . 'al'iyn . b'l	because Ba'lu the Almighty had been defiled.

[tt]bḫ . šbʿm . ṣʾin [k g]mn . ʾalʾiyn . bʿl	She slaughtered seventy sheep, because Baʿlu the Almighty had been defiled.
[tt]bḫ . šbʿm . ʾaylm [k gmn .] ʾalʾiyn . bʿl	She slaughtered seventy harts, because Baʿlu the Almighty had been defiled.
[ttbḫ . š]bʿm . yʿlm [k gmn . ʾal]ʾiyn . bʿl	She slaughtered seventy mountain– goats, because Baʿlu the Almighty had been defiled.
[ttbḫ . šbʿm . y]ḥmrm[62] [k gm]n . ʾalʾiyn . bʿl	She slaughtered seventy roebucks, because Baʿlu the Almighty had been defiled.

In spite of their great similarity the six verses have to be distributed over two strophes of three verses each because the first three deal with cattle, the second with game.[64] It may be added that the canticle consisting of 3 + 3 verses is one of the most common forms in the Hebrew Bible.[65]

Unfortunately it is often much more difficult to establish the

---

62 Cf. H.L. Ginsberg, *JANES* 5 (1973) 131f.

63 As proposed by De Moor: 1971: 199. Ugaritic *gmn* should be connected with Ethiopic *gammana* 'defile', *gᵉmūn* 'defiled, unclean', used where Hebrew employs *ṭmʾ*. We now add that this root is also related to Arab. *maǧana* 'be affronted', Hebr. *māgēn* 'insolent', *māgēnāh* 'insolence'. This kind of metathesis is also attested in: Ugar. *mrḫ* = Hebr., Arab. *rmḥ*; Ugar. *ḥsp* = Arab. *shf*; Ugar. *ʾarbdd* = Arab. *bard*; Ugar. *gml* = Hebr. *mgl*; Ugar., E.S.Arab. *ṭkḫ* = Arab. *kṯḫ*. It is well known that death defiled, cf. K.van der Toorn, *Sin and Sanction in Israel and Mesopotamia* (Assen, 1985) 36f.

No such plausible reason for the sacrifices can be adduced with the proposal of Dietrich and Loretz (*kgmn* would be a Hurrian loan word meaning 'three year old [animals]'), cf. *UF* 8 (1976) 432.

64 Because a *rʾum* 'wild ox' could be born to an *ʾarḫ(t)* 'wild cow' who was also an *ʾalp* 'domesticated ox' (*KTU* 1.10: III.1f.,15f.,19–24,36f.) a *rʾum* was apparently regarded as a more or less domesticated animal.

65 E.g. Isa. 49:5f.; 55:4–7; Hos. 2:16–19; Mic. 6:3–5; Joel 4:4–6; Ps. 21:2–7, 8–13; 34:5–10; 48:10–15; 50:1–6; 97:1–6, 7–12; 140:2–6, 7–12; 142:2–5; Cant. 1:2–4; 4:8–11; Lam. 1:10f.,12f.; 2:4f.,6f.,14f.,16f.

boundaries of a canticle than it is in the cases discussed thus far. Unity of thought, external parallelism between the strophes, ancient divisions like *selah, petuchah* and *setumah*[66] may be helpful here, but it is still impossible to obtain absolutely reliable results. For that reason we consider it imprudent to draw up a list of all forms of canticles we believe to have identified in the poetry of Ugarit and Israel. Thus far we found no less than 67 different combinations of strophes of varying length forming a canticle. Regular patterns like 2 + 2 or 3 + 3 + 3 verses and symmetrical patterns like 2 + 3 + 2 + 3 seem to prevail over canticles with unbalanced numbers of verses.

6.2 The smallest canticle

As might be expected on the basis of what we found for the smaller structural elements *the shortest possible canticle consists of only one strophe*. Of course the latter may comprise only one verse (cf. 5.2). Hebrew examples of canticles of only one verse may be found in Ps. 3:9; 16:1; 21:14; 75:2; 82:8; 146:1; Isa. 5:1; 48:22.

6.3 Expansion / contraction of the canticle

Only parallel transmission might provide us with conclusive evidence of canticles to which strophes were added. As yet we know of no such examples. It seems that the possibilities for expansion and contraction ended with the strophe. In any case such a drastic expansion or contraction, if it was acceptable, must have been very rare. If this proves to be true, it is the most important restriction imposed on the freedom of the singers. It guaranteed that the basic message of a poem always remained inviolate.

6.4 The largest canticle

Because of the difficulties involved in the delimitation of

---

66 On the importance of *selah* see Van der Lugt: 1980:523,587 n.19. On the pre—Massoretic tradition of *petuchah* and *setumah* see J.M. Oesch, *Petucha und Setuma* (Freiburg, 1979).

canticles (6.1) it is impossible to pronounce a definitive judgment on the question what the maximum length of a canticle could be. We found possible examples of canticles of *five strophes* in: Isa. 41:17–20 (1 + 1 + 2 + 2 + 2); 44:1–5 (1 + 2 + 2 + 1 + 2); Ps. 50:7–15, 16–23 (both 1 + 2 + 2 + 2 + 2); Isa. 53:2–6; Mic. 2:6–11; Ps. 132:11–18; Cant. 3:1–5 (all 2 + 2 + 2 + 2 + 2); 1.Sam. 2:4–10 (3 + 2 + 3 + 2 + 3).

7. Beyond the Canticle

One or more canticles could be combined to form higher structural units which we call provisionally sub–canto and canto. The same kind of arguments used in delimiting the canticle are invoked to describe the sub–canto and canto. In lieu of more theorizing we will try to elucidate our approach of these higher structural units by a step–by–step analysis of two short poetical fragments. The first, relatively easy example is Isa. 1:21–26:

A.1 *'ykh hyth lzwnh* (21aA)
    qryh n'mnh (21aB)
 ml'ty mšpṭ (21bA)
   ṣdq ylyn bh (21bB)
    w'th mrṣhym (21bC)

How she became a harlot (21aA),
    the faithful city (21aB) !
She was full of justice (21bA),
    righteousness lodged in her (21bB),
    but now murderers (21bC).

A.2 *kspk hyh lsygym* (22aA)
    sb'k mhwl bmym (22aB)
 šryk swrrym (23aA)
   wḥbry gnbym (23aB)

Your silver became dross (22aA),
    your beer was diluted with water (22aB).
Your princes are rebels (23aA),
    and friends of thieves (23aB).

A.3 *klw 'hb šḥd* (23bA)
    wrdp šlmnym (23bB)
 ytwm l' yšpṭw (23cA)
   wryb 'lmnh (23cB)
    l'–ybw 'lyhm (23cC)

Every one of them loves a bribe (23bA),
and pursues presents (23bB).
The orphan they do not judge (23cA),
and the case of the widow (23cB)
does not come to them (23cC).

p— —

B.1 *lkn n'm h'dwn* (24aA)
yhwh ṣb'wt (24aB)
'byr yśr'l (24aC)
hwy 'nḥm mṣry (24bA)
w'nqmh m'wyby (24bB)

Therefore the declaration of the Lord (24aA),
YHWH of the hosts (24aB),
the Bull of Israel (24aC):
Woe, I will be sorry for my opponents (24bA),
and will avenge myself on my enemies (24bB).

B.2 *w'šybh ydy 'lyk* (25aA)
w'ṣrp kbr sygyk (25aB)
w'syrh kl—bdylyk (25aC)
w'šybh šptyk kbr'šnh (26aA)
wy'ṣyk kbtḥlh (26aB)

And I will bring back my hand against you (25aA),
and I will purify your dross as with lye (25aB),
and I will remove all your slags (25aC).
And I will bring back your judges, as at first (26aA),
and your counsellors as at the beginning (26aB).

B.3 *'ḥry—kn yqr' lk* (26bA)
'yr hṣdq (26bB)
qryh n'mnh (26bC)

Afterward you will be called (26bA),
town of righteousness (26bB),
faithful city (26bC).

The delimitation of the passage is based on the following
considerations. According to ancient tradition already attested in
the first Isaiah scroll from Qumran the separation upwards is
ascertained by the *setumah* after vs. 20. Moreover, *'ykh* is a
typical beginning of a lament (e.g. Lam. 1:1; 2:1; 4:1). It is

more difficult to pinpoint the end of the passage. The verses 27–28 would seem to contradict the message of the preceding oracle of doom. Zion will be redeemed whereas its enemies will be obliterated. This looks suspiciously like a later neutralization of the harsh verdict of the preceding verses. Moreover, in vs. 21 and vs. 26 the prophet uses the word *ṣdq* whereas the author of vs. 27 prefers *ṣdqh*. Therefore it seems admissable to take vs. 26 as the last verse of the poem, with B.Duhm and many others.[67]

Division into strophes:

A.1   Separation upwards: *setumah* – *'ykh*. Separation downwards: tricolon — *w'th*. External parallelism linking the verses of the strophe: *zwnh // mrṣhym, n'mh // mšpṭ, ṣdq*.

A.2   Sep.up: emphasized *kspk*. Sep.down: absent. Ext.par.: *kspk // šryk, sygym // swrrym, mym // gnbym*, explaining the metaphors. Also the end–rhyme –*ym* (4 times).

A.3   Sep.up: emphasized *klw*. Sep.down: tricolon — tautological parallelism *l' // l'* – *petuchah*. Ext.par.: the corrupted judicial system.

B.1   Sep.up: *lkn* – *n'm* – tricolon. Sep.down: *hwy* – cohortative. Ext.par.: absent.

B.2   Sep.up: tricolon — cohortative — tautological parallel *w // w // w* and –*k // –k // –k* (end–rhyme). Sep.down: cohortative — tautological parallel *k* and *h* (end–rhyme). Ext.par.: *w'šybh // w'šybh* – suffixes –*k* in all cola.

B.3   Sep.up/down: tricolon — *'hry–kn*.

Division into canticles:

The *petuchah* at the end of vs. 23 is a strong argument in favour of a division into two canticles of three strophes. It appears to coincide with the borderline between the accusation and the verdict in the classical form of the oracle of doom.[68] This is sufficient proof that here is *a unity of thought* within

67   B. Duhm, *Das Buch Jesaja* (Göttingen, 1922⁴) 35.   See also J. Vermeylen, *Du prophete Isaie à l'apocalyptique.* t.1, (Paris, 1977) 71–105; H. Wildberger, *Jesaja.* 1.Teilband (BKAT X/1; Neukirchen–Vluyn, 1980²) 55–68; O. Kaiser, *Das Buch des Propheten Jesaja. Kap. 1–12* (ATD 17; Göttingen, 1981⁵) 52–58.

68   C. Westermann, *Grundformen prophetischer Rede* (München, 1960) 120ff.; K. Koch, *Was ist Formgeschichte?* (Neukirchen–Vluyn, 1974³) 258ff.

each of the two canticles. Finally we observe that the borderline between the two canticles is marked by two successive long verses (tricola).

But as on the level of the strophe, *external parallelism* is linking the strophes of the two canticles together:

A.*1–3* *hyth l* (21aA) // *hyh l* (22aA) (responsion)
     zwnh (21aA) // *'lmnh* (23cB) (inclusion)
     mšpṭ (21bA) // *yšpṭw* (23cA) (responsion)
     mrṣhym (21bC) // *gnbym* (23aB) (responsion)

B.*1–3* *lkn* (24aA) // *kn* (26bA) (inclusion)
     n'm (24aA) // *n'mnh* (26bC) (assonance, inclusion)
     names of YHWH (24) // names of Zion (26) (inclusion)
     ṣry (24bA) // *špṭyk* (26aA) (responsion)
     'wyby (24bB) // *y'ṣyk* (26aB) (responsion)

Finally it may be observed that the whole *canto* is held together by an intricated web of external parallelism:

    qryh n'mnh (21aB) // *qryh n'mnh* (26bC) (inclusion of the total canto, a very frequent phenomenon)
    mšpṭ (21bA), *yšpṭw* (23cA) // *špṭyk* (26aA)(inclusion as well as responsion)
    ṣdq (21bB) // *ṣdq* (26bB) (responsion)
    'th (21bC) // *br'šwnh, bthlh* (26a) (responsion)
    sygym (22aA) // *sygyk* (25aB) (responsion)
    šryk (23aA) // *špṭyk, y'ṣyk* (26a) (responsion)

Isa. 1:21–26 presents us with a straightforward example of a canto composed of two canticles of three strophes each. The regularity in the structure of this canto is not to be sought in the number of verses per strophe but in the equal number of strophes per canticle.

Our second, more complicated example comes from Ugarit:

KTU 1.3: III.32 – IV.20
A.1 I.1 *hlm . 'nt . tph . 'ilm .*

    Behold ! 'Anatu saw the two gods.

A.1 I.2 *bh . p'nm ttt .*

b'dn . ksl . ṯṯbr
'ln . pnh . td'
tġṣ . pnt kslh .
'anš . dt . ẓrh

With her the feet began to totter,
at her back the spine loosened,
her face above began to sweat,
the joints of her spine shook,
the small of her back too.

– –

A.1 II.1 *tš'u gh . wtṣh .*

She lifted up her voice and cried:

A.1 II.2 *'ik . mġy . gpn . w'ugr*
mn . 'ib . yp' . lb'l .
ṣrt lrkb . 'rpt .

'Why did Gupanu and Ugaru arrive ?
What enemy did rise against Ba'lu,
what opponent against the Rider on the Clouds ?

+ +

A.2 I.1 *l mḫšt . mdd 'il ym .*
l klt . nhr . 'il . rbm
l 'ištbm . tnn .
'ištm . lh

Did I not slay the Beloved of Ilu, Yammu ?
Did I not destroy River, the god of the great ones ?
Did I not muzzle Tunnanu,
did I (not) stop his mouth ?

A.2 I.2 *mḫšt . bṭn . 'qltn*
šlyt . d . šb't . r'ašm
mḫšt . mdd 'ilm . 'arš
ṣmt . 'gl . 'il . 'tk
mḫšt . klbt . 'ilm . 'išt
klt . bt .'il . ḏbb .

I did slay the coiling serpent,
the tyrant with the seven heads !
I did slay the Beloved of Ilu, Arishu,
I silenced the bull–calf of Ilu, 'Atiku !

I did slay the bitch of Ilu, Ishatu,
I did destroy the daughter of Ilu, Dhubabu !

— — — — — — — — — — — — — — — — — — — —

A.2 II.1 *'imthṣ* . *ksp*
  'itrt . *ḥrṣ* .
  ṭrd . *b'l bmrym* . *ṣpn* .
  mšṣṣ . *k'ṣr 'udnh* .
  gršh . *lks'i* . *mlkh*
  lnḫt . *lkhṭ* . *drkth*

I shall battle for the silver,
  shall take possession of the gold
of anyone who tries to expel Ba'lu from the heights
of Sapanu,
  tries to make him fly up like a bird from his aerie,
tries to chase him from the chair of his kingship,
  from the seat of the throne of his dominion !

A.2 II.2 *mnm* . *'ib* . *yp'* . *lb'l*
  ṣrt . *lrkb* . *'rpt*

What enemy did rise against Ba'lu,
  what opponent against the Rider on the Clouds ?"

= =

B.1 I.1 *y'n* . *ġlmm* .
  y'nyn .

The lads answered,
  they answered her:

B.1 I.2 *l* *'ib* . *yp'* *lb'l* .
  ṣrt . *lrkb* . *'rpt*

'No enemy did rise against Ba'lu,
  (no) opponent against the Rider on the Clouds !

— — — — — — — — — — — — — — — — — — — —

B.1 II.1 *thm* . *'al'iyn* . *b'l* .
  hwt . *'al'iy qrdm* .

A message from Ba'lu the Almighty,
  a word from the Mightiest of heroes:

B.1 II.2 *qryy* . *b'arṣ* . *mlḥmt*

št . bʿprm . ddym .
sk. šlm lkbd. ʾarṣ.
ʾarbdd . lkbd . šdm

Oppose war on earth,
    put love—fruit in the ground,
    pour peace in the middle of the earth,
    tranquillity in the middle of the fields !

+ +

B.2 I.1 *hšk ʿṣk . ʿbṣk .*
    ʿmy . pʿnk tlsmn .
    ʿmy . twṯ̲ . ʾišdk

Hurry up ! Press on ! Make haste !
    Let your feet run towards me,
    let your legs rush towards me !

B.2 I.2 *dm . rgm . ʾiṯ . ly . wʾargmk*
    hwt wʾaṯnyk .

For I have a word which I want to speak to you,
    a message which I want to communicate to you,

– –

B.2 II.1 *rgm . ʿṣ . wlḫ̲št ʾabn .*
    rgm . l tdʿ . nšm .
    w l tbn hmlt . ʾarṣ .
    tʾant . šmm . ʿm . ʾarṣ
    thmt . ʿmn . kbkbm .
    ʾabn . brq dl tdʿ . šmm .

a word of trees and a whisper of stones,
    a word that mankind does not know,
        nor the multitude of the earth do understand,
    a groaning of the heavens to the earth,
        of the Flood to the stars:
    I understand the lightning which heavens do not know!

B.2 II.2 *ʾatm . wʾank ʾibġyh .*
    btk . ġry . ʾil . ṣpn
    bqdš . bġr . nhlty

Come, because I am asking it,
    towards my mountain, the divine Sapanu,
        to the holy one, to the mountain of my heritage!

= =

Division into strophes:

A.1. I.1: Sep.up: double line on the tablet — *ḥlm.* Sep.down:
A.1. I.2. See
A.1. I.2: We discussed this strophe above, p.33f.
A.1. II.1: A well—known unicolon introducing direct oration.
A.1. II.2: Sep.up: *'ik.* Sep.down: *mn.* Ext.par.: *'ik // mn,* names.
A.2. I.1: Sep.up: tautological parallel *l // l, 'il // 'il.* Sep.down: absent. Ext.par.: *l // l, ym // tnn.*
A.2. I.2: Sep.up: absent. Sep.down: absent. Ext.par.: *mḫšt // mḫšt // mḫšt, btn // 'gl // klbt, ilm // 'ilm, 'il // 'il.*
A.2. II.1: Sep.up: absent. Sep.down: absent. Ext.par.: *ṭrd // gršh, mrym ṣpn // ks'i mlkh.*
A.2. II.2: Sep.up/down: *mnm.*
B.1. I.1: Sep.up: introduction direct oration.
B.1. I.2: See A.2. II.2.
B.1. II.1: Sep.up/down: introduction direct oration.
B.1. II.2: Sep.up.: imperatives. Sep.down: imperative — tautological parallel *lkbd // lkbd.* Ext.par.: *'arṣ // 'arṣ, mlḥmt // šlm,* etc.
B.2. I.1: Sep.up/down: tricolon — infinitives serving as imperatives — jussives.
B.2. I.2: Sep.up/down: *dm.*
B.2. II.1: Sep.up: tricolon, tautological parallel *rgm // rgm.* Sep.down: absent. Ext.par.: *rgm // t'ant, 'arṣ // šmm, l td' // l td', tbn // 'abn.*
B.2. II.2: Sep.up/down: tricolon — imperative — independent *'ank,* end of message.

Division into canticles:

First we observe there is *a unity of thought per canticle:*

A.1. I: Description of 'Anatu's physical reaction to the approach of the messengers.
A.1. II: Description of her verbal reaction: What enemy?
A.2. I: Her victories over foes of Ba'lu in the past.
A.2. II: Her readiness to defeat them all over again. What enemy?
B.1. I: Answer of messengers: No enemy.
B.1. II: Delivery of their first message from Ba'lu: no more war on earth.
B.2. I: Delivery of their second message from Ba'lu: come to

hear my news.

B.2. II: It is a very special piece of news, so do not tarry and come.

Next we look for *external parallelism linking the strophes of the canticles to each other:*

A.2.I.1 with A.2.I.2:
  mḫšt // *mḫšt* (responsion and inclusion)
  mdd 'il // *bt 'il* (inclusion)
  mdd 'il // *mdd 'ilm*
  monsters // monsters.

A.2.II.1 with A.2.II.2:
  ṭrd, mšṣṣ, gršh // *'ib, ṣrt*
  b'l // *b'l*

B.2.I.1 with B.2.I.2:
  'my // *ly*, suffixes −*k*.

It appears that the eight canticles can be grouped into four *sub- cantos:*
  A.1 'Anatu's reaction at seeing the messengers.
  A.2 Her threatening speech.
  B.1 The pacifying answer of the messengers.
  B.2 Ba'lu's invitation to come.

A.1 is marked by the responsion *'ilm* // *gpn w'ugr.*
A.2 is marked by the responsion *mḫšt* // *'imtḫs.*
The parallel structure of the sub−cantos A.1 and A.2 is underlined by the refrain A.1.II.2 = A.2.II.2.
B.1 is marked by the responsion *b'l* // *b'l.*
B.2 is marked by the chiastic parallelism between B.2.I.1 // B.2.II.2 and B.2.I.2 // B.2.II.1.

Finally it is not difficult to see that we are dealing with two *cantos* here:
  A   'Anatu's premature reaction and speech.
  B   The reaction of the messengers and their speech.
The two cantos are connected by a number of evident links:
  A.1.I.1 *'ilm* // B.1.I.1 *glmm* (responsion)
  A.1.II.2 // B.1.I.2 (refrain)
  A.2.II.1 *mrym ṣpn* // B.2.II.2 *gry 'il ṣpn.*

In spite of the great differences in length between verses and strophes the overall structure on the higher level of canticles, sub—cantos and cantos exhibits a surprising regularity:

CANTOS	SUB-CANTOS	CANTICLES	STROPHES
1	2	4	8
1	2	4	8

8. Some Implications

The results obtained via the analytical method we propose are not just of a purely esthetic nature. We often observed a certain spin—off into other areas of research.

The method may be helpful in solving *textcritical problems*. Two examples may serve to illustrate this. The responsion *mṣrym* 'Egypt' in Isa. 31:1 and *'šwr* 'Assur' in Isa. 31:8 as well as the inclusion *mṣrym* 'Egypt' in 31:3 and the inclusion created by the word—play *'ᵃšer 'ūr lō* 'who has a fire' in 31:9 render it almost certain that we have to vocalize *šwbw l'šr* in Isa. 31:6 as *šūbū lᵉ'aššūr* 'Turn to Assur !'. The second example is found in Ps. 23 where the responsion *yšwbb* (3aA) // *wšbty* (6bA) provides us with an extra argument in favour of the Massoretic vocalization of the latter. Of course this in turn has a bearing upon the interpretation of the Psalm as a song of pilgrimage.

As in the example Isa. 1:21—26 we discussed earlier the meaning of *metaphors* can be clarified through the mechanism of external parallelism. In Ps. 23:4 the metaphorical content of the phrase *šbṭk wmš'ntk / hmh ynḥmny* 'your rod and your staff — they comfort me' is unclear. What did the poet have in mind when he spoke of the 'rod' and the 'staff' of the divine Shepherd? The inclusion *twb wḥsd yrdpwny* 'goodness and faithfulness follow me' in vs. 6 provides us with a clue. Rod and staff would seem to be certain qualities of God, just like 'goodness' and 'faithfulness'. Probably his vigilance and protection are meant. The interesting thing is that the metaphor *yrd pwny* 'follow me' is in turn explained by the imagery of the first canticle of Ps. 23: 'Goodness' and 'Faithfulness' are the pseudo—names of the staffs urging the Psalmist on.[69] That such explanations are far from fanciful is ascertained by an allegory like that of Isa. 5:1—7. Here the explanatory nature of the responsion between vs. 2c and vs. 7c—d is guaranteed by the

---

69 Cf. Zech. 11:7.

explicit explanation of the metaphor of the vine directly preceding it.[70]

Literary criticism too may sometimes benefit from the analytical method we described. As shown by K. Spronk the regular structure of Isa. 14:4b–20aA renders it practically certain that 14:4a and 14:20aB–23 are later additions actualizing a song which originally had nothing to do with the king of Babylon.[71] The regular structure of Isa. 31:1–9 (3 canticles of 3 strophes each counting 2 verses) would seem to indicate that 1c, 4a and 7b are explanatory glosses. One final example: the verses Hos. 1:7 and 2:1–3 are almost universally recognized as later additions. This is confirmed by the circumstance that the regular structure of Hos. 1–2 emerges only if these verses are omitted (4 cantos of 3 canticles, each of which consisting of 2 strophes).

Finally we found the method helpful for the *exegesis* of these ancient poems. We modern readers are conditioned to read a text in a strictly linear way, from beginning to end. However, the skilful exploitation of the repetitive effect of external parallelism tends to lend a more or less concentric structure to the larger building–blocks of ancient North–West Semitic poetry. Verses many lines apart appear to form one and the same concentric shell and as we have seen they explain each other in this way. We for our part are accustomed to look at the end of a composition for the general conclusions, a pithy recapitulation of the main points or the outcome of the captivating story. In the kind of poetry we try to describe here, however, we often find the heart of the matter right in the middle where it belongs as the kernel out of which everything grew in accordance with the laws of parallelistic expansion. Of course it would require too much space to document these observations as fully as might be desirable. One final example will do: Psalm 78, which is especially interesting because the poet deliberately re–arranged historical traditions that had long been fixed by the time he was writing for the sole purpose of a

---

70 M.C.A. Korpel, *De litteraire vorm van het lied van de wijngaard* (Theol.Hogeschool; Kampen, 1985) 19,22,58f. See p.139f., 141ff., 146 below.
71 K. Spronk, *Beatific Afterlife in Ancient Israel and in the Ancient Near East* (AOAT 219; Neukirchen–Vluyn, 1986) 213–220.

well—balanced concentric structure.[72]

We first give the results of our analysis of Ps. 78 in an abbreviated schematic form:

	VERSES	COLA
A.1.I.1	1b−2	2 + 2
A.1.I.2	3−4	2 + 2 + 3
- -		
A.1.II.1	5	2 + 2
A.1.II.2	6−7	2 + 2 + 3
- -		
A.1.III.1	8	2 + 2
A.1.III.2	9−11	3 + 2 + 2
+ +		
A.2.I.1	12−14	3 + 2 + 2
A.2.I.2	15−16	2 + 2
= =		
B.1.I.1	17−18	2 + 2
B.1.I.2	19	2 + 2
B.1.I.3	20	2 + 2
- -		
B.1.II.1	21−22	3 + 2
+ +		
B.2.I.1	23−25	2 + 2 + 2
B.2.I.2	26−27	2 + 2
B.2.I.3	28−29	2 + 2
- -		
B.2.II.1	30−31	2 + 3
= =		
C. I.1	32−33	2 + 2
C. I.2	34−35	2 + 2
- -		
C. II.1	36−37	2 + 2
C. II.2	38−39	3 + 2 + 3
= =		

---

72 Several scholars have advocated a very early date for this Psalm but in view of the deuteronomistic language the late seventh century is a much more realistic date. Cf. R.J.Clifford, 'In Zion and David a New Beginning', in: B. Halpern—J.D. Levenson (eds.), *Traditions in Transformation. FS F.M. Cross* (Winona Lake, 1981) 121ff.

D.1. I.1	40–41	2 + 2
D.1. I.2	42–43	2 + 2

- -

D.1.II.1	44–45	2 + 2
D.1.II.2	46–48	2 + 2 + 2

- -

D.1.III.1	49–50a	2 + 2
D.1.III.2	50b–51	2 + 2

+ +

D.2.I.1	52–53	2 + 2
D.2.I.2	54–55	2 + 3

= =

E.1.I.1	56–58	2 + 2 + 2
E.1.I.2	59–60	2 + 2

- -

E.1.II.1	61–62	2 + 2
E.1.II.2	63–64	2 + 2

+ +

E.2.I.1	65–66	2 + 2
E.2.I.2	67–68	2 + 2

- -

E.2.II.1	69–70	2 + 2
E.2.II.2	71–72	3 + 2

= =

This results in a nice symmetrical structure:

CANTOS	SUB–CANTOS	CANTICLES	STROPHES	VERSES
A	2	4 (3+1)	8 (2+2+2/2)	20
B	2	4 (2+2)	8 (3+1/3+1)	17
C	0	2 (1+1)	4 (2/2)	9
D	2	4 (3+1)	8 (2+2+2/2)	17
E	2	4 (2+2)	8 (2+2/2+2)	17

Disregarding the slight expansion of the number of verses in the introductory canto we find a high degree of symmetry on the level of the higher structural units of this Psalm. This is by no means a rare phenomenon. It is rather fully in accordance with what we found in numerous other cases.

With regard to the exegesis of the Psalm a number of interesting conclusions can now be drawn. The concentric shape of the poem tells us where to look for its central message. Canto C appears to teach the lesson of history in the most

general terms. The ever recurring unfaithfulness of Israel is
contrasted to the enduring faithfulness and mercy of God. We
would expect such a general conclusion at the end of the poem.
Here it is right in the middle. The central position of canto C
is underlined by a fivefold responsion:

C. I.1   t h e y s i n n e d
C. I.1   *they did not believe ('mn)*
C. I.2   HE KILLED THEM
C. I.2   *they turned to Him (šwb)*
C. I.2   they remembered that God was their rock

C. II.1   t h e y d e c e i v e d H i m
C. II.1   *their heart was not steadfast ('mn)*
C. II.2   HE DID NOT DESTROY THEM
C. II.2   *He did turn away his wrath (šwb)*
C. II.2   He remembered that they were flesh.

Just as the verses of a strophe are usually bound together by
external parallelism, so too the higher structural units. The
sub−canto A.1 is bracketed by an inclusion: the 'teaching' in
A.1.I.1 and A.1.III.2. The three canticles of A.1 are linked by
the word 'fathers' (A.1.I.2, A.1.II.1, A.1.III.1). Even more
striking are the responsions between all second strophes of these
canticles forming the sub−canto A.1:

A.1 I.2   knowing   children telling generations God acts
A.1 II.2 knowing   children telling generations God acts
          not forgetting
A.1 III.2 forgetting   children −   cf. III.1   God acts

The elaboration of the very regularly structured sub−canto A.1
starts with A.2. This much smaller sub−canto is linked to A.1
by the words 'fathers', 'He did' (// deeds) and 'wonders'.

The relation between the sub−cantos B.1 and B.2 is indicated
by their contents:

B.1. I The call for bread and flesh
B.1. II *The wrath of YHWH*
B.2. I The gift of manna and birds
B.2. II *The wrath of God*

Note the symmetrical structure which is still preserved even if
the strophes and canticles differ widely in length (law of
expansion and contraction). The responsion between B.1.II. and
B.2.II. *(the wrath of God)* is supported by yet another inclusion:

B.1. I food for their throats
B.2. II food in their mouths.

Also the canticles of B.1 and B.2 are subtly connected by inclusions:

B.1. I.1   sinning against God
B.1. I.3   *water for his people*
B.1.II.1   *fire for Israel*
B.1.II.1   not believing in God.

A striking feature of sub—canto B.2 is the chaining of the strophes (concatenation):

B.2. I.1   the bread of *heaven* r a i n s   down
B.2. I.2   the flesh of *heaven* r a i n s   down
B.2. I.3   it   f e l l   down, they *ate what they craved*
B.2.II.1   *they ate what they craved*
B.2.II.1   *they ate* and died.

The three canticles of sub—canto D.1 are obviously bound together by the plagues of Egypt. The responsions 'in Egypt' // 'in Egypt' and 'in the field of Zoan' // 'in the tents of Ham' mark the beginning and end of this sub—canto.

The relation of D.1 and D.2 is indicated by three responsions:

D.1. I.1 in the desert
D.1. I.2 HIS HAND
D.1.III.2 *in the tents of Ham*
D.2. I.1 in the desert
D.2. I.2 HIS RIGHT HAND
D.2. I.2 *in their tents*

The last canto presents us with a nice concentric structure:

a'   E.1. I.1   Israel is unfaithful to God and does not guard,
b'   it builds high places;
c'   E.1. I.2   God rejects Israel,
d'   abandons the tent of Siloh,
e'   E.1.II.1   gives his inheritance to the enemy,
f'   E.1.II.2   young men are dying in the prime of life.
f"   E.2. I.1   The hero Adonay is awaking,
e"   defeats the enemies,
d"   E.2. I.2   rejects the tent of Joseph,
c"   elects the tribe of Judah,
b"   E.2.II.1   builds his own sanctuary as in high places,
a"   E.2.II.2   elects David who guards his inheritance
             faithfully.

It will be clear that this way of structuring history has a theological and political background. Also it appears to be totally impossible to strike vs. 58 as a deuteronomistic addition (so Campbell) because this would destroy the delicate construc—

tion. The relevance of this kind of poetical analysis to the exegesis would seem obvious. One final detail may illustrate this point. In a linear reading of Ps. 78 it is not easy to determine who the 'enemies' of vs. 66 are. Are they the Israelites who are rejected according to vs. 67? Or are they foreign troops? The concentric correspondence between e' and e'' argues in favour of the latter possibility.

If we adhere to our Western—European ideas about regularity Psalm 78 does not seem to be composed in a very regular way. However, if we are willing to look for *their* idea of poetical order and structure, regularity manifests itself on many levels. Also in the macro—structure of the Psalm. After the introductory canticles A.1.I and II a most remarkable undulatory movement develops:

A.1   Sin of the fathers (canticle III)
A.2   Wonders of God in Egypt and in the desert

B.1   Sin of the fathers (canticle I)
B.2   Wonders of God in the desert

C.I   Sin of the fathers (canticle I)
C.II Mercy of God

D.1   Sin of the fathers (canticle I)
D.2   Wonders of God during Exodus and Conquest

E.1   Sin of the fathers (canticle I)
E.2   Salvation and election of Zion and David

The poet appears to have placed the election of Zion and David on a par with God's great acts of salvation in the past, just as 2.Sam. 7 does. In the past it was God himself who lead the people of Israel as if it was his herd (A.2.I.1 and D.2.I.1). According to E.2.II.1—2 God turns over the pastoral office to David. A second responsion, intimately related to the first one, underlines the intention of the poet: from the beginning the Conquest of Canaan was aimed at the acquisition of the holy precinct, mount Zion (D.2.I.2). This is taken up in E.2.I.2 and E.2.II.1. Apparently we are dealing here with a theology in which the royal dynasty and the temple were closly related. 'My people' (the people of the Psalmist, vs. 1) and 'his people' (the people of God, vss. 20, 52, 62, 71 — inclusion !) become the people of David. His hands (vs. 72) take the place of the hands of God (vss. 42, 52, a doubtlessly deliberately introduced responsion, cf. 'inheritance' and 'Israel'). David is able to fulfil this task because in contrast to the other Israelites whose hearts were unsteadfast (vss. 8, 18, 37) his leadership is rooted in a blameless heart (vs. 72). These examples may suffice to demonstrate that it is worthwhile to unravel the structural framework of such a Psalm.

9. Conclusions

The poetry of Canaan and Israel may be characterized as a breathing universe, expanding and contracting according to the mood and skill of the singers. By adding 'more of the same' every structural unit up to and including the strophe could grow considerably. In theory one word[73] might form the kernel out of which a major work of art was composed by adding ever more balancing parallelistic structures. Because every structural element contained at least one element of the preceding order of magnitude such poems tended to grow in concentric circles, not in the way of ripples caused by a stone in a pond, but much more irregularly, like the rings marking the good and bad years of a tree, with knots indicating the places where new parallelistic structures branch off.

The following table summarizes some of our findings:

Building–block	Smallest	Expandable	Largest
Foot	1 syllable	Yes	8 syllables
Colon	1 foot	Yes	5 feet
Verse	1 colon	Yes	9 cola
Strophe	1 verse	Yes	4 verses
Canticle	1 strophe	No ?	5 strophes ?
(Sub–)canto	1 canticle	?	?

As a result of the concentric structure we described the deeper intentions of the poets may escape the modern reader who is accustomed to a linear interpretation of texts. Conditioned as we

---

73 Compare the titles of the Ugaritic myths and legends: *lbʿl* 'Of Baʿlu', *lkrt* 'Of Kirtu', *ʾaqht* 'Of Aqhatu'.

all are by a society placing its faith in the written word, we find it hard to imagine how an audience used to memorizing every noteworthy scrap of information could savour the intricate webs of allusions created by the skilful exploitation of the stylistic device of external parallelism between verses often many lines of poetry apart. From the level of the verse to that of the canto these poems have often been composed not straightforwardly from A to B, but from A1 via B1 and C1 to C2, B2 and finally A2 explaining A1. Careful analysis of this kind of embracing and repetitive patterns, especially the figures of inclusion, responsion and concatenation, has proved to be extremely helpful in understanding poetic texts from Ugarit and Israel. Sometimes the method we propose has even been useful in solving textcritical problems or identifying later additions to old compositions.

Admittedly the method is still far from perfect. It does not guarantee absolute unanimity with regard to the results. However, what it does achieve is a much higher degree of unanimity among different scholars analysing the same text independently. Their reasoning is fully verifiable and therefore debatable. It does not depend as heavily as current methods on content and therefore on exegesis. Anybody knowing from experience the feeling of bewilderment pervading the scholar who compares the division of a Psalm or a prophetic discourse in a number of Bible translations and commentaries will recognize that this might be at least one step in the right direction.

THE LEGEND OF KIRTU (KTU 1.14–16)

A Study of the Structure and its Consequences for Interpretation

Klaas Spronk

This well–known Ugaritic text describing the adventures of king Kirtu can be classified as epic poetry.[1] As far as its literary form is concerned, this can be determined from the fact that the text is built up of cola. Ilimilku, the writer responsible for the written form of the text, apparently attempted to adhere to the colometric divisions wherever possible, as is evident from the high degree of conformity between the cola and the physical lines on the tablet. Additional indications of poetic structure are also clearly evident.[2] Higher poetic units such as strophes, canticles and cantos are discernible.[3] This in turn raises the question whether a clear structure has been placed upon these units when taken together, and if so, whether the poet employed the usual means of external parallelism and uniformity of structure. Research into the poetic structure of the book of Ruth has produced positive answers to similar questions.[4] It has been demonstrated there that a number of cantos taken together can form a clearly delineated unit (or chapter), and that the division of the chapters into smaller units proceeds according to a uniform pattern.

A study of the larger literary units within the legend of Kirtu is seriously impeded by the badly damaged condition of tablets *KTU* 1.15 and 1.16. Furthermore, we must take into account that at least one tablet is missing.[5] Fortunately the opening portion of the legend is well preserved. And it is probable that literary principles with respect to form and structure of the higher poetic units established on the basis of a study of this section will supply clues for the reconstruction of lost portions

1 W.G.E. Watson, *Classical Hebrew Poetry*. A Guide to its Techniques (JSOTS; Sheffield, 1986[2]) 85.
2 Watson: 1986 gives many examples of this.
3 J.C. de Moor, *UF* 10 (1978) 190–191, 202–205.
4 J.C. de Moor, *Or* 53 (1984) 262–283 and 55 (1986) 16–46.
5 J.C.L. Gibson, *Canaanite Myths and Legends* (Edinburgh, 1978) 20.

of the legend.

The scope of this study, with its focus upon literary structure, does not permit discussion of philological problems.[6] Similarly, the limited length of this article does not allow for a complete reproduction of the text itself. The divisions of the text as here treated are based upon the colometry found in some recently published textbooks of religious Ugaritic literature.[7] In this article we are necessarily limited to a brief description of the content of each canticle, followed by a statistical summary of the strophes, verses and cola.

Chapter 1

Canto 1 (KTU 1.14:I.2−II.9)

Kirtu laments his childlessness, and is approached in this connection by Ilu.

Determination of the boundaries of this canto affords little problem. There can be no doubt about the beginning, and the termination too leaves little room for doubt because *KTU* 1.14:II.9 marks the beginning of Ilu's monologue, which has been demonstrated in a previous study to be a uniformly structured canto.[8]

Canticle 1 (*KTU* 1.14:I.2−21) describes Kirtu's dire circum−stances; he had seven wives but not one of them produced children. Unfortunately the opening lines of the text are damaged. Consequently it is not possible to determine whether the first canticle consisted of four or five strophes. Of the final three strophes, the first consists of two bicola, the second consists of one bicolon, and the final strophe contains three bicola and one tricolon, producing the statistical scheme:

---

6   See J.C. de Moor−K. Spronk, 'Problematical Passages in the Legend of Kirtu', *UF* 14 (1982) 153−190.

7   J.C. de Moor−K. Spronk, *A Cuneiform Anthology of Religious Texts from Ugarit* (Semitic Study Series; New Series VI; Leiden, 1987) 78−101; J.C. de Moor, *An Anthology of Religious Texts from Ugarit* (NISABA XVI; Leiden, 1987) 191−223. The colometrical divisions in these publications agree almost entirely with that of Gibson: 1978:82−102. For a delineation of the verses see the above mentioned translation by De Moor.

8   J.C. de Moor, *UF* 10 (1978) 202−204.

2+2/2/2+2+2+3.

Thus, the strophe concludes with a tricolon, which frequently marks the beginning, or as in this case the end, of a larger literary unit. This canticle is also characterized by frequent employment of numbers, by the external parallelism formed by *šb'* (1. 8 and 20), and by the qinah pattern in the last strophe.[9]

Canticle 2 (*KTU* 1.14:I.21—35) describes how Kirtu cries himself to sleep, heartsick because of his misfortune. Division into smaller units follows the scheme 2/2/2/2+3/2+2. Characteristic here is the repeated emphasis upon Kirtu's mourning and the qinah pattern in the fourth strophe.

According to canticle 3 (*KTU* 1.14:I.35—50) Ilu appears to Kirtu in a dream and suggests that he should not set his demands too high, that he should rather enjoy those riches which are within his grasp. Schematic division: 3/2/2/2/2+2. In this case the tricolon marks the beginning of the larger unit.

Canticle 4 (*KTU* 1.14:I.50—II.9) forms the conclusion of the canto. It relates Kirtu's response in which he states his preference for sons rather than riches. The canto concludes by introducing Ilu's instructions to Kirtu which are elaborated in the following canto. Schematic division: 1/2+2/2/3. Note once again the position of the tricolon.

The decision to include this final strophe with the first canto might upon first glance appear to be debatable. But the suggested division is confirmed by the clear relationship between the tricolon here and the tricolon which heads the preceeding canticle. Both speak of Ilu's approach (*qrb*) to Kirtu, thereby embracing Ilu's proposal and Kirtu's response. Furthermore, it may be noted that the final strophe of the fourth canticle is connected with the second canticle by renewed mention of the mourning of Kirtu, as is also the case in the second strophe of the third canticle. Other clear examples of external parallelism in this canto include *bn(m)* (I.9 and II.4) and the repeated employment of numbers (in addition to the first canticle, mentioned earlier see I.30,48 and II.2). It is noteworthy that the transition from the one canticle to the next coincides with a

---

9   J.C. de Moor, in: Y.Avishur—J.Blau (eds.), *Studies in Bible and the Ancient Near East Presented to S.E. Loewenstamm* (Jerusalem, 1978) 136.

change of subject. The first canticle discusses Kirtu's situation, the second canticle describes Kirtu's reaction, the third focuses upon Ilu, and the final strophe once again calls attention to Kirtu. The tricolon mentioned above as forming the conclusion to the final canticle is an exception to this pattern. But a closer analysis will demonstrate that a larger unit more frequently ends with an indication of what is to follow in the next unit. Finally, it appears that there is a certain degree of balance to the number of strophes per canticle; they all consist of four or five strophes.

Canto 2 (*KTU* 1.14:II.9—III.51)

In this monologue by Ilu, Kirtu is instructed as to how he can win for himself Hariya, the daughter of Pubâla, king of Udumu. She is to bear offspring for him.

Canticle 1 (*KTU* 1.14:II.9—26). Kirtu must wash himself, make preparations for an offering, and then bring the offering in order thereby to summon the gods. Schematic division: 3/1/2+2+2/3/2+2. Once again a tricolon marks the beginning. External parallelism is present in *ydk* (l. 10, 13 and 22) and *dbḥ* (l. 14, 18, 23 and 25). Note too the characteristic employment of verbs indicating coming and going, such as *'rb* (l. 12), *'ly* (l. 20) and *yrd* (l. 24).

Canticle 2 (*KTU* 1.14:II.26—III.1). Kirtu will mobilize a huge army in which all the subjects of state will participate. Schematic division: 1/2+2+3/2+2+2+2/2+2+3/2. The transition from the first to the second canticle is marked by the reversal of movement (*yrd* [l. 26] in contrast to *'ly* [l. 20]), and by the shift from Ba'lu to Kirtu as subject of the verb depicting descent. As is the case with the first canticle in canto 1, this unit is characterized by repeated mention of numbers and by the verb *yṣ'* (l. 32, 34 and 47). Also striking is the neat symmetry by means of which the extensive, central strophe is particularly highlighted.

Canticle 3 (*KTU* 1.14:III.2—19) describes the journey to place the city Udumu under siege. Schematic division: 3/3/2+2+2/3+2/ 2+2+2. A tricolon marks the beginning. A telling characteristic is the twofold mention of a seven day period. After the first week the people outside the city are attacked, and after the second the consequences of the siege are felt in the city itself.

Canticle 4 (*KTU* 1.14:III.19—32). Pubâla will suggest payment of tribute in exchange for Kirtu's departure. Schematic division: 2/1/2+2+1/2/2+2. With respect to content this canticle differs from the preceding one by virtue of the fact that here it is Pubâla who speaks. This canticle, which is repeated a few times in the legend of Kirtu, is clearly marked as a unit via the presence of external parallelism, namely *krt* (l. 20, 26 and 28), *mlk* (l. 21 and 27), and by mention of various places of habitation, *mswn* (l. 21), *bt* (l. 27), *ḫẓr* (l. 28) and *'udm* (l. 30 and 31). Special mention of the fact that the first and last lines of the third strophe begin with *qḥ* is also warranted. The form of the unit is thereby so firmly established that when it is re—employed elsewhere it is kept unchanged, which stands in marked contrast to numerous other situations where the repetition of a given larger unit does show variation.

Canticle 5 (*KTU* 1.14:III.32—51). Kirtu will reject Pubâla's offer and demand Hariya instead. Schematic division: 1/2+2/3/ 2+2+2+2+2/2. The fourth strophe is exceptional because of its length, which also serves to reinforce the great admiration which it expresses for Hariya. Clear indications of the formal unity of this strophe may be detected in the use of the relative *d* and in the divine names with which it begins and ends. In light of the content of the final strophe, which is a description of how Kirtu awakes, there appears to be little reason to join it to the preceding canticle. As was the case in the termination of the first canto, we have an indication here of a transition to the following major unit. The fact that this strophe does belong to what precedes it, as was also the case in canto 1, is made evident by external parallelism formed by *ḥlm* (l. 46 and 50), which is confirmed by the fact that the following lines describe the fulfilment of the instructions. Here Kirtu moves into action for the first time, thus marking a clear transition from the preceding section.

We may conclude that the second canto too forms a well—balanced structure. All of the canticles consist of five strophes. Furthermore, the canticles all demonstrate a similarity in composition; they all begin with a strophe consisting of a single verse. With respect to external parallelism within the canto, mention may be made of the repetition of Pubâla's offer (III.22—27) in Kirtu's response (III.33—37), and especially also the repeated mention of animals, *'irby* (II.50), *ḥsn* (III.1), the animals in Udumu (III.16–19) and *sswm* (III.24 and 36).

Canto 3 (*KTU* 1.14:III.52–V.12)

Kirtu brings offerings and departs with his mighty army for Udumu to besiege the city. Along the way he makes a vow to Athiratu.

Canticle 1 (*KTU* 1.14:III.52–IV.8). Kirtu exercises the rituals as they were prescribed by Ilu in the first canticle of canto 2, which is here repeated virtually verbatim. Schematic division: 3/1/2+2+2/2/2+2. The canticle is slightly shorter than the canticle which it repeats; the first verse of the third strophe is a bicolon instead of a tricolon and the fourth strophe consists of a bicolon instead of a tricolon.

Canticle 2 (*KTU* 1.14:IV.8–31). Kirtu mobilizes a mighty army in accordance with his instructions. Everyone lends a hand. Schematic division: 1/2+2+3/2+2+2/2+2+3/2. Omission of the second verse of the third strophe once again produces a canticle somewhat briefer than the antecedent parallel (canticle 2 in canto 2).

Canticle 3 (*KTU* 1.14:IV.31–43). After three days journey Kirtu arrives at the sanctuary of Athiratu, where he makes a vow. Schematic division: 1/3/1/2/2+2. An inclusion is formed by *ṯn/ṯlṯ* (1.32–33 and 42–43).

Canticle 4 (*KTU* 1.14:IV.44–V.12). The journey to, and seige of, Udumu. Schematic division: 2/3/2+2+2/3/2+2+2. The topic here is the fulfilment of the instructions detailed in canto 2, canticle 3.

The transition to the following canto is indicated by the shift from Kirtu to Pubâla as acting subject. *'apnk* (1. 12) clearly serves as a marker. The response of Pubâla is also more clearly introduced than was the case in the parallel passage of the second canto (*KTU* 1.14:III.19–20), where it does not stand at the beginning of a canto but rather at the beginning of a canticle in the middle of a canto.

An interesting detail is to be noted in the manner in which the conclusion of the third canto is reminiscent of the end of the second; Pubâla cannot sleep, while Kirtu awakes from his slumbers. The third canto repeats large portions of the previous canto, which provides the opportunity to compare the two, and to observe the way in which the poet introduces new elements. The first striking feature is that in the repetition of previous material from the first two canticles, the poet handles a number of points more concisely here. It is only in the third canticle, where Kirtu's vow to Athiratu is discussed, that new information is added, thereby attracting special attention.

Canto 4 (KTU 1.14:V.12—1.15:I.20*)

As predicted Pubâla makes a proposal. Kirtu conveys the response that he is only willing to leave upon the condition that he should receive Hariya as his wife.

Canticle 1 (*KTU* 1.14:V.12—29). The text is regrettably damaged here, but it obviously gave a detailed introduction to the message conveyed by Pubâla to his servants. The estimated length agrees with the average number of lines per canticle in this canto.

Canticle 2 (*KTU* 1.14:V.29—45). Instructions are given to Pubâla's messengers. Kirtu is offered tribute. Schematic division: 2/2/2+2+1/2+2/2. Repetition of canto 2, canticle 4. The major difference is that the previously brief introduction now appears to be expanded to form a self—contained canticle. Furthermore, in comparison with the previous canticle, the order of the last two strophes is reversed. It is striking that now both the first and the last strophe mention 'going/departing', which is probably the reason for the change of order.

Canticle 3 (*KTU* 1.14:VI.1*—15) narrates how the messengers deliver Pubâla's words to Kirtu. Schematic division: 1+2/1+1/2+2+1/2+2/2. As in the previous canticle, an inclusion is formed by repetition of words for 'departure'.

Canticle 4 (*KTU* 1.14:VI.16—35) contains the by now familiar answer of Kirtu. Schematic division: 1/2+2/3/2+2+2+2. Comparison with canticle 5 of canto 2, shows that the third verse of the last strophe, which praises Hariya, is here omitted.

Canticle 5 (*KTU* 1.14:VI.35—15:I.20*) relates the transmission of Kirtu's response. The damaged text is easily reconstructed by comparison with the parallel text. Schematic division: 1+2/1+2/2+2/3/2+2+2+2.

Canto 4 is an elaboration of the final two canticles of the vision of Kirtu described in canto 2. The expanded introduction and the double repetition help to produce a complete and balanced canticle. Characteristic of this canto are the repeated introductory formulas at the beginning of the canticles, with reference to the messengers. In this respect the particles *'apnk* (V.12) and *'idk* (V.29, VI.3* and 36) which function as formal markers of separation are noteworthy. Finally, an inclusion is created via mention of Pubâla's wife (V.13), which corresponds with the reference to Kirtu's future spouse at the end of the canto (1.15:I.9*).

Canto 5 (*KTU* 1.15:I.20*–II.7)

Although the major portion of this canto is lost, the content can be reconstructed with a fairly high degree of certainty. In view of what later follows we can conclude that Pubâla acquiesces to Kirtu's request, though it is difficult for him to do so, as is evident from the fragment *KTU* 1.15:I.1–17. Presumably Kirtu then summons the gods for the wedding festivities. The following canto is marked by *'apnk*, as was the preceding one. This fifth canto would then span approximately 55 cola, which is relatively short but not impossible since the first canto is only slightly longer.

Canto 6 (*KTU* 1.15:II.8–III.19)

Kirtu coerces a blessing from Ilu, who in turn promises him many children but adds that the youngest will receive the rights of the firstborn.

Canticle 1 (*KTU* 1.15:II.8–20) describes how Kirtu coerces Ilu to bless him. Schematic division: 1+1/2/2/2+2/2+3. A tricolon marks the end of this canticle.

Canticles 2 and 3 (*KTU* 1.15:II.21–III.4). Hariya will bear two sons. Unfortunately the tablet here is damaged. But it is evident that canticle 2 begins with a tricolon. Furthermore, it is probable that the repeated lines praising Kirtu (*KTU* 1.15:III.2–4 and 13–15) are also employed in the lost portion because they can be viewed as a reaction to the announcement of the birth of one or more children. That is the case in canticle 4 after the announcement of the birth of six daughters. In canticles 2 and 3 that would also have been the case after the announcement of the birth of Yassubu as well as the birth of Iluha'u.

Canticle 4 (*KTU* 1.15:III.5−19) contains the promise that Hariya will bear Kirtu six daughters, of which the last will receive the birthright. Following the blessing the gods depart. Schematic division: 1/2+2+2/3/1/3. As in the previous canticle, it is concluded with a tricolon.

Canto 6 is clearly a coherent unit. That is evident in the repeated praise of Kirtu, in the inclusion formed via mention of the arrival of the gods at the beginning (II.9) in correspondence with the notation of their departure at the end (III.17−18), and also in the multiple use of the verb *brk* (II.14,18,19 and III.17).

The number of strophes per canticle is consistent throughout, and like cantos 1 and 3 it is composed of 4 canticles. On closer inspection there appear to be more connections between canto 1 and canto 6. A considerable number of responsions are established, by which it is made evident that the blessing recounted in canto 6 is to be viewed as the solution to the grief so vividly depicted in the beginning. That is evident, among other things, in the repetition of the words *'aṭṭ* (1.14:I.12, 14 and 1.15:II.21), *šbʿ/ṯmn* (1.14:I.8−9, 20 and 1.15:II.23−24).

All of these factors together create the impression that the first six cantos, with respect to content and structural considerations, form a complete and coherent unit, the first chapter. This is confirmed by detection of additional external parallelism within the six cantos, e.g., the summons of the gods, their coming and their departure in cantos 2−3 and 5−6, the use of *lqḥ* (1.14:I.45; II.13; III.22, 26 + parallel passages and 1.15:II.21−22), and *ḥẓr* (1.14:III.29 + par. and 1.15:II.23). Finally, mention may be made of the frequent use of numbers, often consecutively in a row.

One important result of the study thus far is that it has given a fairly clear picture of the poet's methodology. His style is frugal. He makes frequent use of unicola, and a given topic is seldom handled extensively. He strives to attain a balanced structure at the level of the higher poetic units, and ordinarily he employs clear markers of separation to distinguish the larger units and their inter−connections. It is probable that the poet maintained this manner of working in the following sections. Unfortunately the clay tablets are often severely damaged from this point. But it may be hoped that the insights gained thus far with respect to the author's manner of writing will assist in the reconstruction of the text.

Chapter 2 (*KTU* 1.15:III.20–1.16:IV.?)

The contention that a new chapter begins here is confirmed by the fact that the same topic as in the beginning of the first chapter, is brought to discussion, namely the birth of children. However, while canto 1 depicted Kirtu's childlessness, now we are told how one wife bears eight children in seven years. Also noteworthy is that the role of Ilu is now taken over by Athiratu. This transition was already forecasted in canto 3. The central focus of this chapter is Kirtu's illness.

Canto 7 (*KTU* 1.15:III.20–IV.40?)

In outrage caused by Kirtu's negligence Athiratu curses him. The arrangements for his funeral must now already be regulated!

Canticle 1 (*KTU* 1.15:III.20–30). The promise of the gods is fulfilled. Hariya bears Kirtu eight children. Athiratu then reminds Kirtu of the unfulfilled vow to her, and begins to list the consequences. Schematic division: 2/3/2/1/1+2. External parallelism: *ndr* (l. 23, 26 and 29).

Canticle 2 is lost. Most likely it contained a curse directed at Kirtu. He will be plagued with a deathly sickness, and the land will also be subjected to suffering (cf. *KTU* 1.19:I; Aqhatu's death results in a severe famine). Thus, as in canto 6 it appears that a divine utterance follows after an extensive introduction spanning the length of a canticle. The form thereby also reflects the fact that cantos 6 and 7 stand as polar opposites.

Canticle 3 (*KTU* 1.15:IV.1?–13). Kirtu has to instruct his wife to prepare a meal and to invite guests. Most likely this is intended to be connected with his own imminent burial. Schematic division: 1?+1/1/2/2+2/2+2. The first line might possibly be reconstructed by comparison with the beginning of canto 4, canticle 1, by virtue of the agreement between *KTU* 1.15:IV.2–3 and 1.14:V.13–14. It is only the name of the one addressed that varies. The first line of this canticle could accordingly, by analogy to *KTU* 1.14:V.12–13, have read *'apnk krt t'*.

Canticle 4 (*KTU* 1.15:IV.14–25). Hariya will carry out her orders and the invited guests will come and eat. Schematic division: 1/2/2+2/3/2. A portion of the preceding canticle is repeated verbatim.

Canticle 5 is to a large extent lost. From the introductory strophe may be gleaned that here a description must have been given of Hariya making the reason for the meal clear to the guests.

That marks the termination of canto 7. The following canticle contains the execution of the orders and the fulfilment of what has been forecasted. We noticed a similar progression in the transition from canto 2 to canto 3. Canto 2 also dealt with the words of a god to Kirtu. But the role of Ilu is assumed in this canto by Athiratu, and the role of Pubâla is taken by the leaders of Khuburu, vassals of Kirtu.

Canto 8 (*KTU* 1.15.IV.41?−VI.15?)

This section describes how the instructions of Athiratu are executed; the vassals come to the banquet and hear the reason for their invitation. But instead of mourning for Kirtu the attention is actually given to his successor Yassubu, Kirtu's firstborn son.

Canticle 1 (*KTU* 1.15:IV.41?−V.8). The first part of this section has been lost. What is clear, however, is that what has been predicted takes place. The last two strophes, which describe the arrival of the guests and their participation at the banquet, employ the same words as are found in the last two strophes of canto 7, canticle 4.

Canticle 2 (*KTU* 1.15:V.9−21). Hariya announces the reason for the banquet and then ascertains that more attention is paid to the coming king than the departing one. Schematic division: 1/2/2+2+2/2/1. It is noteworthy here that the symmetric structure calls particular attention to the central strophe, in which it is stated that they assume that Kirtu is as good as dead.

Canticle 3 (*KTU* 1.15:V.21−?). Kirtu points out the dangers involved in the appointment of a young king. May Ilu spare them from such a person! Schematic division: 1/1/3/2+?/?. Although the final portion is missing, once again the emphasis seems to fall upon the middle strophe, conspicuous because of its length. Here the dangers of a young king for the populace, and especially for the women, is described.

Regrettably the remainder of the canto is only fragmentarily represented in the few preserved lines of *KTU* 1.15:VI.

Nevertheless, it can be concluded from these lines that apparently no significant change took place in the attitude of the guests; Hariya's rebuke is repeated nearly verbatim (l. 4ff.). It is likely that a new canticle begins with the opening words *wt'n mtt hry* (l. 3). This is probably the fifth canticle. It is possible that this canticle ended, as attested more frequently in this text, with a transition to the ensuing canto, in this case by means of an announcement of the arrival of Kirtu's children.

It is tenable to conclude that canto 8 too consisted of five cantos. The inclusion mentioned above places primary emphasis upon Hariya's discourse in the third canticle. Comparison of this canticle with its parallel in canto 3 in the first chapter reveals a number of significant correspondences. Canto 3 centers primary attention upon the vow to Athiratu in the hope of attaining descendants (canticle 3). The fact that this vow entails an exaggerated responsibility for Kirtu himself is already predictive of his imminent jeopardy. Canto 8 once again focuses upon the question of offspring, but now in fear of the danger which can accompany the arrival of the firstborn. The poet later returns again to this theme. Also noteworthy is the exchange of roles between Athiratu and Ilu. In canto 3 hope is invested in Athiratu while Ilu occupies a central position throughout the chapter. But in canto 8 hope is placed in Ilu, in a chapter in which Athiratu is predominant.

Finally, it is significant that Kirtu's caveat concerning his son is strongly reminiscent of the early stages of his own rule as that is described at the beginning of this legend, which is also expressed in the repetition of the words *mlk*, *'att* and the name Khuburu.

Canto 9 (*KTU* 1.15:VI.16?–1.16:I.23)

The opening portion of this canto is not preserved. Presumably, in contrast to the reaction of the vassals, the appropriate mourning of Kirtu's children, with the exception of his eldest, is here described. The transition to canto 10 is marked by a change of grammatical subject; from Kirtu's children to Kirtu (cf. the transition from the third to the fourth canto). The preceding canticle is recognizable as the concluding canticle of canto 9 by virtue of its introduction of a new situation, namely that Iluha'u approaches his father. That this canticle must be included with what precedes it can be deduced from the fact that it repeats large portions from there. In light of the

assumed number of lines which have been lost, the portion
which has been preserved likely constitutes the fourth and fifth
canticle.

Canticle 4 (*KTU* 1.15:VI.?–1.16:I.11) contains the mournful words
of Kirtu's children. Schematic division: ?/2/3/2+2/2. We are
concerned here with a portion which is repeated almost
verbatim in a few other instances (cf. 1.16:I.14–23 and
II.36–49). It is striking that it is precisely here that a higher
than average frequency of external parallelism may be detected.
It concerns the various references to places of habitation, *bt* (l.
2), *ḫšt* (l. 3 and 4; in antithetic parallelism with *ṣrry*, l. 5), *ḫl*
(l. 7 and 8), as well as the many references to the gods, *b'l* (l.
6), *ṣpn* (l. 7), *'il* (l. 10), *ltpn* (l. 11) and *qdš* (l. 11).

Canticle 5 (*KTU* 1.16:I.11–23). Iluha'u comes to his father and
laments for him. Schematic division: 3/2/2/3/2+2. The
preceding canticle finds virtually literal repetition. But one
strophe is left out, and by contrast, the final strophe is
expanded by one bicolon. An expansion of this sort often
signifies the end of a larger literary unit.

Canto 10 (*KTU* 1.16:I.24–III.16)

Kirtu charges Iluha'u to locate his youngest sister to request her
to bring an offering for her father. Iluha'u carries out this
charge.

Canticle 1 (*KTU* 1.16:I.24–38). Kirtu sends his son to
Thatmanatu. Schematic division: 1/2+2/3/2+2/2+2. Emphasis
falls upon the middle strophe, in which Kirtu states that it is
his youngest daughter who cares most for him. The circumspect
manner in which he approaches her demonstrates that the
feelings are mutual.

Canticle 2 (*KTU* 1.16:I.38–45). Iluha'u has to inform
Thatmanatu of Kirtu's present situation and request her to
bring an offering in mourning for her father. Schematic division:
1/2/2/1/2. The canticle is conspicuously brief, and concerns
terse but hefty requests. Inclusion is formed by mention of an
offering in the second and the fifth strophe. The time stipulated
in the preceding canticle for the rendezvous (at night), and the
offering here specified (gold and silver), are reminiscent of the
vow to Athiratu in canto 3, canticle 3. The hint of a possibility
to yet pay the debt is thereby raised.

Canticle 3 (*KTU* 1.16:I.46—55). Iluha'u goes and meets Thatmanatu. Schematic division: 1+2/1/1/2+2/2. Characteristic is the external parallelism established by *aḫ(t)* (l. 51, 53 and 55) and the inclusion formed by mention of mourning in l. 47—48 and l. 55.

Canticle 4 (*KTU* 1.16:I.56—II.2?). In response to Thatmanatu's question Iluha'u relates Kirtu's illness and his request. Schematic division: 2/1/2/2/2?

In canticle 5 (*KTU* 1.16:II.2?—16) the charge is further carried out and mention is also made that Thatmanatu is caring for her father.   This transition marks the end of the canto. The termination of the canto receives extra emphasis via employment of an extra long verse, the tricolon. Just as canto 9 ended with the announcement of Iluha'u's arrival at his father, so too canto 10 concludes with Thatmanatu's coming to visit Kirtu.

Canto 11 (*KTU* 1.16:II.17—?).

Thatmanatu utters grief—stricken lament for her father. Upon approaching him, he charges her with a particular duty.

Canticle 1 (*KTU* 1.16:II.17—25). In response to her inquiries Iluha'u informs his sister of the seriousness of Kirtu's illness. Schematic division: 1/1/2/1/2+2. The conclusion of the canticle is indicated by the relatively lengthy final strophe. Characteristic is the external parallelism generated by *mrṣ/dw* (l. 19—20 and 22—23).

Canticle 2 (*KTU* 1.16:II.25—36) describes Thatmanatu's bitter mourning. Schematic division: 2/2/2/2+2+2. Once again the end of the canticle is indicated by the lengthy final strophe. The extreme imbalance within the canticle can be associated with its content. An obvious inclusion is formed by the elaboration in the final strophe of elements introduced in the first strophe.

Canticle 3 (*KTU* 1.16:II.36—49) is a somewhat modified repetition of the complaint of Kirtu's children mentioned already in canto 9, canticles 4 and 5. Schematic division: 2/2/3/2/2+2/2. It is noteworthy that while the preceding canticle, since it consists of four strophes, is one strophe short of the usual number of strophes per canticle, this canticle, with six strophes, has one extra. We could compare this to the phenomenon of the qinah pattern which also occurs intermittently in this text at the level of the verses.

In canticle 4 is stated that Thatmanatu visits her father. She likely expresses her complaint, as was previously done by Iluha'u at the end of canto 9. Whether that also marks the end of the canto here is not possible to determine with certainty. We may assume, however, that Thatmanatu also receives a commission. This results in the termination of the famine which was connected with Kirtu's illness. All of this is likely taken up in the description which ensues in the following canto.

Canto 12

Merely a fragment is preserved (*KTU* 1.16.III.1–17). On the basis of what preceded, it is logical to conclude that this canto corresponds with canto 10. Both canto 11 and canto 9 are elaborate introductions to the formulation of a particular charge, along with its execution, which are narrated in the following canto.   Accordingly, in canto 12 the charge is given to Thatmanatu. She too, like Iluha'u previously, would have to enlist the assistance of a third party. In the fragment which is preserved we are told how the third party, with recourse to magical actions, is able to bring back the rain. That results in a partial retraction of Athiratu's curse. We may assume that this marks the end of another chapter. As in the first chapter it begins with a problem and concludes with the mention of a possible solution. The enactment of that solution follows in the subsequent chapter.

A formal or structural justification of the supposed divisions in chapter 2 is hampered by the damaged state of the tablets. But what is noteworthy in this respect is that chapter 2 differs from the other chapters by virtue of the repeated mention of mourning, and in the detail that here it is people rather than gods who are assembled.

Chapter 3

Canto 13 (*KTU* 1.16:IV.?–V.9)

Virtually nothing remains of this canto. Nevertheless, from what follows we can determine that here a request is made to assemble the gods. According to *KTU* 1.16:IV.1–16 that takes place in the same manner as the vassals of Kirtu were summoned in canto 7. In canto 7 Athiratu charges Kirtu to have Hariya summon the vassals. In canto 13 it appears to be Ba'lu who orders Ilu to instruct Ilishu to assemble the gods. Another notable parallel with canto 2 is evident in the need for Ilishu to go onto the roof (*KTU* 1.16:IV.14). According to *KTU* 1.14:II.20–22 Kirtu must do likewise to summon the gods. To an extent the same words are employed. In this manner the beginning of the third chapter is connected with the beginning of both the second and the first chapter. It is probable that canto 13 ended with a description of the arrival of the gods, at which time Athiratu would be promised the reward which Kirtu had vowed to give. This too is reminiscent of the commencement of the second chapter (cf. canto 7, canticle 1). It was already foreshadowed by mention of a comparable offering from Thatmanatu to her god, likely Ba'lu (cf. canto 10, canticle 2). All obstacles to Kirtu's healing are thereby removed.

Canto 14 (*KTU* 1.16:V.9–VI.14)

Ilu takes personal charge of the healing of Kirtu. He creates Sha'tiqtu, who in turn dispels death from Kirtu.

Canticle 1 (*KTU* 1.16:V.9–22). Seven times Ilu asks in vain whether one of the gods will dispel Kirtu's sickness. Schematic division: 1/2+1/1+2+1/1+2+1/1+2+1.   This   canticle   is characterized by the seven motif which has also been employed a couple of times in the first chapter (canto 1, canticle 5 and canto 2, canticle 3).

Canticle 2 (*KTU* 1.16:V.23–38). Ilu takes the responsibility upon himself and out of clay creates a healer. Schematic division: 1/2/3/2+3/?. Characteristic of this canticle are the various verbs referring to creating and forming.

Canticle 3 (*KTU* 1.16:V.39–5?). Ilu gives Sha'tiqtu the power and the charge to heal Kirtu. Schematic division 2/3/2/3/?. External parallelism: *yd* (l. 39 and 44).

Canticle 4 is mostly lost, with only the end preserved. Apparently Ilu's charge to Sha'tiqtu ends here with the prediction that he will triumph over death.

Canticle 5 (*KTU* 1.16:VI.2–14). Sha'tiqtu heals Kirtu. Schematic division: 2/2/2/3+2/2. The last strophe corresponds with that of the preceding canticle. An inclusion is formed by the name Sha'tiqtu in l. 2 and l. 13.

The entire canto is typified by the repetition of the words *mrṣ/zbl* in canticle 1 and in V.27–28, 31, 42–43, 50–51 and VI.9.

Canto 15 (*KTU* 1.16:VI.15–?)

Physically restored, Kirtu once again assumes his position as king. His oldest son, Yassubu, appears and demands the throne. Kirtu curses him.

Canticle 1 (*KTU* 1.16:VI.15–21). Kirtu charges Hariya to prepare a meal. She complies and Kirtu dines. Schematic division: 2/1/2/1/2.

Canticle 2 (*KTU* 1.16:VI.21–29). Kirtu reigns once again. Yassubu approaches, and his soul induces him to speak. Schematic division: 1/3/1/1/3. The tricola determine the emphasis upon Kirtu's rule and Yassubu's approach. The final tricolon also serves to indicate the end of the canticle.

Canticle 3 (*KTU* 1.16:VI.29–40). Yassubu must demand the kingship from his father because Kirtu has become too weak. Schematic division: 1/2+1+2/2/2/2. The extra–long second strophe descibes Kirtu's shortcomings as king.

Canticle 4 (*KTU* 1.16:VI.40–54). Yassubu relays what his soul tells him. Schematic division: 1/2/2+1+3+2/2/2. The imputations concerning Kirtu's deficiencies as king receive further expansion here; the last bicolon is expanded into a tricolon and a bicolon is added.

Canticle 5 (*KTU* 1.16:VI.54–?). Kirtu answers with a curse. Schematic division: 1/3/2+?. The text breaks off here. Canto 5 probably ends with this extensive curse upon Yassubu.

This once again brings a blemish upon what appeared to turn out so well. This repeats what happened in chapter 2. Joy initiated by the fulfilment of Ilu's promise is tempered by Athiratu curse. The first hint of this was already alluded in chapter 1. Kirtu's curse of his son accordingly casts a shadow over his own healing. Nor does this come entirely unexpected when one observes Kirtu's thoughts concerning his son expressed already in canto 8, canticle 3.

The logical conclusion to all of this would seem to be that Kirtu's curse would not go without effect. In this way he loses the son for whom he had longed so desperately (canto 16?). In light of Ilu's prophecy that the youngest will become the firstborn (*KTU* 1.15:III.16) we must assume that Iluha'u and the five oldest daughters also die by one means or another (canto 17?) leaving Thatmanatu to take the throne of her father (canto 18?). That concludes the third chapter, and likewise the entire legend of Kirtu.

Accordingly, it is quite possible that the third chapter also consisted of six cantos. Unfortunately the damaged state of the texts and the absence of the last tablet make it difficult to undergird the asserted inner cohesion of the chapter with arguments based upon form and structure. Support for the threefold division of the text is provided, however, by the fact that the third canticle draws undeniable correlations with the first chapter. Both chapters summon the gods (chapter 2 by contrast has people assemble), Ilu stands central (compared to Athiratu in chapter 2), Kirtu's kingship is in question (*mlk/drkt* in *KTU* 1.14:I.41−42 and 1.16:VI.37−38; in contrast to the kingship of Yassubu in *KTU* 1.15:V), and the seven motif is employed.

Conclusion

Our closer investigation confirmed the previously made assumption that the writer of these texts worked a deliberate structure into the arrangement of his story. The entire legend is arranged in three chapters written in a similar manner, with the first and last having a special correspondence. The structure is very uniform; the chapters all appear to consist of 6 cantos, and the cantos consist almost exclusively of 5 strophes.

The style is rather sober when compared, e.g., with myth the Ba'lu, though this was written by the same hand. The strophes are often very brief and external parallelism is minimal. What is striking is that the few portions which do contain a more detailed description are often repeated one or more times in nearly verbatim form. Examples of this are the offer of riches to Kirtu (*KTU* 1.14:III.22−27 + par.), the preparations for the army's departure (*KTU* 1.14:II.27−50 + par.), the description of Hariya (*KTU* 1.14:III.38−49 + par.), the complaint of Kirtu's children (*KTU* 1.16:I.2−11 + par.) and the description of Kirtu's deficiency as king (*KTU* 1.16:VI.30−34.43−50). Whether the lengthy complaint of Thatmanatu (*KTU* 1.16:II.25−36) is repeated cannot be determined with certainty. It is also noteworthy that all of these repetitions take place within the same chapter.

The difference of the above mentioned segments in comparison to the rest of the text with regard to style, and the exceptional place that they are given, is suggestive that they are traditional, established phrases which the poet has reworked in his edition of the story.

The results of this study also produce greater clarity with respect to major and minor emphases in the legend. To begin with, the story of Kirtu focuses upon his succession. That is where it begins, and that is likely also where it ends. The manner in which it ends is foreshadowed by Ilu's blessing at the end of the first chapter; Kirtu will receive offspring, but the youngest will be the firstborn (*KTU* 1.15:III.16). The youngest is Kirtu's eighth child. The writer seems to play upon this conclusion with the frequent employment of the parallelism 'seven'/'eight', and in the seven motif of the first and last chapter.

In the Old Testament too there appear to be examples of the eighth child receiving the rights of the firstborn.[10] Another interesting parallel is found in the Sumerian myth 'Enki and Ninhursag', situated in Dilmun, which is also the focus of its description. The text concludes with a summary of the eight children of Enki and Ninhursag. The eighth one, Enshag, becomes king of Dilmun.[11] This emphasis upon the eighth member in the genealogy could refer to an important transition; once the unit seven is complete something totally new begins.[12]

---

10 See in this respect *UF* 14 (1982) 176. In addition to the examples given there of David (cf. 1 Sam. 16:10) and Solomon (cf. 2 Sam. 3 and 12), mention may also be made of Joseph in light of the fact that he was Jacob's eighth child, not counting the children of the concubines (cf. Gen. 30:20–24), and is exalted as the one 'chosen above his brothers' (Gen. 49:26). Isaac too can be added to this list. From Gen. 25:1–15 can be deduced that Isaac was Abraham's eighth child (cf. the observation by W. Zimmerli, *1. Mose 12–25: Abraham* [ZB 1.2; Zürich, 1976] 136, that the list of six sons from Keturah actually belongs in the period prior to the birth of Ishmael and Isaac).

11 See *ANET* 41 and B. Alster, in: D.T. Potts (ed.), *Dilmun: New Studies in the Archaeology and Early History of Bahrain* (Berliner Beiträge zum Vorderen Orient, Band 2; Berlin, 1983) 52–65.

12 For this meaning of the number eight see W.E. Filmer, *God Counts: A*

In addition to this central concern, each chapter entertains a separate theme, introduced in each case by a new problem. Chapter 1, Kirtu's childlessnes; chapter 2, Kirtu's illness; chapter 3, Kirtu's disagreement with his firstborn. The progression is always such that a chapter ends with an initial indication of the solution to the problem. The following chapter then begins with an extensive description of the solution of the problem, followed by the arisal of a new difficulty. This too is often forecasted already in the preceding chapter (e.g., the vow to Athiratu in chapter 1, and the appearance of Yassubu in chapter 2). A similar observation is valid with respect to the solutions to the problems (e.g., the offering of Thatmanatu in chapter 2 which foreshadows the settlement of Kirtu's debt to Athiratu at the outset of chapter 3).

It is possible to compare the structure of the legend of Kirtu with that of the Book of Ruth. The central theme of this Biblical book is similarly the problem of the continuation of the family name. This is jeopardized by the premature death of Elimelek and his sons, as delineated at the outset. The book ends with the solution, Ruth bore a son 'to Naomi'. In each of the chapters, which in themselves constitute a self—contained literary unit,[13] a secondary problem is raised and then in principle is solved again. In chapter 1, the famine; in chapter 2, the question of whether anyone in Naomi's family will become involved in her plight; in chapter 3, the question of whether Boaz will marry Ruth; and finally, in chapter 4, the problem of Boaz's potential to act as kinsman redeemer.

Comparison with the Book of Ruth also calls attention to the great difference between the role of the God of Israel and the role of the gods in the legend of Kirtu.[14] That too is made evident in the structure of the story. In the first chapter Ilu arises as Kirtu's helper. In the second chapter Athiratu turns against Kirtu, while in the third chapter Ilu finally comes to Kirtu's assistance once again. Thus, the gods work against each other, as is also evident in the unwillingness of any of the gods to assist in the healing of Kirtu. Furthermore, Ilu's assistance appears to be half—hearted. He must continually be urged on by

---

Study in Bible Numbers (Croydon, Surrey, 1947) 20–21.
13   See the articles by De Moor mentioned in n. 4 above.
14   Cf. J.C. de Moor, *OTS* XXIV (1986) 14.

another god. An his blessing is darkened by the foreshadowing of what will happen with respect to the birthright of the firstborn. Man appears to be a victim of the capricious gods. On the other hand, sometimes it seems possible to coerce things from the gods, which often results in playing off the one god against the other. Ultimately, however, man is unable to rise above his fate in life; no sooner had Kirtu disentangled himself from the curse of his childlessness (chapter 1), and the illness deriving from Athiratu's curse (chapter 2), than he finds himself forced to utter a curse which reinstates the original problem (chapter 3).

The results attained from a structural study of the legend of Kirtu inspire admiration for the technical expertise of the poet, but consternation concerning the negative view upon life pervading his beautiful artistry.

THE POETIC PROSE OF JOSHUA 23

William T. Koopmans

1. Introduction

The problem of the relationship between poetry and prose in the Old Testament has generated many stimulating discussions[1] but continues to defy convincing resolution. The present essay does not attempt to solve the prose/poetry differentiation problem, but seeks rather to contribute to the discussion via a detailed analysis of the literary structure of Josh. 23. A number of introductory observations pertaining to the relationship of poetry and prose are first offered. These comments are followed by an attempt to demonstrate that Josh. 23, while traditionally viewed as purely prose, can more correctly be interpreted as poetic prose.

1.1 Meter as the distinguishing characteristic of poetry?

In 1901 E. Sievers produced a voluminous study in which he defended the thesis that metre is the fundamental, constitutive element of O.T. Hebrew poetry.[2] Subsequent studies by Sievers attempted to demonstrate that the books of Genesis[3] and

---

1   R. Lowth, *Lectures on the Sacred Poetry of the Hebrews, Vol. II*, Trans. G. Gregory (London, 1787; [orig. *De Sacra Poesi Hebraeorum*, 1753]) 2–83. G.B. Gray, *The Forms of Hebrew Poetry* (London, 1915; repr. New York, 1972) esp. 37–48; see too D.N. Freedman's 'Prolegomenon, to this reprint edition, XXVI–XXVII. T.H. Robinson, 'Basic Principles of Hebrew Poetic Form', in: *Festschrift für Alfred Bertholet zum 80. Geburtstag* (Tübingen, 1950) 438–450. J. Kugel, *The Idea of Biblical Parallelism* (New Haven/London, 1981) esp. 59–95. J.C. de Moor, 'The Poetry of the Book of Ruth' (Part I), *Or* 53 (1984) 262–283; (Part II) *Or* 55 (1986) 16–46. For additional literature see the studies by Kugel and De Moor.
2   E. Sievers, *Metrische Studien I: Studien zur hebräischen Metrik* (Abhandlungen der philologisch–historischen Classe der königlich sächsischen Gesellschaft der Wissenschaften XXI; Leipzig, 1901).
3   E. Sievers, *Metrische Studien II: Die hebräische Genesis* (Leipzig, 1904–1905).

Samuel[4] were based upon metrical sources and thus had a
poetic background. Defence of his theory, however, was
contingent upon excessive textual emendation and rested upon
theories of metre notoriously difficult to prove. Sievers' views
ultimately failed to command a general following,[5] but the
benefit of his studies has been twofold; he stimulated discussion
both of metre and of the problem of the relationship between
poetry and prose. It is clear, however, that the latter concern
cannot be made contingent upon the question of metre, as was
done in Sievers' methodology. Although the alleged presence of
metre continues to be debated today, it has been convincingly
demonstrated that metre does not constitute an indispensable
characteristic of O.T. poetry.[6] Consequently, the relationship
between poetry and prose must be sought on grounds other
than metrical considerations.

1.2 Parallelism as a means of distinguishing poetry and prose?

If the distinguishing mark between Hebrew poetry and prose is
not to be found in metrical theories, a second logical possibility
to pursue may be sought in the predominant presence of
parallelism, which has long been recognized as fundamental to
O.T. poetry. Fortunately numerous recent studies have subjected
the phenomena of parallelism to rigorous scrutiny.[7] For our
present purposes two conclusions from these studies are of
foundational significance. First, the concept of parallelism in the

---

4   E. Sievers, *Metrische Studien III: Samuel* (Leipzig, 1907).
5   Sievers' position was challenged by G.B. Gray: 1972:143–154, 202–216.
Gray's criticisms receive Freedman's approval in the 'Prolegomena' to this
reprint edition, XXI–XXII.
6   J.C. de Moor, 'The Art of Versification in Ugarit and Israel, I: The
Rhythmical Structure', in: Y. Avishur, J. Blau (eds.), *Studies in Bible and
the Ancient Near East* (Jerusalem, 1978) esp. 121–128. M. O'Connor, *Hebrew
Verse Structure* (Winona Lake, 1980) 138. J. Kugel: 1981:82.
7   In addition to the sources in the previous note, see S.A. Geller,
Parallelism in Early Biblical Poetry (HSM 20; Missoula, 1979). Y. Avishur,
Stylistic Studies of Word-Pairs in Biblical and Ancient Semitic Literatures
(AOAT 210; Neukirchen–Vluyn, 1984). W.G.E. Watson, *Classical Hebrew
Poetry: A Guide to its Techniques* (JSOTSS 26; Sheffield, 1984) esp. 114–159.
A. Berlin, *The Dynamics of Biblical Parallelism* (Bloomington, 1985).

O.T. is extremely complex and defies simple categorization. As Berlin competently demonstrates, a linguistic study of parallelism can be pursued grammatically, lexically, or phonologically, and all of these dimensions can be further subdivided for a more precise delineation of the types of parallelism utilized.[8] Second, increased sensitivity to the diversity of parallelism found in classical biblical poetry alerts the reader to similar phenomena in passages traditionally treated as prose. These two observations already suggest that extreme caution must be used in designating parallelism as the distinguishing mark between prose and poetry. It has been argued already by G.B. Gray[9], and more recently and extensively by J. Kugel[10], that parallelism does not *per se* offer a criterion by which to differentiate poetry and prose.

1.3 'Prose particle counts' and the prose/poetry problem

A new attempt to distinguish poetry and prose is defended by D.N.Freedman who rather confidently asserts, 'We have devised recently a mechanical test to separate poetry from prose in the Bible, and preliminary tests show that it will work efficiently in most cases'.[11] The method referred to is a count of the definite article –ה, the relative אשר and the direct object marker את. A further explanation of this method and the computer statistics thereby attained were published by F.I. Andersen and A.D. Forbes.[12]

Tabulation of the respective scores of these three particles in all the chapters of the O.T. (excluding nine chapters of Aramaic

---

8 These categories provide the major outline for Berlin's discussion in the work mentioned in the previous footnote.

9 G.B. Gray: 1972:37–48.

10 J. Kugel: 1981:63 'the same traits that seem to characterize Hebrew "poetry" also crop up in what is clearly not poetry'. And the flipside of the coin is the recognition that parallelism is not absolutely indispensable for poetry, as is proven by lines in acrostic poems where it is lacking (p. 65).

11 D.N. Freedman, 'Pottery, Poetry and Prophecy: An Essay on Biblical Poetry', *JBL* 96 (1977) 6.

12 F.I. Andersen–A.D. Forbes, ' "Prose Particle" Counts of the Hebrew Bible' in: C.L. Meyers and M. O'Connor (eds.), *The Word of the Lord Shall Go Forth* (Winona Lake, 1983) 165–183.

and twenty chapters of Qohelet and Song of Songs which are
judged to be of a different dialect) demonstrates that classical
poetry has low percentage scores while pure prose has the
highest percentage of these articles. Freedman concludes, 'In
general, these particles occur six to eight times more frequently
in prose passages than in poetic ones'.[13]

What are we to make of these statistical analyses? Has the
prose/poetry problem been virtually solved by these results? In
the first place we may concur that the initial confidence shown
by Freedman, Andersen and Forbes has some warrant. The
statistical patterns demonstrate that passages already recognized
as classical poetry are confirmed as much by the low percentage
scores. Similarly, other passages in prose books which score low
may be suspected of being poetic, whether in whole or in part.
To this extent the statistical analyses have essentially confirmed
what could already be detected from the presence of other
characteristics of poetry.

However, of particular significance for the discussion of the
relationship between poetry and prose is the fact that the study
of Andersen and Forbes also demonstrates a substantial 'middle
range' concerning which they observe, 'The handful of psalms
with such scores attract attention. Prophecy, Pentateuch and
History are well represented'.[14] This 'middle range' immediately
reminds one of the postulation by other scholars on the basis of
literary and stylistic criteria of an 'intermediate' category
between prose and poetry.[15] While it may readily be conceded
that many chapters could fall into this middle range because
they are composed partly of prose and partly of poetry, for
example narratives which contain poetic discourse or oracular
material, such a ready solution appears to be too simple. In
many of the chapters falling within the middle range of
Andersen and Forbes' study it is impossible to separate poetic
and non—poetic portions which balance each other out to
produce a middle range result.[16]

---

13   Freedman: 1977:7.
14   Andersen—Forbes: 1983:166.
15   Kugel: 1981:76.
16   The statistics attained in the three categories are added together to give
a percentage total. Andersen—Forbes suggest that most chapters with scores
below 10% are poetic, 10—20% are mixed, and above 20% are virtually pure

In short, while these statistical studies have convincingly demonstrated a generally low percentage of particle counts in so—called classical Hebrew poetry, they are inadequate as a criterion for a mechanical distinction between poetry and prose. They by no means eliminate the possibility suggested on the basis of other studies that certain passages of the O.T can be best termed poetic prose, prosaic poetry or poetic narrative, in a category (categories?) distinct from the classical Hebrew poetry of the Psalms and portions of the Prophets and Wisdom literature, etc.

At this point we might anticipate the objection that once the distinction has been made between passages which do or do not meet the criterion of classical Hebrew poetry, it becomes a moot point whether one must make further distinctions concerning passages excluded from this category, by designating different sorts of prose, including poetic prose, etc. Such an objection, however, would be fallacious. Precisely the same reasons which initially motivate attempts to distinguish poetry and prose may be cited as reasons for distinguishing prose and poetic prose.[17] Although the 'prose particle' counts are instructive, we must conclude that they do not provide a definitive solution to the problem of distinguishing between prose and poetry. They perhaps demonstrate that prose and poetry, as classically understood, tend to collect at opposite ends of a spectrum. Unanswered is the question where poetry ends and prose begins.

---

prose (1983:166). However, the four chapters of the book of Ruth have respective total percentage scores of 5.846, 15.344, 14.729 and 18.507 (p.177). Thus, the last three chapters fall in the middle range. But in light of De Moor's study it is impossible to argue that the present text is a mixture of poetic and non—poetic material. See now J.C. de Moor: 1984:262—283; 1986:16—46; 'The conclusion would seem to be inevitable that not only a few isolated verses but the entire Book of Ruth is a poetic composition' (p. 45).

17 G.B. Gray's conclusion that, 'Failure to perceive what are the formal elements in Hebrew poetry has, in the past, frequently led to misinterpretation of Scripture' (1972:3) pertains equally to poetic narrative. Concerning the distinction between poetry and prose Freedman aptly states, 'Each has its own rules of operation, and it is obligatory to understand each category according to its own pattern, even if the dividing line is not always certain' (1977: 6). See also P.C. Craigie, 'The Conquest and Early Hebrew Poetry' *Tyndale Bulletin* 20 (1969) 76—78.

The question of an intermediate range, namely the possibility of poetic narrative, remains as vital as ever !

1.4 Analysis of poetic prose

The preceding paragraphs have mentioned certain difficulties encountered when one attempts to precisely differentiate poetry and prose in the Old Testament. Despite the obstacles involved, a more refined analysis of possible types of poetic narratives is highly desirable. R.Lowth's study of poetry in the Prophets, although in itself incomplete and inadequate, revolutionized the literary study of these books by setting into motion a method of poetry—sensitive literary analysis. Similary, a concentrated study of poetic aspects in Old Testament narratives may be expected to pay good returns. U. Cassuto, both in his commentaries and articles, frequently alerted the reader to phenomena which appear to indicate poetic prose.[18] Additional examples of poetic stylistics in passages traditionally treated as prose may be found in the works of *inter alia* Kugel, Avishur, Watson and Berlin. However, increased recognition of 'poetic' elements in narrative texts has frequently led to talk of 'poetic fragments' or of poetry 'embedded' in narrative.[19] Such descriptions usually imply a diachronic explanation for the present form of the text; the poetic aspects are treated either as an indication that the text

---

18   U. Cassuto, *A Commentary on the Book of Genesis,* 2 vols., Trans. I. Abrahams (Jerusalem, 1961 + 1964) [Hebr. orig. 1944 + 1949]; *A Commentary on the Book of Exodus,* Trans. I. Abraham (Jerusalem, 1967) [Hebr. orig. 1951]. Many of Cassuto's articles are offered in translated form in *Biblical & Oriental Studies,* 2 vols. (Jerusalem, 1973 + 1975). See esp. vol. 1: 7—16; vol. 2: 69—109.

19   One approach to the presence of poetry and prose collocated in numerous books of O.T. history and prophecy was suggested in the now famous 'epic theory' of W.F. Albright. See his *Yahweh and the Gods of Canaan* (London, 1968) esp. 1—46. Cf. F.M. Cross, *Canaanite Myth and Hebrew Epic* (Cambridge, Mass., 1973). See now the reservations expressed by S. Talmon, 'The "Comparative Method" in Biblical Interpretation — Principles and Problems', in: *Congress Volume Göttingen 1977* (VTS 29; Leiden, 1978) 351—356. For a further review and evaluation of various epic theories see C. Conroy, 'Hebrew Epic: Historical Notes and Critical Reflections', *Bib* 61 (1980) 1—30.

was previously more pervasively poetic, or that the poetic 'fragments' are taken up from another source.[20] It lies beyond the purview of this study to discuss the validity of such terminology or the diachronic theories presupposed, but one caveat must be made. A ready tendency to assume a diachronic explanation for what at first sight appears to be an indiscriminate collocation of prose and poetry often hinders recognition of the true character of a larger unit of poetic narrative. More justifiable from a literary point of view is an approach which initially takes the presence of poetic characteristics in a narrative as a hint that the larger literary unit may possibly be structured as poetic prose.

This caveat is by no means intended to obviate the possibility that certain O.T. narratives may at one time have had a form more clearly poetic than is presently discernible, or that in some passages prose and poetry may in fact be collocated within a given literary unit. Nevertheless, the modern scholar has much to learn in the recognition of the presence as well as the form of poetry in the O.T.[21] It is primarily to the goal of *recognition* that this study hopes to contribute. The principles of poetic analysis developed elsewhere[22] are used here to demonstrate that Josh. 23 is poetic narrative. Due to the novelty of this thesis it is deemed necessary to present a very detailed justification of the proposed literary structure of this passage. Textual—critical questions are kept minimal, in accordance with the primary goal of *recognition* rather than *reconstruction* of poetry. However, by virtue of its contribution

---

20 Somewhat unique is the emphasis of E.F. Campbell Jr., *Ruth* (AB 7; Garden City 1975) who defends the theory that the present text contains embedded poetry written by the same author as the prose, in order to heighten the style of the narrative (see esp. 5—23). But, compare now the conclusions attained by J.C. de Moor (see notes 1 and 16 above).

21 Watson: 1984:45, makes a crucial distinction between *recognition* and *reconstruction* of poetry. He suggests that recognition of poetry is facilitated by discernment of certain characteristics, for which he offers a table of nineteen indicators (45—46). The characteristics included in this table of indicators are all helpful, but they do not yet provide a systematic, step—by—step method of analysing a poetic unit.

22 See M.C.A. Korpel—J.C. de Moor, 'Fundamentals of Ugaritic and Hebrew Poetry', *UF* 18 (1986) 173—212 (reprinted in this volume).

towards a clearer understanding of the structure of a given passage, the method here employed can often constitute an important tool for solving textual problems. In accordance with the assumption that literary structure is employed deliberately by the Biblical authors as a means of conveying and heightening theological meaning, numerous comments will also be offered pertaining to the theological insights gained by reading Josh. 23 as poetic narrative.

2. Colometrical delineation and justification

In the ensuing study Josh. 23 is reproduced in colometrical format. To avoid possible confusion the numbering of the respective poetic units merits explanation. For example, in the designation I.A.i.1 the following components are to be recognized: I = canto; A = sub—canto; i = canticle; 1 = strophe, etc. And the designation of the verse and colon is placed in brackets by the respective cola. Following the colometrical delineation of Josh. 23 in its entirety, a detailed justification for the proposed structure is offered.

2.1 *Colometrical delineation of Josh. 23*

I.A.i.1   (1aA) ויהי מימים רבים
    (1aB) אחרי אשר־הניח יהוה לישראל
    (1aC) מכל־איביהם מסביב
    (1bA) ויהושע זקן
    (1bB) בא בימים

I.A.i.2   (2aA) ויקרא יהושע לכל־ישראל
    (2aB) לזקניו ולראשיו
    (2aC) ולשפטיו ולשטריו
    (2bA) ויאמר אלהם
    (2bB) אני זקנתי
    (2bC) באתי בימים

I.A.ii.1   (3aA) ואתם ראיתם
    (3aB) את כל־אשר עשה יהוה אלהיכם
    (3aC) לכל־הגוים האלה מפניכם
    (3bA) כי יהוה אלהיכם
    (3bB) הוא הנלחם לכם

I.A.ii.2   (4aA) ראו הפלתי לכם
    (4aB) את־הגוים הנשארים האלה
    (4aC) בנחלה לשבטיכם

מן־הירדן (4bA)

[וכל־הגוים אשר הכרתי (4bB)]

והים הגדול מבוא השמש (4bC)

I.A.ii.3   ויהוה אלהיכם (5aA)

הוא יהדפם מפניכם (5aB)

והוריש אתם מלפניכם (5aC)

וירשתם את־ארצם (5bA)

כאשר דבר יהוה אלהיכם לכם (5bB)

I.B.i.1   וחזקתם מאד (6aA)

לשמר ולעשות (6aB)

את כל־הכתוב (6aC)

בספר תורת משה (6aD)

לבלתי סור־ממנו (6bA)

ימין ושמאול (6bB)

I.B.i.2   לבלתי־בוא בגוים האלה (7aA)

הנשארים האלה אתכם (7aB)

ובשם אלהיהם לא־תזכירו (7bA)

[ולא תשביעו (7bB)]

ולא תעבדום (7bC)

ולא תשתחוו להם (7bD)

I.B.ii.1   כי אם־ביהוה אלהיכם תדבקו (8aA)

כאשר עשיתם (8aB)

עד היום הזה (8aC)

ויורש יהוה מפניכם (9aA)

גוים גדלים ועצומים (9aB)

I.B.ii.2   ואתם לא־עמד איש בפניכם (9bA)

עד היום הזה (9bB)

איש־אחד מכם ירדף־אלף (10aA)

כי יהוה אלהיכם (10aB)

הוא הנלחם לכם (10aC)

כאשר דבר לכם (10aD)

II.A.i.1   ונשמרתם מאד לנפשתיכם (11aA)

לאהבה את־יהוה אלהיכם (11aB)

II.A.i.2   כי אם־שוב תשובו (12aA)

ודבקתם ביתר הגוים האלה (12aB)

הנשארים האלה אתכם (12aC)

והתחתנתם בהם (12bA)

ובאתם בהם (12bB)

והם בכם (12bC)

II.A.ii.1

ידוע תדעו (13aA)
כי לא יוסיף יהוה אלהיכם (13aB)
להוריש את־הגוים האלה מלפניכם (13aC)
והיו לכם לפח ולמוקש (13bA)
ולשטט בצדיכם (13bB)
ולצננים בעיניכם (13bC)

II.A.ii.2

עד־אבדכם (13cA)
מעל האדמה הטובה הזאת (13cB)
אשר נתן לכם (13cC)
יהוה אלהיכם (13cD)

II.B.i.1

והנה אנכי הולך היום (14aA)
בדרך כל־הארץ (14aB)
וידעתם בכל־לבבכם (14bA)
ובכל־נפשכם (14bB)

II.B.i.2

כי לא־נפל דבר אחד (14cA)
מכל הדברים הטובים (14cB)
אשר דבר יהוה אלהיכם עליכם (14cC)
הכל באו לכם (14dA)
לא־נפל ממנו דבר אחד (14dB)

II.B.ii.1

והיה כאשר־בא עליכם (15aA)
כל־הדבר הטוב (15aB)
אשר דבר יהוה אלהיכם אליכם (15aC)
כן יביא יהוה עליכם (15bA)
את כל־הדבר הרע (15bB)

II.B.ii.2

עד־השמידו אותכם (15cA)
מעל האדמה הטובה הזאת (15cB)
אשר נתן לכם (15cC)
יהוה אלהיכם (15cD)

II.B.ii.3

בעברכם את־ברית יהוה אלהיכם (16aA)
אשר צוה אתכם (16aB)
והלכתם ועבדתם אלהים אחרים (16bA)
והשתחויתם להם (16bB)
וחרה אף־יהוה בכם (16cA)
ואבדתם מהרה (16cB)
מעל הארץ הטובה (16cC)
אשר נתן לכם (16cD)

2.2 *Justification of the colometrical divisions*[23]

2.2.1 Sub—canto I.A (Josh. 23:1—5)

I.A.i.1 (Josh. 23:1)

Int.par.:	[24]בא בימים // זקן
Inclusion:	[25]בא בימים // מימים רבים
Sep.up:	*petucha*; tricolon; ויהי
Sep.down:	בימים // מימים (inclusion and tautological parallelism).

I.A.i.2 (Josh. 23:2)

Int.par.:	// לזקניו ולראשיו // לכל־ישראל
	באחי בימים // זקנתי[26]; ולשפטיו ולשטריו
Ext.par.:	זקנתי // לזקניו // ויאמר // ויקרא
Allit.:	ולשפטיו ולשטריו
Sep.up:	taut.par. (ל // ל // ל); tricolon
Sep.down:	אמר; tricolon; refrain[27]

Ext.par. between strophes I.A.i.1 and I.A.i.2:

לכל // מכל (1a, 2a); לכל־ישראל // לישראל (1a, 2a)

אני זקנתי // יהושע זקן (1b, 2b; responsion)

באחי בימים // בא בימים (1b, 2b; responsion)

יהושע // יהושע (1b, 2a; concatenation)

לזקניו // זקן (1b, 2a; concatenation)

בימים // מימים (1a, 2b; inclusion)

---

23 I wish to thank Prof. J.C. de Moor for reading a preliminary draft of this part of my study and offering suggestions for improvements.

24 The apposition בא בימים may be taken as a semantic parallel of זקן. The same idiomatic expression is used in Josh. 13:1 and Gen. 18:11; similar expressions are found in Jer. 6:11 (poetry) and Job 42:17. Cf. Isa. 65:20; Job 32:4.

25 Note that M. Dahood, 'Ugaritic—Hebrew Parallels' in: L. Fisher (ed.), *Ras Shamra Parallels* (AnOr 49; Rome, 1972) 336—337 lists examples of זקן // רבים, which strengthens the case for parallelism between 1a and 1b here.

26 Cf. Josh. 8:33; 24:1; Ezra 10:14, and more importantly for our argument here, the chiastic enumeration in Isa. 3:2, which is clearly poetic.

27 Cf. the final cola (1b) of the preceding strophe.

I.A.ii.1 (Josh. 23:3)

Int.par.:   // יהוה (3a); ‏כם‏- // ‏כם‏- // ‏חם‏-; לכל‏- // כל‏-
          (3b) ‏כם‏- // ‏כם‏-; הוא

Ext.par.:   יהוה אלהיכם // יהוה אלהיכם

Rhyme: ‏כם‏- // ‏כם‏- // ‏כם‏- // ‏חם‏-

Inclusion: לכם // ואתם

Sep.up: tricolon; ואתם; tautological parallelism (כל // כל);
          האלה

Sep.down: כי and הוא

I.A.ii.2 (Josh. 23:4)

Int.par.:   בנחלה לשבטיכם // הפלתי לכם;
          [28]‏והים הגדול // מן‏-הירדן

Ext.par.:   את‏-הגוים הנשארים האלה //
          [29]‏וכל‏-הגוים אשר הכרתי

Sep.up: ראו (imperative); tricolon; האלה

Sep.down: tricolon

---

28 Note that this parallelism forms a merismus for the land of Palestine proper. Dahood: 1972:204 suggests that a parallel pair may be identified in the words השמש // והים, which in this case would mark the beginning and end of the final colon of this strophe. Transjordan is not mentioned because that was already allotted by Moses (Num. 32; Deut. 3:12—22; Josh. 1:12—15, etc.).

29 The awkwardness of the phrase in 4b has long been noted by commentators. See C. Steuernagel, *Deuteronomium und Josua* (HK I.3; Göttingen, 1900) 240; H. Holzinger, *Das Buch Josua* (KHC VI; Leipzig und Tübingen, 1901) 94; G.A. Cooke, The Book of Joshua (Cambridge, 1918) 210—211; M. Noth, *Das Buch Josua* (HAT 7; Tübingen, 1953) 134; J.H. Kroeze, *Het Boek Jozua* (COT; Kampen, 1967) 245; J.A. Soggin, *Joshua* (OTL; London, 1972) 217; R.G. Boling, *Joshua* (AB 6; New York, 1982) 523; J. Gray, *Joshua. Judges. Ruth* (New Century Bible Commentary; Basingstoke/Grand Rapids, 1986 [revised edition]) 174. Most of the commentators here listed solve the problem by placing this phrase before מן‏-הירדן. But that leaves unexplained how the word order was transposed, unless if Boling is correct that it is a garbled envelope construction (1982:523). It can also be explained as simply a gloss, perhaps based upon 13:1ff. At this point it is sufficient to note the problem; additional considerations will be given below in the context of the macro—structure of the entire canto.

I.A.ii.3 (Josh. 23:5)

Int.par.:   ‎30‏והוריש אתם מלפניכם // יהדפם מפניכם
Ext.par.:   וירשתם את־ארצם // והוריש אתם מלפניכם
Rhyme: ‎־כם // ־צם // ־כם // ־כם // ־כם
Inclusion: יהוה אלהיכם // ויהוה אלהיכם
Sep.up: הוא; tricolon; taut.par. ‎־כם // ־כם // ־כם
Sep.down: tautological use of ‎לכם‏31; inclusion; refrain‏32

Ext.par. between I.A.ii.1 and I.A.ii.2:

ראו הפלתי לכם // ואתם ראיתם (3a; 4a; chiastic responsion)
‎־הגוים...האלה // ־כם // ־כם (3a; 4a;‏ ‏־הגוים; ־הגוים האלה
responsion)
וכל־הגוים // לכל־הגוים (3a, 4b)
לכם // לכם (concatenation)

Ext.par. between I.A.ii.2 and I.A.ii.3:

entire tricolon 4a // entire tricolon 5a‏33
לכם // לכם (4a, 5b; inclusion)

Ext.par. between I.A.ii.1 and I.A.ii.3:

יהוה אלהיכם // יהוה אלהיכם (3a//5a, and 3b//5b,
responsions)
כאשר דבר // כל־אשר עשה (3a, 5b; inclusion)‏34
מלפניכם // מפניכם and מפניכם (3a, 5a; responsion)
הוא // הוא (3b, 5a)

---

30 Cf. Deut. 30:4.
31 The word לכם is grammatically unnecessary. Specification in 5a of the
people as beneficiaries of Yahweh's assistance, and the people as subject in
5b, would have been sufficient to show that the people are the recipients of
God's word in 5bB, without a need to specify the indirect object.
Furthermore, לכם is not necessary to maintain the rhyme at the end of
the colon, which would have been present in אלהיכם. Stylistically the
presence of לכם seems to be primarily due to the inclusion that it forms
with לכם in 4aA, and to mark sep.downwards.
32 See 10aD below, which similarly marks the end of the next sub−canto.
33 Verse 4a details Joshua's action in allotting the inherited land to the
tribes, 5a attributes facilitation of the inheritance to Yahweh.
34 This parallelism, with the subject יהוה אלהיכם, forms an inclusion
of the canticle.

Detection of the responsions and inclusion formed by strategic placement of the divine subject in the first and last strophe of this canticle reveals the symmetrical effect of the three strophes. Yahweh's action on behalf of his people constitutes the framework within which Joshua, the divinely commissioned real—estate agent, could parcel out the land which 'fell' to the tribes.

   A number of observations may now also be made concerning the relationship between the two canticles (I.A.i and I.A.ii) of this sub—canto:

(1a, 5b; לכם // לישראל; יהוה // יהוה; כאשר // אשר
inclusion)

(1a, 3a; responsion) כל־אשר עשה יהוה // אשר־הניח יהוה

(1a, 3a; לכל־הגוים האלה מפניכם // מכל־איביהם מסביב
responsion)

(1b, 2b, 4b; מבוא השמש // באתי בימים // בא בימים
responsions)

(Joshua to Israel, 2a, 4a; הפלתי לכם // יהושע לכל־לישראל
responsion)

(2b, 3a; concatenation)[35] ואתם // אני

2.2.2 Sub—canto I.B (Josh. 23:6—10)

I.B.i.1 (Josh. 23:6)

Hendiadys: ימין ושמאול[37]; [36]לשמר ולעשות

---

35   B. Holwerda, *Jozua en Richteren* (Kampen, 1971³) 75f.

36   Note that each of these verbs occurs frequently in collocation with חזק, which is found here in the preceding colon. In numerous cases they form virtual parallelisms with חזק. For חזק and שמר see especially Isa. 56:2,4,6; Jer. 51:12 and 1.Chr. 22:13. For חזק and עשה see especially Isa. 27:5; 56:2; Jer. 51:12; Ez. 22:14; Hag. 2:4. For verses in which all three of these verbs occur see Josh. 1:7; 23:6; Isa. 56:2 and Jer. 51:12.

37   This word—pair occurs elsewhere in poetic parallelism and in syndetic parataxis, in Akkadian, Ugaritic and Aramaic as well as in Hebrew. See now C.I.K. Story, 'The Book of Proverbs and Northwest Semitic Literature', *JBL* 64 (1945) 326—327. E.Z. Melamed, 'Break—up of Stereotype Phrases as an Artistic Device in Biblical Poetry', in: Ch. Rabin (ed.), *Studies in the Bible* (Scripta Hierosolymitana 8; Jerusalem, 1961) 146—147. Avishur: 1984:47, 579, 588—589, 599.

Sep.up: quadrocolon; מאד לשמר[38]; infinitive constructs
Sep.down: syndetic parataxis ?[39]

I.B.i.2 (Josh. 23:7)

Int.par.:   // אליהם // בגוים האלה // הנשארים האלה;
            // ולא תשביעו // לא־תזכירו; בהם[40] //
            ולא תשתחוו // ולא תעבדום[41]
Ext.par.:   להם // אתכם
Sep.up: האלה // האלה (tautological parallelism)[42]
Sep.down: quadrocolon; taut.par. ולא // ולא // ולא // לא

---

38 Cf. below at 11a.

39 This is questionable as a marker of separation, but cf. 9aB. A larger corpus of comparative material of this type of poetic narrative should help to clarify whether syndetic parataxis is employed elsewhere as a formal marker of separation.

40 Forming inclusion at the level of the poetic verse.

41 Various combinations of the four prohibitions listed here in syndetic parataxis are found elsewhere in poetic parallelism. For זכר // שבע see Isa. 48:1. Note that frequently a form of the root זכר is found in poetic parallelism with שם; see Cassuto: 1967:39; Avishur, 1984:83, 317, 579, 598–600 (including examples in Aramaic, Phoenician and Akkadian). The verbs עבד and שחה occur 31 times together in the same verse. Of particular interest here are 5 occurences in Jeremiah (8:2; 13:10; 16:11; 22:9; 25:6) all printed in BHS as prose. The first four are found in the immediate context of poetry. More significantly, all are part of divine oracles spoken by Yahweh through Jeremiah as prophetic spokesman. עבד and שחה occur together in Isaac's poetic blessing of Jacob in Gen. 27:29. They stand as poetic parallels in a chiastic bicolon in Ps. 72:11 and as a poetic pair in the tricolon of Ps. 97:7. Cf. the prohibitions in Ex. 20:5 and 23:24 as well as the divine discourse to Solomon in 2.Chron. 7:22. The remaining occurrences are found in Deut. – 2 Kgs. (plus once in 2 Chron. 33:3) either as prophetic admonitions from Moses to Joshua (cf. 23:16) or as the historical narrator's judgement concerning unfaithfulness. It would take too much time to demonstrate that most of these verses can be read as poetry. For a poetic verse in which שבע and שחה are both used twice as nominal participles see Zeph. 1:5. Note the asyndetic parataxis here. In Ps. 22:28 the syndetic hendiadys ידכרו וישבו stands parallel to וישתחוו. For שבע and עבד Deut. 6:13 and 10:20 are of interest because these verses demonstrate the principle of expansion and/or contraction.

42 This marker of separation is of particular significance because of the relative weakness of the formal indicator of separation downwards in the

Ext.par. between strophes I.B.i.1 and I.B.i.2:

(6b, 7a;   לבלתי־בוא בגוים // לבלתי // סור־ממנו
concatenation)

Mention must also be made of the contrasting parallelism formed between 6a and 7b. The former constitutes a positive injunction to maintain the law. The latter contains prohibitions related to transgression of the divine law. These two strophes balance very well to form a symmetrical canticle.

I.B.ii.1 (Josh. 23:8—9a):

Ext.par.:   יהוה מפניכם // ביהוה אלהיכם
Allit.:   גוים גדלים
Asson.:   גוים גדלים ועצומים
Sep.up: כי; כאשר; tricolon
Sep.down: גדלים ועצומים (tautological parataxis)[43]

I.B.ii.2 (Josh. 23:9b—10):

Int.par.:   // כם- // כם // כם-;הוא הנלחם לכם // יהוה אלהיכם
             לכם // לכם
Ext.par.:   (4x)[44] כם- // כם // כם-;איש- // איש // מכם; ואתם
Juxtaposition: אלף // אחד
Rhyme: כם- // כם- // כם // כם-

---

previous strophe and because of the external parallelism between לבלתי // לבלתי (6b, 7a). The second independent pronoun האלה is superfluous to the Hebrew, as is also reflected by its absence in the Syriac Peshitta. It is probably present in the Hebrew primarily to mark the border of the strophe. Recognition of this literay device in MT makes it unnecessary to resort to the theory of scribal conflations and haplographies proposed by R.G. Boling, 'Some Conflate Readings in Joshua—Judges', *VT* 16 (1966) 296f.

43 This syndetic hendiadys, with alliteration and assonance, forms a satisfactory literary ending for the strophe. Reference to this parataxis as being 'tautological' is a judgement upon the grammatical and semantic redundancy, and does not suggest that it does not have a meanigful role with respect to stylistics and content.

44 Perhaps an additional external parallelism should be identified in the semantic equivalency formed by ירדף // לא־עמד. Cf. 2 Sam. 2:28 where ויעמדו and ולא־ירדפו are used synonymously. Incidentally, the latter text should likely be read as four poetic cola.

Inclusion: ולכם // ואתם[45]
Sep.up: ואתם; negative particle
Sep.down: quadrocolon; taut.par. ‎-כם // ‎-כם // ‎-כם // ‎-כם // ‎-כם;
כי; הוא; כאשר; inclusion; refrain[46]

Ext.par. between strophes I.B.ii.1 and I.B.ii.2:

עד היום הזה // עד היום הזה (8a, 9b; responsion)
יהוה // יהוה (9a, 10a; responsion)
כי יהוה אלהיכם // כי אם־ביהוה אלהיכם (8a, 10a; inclusion)
כאשר דבר // כאשר עשיתם (8a, 10a; inclusion)
איש // גוים גדלים ועצומים (9a, 9b; concatenation of contrast)
לא־עמד איש בפניכם // ויורש יהוה מפניכם (9a, 9b; concatenation; semantic parallelism)

A couple of parallelisms must also be noted at the level of the sub–canto:

עשיתם // ולעשות (6a, 8a; responsion)
לכם // להם (7b, 10a; responsion)

The four strophes of these two canticles form a well–balanced sub–canto (2+2).[47]

_____

45 Cf. I.A.ii.1 above.
46 Note that of the last three cola of the verse, the first two cola are identical to the bicola forming separation down in the canticle I.A.ii.1 (3bA and 3bB), while the final colon here is a contracted form of the final colon forming separation downwards at the end of sub–canto I.A (5bB). The strong markers of separation combine here to show the termination of the strophe, canticle, sub–canto and canto.
47 Even the number of cola per canticle shows close uniformity. As now divided there are 4+2/2+4=12 and 3+2/2+4=11 cola. Furthermore, 7bB is suspect. Although it fits the parallelism of the strophe well it is absent in LXX. It could be an expansion in MT, perhaps prompted by correlation with שם; cf. Lev. 19:12; Deut. 6:13; 10:20; Isa. 48:1; Jer. 12:16; 44:26 and Zech. 5:4, etc. Deletion of this colon would slightly reduce the symmetry of the canticle, but would perfect the symmetry of the sub–canto, producing the scheme: 4+2/2+3//3+2/2+4. This would mean that the sub–canto would only begin and end with a quadrocolon. Sep.down at 7b would not be weakened because it would still be marked by a tricolon, taut.par., etc. All things considered, 7bB is likely a later expansion in MT.

100   *William T.Koopmans*

2.2.3 Sub–canto II.A (Josh. 23:11–13)

II.A.i.1 (Josh. 23:11)

Int.par.:   ‏48לאהבה // ונשמרתם ;כם- // כם-

Sep.up: ‏49ונשמרתם מאד; // -ל // -ל and כם- // כם- // כם-
(tautological parallelism)‏50

II.A.i.2 (Josh. 23:12)

Int.par.:   ‏51;הנשארים האלה // ביתר הגוים האלה
בכם // בהם // בהם ‏52(12a); -כם // -חם

Ext.par.:   ‏53בכם // אתכם

Asson. and allit.: entire tricolon 12b.

Rhyme: בכם // בהם // בהם // אתכם

Sep.up: כי; infinitive absolute; tricolon; האלה // האלה
(taut.par.);‏54 beginning of hypothetical transgression

Sep.down: בכם // בהם // בהם (taut.par.); tricolon; end of

---

48   While the first form is a Niphal functioning imperatively and the second is a Qal infinitive construct completing the imperatival sense of the first colon, we are likely justified in seeing these two verbs as forming a parallelism here. Cf. now Isa. 56:6; Ps. 97:10; 119:167 and the parallelism in 146:8–9; see M. Dahood, *Psalms II* (AB 17; Garden City, 1968) 362. See too Josh. 22:5; Dan. 9:4 (Daniel's prayer) and Neh. 1:5 (Nehemiah's prayer). In Ps. 37:28 the two verbs occur together, but by virtue of the acrostic form of the poem it is clear that they are not part of the same poetic line. Nevertheless, external parallelism seems likely here.

49   Cf. in 6aA above, also at the beginning of a sub–canto. Also compare Jer. 17:21, following a *setuma*, and Deut. 4:15.

50   Since our colometrical division here suggests that the strophe is coterminous with the bicolon verse, it is technically not possible to argue for separation downwards apart from the markers of separation upwards already listed here. But more important for justification of the division made between this strophe and the following one are the markers of separation upwards which may be listed for the next strophe. The strength of those markers helps to confirm the division made here.

51   For יתר and שאר in poetic parallelism see Isa. 4:3.

52   It is also possible to see a semantic parallelism between the verb 'to cling' and the preposition 'with'.

53   An additional external parallel may possibly be seen in the verbs שוב and חתן. They occur together in Ezra's prayer (Ezra 9:14) in what appears to be poetic parallelism.

54   Cf. above, I.B.i.2.

hypothetical transgression

Ext.par. between strophes II.A.i.1 and II.A.i.2:

⁵⁵ודבקתם ביתר הגוים האלה // לאהבה את־יהוה אלהיכם

‎-כם, -הם, -הם // -כם, -הם // -כם, -כם

II.A.ii.1 (Josh. 23:13a,b)

Int.par.:	‎-כם // -כם (13a); ⁵⁶לפח ולמוקש // ולשטט //
	‎⁵⁷ולצננים; לכם // בצדיכם // בעיניכם⁵⁸
Ext.par.:	‎-יכם, -יכם // -יכם // -יכם, -יכם⁵⁹
Sep.up:	infin. absol. functioning imperatively; כי; negative particle; infin. const.; tricolon
Sep.down:	tricolon; taut.par. of ‎-כם (3x) in 13b and ל // ל // ל

II.A.ii.2 (Josh. 23:13c)

Int.par.:	‎-כם // -כם // -כם
Sep.up:	particle עד; quadrocolon; taut.par. ‎-כם (3x); הזאת⁶⁰
Sep.down:	entire strophe as refrain⁶¹

---

55 An explicit contrast is established between loving God and clinging to the remaining nations.

56 This hendiadys also occurs in syndetic parataxis in Isa. 8:14 (poetry), and in parallelism in Amos 3:5; Ps. 69:23; 140:6 and 141:9. These places, along with Josh. 23:13, are all poetic and are the only places where these two words are collocated in a verse. See now Melamed: 1961:126f.; Avishur: 1984:317 (it is not clear why Avishur omits reference to Ps. 69:23 and 140:6).

57 The plural forms of שטט and צך occur in asyndetic parataxis in Prov. 22:5; see Avishur: 1984:144.

58 The last two words listed here form a clear parallelism, not only because of the identical preposition and suffix, but also because of the fact that both nouns refer to body parts. See the collocation in Isa. 60:4. The closest parallel to Josh. 23:13 is found in Num. 33:55.

59 In מלפניכם and בעיניכם the parallelism is heightened by the association of 'face' and 'eyes'.

60 The independent pronoun is grammatically redundant here after the adjective and before the modifying clause of the subsequent colon. While it may be of some significance for the theological emphasis placed upon the land as a realized gift, it is also possible to see its function here as being similar to the tautological האלה discussed above.

61 Cf. below at II.B.ii.2 and II.B.ii.3.

Ext.par. between strophes II.A.ii.1 and II.A.ii.2:

יהוה אלהיכם // יהוה אלהיכם (13a, 13c; inclusion)

כם- (3x) // כם- (4x) (rhyme; responsion; concatenation)

In addition to the many observations already made at the level
of the strophes and the canticles, it is now necessary to list the
literary connections between the two canticles (II.A.i and II.A.ii)
of this sub−canto (II.A). An inclusion is formed by יהוה-
אלהיכם // יהוה אלהיכם (11a, 13c). Of particular significance
are the literary connections between II.A.i.2 and II.A.ii.1 which,
along with the inclusion mentioned, serve to give a coherence to
the entire sub−canto. For convenience we list these parallelisms
in the format used in the previous analyses:

ידוע תדעו // שוב תשובו (12a, 13a; syntactic parallelism of
infin. absolute constructions; responsion)

כי // כי (12a, 13a; responsion)

את־הגוים האלה // הגוים האלה (12a, 13a; responsion)
suffixes // suffixes[62]

Syntactically it is important to note that the section 12aB −
12bC stands in apposition to the inf. abs. construction שוב
תשובו. The inf. abs. construction of 13aA reads directly back
to 12aA. The explication of the hypothetical transgressions in
the tricolon 12b is balanced by the tricolon of curses in 13b.
These two strophes are framed by the connection made between
II.A.i.1 and II.A.ii.2, thereby creating a very symmetrical
sub−canto.

2.2.4 Sub−canto II.B (Josh. 23:14−16)

II.B.i.1 (Josh. 23:14a,b)

Int.par.:   בכל־נפשכם // בכל־לבבכם[68]

Ext.par.:   ובכל־ and בכל־ // כל־ // חם־;[64] // אנכי

---

62   Note that of the 12 cola in these two strophes 6 end with כם- and 2
with הם-. Of the 18 cola in the sub−canto, 11 end with כם- and 2 with
הם-, thus all but 5 end with ם.

63   There are 48 verses in which לב or לבב occurs along with נפש.
Many are poetic, e.g. Jer. 4:19; Ps. 13:3; 24:4; 35:25; 78:18; 84:3; Prov. 2:10;
6:32; 14:10; 15:32; 19:8; 23:7; 24:12; 27:9; Lam. 2:19.

64   It is noteworthy that Dahood lists ידע and הלך as a poetic pair

Sep.up: 65‎והנה אנכי

Sep.down: -בכל // ‎ובכל- (taut.par.)

II.B.i.2 (Josh. 23:14c,d)

Int.par.:   דבר // דבר הדברים‎66; באו //
             לא-נפל ?‎67

Ext.par.:   ‎68;לא-נפל ממנו דבר אחד // לא-נפל דבר אחד
             באו לכם // עליכם ;הכל // מכל

Asson.:   אליהכם עליכם

Sep.up: // הדברים // דבר ;‎כי; negative particle; tricolon;
             דבר (taut. par.)

Sep.down: ‎ממנו; inclusion of the strophe

Ext.par. between strophes II.B.i.1 and II.B.i.2:

---

occurring both in Hebrew and Ugaritic: *RSP*, vol.2 (1975) 198; *Psalms III* (AB 17a; Garden City, 1970) 449. The frequency with which these two words are collocated in the same verse is indeed striking; a computer search lists 62 such verses, many of which are poetic. It is thus possible that we should include הלך and ידע as part of the parallelism here. The closest similarity to this verse is found in David's farewell speech to Solomon (1 Kgs. 2:2).

65 Note that in 1 Kgs. 2:2 the idiomatic phrase -אנכי הלך בדרך כל הארץ stands at the beginning of direct discourse.

66 This is a 'noun // noun (pl.) // verb' type of parallelism. The phenomenon of noun // verb constructions has received some discussion in recent studies, but parallelisms formed by nouns and verbs from the same root consonants have not been adequately studied. See now S.E. Loewenstamm, *UF* 3 (1971) 93 n.2; D. Grossberg, 'Noun / Verb Parallelism: Syntactic or Asyntactic?', *JBL* 99 (1980) 481−488; Avishur: 1984:311−315; Beyerlin: 1985:34; Watson: 1984:157−158. Watson states that Grossberg was the first to notice noun / verb parallelism in Hebrew poetry (157), but Watson is mistaken unless if he means more specifically the type of parallelism in which a verb is nominalized to stand parallel to a noun, which is the focus of Grossberg's study.

67 This is a questionable parallelism. However, it is suggested by W.G.E. Watson, 'Fixed Pairs in Ugaritic and Isaiah', *VT* 22 (1972) 463, that these verbs can be poetic pairs in both Hebrew and Ugaritic. In addition to Isa. 47:11 mentioned by Watson, Jer. 15:8 and Ps. 35:8 may be listed. In Josh. 23:14, the strongest parallelisms are formed by 14cA and 14dB on the one hand, and 14dA and 15aA on the other.

68 Inclusion at the level of the strophe is also formed by this parallelism.

repetition of כל (14a, 14b [2x] // 14c, 14d)

Perhaps an inclusion is intended with אנכי (14a) and ממנו (14d). This possibility would be strengthened if we are to see a connection between הולך and לא־נפל.

II.B.ii.1 (Josh. 23:15a,b)

Int.par.:	דבר // ־הדבר ;אליכם // עליכם ;אשר // כאשר
Ext.par.:	;עליכם // עליכם ;יביא // בא [69]כל־הדבר הרע // כל־הדבר הטוב
Sep.up:	;אשר // אשר ;והיה כאשר; taut. par. (כאשר // (דבר // הדבר ;אליכם // עליכם; tricolon
Sep.down:	את ;כן (cf. 15a); inclusion

II.B.ii.2 (Josh. 23:15c)

Int.par.:	־כם // ־כם // ־כם
Sep.up:	עד[70]; הזאת[71]; quadrocolon
Sep.down:	refrain[72]

II.B.ii.3 (Josh. 23:16)

Int.par.:	־כם // ־כם (2x); והשתחויתם להם // ועבדתם אלהים
Ext.par.:	בעברכם את־ברית יהוה אליכם // ;והלכם ועבדתם אלהים אחרים // והלכתם ועבדתם ;יהוה // יהוה // ;[73]ואבדתם מהרה

---

69   The adjectives 'good' and 'evil' make a natural, antonymous pair. See Dahood, *Psalms I* (AB 16; Garden City, 1966) 219–220; Avishur: 1984:93, 122, 281.

70   See above at II.A.ii.2.

71   It has already been argued at V. 13c above that the independent pronoun is superfluous here. Cf. V. 16c where it is absent.

72   Cf. V. 13c and V. 16c.

73   A neat wordplay is established between the hendiadys designating transgression and the destructive results which may be anticipated. Although the phonology of the original pronunciation remains somewhat hypothetical, the words ועבדתם and ואבדתם must have been nearly homonyms. Cf. the wordplay in Isa. 60:12. It is also noteworthy that הלך and מהרה occur as a pair in Isa. 58:8. The two words are also employed in a literary device in 2 Sam. 17:18,21.

[74]אשר נתן לכם // אשר צוה אתכם

Allit. and asson.: אלהים אחרים

Rhyme: כם- // כם- // הם- // כם- // כם-

Wordplay: ואבדתם // ועבדתם ;מהרה // וחרה

Sep.up: בעברכם

Sep.down: quadrocolon; refrain[75]; *petucha*

Ext.par. between strophes II.B.ii.1 and II.B.ii.2:

הטוב // הטובה (15a, 15c; responsion)

אשר // אשר (15a, 15c; responsion)

יהוה אלהיכם // יהוה אלהיכם (15a, 15c; responsion)

הרע // הטובה (15b, 15c; antonymical concatenation)

Ext.par. between strophes II.B.ii.2 and II.B.ii.3:

מעל הארץ הטובה // מעל האדמה הטובה (15c, 16c; inclusion)[76]

אשר נתן לכם // אשר נתן לכם (15c, 16c; inclusion)

יהוה אלהיכם // יהוה אלהיכם (15c, 16a; concatenation)

Ext.par. between strophes II.B.ii.1 and II.B.ii.3:

הטוב // הטובה (15a, 16c; inclusion)

אשר דבר // אשר צוה (15a, 16a; responsion)

יהוה אלהיכם // יהוה אלהיכם (15a, 16a; responsion)

יהוה // יהוה (15b, 16c)

These observations conclude our discussion at the level of the strophes within the canticles. However, as was the case above, it

---

74 This parallelism also forms inclusion at the level of the strophe.

75 This refrain was already mentioned above at vs. 13c and vs. 15c. The position of the *petucha* here serves to confirm our conclusion that the quadrocolon refrain marks separation downwards in each of these cases. The refrain in the last two strophes serves to mark the end of the sub—canto and canto as well. It is significant that both canto I and canto II are concluded by employment of refrains constructed from elements introduced earlier in the respective cantos.

76 For the parallelism of האדמה // הארץ consult S. Talmon, 'Synonymous Readings in the Textual Traditions of the Old Testament', in: Ch. Rabin (ed.), *Studies in the Bible* (Scripta Hierosolymitana 8; Jerusalem, 1961) 348–349.

is worthwhile to indicate numerous parallelisms operative at the higher level of the sub—canto, in other words, in the form of parallelisms evident between, rather than within, the canticles. There is inclusion at the level of the sub—canto, הארץ // הארץ (14a, 16c), as well as והלכתם // אנכי הולך (14a, 16b). Furthermore, there is strong external parallelism between strophes II.B.i.2 and II.B.ii.1:

כל־הדבר הטוב // מכל הדברים הטובים (14c, 15a; responsion)

אשר דבר יהוה אלהיכם עליכם // (14c, 15a; responsion)[77] אשר דבר יהוה אלהיכם אליכם

כן יביא יהוה עליכם // הכל באו לכם (14d, 15b; responsion)

כל־הדבר // דבר אחד (14d, 15b; responsion)

כל־הדבר // דבר אחד (14c, 15b; inclusion)

הרע // הטובים (14c, 15b; antonymical inclusion)

כל־הדבר // דבר אחד (14d, 15a; concatenation)

־בא עליכם // באו לכם (14d, 15a; concatenation)

This high degree of parallelism demonstrates that these two strophes are virtually 'identical twins' with respect to literary structure. The close identity of structure and content makes it imperative to recognize the strong markers of separation upwards present in 15a, for apart from these literary indicators it would be questionable whether one could justifiably divide these strophes into separate canticles. It is noteworthy that in the two preceding sub—cantos (I.B and II.A) we also discovered a very close relationship between the last strophe of the first canticle and the first strophe of the second canticle. With respect to the last canto, in each of the sub—cantos the central strophes are followed by a quadrocolon refrain. And in sub—canto II.B the quadrocolon of 15c is followed by a final strophe somewhat lengthier than the other strophes of the canto, thereby marking the end of the entire literary unit.[78]

---

77 With a variance of one consonant, this is virtually an identical parallelism.

78 A somewhat longer final strophe is not unusual in Biblical poetry. See P. van der Lugt, *Strofische structuren in de bijbels—hebreeuwse poëzie* (Kampen, 1980) 502—505.

3 The macro—structure of Joshua 23

3.1 *The function of the refrains*

We have noted in our discussion of II.A.ii.2 and II.B.ii.2 above that the separation downwards is marked by a quadrocolon which is at the same time a strophe.[79] A similar quadrocolon verse marks final separation downwards of the canto in II.B.ii.3. In order to show the striking correspondence between these verses it is beneficial to list all three together in sequence :

II.A.ii.2

עד־אבדכם (13cA)
מעל האדמה הטובה הזאת (13cB)
אשר נתן לכם (13cC)
יהוה אלהיכם (13cD)

II.B.ii.2

עד־השמידו אותכם (15cA)
מעל האדמה הטובה הזאת (15cB)
אשר נתן לכם (15cC)
יהוה אלהיכם (15cD)

II.B.ii.3

וחרה אף־יהוה בכם (16cA)
ואבדתם מהרה (16cB)
מעל הארץ הטובה (16cC)
אשר נתן לכם (16cD)

Repetition of key lines in key places generates a cumulative effect. We have called attention to this phenomenon above with respect to canto I. For purpose of comparison it is also helpful to list those cola together.

כי יהוה אלהיכם (3bA)
הוא הנלחם לכם (3bB)

כאשר דבר יהוה אלהיכם לכם (5bB)

The last verse of strophe I.A.ii.1 and the final colon of I.A.ii.3 are combined, along with an extra colon, to form a new quadrocolon refrain marking separation downwards for canto I:

---

79   Cf. Korpel—De Moor: 1986:197.

איש־אחד מכם ירדף־אלף (10aA)

כי יהוה אלהיכם (10aB)

הוא הנלחם לכם (10aC)

כאשר דבר לכם (10aD)[80]

Thus, the same means is used to form refrain strophes in both cantos of Josh. 23. The symmetry between the three refrain verses in canto II is readily apparent. All three are quadrocola. The first strophe counts either ten or eleven poetic feet, depending on whether עד־אבדכם is seen as one or two feet. The latter is more likely in view of the number of feet in the subsequent cola. The remaining two strophes contain either 11 or 12 feet, again depending upon how the two words joined by a *maqqep* in the first colon of each strophe are scanned.

It is precisely the symmetry and tremendous correspondence of detail in all three of these 'final' strophes which should also alert us to pay careful attention to the difference which may be detected. We may confidently assert that when three strophes show as much unity as these do, the diversity is as important as the correspondence.[81]

A few differences immediately spring to view when these strophes are placed parallel. The first two end with the colon יהוה אלהיכם, which is absent in the third. The absence of this colon is compensated for in the third strophe by adding a colon at the beginning of the verse, וחרה אף ־יהוה בכם. Of course we would also state the matter conversely — that the addition of this colon causes the last colon (יהוה אלהיכם) to drop off. The first and third strophe utilize the verb אבד while the second has שמד in the Hiphil, with יהוה as the understood subject, carried over from the previous reference in 15bA. The third strophe has an added adverb (מהרה), it has הארץ in the place of האדמה, and it does not include the demonstrative הזאת.

---

80 Note the contracted form of the colon as compared to 5bB. In 5bB יהוה אלהיכם was necessary in the colon to form inclusion at the level of the strophe, canticle and sub-canto. Since that is not the case in 10aD it does not need to be included. Regarding expansion and contraction see the colon see now Korpel—De Moor: 1986:178—180.

81 See now Berlin: 1985:11—13 for a discussion of poetic contrast and equivalence.

What is to be made of these variances? An increasing level of urgency and threat has been built into the successive strophes. In II.A.ii.2 the remaining nations will be the cause of Israel's destruction if Israel is not faithful to keep the law. In II.B.ii.2 Yahweh himself will bring upon them the curses contained in the law, thereby causing them to be destroyed. In II.B.ii.3 is warned that if they break the covenant 'Yahweh's face' will burn against them, and they will perish in a hurry ! And not only from this good ground, but off the very earth ! And, do we read too much into the contrasting lines if we note that in the first two strophes יהוה אלהיכם at least remains in the picture, while in the final strophe the transgression of the covenant jeopardizes this relationship, as dramatically illustrated by the absence in the last line of יהוה אלהיכם ?

With respect to the composition of Josh. 23:16 it is also instructive to note evident correspondence with a couple of passages from Deuteronomy. As Talmon has observed,[82] Josh. 23:16b is virtually identical to Deut. 11:16b, with the substitution of והלכתם for וסרתם. The rationale for the substitution in Josh. 23:16b can now be explained on the basis of the inclusion which is thereby formed with הולך in 23:14a. By means of this inclusion Joshua's impending death, 'going the way of all the earth', stands parallel with the hypothetical destruction of the people from the earth in the event of disobedience. Josh. 23:16c is a contracted form of Deut. 11:17, thereby recalling the warning issued by Moses prior to his death.[83]

The theological impact of the formation of refrain strophes is most powerful when the passage is viewed as a symmetrical composition rather than as a linear story. It is only when Josh. 23 is read as a balanced literary construction that one can appreciate how fully the emphasis in canto II complements the message of canto I. Ironically, to this point we have discussed the larger unity of Josh. 23 primarily from the starting point of the repetitions noted in final lines ! These connections are so overwhelming that we are coerced to pursue additional

---

82 Talmon: 1961:357.
83 The scope of this article does not permit further elaboration of the many points of contact with Deut. 11, and with numerous other passages of the book of Deuteronomy.

indicators of a coherent macro—structure connecting the cantos.

3.2 The relationship between cantos I and II

Clues to the final organization and unity of a given passage must be drawn from formal, literary markers as well as from content. When content and formal markers concur, one has the highest degree of certainty regarding the correctness of a structural analysis. The strength of the method here employed is that it offers a systematic avenue by which to correlate form and content, and to allow their combined results to dictate one's understanding of the text.

The first canticle (I.A.i) is introductory to the entire pericope in the sense that it sketches the setting and circumstances of the gathering, in preparation for the monologue which follows. 'All Israel' (2aA) remains silent throughout the entire discourse. 2bA states specifically that the oration begins. It is noteworthy that the unity between canticles I.A.i and I.A.ii is heightened by responsion at the level of the canticles (see 2.2.1 above). The resulting effect is that I.A.ii.1 stands as a brief paradigmatic unit at the beginning of Joshua's oration. The theme of this paradigmatic unit is expanded upon in the following two strophes (A.II.2—3), and then elaborated in yet greater detail in the sub—canto I.B, demonstrating a strong thematic and literary unity to canto I. Justification for distinguishing cantos I and II is supported by thematic considerations as well as the cumulative separation downwards found in strophe I.B.ii.2, which finds a parallel phenomenon in II.B.ii.3. The ensuing paragraphs will demonstrate how sub—cantos I.A and I.B are symmetrically balanced by sub—cantos II.B and II.A respectively with regard to both content and structure, suggesting a concentric or chiastic arrangement at the level of the cantos.

3.3 The correspondence between sub—cantos I.A and II.B

A strong parallelism is established between the beginning of direct discourse in sub—canto I.A and the commencement of sub—canto II.B:[84]

---

84   C.F. Keil—F. Delitzsch, *Joshua, Judges, Ruth* (Biblical Commentary on the Old Testament, trans. J. Martin; Grand Rapids, 1950) 223.

ויאמר אלהם (2bA)
אני זקנתי (2bB)
באתי בימים (2bC)

והנה אנכי הולך היום (14aA)
בדרך כל־הארץ (14aB)

Both strophes refer to the age of Joshua, the hoary leader of
Israel, who now gives his parting admonitions to Yahweh's
covenant people. Sub-canto I.A.ii delineates את כל־אשר עשה
יהוה אלהיכם and is bracketed by the corresponding line of the
inclusion, כאשר דבר יהוה אלהיכם לכם (5bB). Now it is
important to note that colon 5bB is taken up almost *verbatim*
in the central cola (14cC and 15aC) of the twin strophes in
II.B. These cola are thereby elevated to a position of primary
emphasis. Mention must also be made of the concatenation
הארץ // ארצם (5bA, 14aB).

In I.A Joshua reminds the people that they possess the land
because Yahweh fought for Israel as he said he would. In II.B
the people are reminded that not a word of what Yahweh had
said had failed; the blessings came about as Yahweh had said
they would. But just as surely, the curses would come in the
case of disobedience. The cross-connection between these two
sub-cantos is heightened by the closing lines of each.
Sub-canto A concludes, 'as Yahweh your God said to you',
which in retrospect we now see standing literarily not only as a
summary of what preceded, but also as a clear anticipation of
the theme more fully elaborated in sub-canto II.B. Sub-canto
II.B, conversely, ends with the reminder that the land as
inheritance is jeopardized by unfaithfulness to Yahweh. In short,
Josh. 23:14-16 places a question mark, contingent upon Israel's
response to Yahweh's word, behind all that was described as
inherited in vss. 3-5. As a final point of contact between I.A
and II.B mention may be made of the fact that the first 8 cola
of I.A constitute an introduction to the entire pericope. With
the 9th colon (2bA) direct discourse begins. In II.B, the final 8
cola (23:16) form a conclusion to the entire pericope, as is
indicated by employment of the refrain in II.B.ii.2.

3.4 The correspondence between sub-cantos I.B and II.A

Obedience to the divine law, implicit in sub-cantos I.A and

II.B, is made the explicit subject of I.B and II.A. Once again we note an unmistakable *literary and thematic* correlation being drawn between these sub—cantos, as is clear from the outset with the opening words of each, and strengthened by responsions at the level of all four corresponding strophes:

‏(6a, ‏לאהבה // ולעשות; ונשמרתם // לשמר; מאד // מאד‏
11a; responsions)

‏(7a, 12a; responsion) ‏הגוים האלה // בגוים האלה‏

‏(7a, 12a; ‏הנשארים האלה אתכם // הנשארים האלה אתכם‏
responsions)

‏(8a, 13a; ‏כי ... יהוה אלהיכם // כי אם־יהוה אלהיכם‏
responsion)

‏(9a, 13a) ‏להוריש ... מלפניכם // ויורש ... מפניכם‏

‏(9a, 13a) ‏את־הגוים האלה // גוים גדלים‏

‏(9b, 13c; responsion) ‏עד־אבדכם // ואתם לא־עמד‏

‏(10a, 13c; responsion) ‏יהוה אלהיכם // יהוה אלהיכם‏

‏(10a, 13c; responsion) ‏אשר נתן לכם // כאשר דבר לכם‏

In addition to these overwhelming responsions at the level of the four respective strophes of each sub—canto when taken simply in the consecutive order in which they stand, a clear responsion must also be mentioned between I.B.ii.1 and II.A.i.2:

‏כי אם־שוב תשובו ודבקתם // כי אם־ביהוה אלהיכם תדבקו‏
(8a, 12a)

When this responsion is viewed along with the parallelisms between I.B.i.2 and II.A.ii.1[85] the possibility arises that these four strophes are not only to be read parallel to each other, but also in a chiastic ordering (i.e., prohibitions against transgression, clinging [positive], clinging [negative], curses resulting from transgression).[86]

When these passages are read as intricate, symmetrical poetry, a richer interpretation is possible than when they are

---

85 Note the parallelism ‏הגוים האלה // בגוים האלה‏־ (7a, 13a; responsion). Also important is the correspondences between the prohibitions (7b) and the curses (13b). This parallelism between 7b and the tricolon in 13b is an additional argument for seeing 7bB as a later insertion, in which case the original reading would have had a tricolon here, matching the tricolon of hypothetical transgressions (12b) and the tricolon of curses (13b).

86 Employment of the verb ‏דבק‏ is crucial here. It does not occur elsewhere in the chapter.

read linearly as 'simply prose'. A parallel reading of the corresponding sub–cantos forces one to digest the contents of both sections in direct comparison and contrast with each other. Both sub–cantos demand obedience to the Mosaic law, with primary emphasis falling upon the first commandment. In both cases this obedience is placed immediately within the framework of Israel's relationship to the remaining nations, the גוים :

cf. (7aA)   לבלתי־בוא בגוים האלה
     (7aB)   הנשארים האלה אתכם

     (12aB)   ודבקתם ביתר הגוים האלה
     (12aC)   הנשארים האלה אתכם

But once again the contrasts are as telling as the equivalencies. While sub–canto I.B proceeds on a very positive note, recounting the benefits of reliance upon Yahweh, sub–canto II.A anticipates potential unfaithfulness, and graphically describes the curses which would ensue. Obedience to the law would result in the continuation of the conquest; disobedience would mean abortion from the land. The two sides of the law are placed in perfect balance. The first is summarized in the final strophe of sub–canto I.B, the negative reciprocal is stated in the final strophe of II.A and twice subsequently, as discussed above. In light of our analysis we may go a step further and assert that the final quadrocolon verse of sub–canto I.B, which is a summary of the first two sub–cantos, contains the central kernel of the entire chapter. The repetition עד היום הזה (8aC, 9bB)[87] serves to highlight the final quadrocolon verse at the end of the sub–canto I.B.[88] This quadrocolon is the pivotal point

---

87 B.S. Childs, 'A Study of the Formula "Until this Day" ', *JBL* 82 (1963) 279–292. Childs notes that the nonetiological idiom used to express *terminus ad quem* always occurs in direct discourse (280–281). To Childs' observation we may add that many of these cases are in poetic texts, e.g., Gen. 48:15 and Jer. 3:25, and this formula often forms a parallelism with another clause containing the word יום (e.g., Ex. 10:6; 1 Sam. 29:8; Isa. 39:6; Jer. 7:25; 11:7; 32:20, 31; 36:2).

88 In light of the observations in the preceding footnote concerning texts in which the formula עד היום הזה stands parallel with another phrase containing the word יום we now note that an inclusion is formed here in

around which the four sub—cantos are symmetrically balanced in chiastic sequence. The division of the cantos as defended above produces a perfectly symmetrical strophic scheme: 2+3 / 2+2 // 2+2 / 2+3, with 9 strophes per canto. At risk of over—kill I diffidently also suggest that even the number of cola per canto adds to the symmetrical perfection of the entire chapter as scanned in the preceding analysis.

Introduction (preceding discourse)	8 cola
Sub—canto I.A (minus intro.)	18 cola[89]
Sub—canto I.B (preceding kernel)	18 cola[90]
kernel (10aA — 10aC)	4 cola
Sub—canto II.A	18 cola
Sub—canto II.B (preceding conclusion)	18 cola
Conclusion (II.B.ii.3)	8 cola

It must be kept in mind that although the Masoretic accentuation proved to be generally very reliable in suggesting the delineation of the cola in the colometrical structure of Josh. 23, the counting of cola is always somewhat uncertain, due both to an unavoidable margin of subjectivity in determining the termination of one colon and the beginning of the next, and the possibility of textual corruptions in the process of transmission. Nevertheless, the symmetry of this carefully constructed poetic narrative appears to be confirmed by the respective statistical totals. The uniformity at all the various structural levels becomes visible at a glance when the relevant statistics are charted.

_____

canto I by עד היום הזה // מימים רבים (1aA, 9bB), setting off the refrain quadrocolon in 10a as the central kernel around which the two cantos are structured. This structure is supported by the employment of the inclusions ואתם // לכם in I.A.ii.1 and I.B.ii.2, marking the beginning and end of the personal charge to the people in the first canto. These observations confirm the conclusions already attained from analysis of the cantos above. Furthermore, this literary technique is identical to the employment of the refrain in canto II to highlight the conclusion to the entire passage of Josh. 23:1—16.

89   This total does not include 4bB for the reasons discussed above.
90   7bB is not included in this count.

Canto	Sub-canto	Can-ticle	Strophe	Verses	Cola
I	A	i	1	2	(3+2)
			2	2	(3+3)
		ii	1	2	(3+2)
			2	2	(3+2)
			3	2	(3+2)
	B	i	1	2	(4+2)
			2	2	(2+3)
		ii	1	2	(3+2)
			2	2	(2+4)
totals:	2	4	9	18	48
II	A	i	1	1	2
			2	2	(3+3)
		ii	1	2	(3+3)
			2	1	4
	B	i	1	2	(2+2)
			2	2	(3+2)
		ii	1	2	(3+2)
			2	1	4
			3	3	(2+2+4)
totals:	2	4	9	16	44

Refinement of the preceding analysis may be expected and welcomed at various points, but the general structure as here delineated seems incontrovertibly marked by the numerous parallelisms, repetitions, responsions, concatenations and inclusions delineated above. The abundant and sophisticated employment of these literary devices can not be coincidental.

4 Conclusions

On the basis of the preceding structural analysis a number of conclusions are warranted. Josh. 23 is clearly poetic narrative.[91]

---

91 Moses ibn Ezra classified Josh. 23:1, along with numerous other pas—

Its poetic structure relies to a high degree upon repetitive and external parallelism rather than internal parallelism at the level of the verse. Consequently, this study supports observations made by de Moor regarding the poetic narrative of the book of Ruth.[92]

Furthermore, the symmetry detected at the level of cola, verses, strophes, canticles, sub—cantos and cantos suggests that the narrative structure of Josh. 23 is as carefully crafted as most so—called 'classical poetry' in the Old Testament. The results of our study contradict the conclusions drawn by Anderson and Forbes that, 'The 122 chapters with scores above 20% are virtually pure prose'.[93] By their count Josh. 23 has a total 'prose particle count' of 22.408%,[94] which brings it close to the high frequency end of their scale.

Consequently, it is not only the 'middle range' in which their method of prose particle counts is inadequate as a device for mechanical recognition of poetry. Poetic narrative clearly exists even in the higher ranges of their charts. There is no mechanical test for distinguishing poetry and prose. The only real test that exists is to apply a precise method of poetic analysis, incorporating what is known of poetic characteristics in Ancient Near Eastern literature, to a given passage, and then finally to tabulate the results. The method which has been adopted in this study appears to provide one important avenue for such research.

It is neither warranted nor advisable to make comprehensive generalizations concerning the prose/poetry problem upon the basis of this study, but perhaps this analysis will stimulate a broader recognition and analysis of poetry in the historical books of the Old Testament. On the one hand such studies ought to go beyond the texts traditionally viewed as ancient historical poetry, and on the other hand they should suspend speculation

---

sages, as belonging to the *ḫuṭba*, 'the rhetorical, somewhat parallelistic sermon style', Kugel: 1981:133. Unfortunately, ibn Ezra's emphasis was that this was prose, in contrast to poetry. See now M. ibn Ezra, *Kitab al-Muḥāḏara wal-Mudhākara*, A.S. Halkin, ed. (Jerusalem, 1975) 19—21 [Hebrew].

92   De Moor: 1984:264; 1986:46.
93   Anderson—Forbes: 1983:166.
94   Anderson—Forbes: 1983:173.

about an epic background to Israel's historical poetry. It is quite conceivable that there existed an ancient tradition of non—epic, historical poetry or poetic narrative.[95]

While it is not possible here to consider all the exegetical and methodological implications which arise from recognition of the poetic structure of Josh. 23, it is apparent that a more objective basis has been established upon which to judge literary critical and form critical considerations pertaining to this passage. For example, it has often been asserted that the literary structure of Josh. 23 is more or less dependent upon a treaty or covenant form.[96] However, on the basis of the analysis above it is dubious that Josh. 23 was ever intended to simulate the structure of ancient treaty texts. The emphasis upon covenant is of great significance, but with primary emphasis placed upon Yahweh's word which has been faithfully fulfilled in the first stages of the conquest of the land, and which will become a curse to Israel, actualized via the remaining nations, in the case of failure to uphold his law.[97] The form of this poetic oration by Joshua is perhaps best summarized by the title *Abschiedspredigt*, or

---

95 Although Talmon: 1978:351—356 correctly raises important warnings against methodologically assuming an ancient Hebrew epic tradition, I do not agree that the problem is solved by asserting that the writers of the Old Testament 'purposefully nurtured and developed prose narration to take the place of the genre which by its content was intimately bound up with the world of paganism and appears to have had a special standing in the polytheistic cults' (354). The 'straightforward prose narration' versus 'epic' polarity breaks down with increased recognition of poetic narrative. The distantiation from epic is more a matter of content than literary form.

96 K. Baltzer, *Das Bundesformular* (Neukirchen, 1960) 70—73. J.A. Thompson, *The Ancient Near Eastern Treaties and the Old Testament* (London, 1964) 31. M.G. Kline, *The Structure of Biblical Authority* (Grand Rapids, 1972) 55. Soggin: 1972:218. F.B. Knutson, 'Literary Genres in PRU IV', in: L.R. Fisher (ed.), *Ras Shamra Parallels, vol.II* (Analecta Orientalia 50; Rome, 1975) 174—175. D.J. McCarthy, *Treaty and Covenant* (Analecta Biblica 21a; Rome, 1978) 200—203.

97 Contrary to the opinion of Soggin: 1972:218—219, the threat of loss of land in Josh. 23 does not need to be seen as a 'deliberately enigmatic' reference to the Babylonian exile. See K.A. Kitchen, 'Ancient Orient, "Deuteronomism", and the Old Testament', in: J.B. Payne (ed.), *New Perspectives on the Old Testament* (Waco, 1970) 5—7.

farewell sermon, as suggested by Hertzberg.[98] The style, structure and content of Josh. 23 suggest its appropriateness for liturgical use in ancient Israel's subsequent worship.

Emphasis upon the conquest as completed, and the potential of hardship on account of remaining nations, are deliberately placed parallel within this poetic unit.[99] Recognition of the poetic character of this narrative adds one additional dimension to be considered in the complex of literary—critical questions focusing upon the relationship of texts such as Josh. 1; 13:1—7; 22:1—6; 23—24; Judg. 1:1—2:10, etc.[100]

I conclude this article on the poetic prose of Josh. 23 with one final remark. It is noteworthy that of the 92 cola as delineated above, 57 end with ם, a high majority of which are found in either אלהיכם or second person plural references.[101] This not only provides structural cohesion and rhyme but also calls repeated attention to the subject at hand — your relationship to your God.

---

98 H.W. Hertzberg, *Die Bücher Josua, Richter, Ruth* (ATD 9; Göttingen, 1953) 128.

99 M.H. Woudstra, *The Book of Joshua* (NICOT; Grand Rapids, 1981) 332—333.

100 Noth: 1953:9—11, 15—16, 133—141. R. Smend, 'Das Gesetz und die Völker', in: H.W. Wolff (Hrsg.), *Probleme biblischer Theologie. Gerhard von Rad zum 70. Geburtstag* (München, 1971) 494—509. A.G. Auld, *Joshua, Moses & the Land* (Edinburgh, 1980) 52—55. A.D.H. Mayes, *The Story of Israel between Settlement and Exile* (London, 1983) 40—60.

101 In many verses, and in numerous strophes, every colon ends with ם, creating an obvious poetic rhyme. I consequently find it impossible to concur with the opinion of R.K. Harrison, *Introduction to the Old Testament* (Grand Rapids, 1969) 965, who states, 'In the first instance there is nothing that can be recognized as rhyme in Hebrew poetic compositions. The nearest approach to rhyme occurs when the same pronoun suffix appears at the end of two or more *stichoi* (Isa. 41:11f.), but it is difficult to believe that this is anything more than purely accidental'.

THE LITERARY GENRE OF THE SONG OF THE VINEYARD
(ISA. 5:1—7)

Marjo C.A. Korpel

1 Introduction

The Song of the Vineyard has been discussed time and again.
The main question raised in most articles on Isa. 5:1—7
concerns the genre to which the text should be attributed. In
1977 J.T. Willis summed up the different views proposed until
then, counting no less than 12 different genres.[1] The most
important proposals put forward are love song, lawsuit, fable,
parable and allegory.

In general it is said that Isa. 5:1—7 is written in the form of
a parable. But if this is true, there should be only *one* point of
comparison. Nevertheless, a mere glance at the explanation of
vs. 7 immediately shows us *more* than one point of comparison.

The Song of the Vineyard has not always been taken as a
parable. Already the Targumists interpreted the song as an
allegory. In the Targum, metaphors usually are replaced by
their abstract meanings. In Isa. 5:1—7 the Targumists have
discovered *many* different metaphors!

The most interesting and recent views on the song we will
sketch in outline below. In advance it has to be stated here
that most scholars distinguish more than one literary genre in
the text.

1.1 Love song

In a love song the singer may simply express his state of mind
in an ordered form, or he may elaborate a compliment to his
lady, or he may deploy an argument to persuade his mistress to
take advantage of opportunity and fleeting youth.[2] In short, this
genre indicates the outpouring of the lover's feelings concerning

---

1   J.T. Willis, 'The Genre of Isaiah 5:1—7', *JBL* 96 (1977) 337—362.
2   Cf. M.H. Abrams, *A Glossary of Literary Terms* (New York, 1981⁴) 99.

his beloved.[3]

Many scholars discern the genre of the love song in the introduction to the song.[4] Most of them are of the opinion that the song has a negative sense then. Bentzen[5] and Junker[6] argue for taking the *entire* song as a complaint of the frustrated lover. Bentzen therefore calls the song an 'erotic allegory'.[7] Squarely against the genre of the love song are the opinions of Delitzsch[8] and Duhm.[9]

1.2 Lawsuit

The prophetic lawsuit is well—known in the Old Testament. The main features are (1) the indictment (2) a logical connective, e.g., 'therefore ...' (3) the announcement of judgment.[10] Some scholars suppose the middle part of the song to be related to the prophetic judgment[11] and others defend the lawsuit as the genre of the entire song.[12]

---

3   Cf. R.E. Murphy, *Wisdom Literature* (Grand Rapids, 1981) 177. See also F. Horst, 'Die Formen der althebräischen Liebeslieder', in: R. Paret (ed.), *Orientalische Studien E. Littmann ... überreicht* (Leiden, 1935) 45–47; M.V. Fox, *The Song of Songs and the Ancient Egyptian Love Songs* (London, 1985) xix–xxvii.

4   H. Wildberger, *Jesaja* (BKAT X/1; Neukirchen–Vluyn, 1972) 166; D. Lys, 'La vigne et la double je', *SVT* 26 (1974) 1; W. Eichrodt, *Der Heilige in Israel* (BAT 17/1; Stuttgart, 1976²) 66; W. Zimmerli, *Grundriß der alttestamentlichen Theologie* (Stuttgart, 1978³) 170.

5   A. Bentzen, 'Zur Erläuterung von Jesaja 5,1–7', *AfO* 4 (1927) 209.

6   H. Junker, 'Die literarische Art von Is 5,1–7', *Bibl* 40 (1959) 263.

7   Bentzen: 1927:210.

8   F. Delitzsch, *Das Buch Jesaia* (Leipzig, 1889) 103.

9   B. Duhm, *Das Buch Jesaia* (Göttingen, 1922⁴) 54.

10   B.O. Long, *1 Kings* (Grand Rapids, 1984) 257.

11   J. Vermeylen, *Du Prophète Isaïe à l'Apocalyptique.* Tome 1 (Paris, 1977) 161: 'plusieurs éléments caractéristiques du *rîb*'; Zimmerli: 1978³:170; P. Höffken, 'Probleme in Jesaja 5,1–7', *ZThK* 79 (1982) 409; M. de Roche, 'Yahweh's *RîB* against Israel', *JBL* 102 (1983) 563–574.

12   Wildberger: 1972:166; C. Schedl, *Rufer des Heils in heilloser Zeit* (Paderborn, 1973) 107: 'Prozessrede mit Anklage und Urteilsverkündigung'; C. Westermann, *Grundformen Prophetischer Rede* (München, 1978⁵) 143ff.; G.A. Yee, 'A Form—Critical Study of Isaiah 5:1–7 as a Song and a Juridi-

1.3 Fable

'A fable is a short story that exemplifies a moral thesis or a principle of human behavior; usually in its conclusion either the narrator or one of the characters states the moral in the form of an *Epigram*'.[13] Usually the acting figures are animals or (less frequently) plants.[14]

Gunkel, who at the beginning of this century pointed to the folk tale in the Old Testament, regarded Isa. 5:1−7 as a fable.[15] Eissfeldt saw the song as related to the fable but not as a real fable in itself.[16] More recently W. Schottroff has elaborated the view of Isa. 5:1−7 as a fable.[17]

1.4 Parable

A parable is 'a short narrative presented so as to stress the tacit but detailed analogy between its component parts and a thesis or lesson that the narrator is trying to bring home to us'.[18] The fundamental difference between a parable and an allegory should be that the former contains a comparison on just *one* point.[19] But nowadays there is great disagreement among scholars as to the precise definition of the parable.[20] It has become clear that 'it is very difficult to make a fine distinction between a parable that conveys one message but whose message has two or more secondary points or characters and an allegory'.[21]

As already said above most scholars consider Isa. 5:1−7 to be

---

cal Parable', *CBQ* 43 (1981) 30−48; G.T. Sheppard, 'More on Isaiah 5:1−7 as a Juridical Parable', *CBQ* 44 (1982) 45−47.

13   Abrams: 1981[4]:6.

14   L. Röhrlich, 'Fabel', *RGG*[3], Band II, 851.

15   H. Gunkel, 'Fabel', *RGG*[2], Band II, 490f.

16   O. Eissfeldt, *Einleitung in das Alte Testament* (Tübingen, 1976[4]) 48.

17   W. Schottroff, 'Das Weinberglied Jesajas', *ZAW* 82 (1970) 68−91, followed in his ideas by A. Schoors, *Jesaja* (Roermond, 1972) 51.

18   Abrams: 1981[4]:6.

19   Cf. A. Jülicher, *Die Gleichnisreden Jesu* (Darmstadt, 1969[2]) 80; Willis: 1977:356.

20   Willis: 1977:356.

21   Willis: 1977:358.

a parable.[22] Only a few of them have given real arguments for taking Isa. 5:1–7 as a parable. Especially Willis has worked out his arguments in favour of this position in an admirable way.[23]

1.5 Allegory

'An allegory is a narrative in which the agents and action, and sometimes the setting as well, are contrived both to make coherent sense on the "literal", or primary level of signification, and also to signify a second, correlated order of agents, concepts, and events'.[24] Mostly it is said that an allegory is an elaborated metaphor. This implies that all things and persons mentioned in the text ought to be metaphors and therefore should have secondary meanings too.

Only a few scholars have interpreted Isa. 5:1–7 as an allegory. Bentzen took the entire song as an erotic allegory. The text of the grower and his vineyard in reality points to the complaint of the deceived husband against his unfaithful wife, who bore him illegitimate children. Using this allegory was a trick of Isaiah to misguide his audience.[25] Höffken interprets the lay–out of the vineyard as the conquest ('Landnahme') of Israel. He points to Ps. 80:8ff. to demonstrate the antiquity of the allegorical interpretation of the Song of the Vineyard.[26]

Some scholars reject the allegorical interpretation of Isa. 5:1–7 categorically. Von Rad states that it will be impossible to take all details in an allegorical sense.[27] Willis asserted, 'The

---

22   Delitzsch: 1889:103; Duhm: 1922[4]:54; Eichrodt: 1976[2]:67; Eissfeldt: 1976[4]: 48; O. Kaiser, *Das Buch des Propheten Jesaja* (ATD 17; Göttingen, 1981) 98. Sometimes a distinction is made between a parable and an elaborated simile (in German it is possible to speak about *Parabel* and *Gleichnis*, in Dutch *parabel* and *gelijkenis*). In this study we take both genres together. Therefore we also refer to J. Ridderbos, *Jesaja*. Deel I (Kampen, 1922) 26; E. König, *Das Buch Jesaja* (Gütersloh, 1926) 81; O. Procksch, *Jesaja I* (Leipzig, 1930) 90; Westermann: 1978[5]:144.

23   Willis: 1977:356ff.

24   Abrams: 1981[4]:4.

25   Bentzen: 1927:210.

26   Höffken: 1982:409.

27   G. von Rad, *Theologie des Alten Testaments*. Band II (München, 1980[2]) 187.

alleged allegorical meanings of specific elements in the text do not come naturally from the text itself, but betray a great deal of ingenuity on the part of the interpreter. It is impossible to explain each element of Isa. 5:1—7 allegorically without being fanciful'.[28]

1.6 The Problem

As we have seen, the question of the literary genre of the Song of the Vineyard was addressed by many scholars and was answered in many different ways. The present author will now examine the poetic structure of the text to show that this procedure is helpful in defining the genre of the text.

2 The Structure

2.1 Division into Verses

Firstly we will divide the entire song into verses according to the method the Kampen team uses, as explained in the introductory article of this volume.

Although the text of Isa. 5:1—7 has been examined over and over again, until now only three scholars have bothered to undertake a structural analysis of the Song, namely O. Loretz,[29] H. Wildberger[30] and H. van Grol.[31] Below we also will discuss some of the most debatable colometric verse divisions of the text.

Verse 1a

אשירה נא לידידי   *'āšīrā nā lidīdī*
שירת דודי לכרמו   *šīrat dōdī l^ekarmō*

Many strong separation markers can be observed in this verse,

---

28 Willis: 1977:355.
29 O. Loretz, 'Weinberglied und prophetische Deutung im Protest—Song Jes. 5,1—7', *UF* 7 (1975) 573—576.
30 H. Wildberger, *Jesaja* (BKAT X/3; Neukirchen—Vluyn, 1982) 1689ff.
31 H. van Grol, *De versbouw in het klassieke hebreeuws.* Fundamantele verkenningen. Deel 1: Metriek (Amsterdam, 1986) 114—116, 178—180. [The article 'A Literary Analysis of "The Song of the Vineyard" (Is. 5:1—7)' by M.L. Folmer in *JEOL* 29 (1985—86 [appeared January 1988]) 106—123, appeared too late to be considered here.]

e.g. the cohortative, the repetitive parallelism[32] caused by the use of both אשירה and שירח, and the synonymous and alliterative parallelism between לידידי and דודי. Also striking in this verse is the rhyme. Later on we will see that rhyme and assonance play an important role in (the structure of) the song. In comparison to the other verses this verse contains an abundance of separation markers. Therefore we conclude that this verse may well be the introductory verse, as a single strophe containing the title of the song separated from the other strophes. This hypothesis is shared by O. Loretz and G.R. Williams.[33] The verse divider here is the *zaqeph parvum*.

This verse could raise the expectation of a song containing a metaphorical description of a man and his bride. The vineyard, כרם, was a common metaphor for a beloved woman in the Ancient Near East (cf. Cant. 1:6; 2:15; 8:11,12), and a vineyard, or more generally a field as a designation of one's beloved is attested in Sumerian,[34] Egyptian[35] and Ugaritic[36] texts.[37]

---

32 The present author employs the term *repetitive parallelism* for the repetition of exactly the same words (pronouns, verbs, suffixes, etc.) in different cola, and also for the parallelism between words derived from the same root. E.g., אשירה and שירח. Hitherto other members of our team have used the term *tautology*. But in our opinion tautology means saying something twice, in different terms. E.g., 'The man was *glad* and *happy*'. (Cf. H. Shaw, *Dictionary of Literary Terms* [New York, 1972] 373). As a result tautological sentences seem a little bit overdone. A repetitive pattern shows a real repetition of words. E.g., 'He *smiled* to the boy, and the boy *smiled* to him'. The *repetitive parallelism* (or related terms as *repetitive pattern* and *repetition*) has become a common term in many publications on the Ancient Hebrew poetry. (Cf. N.H. Ridderbos, *Die Psalmen*. Stilistische Verfahren und Aufbau. Mit besonderer Berücksichtigung von Ps. 1–41. [BZAW 117; Berlin/New York, 1972] 19ff.; S.A. Geller, *Parallelism in early Biblical Poetry* [Missoula, 1979] 297f.; Y. Avishur, *Stylistic Studies of Word-Pairs in Biblical and Ancient Semitic Literatures* [Neukirchen–Vluyn, 1984] 639ff.; W.G.E. Watson, *Classical Hebrew Poetry*. A Guide to its Techniques [JSOTS 26; Sheffield, 1984] 274ff.; A. Berlin, *The Dynamics of Biblical Parallelism* [Bloomington, 1985] 69–71.).

33 Loretz: 1975:574; G.R. Williams, 'Frustrated Expectations in Isaiah V 1–7: A Literary Interpretation', *VT* 35 (1985) 459.

34 S.N. Kramer, *The Sacred Marriage Rite* (London, 1969) 81, 100.

35 Cf. S. Schott, *Altägyptische Liebeslieder* (Zürich, 1950²) 50, 56, 82 and 107; J.B. White, *A Study of the Language of Love in the Song of Songs and*

A second meaning of כרם is attested in Isa. 3:14; 27:2 and Jer. 12:10: the vineyard as (the land of) Israel.

Verse 1b

כרם היה לידידי   *kèrèm hāyā līdīdī*
בקרן בן־שמן   *b^eqèrèn bèn šāmèn*

The assonance concatenates the two cola of the verse: *kèrèm/qèrèn*. And rhyme delimits the second colon: *qèrèn/ bèn/šāmèn*. Furthermore, it will be clear that the two cola belong together because of the synthetic parallelism. The second colon furnishes additional information on the situation of the vineyard.

The parallel to this verse in Cant. 8:11 (כרם היה לשלמה) is striking, which indeed makes it very likely that the vineyard could be interpreted by the hearers as a beloved woman. The קרן בן־שמן also can be taken as a part of the love song. Perfumed oil played an important role in the Ancient Near Eastern love poetry (cf. Cant. 1:3; 4:10). In Egypt the lovers were anointed with oil[38] and in the Sumerian Rite of the Sacred Marriage it was the custom to sprinkle the ground in front of the sanctuary with fragrant oil.[39] In Ugarit the use of oil is mentioned too.[40] In the Ancient Near East a bride was also

---

ancient Egyptian Poetry (Missoula, 1978) 176f. See now also Fox: 1985:17, 26ff.

36   In the Ugaritic text *KTU* 1.23, which has to be seen as a religious text describing the ritual of the sacred marriage, it is said in line 28:

> *The field of the two gods*
>   *is the field of Athiratu and the Damsel.*

The moon god Yarikhu expresses himself concerning his beloved bride Nikkalu as follows (*KTU* 1.24:22–23):

> *I will make her field into a vineyard,*
>   *the field of her love into a flower–garden !*

37   Compare also Koran 2:223: '*Your women are your tillage*'.
38   Schott: 1950²:58. Compare also pp. 65, 68, 111, 126, 127, 130.
39   Kramer: 1969:65.
40   In *KTU* 1.10:II.21–23 the God Ba'lu declares his love for the goddess 'Anat in this way:

> *Ba'lu will anoint the horns of your headdress.*
> *Ba'lu will anoint them while flying !*

anointed with oil. This is the background of an Old Akkadian love incantation, in which the groom is described with a cruse of oil in his hand.[41] So it would by no means be odd if the audience of the prophet Isaiah had interpreted the first verses of his song as a rather cheeky love song. This was bound to capture their full attention.

It must not be overlooked that שמן also can call forth associations with the land of Canaan, flowing with milk and honey (cf. Num. 13:20, 27; Neh. 9:35).[42]

Verse 2a

וייעזקהו ויסקלהו	*wayᵉʿazzᵉqēhū wayᵉsaqqᵉlēhū*
ויטעהו שרק	*wayyiṭṭāʿēhū śorēq*

This verse is marked by repetitive parallelism creating the assonance and striking rhyme (3ms suffix).

To the hearers it must have been a much more arduous task to place this verse in the context of love poetry. Verbs like עזק, *to plough*, and סקל, *to clear of stones* require a lot of fantasy to interpret them as erotic metaphors. The Old Testament itself does not contain any examples of the metaphorical use of 'ploughing' and 'clearing of stones' within the context of love poetry.

Nevertheless, this lack of Old Testament proof does not mean that the verbs *could* not have had an erotic meaning in the love poetry of those days. Outside the Old Testament examples of the metaphorical, erotic meaning of 'ploughing' are attested in Egypt (Amarna)[43] and Sumer (in the Sacred Marriage Rite).[44]

So, in theory it was within the realm of possibility that the hearers interpreted the verb עזק as applying to the groom and his bride. But the parallel verb סקל would have defeated them. It would have become increasingly difficult for the audience to

---

41   J. and A. Westenholz, 'Help for Rejected Suitors: The Old Akkadian Love Incantation *MAD* V.8', *Or* 46 (1977) 203.

42   שמן as a designation for moist and fertile soil is attested in Num. 13:20; Isa. 28:1, 4; Ezek. 34:14; Neh. 9:25; 1 Chron. 4:40.

43   In an Amarna–text it is said: *'My field, for lack of ploughing, is like a woman without a man.'* Cf. D. Marcus, 'A Famous Analogy of Rib–Haddi', *JANES* 5 (1973) 281. Compare now also Fox: 1985:28.

44   Kramer: 1969:59.

interpret this verb too as belonging to the vocabulary of love poetry.

A text related to this verse is Ps. 80:10, in which the preparation of the soil is described by the verb פנה. Interesting are verses 9 and 10a of Ps. 80 where it is said:

> גפן ממצרים תסיע - *Thou didst dig out a vine from Egypt;*
> תגרש גוים ותטעה   *thou didst drive out nations and*
>   *plant it.*
> פנית לפניה - *Thou didst clear the ground for it, ...*

Noteworthy is the mixing of both literal and metaphorical use of words. Comparison with Isa. 5:2b shows that in Ps. 80:9 the action of the digging up and clearing of stones has been replaced by the literal concept of driving out the nations. A similar text is Ps. 44:3:

> אתה ידך - *Thou, with thy hand,*
> גוים הורשת ותטעם   *didst drive out the nations,*
>   *but them thou didst plant;*
> תרע לאמים ותשלחם - *thou didst afflict the peoples,*
>   *but them thou didst let go.*

Other texts where the 'planting' (נטע) of Israel by God is preceded by the driving out of the enemies include Ex. 15:16f.; 2 Sam. 7:9—10; 1 Chron. 17:8ff. On the basis of these texts, and with the vineyard as metaphor for Israel in mind, it would be possible that some of the hearers began to discern the real intention of the prophet as early as this verse.

The שרק is mentioned only twice in the Old Testament apart from Isa. 5 (Gen. 49:11; Jer. 2:21). In Jer. 2:21 שרק is a metaphor for the people of Israel and both texts contain the parallel גפן/שרק. Other texts in which גפן is used metaphorically as a designation for the people of Israel (or a part of them) are Deut. 32:23; Jer. 8:13; Ezek. 19:10; Hos. 10:1; 14:8. The relatively early texts of Hosea prove that the hearers were quite capable of changing their mind by interpreting גפן as the people of Israel.

Nevertheless, גפן could also have a different metaphorical meaning, namely that of a woman (cf. Ezek. 19:10 where the woman indicated by the vine metaphor is at the same time a metaphor for the people of Israel; see Ps. 128:3; Cant. 6:11 and also the use of the word גפן in Cant. 2:13 and 7:13). In the Ancient Near East the vine as a metaphor for a woman was quite common.[45] So, the more hardy listeners who still expected a love song could take heart in hearing the word שרק.

Verse 2b

ויבן מגדל בתוכו	*wayyibèn migdāl b^etōkō*
וגם־יקב חצב בו	*w^egam yèqèb ḥāṣēb bō*

End rhyme, the ellipsis of the verb in the second colon, and the repetitive parallelism between בתוכו and בו, serve to link the two cola together.

With the description of the building of the tower and the hewing out of the winepress the interpretation of the song in an erotic sense must have ended. Only one metaphorical interpretation was left; Israel was the vineyard, and God was building a 'tower' in it and hewing out a 'winepress.' The verb בנה with God as the subject is attested in many texts of the Old Testament (cf. 1 Sam. 2:35; 2 Sam. 7:27; Ps. 78:68f.; 102:17; 147:2; 1 Chron. 17:10. See also the texts containing synonyms for בנה, e.g. Ex. 15:17 and 2 Sam. 7:11). In these texts it is said that God builds his sanctuary on Zion, or He builds Jerusalem, or He builds a palace for the king. Interesting in connection with these texts is Mic. 4:8 where the עפל of Zion is paralleled by the מגדל עדר. In light of vss. 6f. this indication has to be seen as an *ad hoc* name ('Tower of the Flock') for the Tower of David, which was standing on the top of the Ophel (cf. Neh. 3:25; Cant. 4:4; Isa. 32:14). So it could be that the 'tower' of Isa. 5:2 was meant as a designation of the temple or the citadel.

יקב is nowhere in the Old Testament used in conjunction with Israel as the vineyard. The only text where מגדל and יקב occur together is Zech. 14:10. In this text the North–South line of Jerusalem is indicated with the words ומגדל חננאל עד יקבי המלך. Probably Isaiah has thought of the highest point of Jerusalem when choosing the metaphor 'tower', and of the lowest point when choosing the 'winepress'.

In this connection it is striking that neither the מגדל nor the יקב is involved in the judgment passed in verses 5 and 6

45　Cf. M.H. Pope, *Song of Songs* (The Anchor Bible, 7C; New York, 1977) 646. B.H. Stricker, *De geboorte van Horus*, Deel III (Leiden, 1975) 240; Deel IV (Leiden, 1982) 458.

of Isa. 5. If it is true that Isaiah intended the Temple and Jerusalem when speaking about the tower and the winepress, his belief in the theology of Zion may have prevented him from drawing the ultimate consequence. According to this theology, Zion with the temple would always be saved by God (see the disillusion of the people in Lam. 2:1).[46]

Verse 2c

ויקו לעשות ענבים   *wayᵉqaw laᶜᵃśōt ᶜᵃnābīm*
ויעש באשים   *wayyaᶜaś bᵉ'ušīm*

The 3ms imperfects with alliteration, the end rhyme of *ᶜᵃnābīm* and *bᵉ'ušīm* as well as the repetitive parallelism of the verb עשה connect the two cola.

ענבים is a common word for grapes (cf. Gen. 49:11, Num. 6:3; Deut. 23:25). The ענבים have been used in a metaphorical sense in Deut. 32:32 (deeds); Jer. 8:13 (deeds) and Hos. 9:10 (people). There are other texts in the Old Testament in which the metaphor of the grapes appears as a designation for either the deeds of man or the people themselves, even though the word ענבים or a clear synonym is lacking (cf. Isa. 63:2f.; 65:8; Hos. 10:1; Joel 4:13; Mic. 7:1f.; Lam. 1:15). On the basis of these parallels it would seem impossible to decide between the meaning 'deeds' and 'people' for the interpretation of the metaphor in Isa. 5. Of some relevance in this respect is the interpretation given in the Targum:

אמרית דיעבדון עובדין טבין -   *I thought that they would do good deeds,*

ואינון אבאישו עובדיהון   *but they did evil deeds.*[47]

But whichever way we look at it, the Old Testament itself clearly proves the metaphorical use of the 'grapes' to be related to the conceptual metaphor 'Israel is a vineyard'. But if the grapes surely have a metaphorical meaning it must be assumed that also the 'tower' and the 'winepress' which are situated between the vines had to be interpreted in a metaphorical sense.

---

46 Cf. J. Renkema, *'Misschien is er hoop ...'* De theologische vooronderstellingen van het boek Klaagliederen (Franeker, 1983) 311ff.
47 Cf. J.F. Stenning (ed.), *The Targum of Isaiah* (Oxford, 1949) 16f.

Just as the 'digging up' and the 'clearing of stones' in verse 2a are *two* metaphors for only one idea, it is obvious that exactly the same may be the case for the 'tower' and the 'winepress' in verse 2b. Probably the two metaphors point to (the building of) Jerusalem with the temple and the palace of the king.

According to Williams[48] the grapes in verse 2c might be seen as a metaphorical designation of the children of the man and his beloved. But the Old Testament itself does not provide clear examples of this metaphorical use of the word 'grapes'. From vs. 2b onwards the listeners must have realized that they would not hear a love song. But what else? A joyful vineyard song?[49] The final word of our verse kills this hope too.

Verse 3a

ועתה יושב ירושלם	*wᵉʿattā yōšēb yᵉrūšālaim*
ואיש יהודה	*wᵉʾīš yᵉhūdā*

Noteworthy is the <u>lack of rhyme</u> in this verse. In this respect the verse strikes a false note in the song. The cola are connected by the clear parallelism of יושב ירושלם and איש יהודה. ועתה is the separation marker, as is the vocative.

It cannot be doubted that in this verse the prophet momentarily leaves the metaphorical setting of his song. The words have to be taken in a fully literal sense. The hearers, tense and confused by now, expect the dénouement.

Verse 3b

שפטו־נא ביני	*šipṭū nā bēnī*
ובין כרמי	*ūbēn karmī*

End rhyme of *bēnī* and *karmī* and repetition of the preposition בין link the two cola. The imperative שפטו־נא forms a separation marker.

Given the appeal שפטו־נא the literary genre suddenly seems to change here into a form related to the *rîb*–pattern. In this verse the introductory formula by which a complainant addresses the court and by which he demands a judicial verdict

---

48 Williams: 1985:460f. Compare also the interpretation of Bentzen: 1927: cited above, §1.5.
49 Cf. Judg. 9:27; 21:21; Isa. 16:10.

can be discerned.[50] As in a real lawsuit there are two parties, but in this case the defendant is a rather strange party, namely a vineyard. Although it is not unusual in the Old Testament for inanimate subjects to play a role in a lawsuit,[51] the hearers must have been uncertain about the semantic sphere within which they could interpret the prophet's words.

In actual fact, however, the form of the verse shows a striking resemblance to Mic. 6:3 where in a similar way YHWH makes a demand for a lawsuit:

ענה בני   *Give evidence against Me !*

Here too, the accused themselves are summoned to administer justice. The difference with Isa. 5:3b is that Micah clearly points out that it is YHWH who enters into a lawsuit with His people (Mic. 6:2), while in Isaiah the addressed can still consider themselves as outsiders.

Verse 4a

מה־לעשות עוד לכרמי   *ma laʿᵃśōt ʿōd lᵉkarmī*

ולא עשיתי בו   *wᵉlō ʿāśītī bō*

Assonance of the vowel 'o', the repetition of the verb עשה, and the interrogative מה are separation markers in this verse.

Verse 4 (both a and b) is dominated by the verb עשה. The grower has 'worked' in his vineyard and he now expects the corresponding 'working' of the vineyard. The use of עשה in connection with מה recalls formulas used in court. Well—known is the formula of accusation מה עשית *'What have you done?*'[52]

So, in the first place the verb עשה belongs to the block of metaphors related to the image of the vineyard. In 4aA עשה is 'preparing' the vineyard and in 4aB the verb is meant as the 'producing' of grapes. In the second place, however, the verb is related to the genre of the lawsuit. The hearers must have thought, 'What are we witnessing here? A farmer's complaint? A lawsuit?'

---

50   H.J. Boecker, *Redeformen des Rechtslebens im Alten Testament* (Neukirchen—Vluyn, 1970²) 72.

51   More than once heaven and earth are called as witnesses (cf. Isa. 1:2; Jer. 2:12; Mic. 6:1f.).

52   Boecker: 1970²:26—31.

Wildberger has taken this verse as a tricolon. The first colon then contains the words מה־לעשות, but it will be clear that the Massoretic accents do not favour a separation at this point. The *mêrkā* below the word לעשות is a conjunctive accent and not a separation marker. Moreover, the Massoretes have joined מה and לעשות by a *maqqeph* in order to achieve an equal number of stressed units in both halves of the verse.

Verse 4b

מדוע קויתי לעשות ענבים   *maddūaʿ qiwwētī laʿᵃśōt ʿᵃnābīm*
ויעש באשים   *wayyaʿaś beʾūšīm*

Verse 4b repeats verse 2c (see above). It can be taken as a refrain within the song. Van Grol views this verse as a tricolon (as does Wildberger). He argues as follows: 'Verse 4b is an intentional expansion of verse 2c. The essence is *now* situated in the first two words מדוע קויתי. Therefore these words have to be taken together as a separate colon. The strophe is very rhetorical and extremely emphatic. In that case a tricolon is appropriate'.[53]

The only Massoretic accent justifying a division of verse 4b in the way Van Grol proposes is the *tebîr* below the word קויתי. However, nowhere in the immediate context is this accent used as a real separation marker, neither below עתה (verse 3a), nor below את (verse 5b).

Furthermore, it has to be asked whether the word מדוע should be connected with קויתי or with the following colon. Logically we are inclined to combine מדוע with the result of the arduous work of the winegrower, i.e. the bad grapes. In light of a similar construction with מדוע in Isa. 50:2 it is possible to take the interrogative מדוע as referring to the second part of the verse.[54]

A final argument against the view of Van Grol concerns the division of verse 7. In all three refrain verses (2c, 4b and 7c)

---

53 Van Grol: 1986:178: 'Anderzijds is v.4b een bewuste uitbreiding van v.2c. De pointe ligt *nu* bij de eerste twee woorden *madduᵃ⁽ qiwweti*, die dan ook met een zekere nadruk apart te plaatsen zijn als colon. De strofe is zeer retorisch en uiterst nadrukkelijk. Hierin past het tricolon'.
54 Cf. P. Joüon, *Grammaire de l'Hébreu Biblique* (Rome, 1923) §161k. See also the commentaries of Procksch: 1930 and Wildberger: 1972 on this verse.

the construction קוה plus ־ל is used. Verse 7c clearly proves that this construction together with its addition belongs to *one* colon. Van Grol himself has to admit this. In our opinion the original structure of the text is clear enough. There is no reason to divide verse 4b into three cola instead of two.[55]

By now some hearers must have concluded that they were listening to a disappointed winegrower thinking aloud and only formally asking their advice. Others, however, would still have been disturbed. They probably knew Isaiah well. Did he possess a vineyard? Did he not start by saying that it was the vineyard of a *friend*? Why, then, does he now speak in the first person?

Verse 5a

ועתה אודיעה־נא אתכם	*wᵉʿattā ʾōdîʿā nā ʾetkèm*
את אשר־אני עשה לכרמי	*ʾēt ᵃšèr ᵃnî ʿōśè kᵉkarmî*

Also in this verse the subtle rhyme is striking. In 5aA the vowel 'a' is used in 'attā/'odîʿā/nā and the vowel 'i' in 5aB ᵃnî/kᵉkarmî. We also note the external repetition of את. Separation markers include עתה, the cohortative, and the grammatical construction of the participle with the emphasized אני instead of the normal imperfect form.

The reading Loretz presents here is incomprehensible. He has taken verse 5a as one colon, neglecting the *zaqeph parvum* above אתכם. So he gets a verse of too many letters, according to his method of counting letters, and has to modify the transmitted text. There is no reason, however, to ignore the *zaqeph* as a separation marker at this point.

Verse 5b

הסר משוכתו	*hāsēr mᵉśukkātō*
והיה לבער	*wᵉhāyā kᵉbāʿēr*
פרץ גדרו	*pārōṣ gᵉdērō*
והיה למרמס	*wᵉhāyā kᵉmirmās*

The cola are linked by the absolute infinitives, the repetition of the 3ms suffix, and the formula ־והיה ל.

The Hiphil verb סור *'to take away'* occurs some 40 times in

---

55 For other examples of קוה and ־ל in one colon cf. Gen. 49:18; Isa. 59:9; 59:11; Jer. 8:15; 13:16; 14:19; Ps. 69:21.

the Old Testament with YHWH as the subject. Often it is used for the removing of sanctuaries, altars and sacred poles.[56]

Comparison with verse 7 may raise the question why verse 5b is divided into four cola whereas we have subdivided verse 7c into two cola. Justification for this quadrocolon is found in a number of other texts of Isaiah in which the construction היה plus ל- also appears, and of which it is clear that all consequences of the היה plus ל- construction have to be read in one verse, e.g. Isa. 7:25b (bicolon), 8:14a (tricolon), 19:20 (unicolon). On this point we are glad to agree with Watson who argues that verse 5b of Isa. 5 is a so—called *quatrain*, in the ABCB—form.[57]

Both Loretz and Van Grol have divided verse 5b into two cola.[58] Wildberger, on the contrary, also has taken the verse as a quadrocolon.[59]

On the basis of Ugaritic *bᶜr* II, '*to remove*' with the special meaning of '*to destroy*' (cf. *KTU* 1.103:41,58; 2.41:22) we translate היה לבער in this text as '*and it will be destroyed*'.[60] Comparison with Ps. 89:41ff. may perhaps justify the assumption that this expression too is used metaphorically. Its meaning could be the destruction of the vineyard (the land of Israel) by its enemies (cf. Ps. 89:43ff.).

The demolition of the walls of the vineyard is paralleled by Ps. 89:41:

פרצת כל־גדרתיו - *Thou hast broken through all its walls;*
שמת מבצריו מחתה   *thou hast reduced its strongholds to ruins.*

It is absolutely certain that in Ps. 89 the walls of the vineyard (גדרתיו) are paralleled by the literal מבצריו. In any case גדר has been used metaphorically in Ps. 89 as a designation for the strongholds in the land of Israel.[61] So it is legitimate to

56   S. Schwertner, 'סור', *THAT*, Band II (München, 1979) 150.

57   Watson: 1984:186. It makes no difference that he calls a *strophe* what we call a *verse*.

58   Loretz: 1975:574; Van Grol: 1986:115.

59   H. Wildberger, *Jesaja* (BKAT X/3; Neukirchen—Vluyn, 1982) 1690.

60   Cf. *HAL*, Band I, 140; Gesenius—Buhl, *Handwörterbuch*, 108.

61   See also Mic. 7:11.

interpret the walls of the vineyard in Isa. 5:5 metaphorically as being included in the conceptual metaphor 'Israel is a vineyard'.

The Targumists too have taken the walls as a metaphor. But they chose for the interpretation *'their sanctuaries'*. This view does not convey the intention of verse 2. With the sanctuaries the Targum points to the illegal altars, built by the Israelites, against the will of God. But the walls of the vineyard usually were built by the grower, using stones found during the clearing of the soil.[62] So when the metaphorical vineyard walls are destroyed, their literal meaning ought to be buildings 'built' by God (the 'grower').[63]

The construction used in this verse (infinitive + perfect tense) reminds us of the special formula commonly found in a lawsuit for the announcement of the verdict.[64]

The verb רמס is used in a literal sense in 2 Kgs. 7:17,20; 9:33; Isa. 1:12; Ezek. 26:11. It appears in a metaphorical sense in the fable of the thistle in 2 Kgs. 14:9 (=2 Chron. 25:18) where the thistle will be trampled down. This refers to king Amaziah who will be defeated by Jehoash, king of Israel. Other cases include Isa. 16:4 (the enemies are the ones who trample underfoot), 41:25 (the rulers will be trampled by the enemy), 63:3 (the enemies will be trodden in the winepress).

מרמס is attested in Isa. 7:25 where the imagery of Isa. 5:5–6 is evoked. The land will be trampled by sheep. The same metaphorical usage appears in Ezek. 34:19. Also used in a metaphorical sense, but connected with a literal subject (enemies), it occurs in Isa. 10:6 and Mic. 7:10 (cf. also Isa. 28:18). So, רמס is in the first place used for the trampling of land by animals (sheep, cows). In a metaphorical sense it stands for the destruction of a land by the enemy. It may be concluded that the more perceptive hearers may have suspected that also the trampling down of the vineyard had to be interpreted metaphorically.

---

62 G. Dalman, *Arbeid und Sitte*, Band IV (Gütersloh, 1935) 309.

63 See Ex. 15:17; 2 Sam. 7:11; Ps. 51:20; 78:69, etc.

64 Boecker: 1970²:143ff. The most frequently used formula consists of an infinitive + imperfect tense (the so-called 'Kurzformel'). More elaborated judgments have to be distinguished from this 'Kurzformel'. Under the latter Boecker classes also Isa. 5:5–6 (p. 151).

Verse 6a

ואשיתהו בתה	*wa'ᵃšītēhū bᵉtōhū*
לא ידמר	*lō yizzāmēr*
ולא יעדר	*wᵉlō yēʿādēr*
ועלה שמיר ושית	*wᵉʿālā šāmīr wāšāyīt*

End rhyme of *wa'ᵃšītēhū/bᵉtōhū* and *yizzāmēr/yēʿādēr*, repetition of לא, assonance of *šāmīr wāšāyīt* and inclusion on the basis of assonance of *wa'ᵃšītēhū/wāšāyīt* form the markers in this verse.

In this verse we have to decide between a tricolon and a quadrocolon. We are inclined to read verse 6a as a quadrocolon on the basis of a similar construction (imperfect + לא // imperfect + לא) as e.g. in Isa. 5:27; 40:28; 42:2,4. Loretz and Van Grol have both decided for a tricolon, without substantiating their argument. The Massoretes placed a disjunctive accent at ידמר (*paštā*).

A *crux interpretum* is בתה, by the Massoretes vocalized as *bātā*. *BHS* proposes to read ואשביתהו, an imperfect Hiphil form of שבת '*And I shall put an end to it*'. But this proposal implies major alterations in the Massoretic text.

Gesenius has derived בתה from the identical root. He translates, '*I will destroy him fully*'.[65] Wildberger has followed G.R. Driver in his view on בתה.[66] He proposes a relation with Akkadian *batû* '*zerstören*'. At first sight this seems a good solution, but neither of the major two Akkadian dictionaries[67] mentions the Akkadian root *batû*.

Several ancient versions relate the word to desolation. The LXX translate: Καὶ ἀνήσω τὸν ἀμπελῶνά μου — '*And I will abandon my vineyard*,' and the Targum paraphrases: ואשוי נון רטישין — '*And I will make them abandoned ones*', and the Vulgate reads: *et ponam eam desertam* — '*And I will put him to desolation*'. This idea of desolation is understandable if בתה may be derived from the root *bw/yt*, '*to spend the night*,' which

---

65 W. Gesenius, *Thesaurus philologicus criticus linguae hebraeae et chaldaeae Veteris Testamenti*, Tomus primus (Leipzig, 1835) 251 (*sub voce*: בתה): '*Ich will ihm das Garaus machen*.'
66 Wilberger: 1972:164.
67 See W. von Soden's *Akkadisches Handwörterbuch* and *The Assyrian Dictionary* published by the University of Chicago (*CAD*).

is attested in several Semitic languages. In that case בתה
should be a feminine noun of the root *bw/yt* meaning
'*night-quarters*', in a bad sense, like the night—hut mentioned
in Isa. 1:8 and 24:20.

A. Schoors and J. Vermeylen point to the view of P.R.
Berger, who proposes to vocalize בתה as *bᵉtōhū*. For this
proposal the latter adduces Ps. 12:6 which is the only place
where the expression שׁית בּ— means '*to turn into*'.[68] Oddly
enough Berger does not support his excellent proposal by a
reference to Theodotion who translated בתה as αβατον —
'*inaccessible*'.[69]

Noteworthy in this respect is that the LXX reading ἐν ἀβάτῳ
in Ps. 106:40 (Hebrew 107:40) is the translation of בתהו. It is
imaginable that Theodotion has taken the consonants of בתה as
those of בתה(ו). Therefore we prefer the reading as proposed
by Berger. A third argument for this alteration of the
vocalization is the rhyme which dominates the entire song apart
from this colon (and, as mentioned above, verse 3a). The
reading *bᵉtōhū* restores the rhyme in this colon too. Finally, this
version matches with the string of metaphors in this verse. The
vineyard will be turned into wilderness, and thorns and thistles
will grow there. In this interpretation the בּ has to be taken as
a so—called *beth essentiae*.[70]

Many commentators have viewed the vineyard as the subject
of עלה.[71] All of them have to insert a preposition like '*in*' into
their translation. Duhm and Joüon justify their view by referring
to Prov. 24:31. In our opinion this reference proves nothing.[72]

---

68 P.R. Berger, 'Ein unerklärtes Wort in dem Weinberglied Jesajas (Jes.
5:6)', *ZAW* 82 (1970) 116f., followed by A. Schoors, *Jesaja* (BOT; Roermond,
1972) 51; Vermeylen: 1977:164.

69 J. Ziegler (ed.), *Septuaginta Vetus Testamentum Graecum*. Vol. XIV.
Isaias (Göttingen, 1939) 138. Symmachus has translated: αφησω αυτον ως
ανεπιβατον — '*I will abandon him and he will become inaccessible*'. (p. 137).

70 Cf. Joüon: 1923:§133c; *HAL*, Band 1, 100 *sub* 3.

71 E.g., Delitzsch: 1889; Duhm: 1922⁴; Wildberger: 1972; Eichrodt: 1976²,
and also Joüon: 1923:§125o.

72 The two parallel cola in Prov. 24:31 argue in favour of taking the
thistles instead of the vineyard as the subject in this verse; the vineyard is
already mentioned implicitly in כלו, and is paralleled by פניו and וגדר
אבניו.

Grammatically it is not impossible that a singular form of עלה
is used in combination with a multiple subject (cf. Judg. 6:3;
Isa. 43:13; Ezek. 37:8). Also, עלה in the sense of *'growing up'*
in reference to a plant is not unknown in the Old Testament
(cf. Gen. 40:10; 41:5,22; Deut. 29:22; Isa. 34:13; 54:13). If the
vineyard had been the subject, the poet could have repeated the
construction היה ל-. Moreover, a Hiphil of עלה would be
expected rather than a Qal if it were the vineyard that *makes*
the thorns and thistles grow. So it is much more attractive to
take the thorns and thistles as the subject of עלה.

The refusal of the grower to prune and cultivate the vineyard
definitely means that God gives up the land of Israel totally.
However, there are no clear parallels to be found in the Old
Testament to prove that this is the correct interpretation of the
metaphors, so we can only rely on the context.

Thorns and thistles will grow up. The use of שמיר ושית is
characteristic of the prophet Isaiah and the authors working in
his tradition (cf. Isa. 7:23ff.; 9:17; 10:17; 27:4; 32:13). On the
basis of these texts it has to be stated that probably the thorns
and thistles must be interpreted in the general meaning of 'total
desolation'.

Verse 6b

ועל העבים אצוה	wᵉ'al hèʿābīm 'ᵃṣawwè
מהמטיר עליו מטר	mēhamṭīr ʿālāw māṭār

Loretz has taken this verse as one colon, again neglecting the
zaqeph parvum, and also paying insufficient attention to the
semantic parallelism between העבים and מטר, and between ועל
and עליו.

Repetition of the preposition על marks this verse. No rhyme
or assonance can be discerned. As in verse 3a, it sounds like a
false note in an otherwise well—balanced whole.

'And I will command the clouds'. – Now it becomes suddenly
clear why the speaker strikes a different tone. Up till now the
hearers may have thought that they were listening to the tirade
of an angry winegrower. But now they realize that the grower
cannot be a human being. It is interesting in this respect that
the subject of the verb צוה with meteorological objects can only

be YHWH/God.[78]

Some scholars[74] suggest that man too can command the clouds. Certainly David in 2 Sam. 1:21 calls out to the land: *'May you have neither dew nor rain !'* And in the Ugaritic text *KTU* 1.19:I.40f. it is also a man who makes an appeal to the clouds: *'May the clouds pour rain on the summer-fruit'*. But in neither of these two texts has a verb meaning 'to command' been inserted. In both texts we have the expression of an ardent wish. Man is unable to command the rain (cf. Job 28:23—28; 38:22—28, 34—38), except if God authorizes him to do so (1 Kgs. 17:1; 18:36).

The verb מטר is attested 36 times in the Old Testament, of which 29 times are with YHWH as the Giver of the rain. The Targum has paraphrased Isa. 5:6b as follows: *'And my prophets I will command not to utter a prophecy concerning them'*. This interpretation is not without proof in the Old Testament. Most interesting are the texts in which מטר is used metaphorically, e.g. Deut. 32:2 (the teaching of Moses is like rain, cf. Job 29:22) and Isa. 55:10 (the Word of God is compared with rain on the earth).

Verse 7a

כי כרם יהוה צבאות	*kī kèrèm YHWH ṣᵉbā'ōt*
בית ישראל	*bēt yiśrā'ēl*

As in verse 3a, there are no veiled terms here, no rhyme and no assonance. The marker in this verse is the emphatic כי. Furthermore, it will be clear that the two cola form a synthetic unity.

Both Loretz and Van Grol have taken verse 7a as one colon. We have taken the *paštā* and the *zaqeph parvum* as separation markers. In our opinion the *paštā* should be interpreted as the marker of the end of a colon here, as in 5bA and 6aB. The result is a short pause, in which the hearers were allowed to recall the כרם היה לידידי of the beginning; so *He* is the friend! And to remove all ambiguity, the following colon identifies the vineyard as the house of Israel, for those who have

---

73   G. Liedke, 'צוה', *THAT*, Band II, 533, 4a.
74   Bentzen: 1927:210; Schoors: 1972:51.

missed all metaphorical clues in the preceding lines. Note the deliberate choice of balancing, ponderous titles i.e., not יהוה, but יהוה צבאות; not ישראל, but בית ישראל; not יהודה, but איש יהודה.

Verse 7b

ואיש יהודה   *wᵉ'īš yᵉhūdā*

נטע שעשועיו   *nᵉṭaʿ šaʿᵃšuʿāw*

The word שעשע can be derived from the root שעע II, 'to fondle, to caress'. In a subtle way it brings back the idea of a love song. Israel/Judah was the beloved of YHWH (cf. Hos. 2).

Verse 7c

ויקו למשפט   *wayᵉqaw lᵉmišpāṭ*

והנה משפח   *wᵉhinnē miśpāḥ*

In this verse the alliterative assonance recurs (*mišpāṭ/miśpāḥ*). The demonstrative interjection והנה is a separation marker. Here and in verse 7d the genre of the lawsuit of verse 3 is explained by the words משפט and צדקה.

Verse 7d

לצדקה   *liṣdāqā*

והנה צעקה   *wᵉhinnē ṣᵉʿāqā*

Again we register a form of alliterative assonance (*liṣdāqā/ṣᵉʿāqā*). Here too we find the separation marker והנה.

Is 7c—d one verse or do we have to divide the strophe into two verses? Similar והנה constructions occur in Isa. 29:8 and Jer. 4:23—26. Constructions of קוה and והנה in Jer. 8:15 and 14:19 argue for the distribution of the והנה cola over two verses, and not to take verse 7c as a quadrocolon. Wildberger and Loretz agree with this division, although the latter supposes that in the first colon of 7d one word (perhaps קויתי) is missing. In our opinion this is an unnecessary supposition. It is due to the power of the end of the song that the cola are getting shorter and shorter as they become sharper! Similar texts prove that the omission of the verb קוה in verse 7d was deliberate, cf. Isa. 59:9,11; Jer. 8:15 (cf. Jer. 14:19); Ps. 69:21. For cola consisting of only one word we refer to an earlier study by our team.[75]

What is highly significant is the fact that the prophet, while explaining the tenor of all other metaphors, still refrains from specifying the bad grapes (באשים). He only *hints* at what is meant by introducing two new metaphors, namely משפח, literally 'scab' as a sign of social disease (cf. Isa. 3:17), and צעקה, a cry for help (cf. Ps. 9:13; Job 34:28).

2.2 *Textual Analysis*

A first, provisional division of the song can be made on the basis of the textual contents:

0. INTRODUCTION
===
I. DESCRIPTION OF THE VINEYARD'S LAY–OUT (=PAST; 3rd person sing.).
　1b. The vineyard is situated on fertile ground.
　2a. The soil is cultivated, a vine is planted.
　2b. A tower is built, a winepress is cut out.
　2c. The expectation of good grapes and the disappointment.

II. THE APPEAL FOR A LAWSUIT (=PRESENT; 1st person sing.).
　3. Appeal to the hearers to administer justice.
　4. The grower's question whether he has forgotten to do anything.

III. JUDGMENT (=FUTURE; 1st person sing.).
　5. The hedge will be taken away.
　6. The vineyard will neither be cultivated nor sprinkled.

IV. EXPLANATION (=PRESENT; 3rd person sing.).
　7. The vineyard is the people of Israel in its entirety; the bad grapes are their bad deeds.

75　M.C.A. Korpel–J.C. de Moor, 'Fundamentals of Ugaritic and Hebrew Poetry', *UF* 18 (1986) 177f., reprinted in this volume.

2.3 Structural Analysis of Isa. 5:1–7

Heading   – אשירה נא לידידי (1aA)
שירת דודי לכרמו (1aB)

===

I. 1   – כרם היה לידידי (1bA)
בקרן בן־שמן (1bB)
– ויעזקהו ויסקלהו (2aA)
ויטעהו שרק (2aB)

I. 2   – ויבן מגדל בתוכו (2bA)
וגם־יקב חצב בו (2bB)
– ויקו לעשות ענבים (2cA)
ויעש באשים (2cB)

II. 1   – ועתה יושב ירושלם (3aA)
ואיש יהודה (3aB)
– שפטו־נא ביני (3bA)
ובין כרמי (3bB)

II. 2   – מה־לעשות עוד לכרמי (4aA)
ולא עשיתי בו (4aB)
– מדוע קויתי לעשות ענבים (4bA)
ויעש באשים (4bB)

III. 1   – ועתה אודיעה־נא אתכם (5aA)
את אשר־אני עשה לכרמי (5aB)
– הסר משוכתו (5bA)
והיה לבער (5bB)
פרץ גדרו (5bC)
והיה למרמס (5bD)

III. 2   – ואשיתהו בתה (6aA)
לא יזמר (6aB)
ולא יעדר (6aC)
ועלה שמיר ושית (6aD)
– ועל העבים אצוה (6bA)
מהמטיר עליו מטר (6bB)

IV. 1 — כי כרם יהוה צבאות (7aA)
בית ישראל (7aB)
— ואיש יהודה (7bA)
נטע שעשועיו (7bB)

IV. 2 — ויקו למשפט (7cA)
והנה משפח (7cB)
— לצדקה (7dA)
חהנה צעקה (7dB)

==

Separation markers:

Heading Internal parallelism: אשירה/שירת (repetitive
parallelism); לידידי/דודי.
Separation upwards/downwards: אשירה נא
(cohortative); repetitive par.

==

I.1   Int. par.: (1b) כרם/קרן (assonance); (2a) consecutive
imperfects; 3ms suffix (ו‪ה‬–).
Ext. par.: כרם/שרק; ו‪ה‬– (3x 3ms suffix)/כרם.
Sep. up: emphatic positioning of כרם.
Sep. down: ו‪ה‬– (repetitive par.).

I.2   Int. par.: (2b) בתוכו/בו (repetitive par., rhyme);
(2c) מגדל/יקב; לעשות/ויעש (repetitive par.);
ענבים/באשים (antithetical par., rhyme).
Ext. par.: ויבן/ויקו (consecutive imperfects).
Sep. up: וגם; repetitive par.
Sep. down: repetitive par.

II.1 Int. par.: (3a) יושב ירושלם/ואיש יהודה; (3b)
ביני/וביך (repetitive par.); rhyme.
Ext. par.: absent (although in fact verse 3a parallels
כרמי in 3b!).
Sep. up: ועתה; vocatives.
Sep. down: שפטו־נא (imperative); ביך/בין; 1cs suffix
(repetitive par.).

II.2   Int. par.: (4a) לכרמי/עשיתי בו ... לעשות; assonance;
        ענבים/באשים. (4b) לעשות/וייעש (repetitive par.);
        Ext. par.: עשיתי/וייעש 2x (interrogatives); מה/מדוע
        לעשות.
        Sep. up: מה; repetitive par. (עשה).
        Sep. down: מדוע; repetitive par. (עשה); rhyme.

III.1   Int. par.: (5a) verbal forms and 1cs suffixes; את
        (repetitive par.); rhyme; (5b) הסר/פרץ (infinitives);
        והיה לבער/והיה לצרצם (repetitive par.);
        משוכתו/גדרו (with repetition of the 3ms suffix).
        Ext. par.: לכרמי/משוכתו/גדרו (3ms suffix referring
        to כרם).
        Sep. up: ורעתה; cohortative; אני (emphasized).
        Sep. down: repetitive par.; quadrocolon.

III.2   Int. par.: (6a) ואשיתהו/ושית (alliterative assonance);
        ידמר/שמיר לא/ולא (alliterative assonance);
        ועל/עליו (repetitive par.); rhyme; assonance; (6b)
        העבים/מטר (repetitive par.).
        Ext. par.: ועל/עליו/עלה (1cs); ואשיתהו אצוה
        (assonance and repetitive par.); common intention of
        the canticle, namely the destruction of the vineyard.
        Sep. up: repetitive par.; quadrocolon.
        Sep. down: emphasized adjunct; מטר ... מהמטיר
        (pleonasm); repetitive par.

IV.1   Int. par.: (7a) כרם יהוה צבאות/בית ישראל (7b);
        ואיש יהודה/נטע שעשועיו.
        Ext. par.: בית ישראל/ואיש יהודה; כרם/נטע; chiasm.
        Sep. up: כי; emphasized position of כרם.
        Sep. down: absent.

IV.2   Int. par.: (7c) משפט/משפח (antithetical par. and
        alliterative assonance); (7d) לצדקה/צעקה (antithetical
        par. and alliterative assonance).
        Ext. par.: והנה משפח/צעקה; למשפט/לצדקה
        (repetitive par.).
        Sep. up: extremely short colon; והנה.
        Sep. down: והנה.

2.4 Remarks on the Higher Structural Units of Isa. 5:1–7

2.4.1 Relation of the Strophes within the Canticles

The coherence between the strophes of the separate canticles is easily recognized.

<u>Canticle I</u>: The consecutive imperfects, כרם/suffix הו–/suffix ו– are the formal links between the two strophes. This canticle tells us about the *past*. It is a description of the laying out of the vineyard. The vineyard was situated on fertile soil. A choice vine had been planted, a watch–tower had been built and a winepress had been hewn out. The time has come to look for good fruit, but the vine has produced only bad fruit.

The whole canticle is dominated by the 3rd person sing. The strophes tell us *about* the winegrower and his vineyard. Subtle inclusions bind the strophes together. באשים stands in apparent contrast to בן־שמן, and as was customary, the stones that had been cleared away (סקל) were used in making the tower (מגדל).

<u>Canticle II</u>: Here we observe the change from 3rd person sing. to 1st person sing. The prophet is speaking as if he himself were the winegrower, '*Judge between me and my vineyard*'. The canticle shows us the *present* time. It contains an appeal for the administration of justice. A tragical paradox is coming through; those who are guilty are summoned to judge themselves, although they are not aware of it. Therefore, a relation can be noticed between the inhabitants of Jerusalem, the men of Judah (verse 3a) and the vineyard (verse 4aA). What is more, if we assume the same kind of inclusion that we have observed in the first canticle, it is intimated already at this point that the בית ירושלם is an עשה באשים 'doer of bad (deeds)'. Besides, we have the clear repetitive parallelism between כרמי (3bB) and לכרמי (4aA). Of course the 1cs suffixes dominate this canticle.

It is clear that both canticles I and II end with a refrain; although it was expected to '*make*' good fruit, the vineyard '*makes*' bad fruit. This very prominent responsion puts us on the track of three further, highly significant responsions:

(3a) יושב ירושלם/איש יהודה – (1b) כרם/קרן
(again !)

סקל (2a) – שפט (3b)
(clear the soil)   (judge, clear people of badness)
בנה (2b) – עשה (4a)

Finally the winegrower asks what more he could have done. A negative answer is taken for granted between the canticles II and III. The audience has judged itself.

Canticle III: After this imaginary answer, the winegrower gives his own verdict, *'But now, I will tell you my own plan'*. The judgment has been passed, and canticle III shows the *future* of the vineyard. It seems as if canticles I and III are each other's opposites. Also in canticle III the arduous labour of the winegrower is described, but now with a totally different intention, namely the destruction of the vineyard.

The inner coherence between the strophes of canticle III is to be recognized in the 1st person sing. of the verbs and the emphatic אני (5aB). עשה (5aB) is worked out in פרץ ,הסר, אצוה מהמטיר and ואשיתהו בתה. The winegrower's only aim now is the destruction of the vineyard. This time he will not 'wait' (קוה).

Canticle IV: After the canticles which have shown us the past, present and future of the vineyard, the explanation of the song is given, clearly indicated by the marker כי. The vineyard is the House of Israel, the men of Judah. The refrain follows again, but now with the use of plain language. The prophet does not disguise the truth any longer. In obvious anger he contracts the cola of the refrain to only a few terse words. No more than the interpretation of the good fruit is given (justice and righteousness). For the bad fruit new metaphors are introduced ('scab', 'cry for help'). It is as if the divine speaker does not want to name the abominations committed.

2.4.2 The Interrelations between the Canticles

Canticles I and IV both start with the word כרם (כי), canticles II and III both start with ועתה – a clear case of embracing responsions. Canticles I and IV are written in the 3rd person sing., canticles II and III in the 1st person sing.

In canticle I we can discern a kind of love song; the prophet is singing about the 'vineyard' of his best friend. Doubtlessly, some of the hearers took the vineyard as a metaphor for a

beloved woman. As a result the following verses were
interpreted out of this framework of love. But in the second
strophe of canticle I it became increasingly difficult to reconcile
the metaphors with the genre of love poetry.

Canticle II cruelly thwarts all associations with love poetry by
ועתה and the appeal to give verdict on the vineyard. The genre
of the song changes from love song (I) to the genre of the
lawsuit (II and III). Interesting is the subtle way in which the
theme of love is reintroduced in canticle IV. It is said of the
men of Judah that they are the plantation of YHWH's 'caress'.
On the semantic level we notice an external parallelism between
canticle I and IV, by the words לידידי (1bA) and שעשועיו
(7bB). נטע in 7bB parallels ויטעהו in 2aB (responsion) but
also כרם in 1bA (inclusion).

Canticle II is related to canticle IV by שפטו־נא (3bA) and
למשפט (7cA). In canticle II the audience is summoned to judge
the metaphorical vineyard, but in canticle IV it has become
clear that the audience is the vineyard and that people who
have shown contempt of justice have just been forced to
condemn themselves.

Interesting are the first cola of each canticle. Even if we
would have failed to hear the explanation of the song at the
end, we could have observed the identification of the men of
Judah with the vineyard on the basis of the external parallelism:

vs.1b: tells about a vineyard.
vs.3a: summons up the inhabitants of Jerusalem//the men of
       Judah.
vs.5a: tragically parallels אתכם (5aA) and לכרמי (5aB).
vs.7a: tells the truth; the vineyard is the house of Israel.

Verse 5a looks like a synthetical bicolon, but in reality it is
more synonymous than synthetical.

The verb עשה connects canticles I–III, and in IV it is tacitly
assumed.

The canto as a whole exhibits a beautiful, concentric
structure of external, often antithetical pairs:

A¹　שירת דודי　　song about my beloved
B¹　קרן בן־שמן　anointed horn (headdress !)
C¹　נטע　　plant
D¹　שרק　　vine
E¹　בנה　　build
F¹　עשה　　make
G¹　ועתה　　and now
H¹　ירושלם/יהודה　Jerusalem, Judah
I¹　כרמי　　my vineyard
I²　כרמי　　my vineyard
H²　באשים　　bad grapes
G²　ועתה　　and now
F²　עשה　　make
E²　פרץ　　break down
D²　שמיר ושית　thorns and thistles
C²　נטע　　plantation
B²　משפח　　scab, scurf
A²　צעקה　　cry for help

2.4.3 The overall Structure of Isa. 5:1—7

The structure of the entire song of Isa. 5:1—7 exhibits a certain
regularity on the level of the higher units:

CANTICLES	STROPHES	VERSES	COLA
—	—	1	2
I	2	4(2+2)	8(2+2+2+2)
II	2	4(2+2)	8(2+2+2+2)
III	2	4(2+2)	12(2+4+4+2)
IV	2	4(2+2)	8(2+2+2+2)

3 The Genre of the Text

The Song of the Vineyard seems to be intentionally constructed
for misinterpretation.[76] The heading of the text rouses the
expectation of a love song, and the first canticle can be
conceived as a metaphorical description of a man and his
beloved. However, the verbs עזק and סקל will have made it
difficult for the audience also to interpret verse 2a on the basis

---

76　With Williams: 1985.

of the genre of love poetry. So, the interpretation of the first canticle in an erotic sense stops with the 'digging up' of the ground in vs. 2aA. And the hearers have to look for a different interpretation of the actions enumerated in vss. 2a—b.

At this point the hearers may have tried to re—interpret the song as an agricultural song about a *literal* vineyard. Eissfeldt mentions the existence of many different secular songs in the Ancient Near East, among them wine songs, drinking songs and harvest songs.[77] Within this context the 'digging up' and the 'clearing of stones' of the vineyard and the description of the planting of the vine, the building of the tower and the hewing out of a winepress could be taken literally. In summary: vs. 1 supposes the genre of a love song, in which an allegorical interpretation of the text (almost every word is a metaphor) is required. Vs. 2, however, seems to point to a type of agricultural song. The prophet is singing of a literal vineyard. The hearers have to change their mind. From the metaphorical framework of love poetry they have to switch over to the context of agriculture.

After the description of the past in very ambiguous words in canticle I, and at the moment that the hearers have been thrown into confusion, the second canticle starts with a new, third genre. It is said to the audience, '*Judge!*' Also, the grammatical person has changed. The prophet is speaking now in the 1st person sing. Is Isaiah himself the owner of the disappointing vineyard? This is confusing and the hearers have to look again for a more suitable interpretation. Now that a lawsuit is introduced, it would still be possible to take the vineyard in a literal sense. Perhaps the prophet has an agricultural problem, and he solicits some advice from his audience. In any case it is clear that the song can no longer become a cheerful vintage song or the like. The introduction of the genre of the lawsuit prevents this.

The third canticle contains the announcement of doom, the verdict of the grower on his vineyard. The parallelism in all first lines of the canticles could have suggested to the hearers that the inhabitants of Jerusalem and the men of Judah were the vineyard. In fact the disguised parallelism between אתכם

---

77   Eissfeldt: 1976[4]:118f.

and כרמי renders such an identification all too obvious. The genre of the lawsuit remains, but the meaning of the vineyard becomes more and more difficult to discern.

It is the last canticle that discloses the truth. Now the hearers no longer have the option to take the word כרם literally, and as a result the *entire* song has to be re—interpreted.[78] The vineyard is the land of Israel, situated on fertile ground. The grapes are the deeds of the Israelites. So it is quite possible that also the other words related to the image of the vineyard are metaphors, referring to the history of Israel in the land of Canaan.

On the basis of our research, it now can be stated that the prophet has used the genre of the allegory, in which he has veiled his real intention by using first the genre of the love song (which has to be taken allegorically too!) and then the genre of the lawsuit.

The transition from one genre to another can be outlined against the macro—structure of the text:

Introduction: Love song?
Canticle I: No! — Vintage song?
Canticle II: No! — Lawsuit?
Canticle III: No! — Still a winegrower's complaint?
Canticle IV: No! — Announcement of God's judgment on
                      Israel.

In canticle IV, elements of all three genres return, cf. כרם (vs. 7aA, vintage song), שעשועיו (vs. 7bA, love song), משפט and צדקה (vss. 7cA, 7dA, lawsuit).

In a table it looks like this:[79]

---

78 Cf. Williams: 1985:463.
79 We distinguish four supposed genres and levels in the song:
1. Is the vineyard meant literally? Is it a <u>vintage</u> song?
2. Is the vineyard a beloved woman? Is it a <u>love</u> song?
3. Is the genre of the song the <u>lawsuit</u>?
4. Is the vineyard <u>Israel</u>?
Brackets indicate that we were unable to prove that the word in question does apply.

CANTICLE	HEBREW	TRANSLATION	VITI-CULTURE	LOVE	LAW-SUIT	ISRAEL
Heading	שיר	sing	*	*		
	ידיד	beloved		*		
	דוד	beloved		*		
	כרם	vineyard	*	*		*
I	קרן בן־שמן	horn of oil	*	*		(*)
	עדק	dig up	*	(*)		(*)
	סקל	clear of stones	*			(*)
	נטע	plant	*			*
	שרק	vine	*			
	מגדל	tower	*			
	יקב	winepress	*			(*)
	ענבים	grapes	*			(*)
	באשים	bad grapes	*			(*)
II	שפט	judge			*	*
	כרם	vineyard	*		*	*
	עשה	make	*		*	*
	ענבים	grapes	*			(*)
	באשים	bad grapes	*			(*)
III	סור	remove	*		*	*
	משוכה	hedge	*			(*)
	בער	destroy	*		*	(*)
	פרץ	break down	*		*	(*)
	גדר	wall	*			*
	רמס	trample	*		*	*
	תהו	wilderness	*			*
	לא זמר	no pruning	*		*	
	לא עדר	no cultivation	*		*	
	שמיר ושית	thorns & thistles	*			*
	מטר	rain	*			*
IV	כרם	vineyard	*			*
	שעשועיו	caress		*		*
	משפט	justice			*	*
	משפח	'scab'			(*)	*
	צדקה	righteousness			*	*
	צעקה	cry for help			*	*

4 Conclusions

In our discussion of the individual verses, rhyme and assonance proved to be relevant to the structure of the text. Obviously these stylistic means could be used as markers in the text, as are parallelism and particles like כי, עמה and הנה.

The lack of rhyme in verses 3a, 5a, 6b, 7a and 7b brings these verses to the fore. Exactly these verses reveal something of the real intention of the song. In all four verses the metaphorical setting is momentarily abandoned.

If we analyse Isa. 5:1−7 according to the method developed by our team at Kampen the structure of the song appears to be very regular, consisting of four canticles, preceded by an introductory verse (or strophe). No doubt the song was composed consciously in this way.

In paragraph 2 we registered several examples of illuminating instances of external parallelism. Canticles I and IV are linked together by (among other things) לידידי in vs. 1 and שעשועיו in vs. 7. Although the prophet announces God's judgment upon the Israelites it is striking that they are nevertheless still called the plantation of God's *caress*! The entire song is bracketed by words of love, the love of God. Whatever may happen, Israel remains his vineyard.

Noteworthy are also the key−words in the song. Of course the word כרם plays and important role, but also the words עשה and קוה have to be noted as key−words. YHWH has worked hard for his vineyard, and after his work He is expecting good grapes. In the end it appears that He expected justice and righteousness. The grower, YHWH, works (עשה) out of love, and because of his arduous labour He expects the satisfactory result of the working (עשה) of the vineyard. It is not only God who works, but also man who has to work. An interaction is required between the initiating עשה of YHWH and the implementing עשה of man. The wonderful acts of God should have been reflected in what Israel did with them.

Above we have seen that at least three levels of interpretation may be discerned in the Song of the Vineyard:

1. literal: the complaint of a farmer against his vineyard.
2. metaphorical: the vineyard as a beloved woman.
3. metaphorical: the vineyard as Israel, the people of God.

In the end it appears that the last two levels can be combined. Israel is the vineyard of YHWH, which is a common symbol in the Old Testament, as we have shown above. But Israel is also the beloved of YHWH, a common symbol in the Old Testament pointing to the covenant of God with his people.

With the help of the structural analysis it now becomes clear how the prophet has duped his audience. The first canticle could be interpreted as an ambiguous *love song*. By choosing this particular genre the prophet was assured of the complete attention of his audience and at the same time he forced his hearers to apply an allegorical interpretation to the song. The people were expecting a love song. Automatically they would have started interpreting the song in a metaphorical (or allegorical) way, since well—elaborated imagery was characteristic of the Hebrew love song. It has rendered an allegorical nature to large parts of the Song of Songs.

But the transition between the canticles I and II also marks the transition to another genre in the text. In verse 3 the *lawsuit* is introduced and the expectations of the hearers are frustrated. There are no longer ambiguous terms that could be applied to a beautiful woman. At the same time those who have taken the vineyard literally are put to confusion. An inanimate subject could not be a realistic party (here the accused) in a lawsuit.

The third canticle confirms the genre of the lawsuit, as judgment is given. But it is still unclear what or who is meant if the vineyard is *not* a beloved woman.

Of course the image of Israel as the vineyard should have been well—known, and some of the hearers may already have guessed the true meaning of the song. But only in the last canticle does the intention of the text become fully clear to everyone. The consequence for the hearers is, that they have to re—interpret the song from beginning to end.

At this point it has to be asked which genre, mentioned above (paragraph 1), can be applied to the entire song. It is certain that the genres of *love song* and *lawsuit* cover some parts of the song. But what about the whole? Is it a fable? Is it a parable? Or is it still an allegory?

Obviously some scholars consider the song a *fable*. The abundant imagery related to viticulture seriously points in that direction. Two arguments, however, plead against the genre of the fable.

1. Although it is the vineyard that '*makes*' the grapes, it is impossible to take it as an acting person. Doubtlessly a dispute

between the winegrower and his vineyard would be expected, if
Isa. 5:1—7 were a fable.
2. Verse 7 cannot be taken as a moral thesis or a principle of
human behaviour in a general sense. The verse only contains
the explanation of the most important metaphors mentioned in
the preceding part of the song. This explanation indicates an
explicit and concrete situation.

A *parable*, like a fable, is also supposed to exemplify a
universal thesis or lesson. Therefore the same two arguments
mentioned above can be applied to the genre of the parable.

Elaborated imagery is characteristic of both parable and
allegory. In paragraph 3, however, we have seen that the
metaphors used in the song cannot be reduced to only one
semantic sphere. They belong to the domains of *love poetry* (the
vineyard is a beloved woman), *lawsuit* (the judgment on the
vineyard) or they are related to the conceptual metaphor 'Israel
is a vineyard'. This argument argues against the parable as the
genre of the entire song. Such a multiple and ambiguous
imagery would be unacceptable to the genre of the parable in
its traditional meaning.

There was sufficient reason to assume that already from the
beginning of the song the prophet aimed to force his hearers to
an *allegorical* interpretation of his words. He attained this goal
by starting with an introduction that raised the expectation of a
love song. Both the explanation in verse 7 and the subtle hints
indicated by the external parallelism prove that the prophet had
more than one tenor in mind when choosing the different
metaphors. It was possible for him to link up with an older
prophetic tradition. Before him the prophet Hosea already had
compared Israel to a vine (Hos. 10:1).

Later on the imagery of the vineyard is still interpreted in an
allegorical way.[80] Not only the New Testament (cf. Mk.
12:1—12; Jn. 15:1—8) but also the ancient Targum tradition (cf.
the paraphrases on Isa. 5:1—7 and Ps. 80:6—16) prove this.

In the table above (paragraph 3) it is demonstrated that
almost every metaphor in Isa. 5:1—7 is related to the conceptual

---

80 Cf. Isa. 3:14 (still dated to the early period of Isaiah); Ps. 80:8ff.
(pre—exilic, presumably an application to Isa. 5); Isa. 7:23—25 (addition to
the book of Isaiah); 27:2 (post—exilic); Jer. 12:10 (post—exilic).

metaphor 'Israel is a vineyard'. If the parable is redefined according to the newer insights, which suggest that it is not one *point* of comparison (one *tenor* of a metaphor) but one *basic metaphor* that is qualifying it, Isa. 5:1—7 could be called an 'allegorical parable'. But the *allegory* still remains the leading feature, in which almost every word (metaphor) has its literal tenor.

In our opinion the genre of Isa. 5:1—7 can best be described as an *allegory*. This genre offered the prophet a limited freedom to disguise his intention in the beginning of the song by also using the genre of the *love song*. Furthermore the genre of the *lawsuit* was introduced to lift a corner of the veil.

THE BOOK OF JONAH AS POETRY
An Analysis of Jonah 1:1–16

Raymond de Hoop

1 Introduction

The book of Jonah, with the exception of the prayer (or 'psalm') of Jonah (2:3–10 [ET 2:2–9]), is generally viewed as prose.[1] It is evident that the prayer of Jonah with 'die uns von Psalter her vertraute dichterische Struktur des *strengen* Parallelismus der Glieder' (emphasis mine, RdH),[2] is stylistically different from the narrative portions of the book. But this difference between prayer and story does not necessarily entail that the narrative portions are not formulated as poetry.[3] The articles by J.C. de Moor regarding the book of Ruth[4] demonstrate that strong internal parallelism at the level of the verse is not the exclusive norm for poetry. Absence of internal parallelism can be compensated for by predominant external parallelism at the level of the strophe. Furthermore, as a characteristic of so called narrative poetry, mention may be

---

1   Stated explicitly for example in H.W. Wolff, *Dodekapropheton 3. Obadja und Jona* (BK XIV/3; Neukirchen–Vluyn, 1977) 57; W.H. Schmidt, *Einführung in das Alte Testament* (Berlin/New York, 1979) 286. Furthermore, most introductions give the impression that the designation 'story', 'Erzählung' or 'verhaal', in contrast to the psalm as poetry, is adequate. Noteworthy, (but in a sense also misleading) is the observation of O. Eissfeldt, *Einleitung in das Alte Testament* (Tübingen, 1976[4]) 546: 'Unserem Buch liegen aber eigentlich zwei Legenden dieser Art zugrunde' (legendary, prophetic accounts as in 1 Kgs. 19:4–8, RdH) [ET=*The Old Testament: An Introduction,* Trans. P.R. Ackroyd (New York/Londen, 1965) 405]. Legends belong to the so–called 'poetische Erzählungen..., die aus einer dichterischen oder auch willensmäßigen Einstellung zu Leben und Welt heraus gestaltet sind...', p. 41 [ET= p.32]. However, for Eissfeldt 'poetic' is not yet 'poetry', cf. pp. 75ff. [ET= pp.57ff.].
2   H.W. Wolff *Studien zum Jonabuch* (BS 47; Neukirchen–Vluyn, 1965) 61.
3   Wolff: 1965:60.
4   J.C. de Moor, 'The Poetry of the Book of Ruth, I', *Or* 53 (1984) 262–283; II, *Or* 55 (1986) 16–46.

made of the presence of wordpairs, so—called synthetic parallelism and expansion and contraction of the various literary units. Recognition of these poetic characteristics suggest that a denial of poetic structure in the book of Jonah, if based upon an observed absence of *internal* parallelism, is premature. When viewed in light of the articles concerning the book of Ruth as poetry, the literary similarity emphasized by various authors[5] between the book of Jonah and the book of Ruth would actually appear to support a conclusion to the contrary. Accordingly, in this article we wish to use Jonah 1:1—16 as a basis upon which to investigate the extent to which the book of Jonah belongs to the genre of narrative poetry.[6]

2 Recent approaches

Most studies of the Book of Jonah call attention to the many verbal repetitions which appear in the book.[7] These repetitions are usually treated in connection with the structure of a specific

---

5   Schmidt: 1979:286; S. Segert, 'Syntax and Style in the Book of Jonah: Six Simple Approaches to Their Analysis', in: J.A. Emerton (ed.), *Prophecy*. Essays Presented to Georg Fohrer on his Sixty—fifth Birthday (BZAW 150; Berlin/New York, 1980) 121—130, esp. 121, 130.

6   D.L. Christensen, 'The Song of Jonah: A Metrical Analysis' *JBL* 104 (1985) announces a comparable study with the title 'The Book of Jonah as a Narrative Poem' (p. 222, n.22); however, since his methodology is based upon a metrical approach and therefore differs radically from the method here employed, I take the liberty to publish this article. Furthermore, a metrical approach is vulnerable to criticism, cf. J.C. de Moor, 'The Art of Versification in Ugarit and Israel, I' in: Y.Avishur—J.Blau (eds.), *Studies in Bible and the Ancient Near East Presented to S. E. Loewenstamm* (Jerusalem, 1978) 119—139, esp. 121—128.

7   To mention only a few works, see G.H. Cohn, *Das Buch Jona im Lichte der biblischen Erzählkunst* (Studia Semitica Neerlandica 12; Assen, 1969) 47—61, 66ff.; J. Magonet, *Form and Meaning: Studies in Literary Techniques in the Book of Jonah* (BET 2; Frankfurt a.M./Bern, 1976) e.g. 16—19; A.S. van der Woude, *Jona/Nahum* (POT; Nijkerk, 1978) 11; P. Weimar, 'Literarische Kritik und Literarkritik, Unzeitgemäße Beobachtungen zu Jon 1:4—16', in: L. Ruppert et al. (Hrsg.), *Künder des Wortes*. Beiträge zur Theologie der Propheten. Josef Schreiner zum 60. Geburtstag (Würzburg, 1982) 217—235; Th.J. Naastepad, *Jona* (Kampen, n.d.); Wolff: 1965:36—40; Wolff: 1977:61.

scene. What remains beyond purview, however, is the employment of repetitions in one or more verses.[8] But it is precisely this repetition of words, so striking in a careful reading of the text, that is a significant indicator of the poetic character of the book.[9] Attention is also called to the 'growing phrase'[10], a phenomenon to which we have already referred above with the designation 'expansion (and contraction)'.[11] This is a regularly occurring phenomenon in West−Semitic poetry and can accordingly also constitute an indication of the poetic character of the book. Exegetically however, the emphasis has consistently been placed upon the content of the expansion and its position within the structure of the narrative, with a view to the effect that this has upon the reader. But it was always assumed that the narrative was prose, which has caused numerous characteristics to remain undetected.[12] For example, word selection and the so−called 'growing−phrase' were accounted for in the structural analysis of the various scenes, and usually a concentric structure was maintained for these narratives.[13] However, since in ch. 1 the concentric structure is primarily detected in vss. 4−16, that produces two more or less

---

8   An exception is found in Weimar: 1982:219f., with strong emphasis placed upon the repetition of words in 1:4f., 15f., but the possibility that the repetitions in these verses could indicate poetry does not appear to be entertained. This is also the case in *idem* 'Jona 2:1−11; Jonapsalm und Jonaerzählung', *BZ* NF 28 (1984) 43−68. Cf. also Magonet: 1976:18: 'The neutral effect of the repetition of a technical term, e.g. נפל' and cf. in this respect the analysis of vs. 7.

9   Cf. 1:3, the triple occurrence (תרשיש)ה (vs. 3aB, bB and cC), the occurence of מלפני יהוה twice, in parallelism (vs. 3aC and cD), the root בוא twice (vs. 3bB and cC) and the root ירד twice (vs. 3bA and cB) antithetical to the root קום (vs. 3aA). See also the analysis below.

10   Magonet: 1976:31ff., 40.

11   Cf. De Moor, Fs Loewenstamm: 1978; II, *UF* 10 (1978) 187−217; III, *UF* 12 (1980) 311−315. See also M.C.A. Korpel−J.C. de Moor, 'Fundamentals of Ugaritic and Hebrew Poetry', *UF* 18 (1986) 173−212.

12   E.g. Cohn: 1969:47−55.

13   Among others, Cohn: 1969:51−52; Magonet: 1976:55−58; Weimar: 1982:218−223 (for bibliography concerning the predecessors of this analysis see Weimar, p.232 n.6 and n.7); L. Alonso Schökel, J.L. Sicre Diaz, *Profetas* (Nueva Biblia Española, t.2; Madrid, 1980) 1020.

independent units, namely 1:1–3 and 4–16. And the only criterion for this caesura between the two pericopes appears to be the concentric structure; additional justification for a break here is absent.[14] Although the concentric structure theory has been criticized, these criticisms have produced little result and have been unable to convince the advocates of the concentric structure.[15] By means of the following analysis we hope to demonstrate that vss. 1–3 and 4–16 are more tightly intertwined than is generally assumed and that this does not necessarily exclude the possibility of a concentric structure.

3 Structural analysis

3.1 Preliminary remarks

The analysis offered here essentially follows the model of analysis employed for the book of Ruth.[16] The colometrical divisions are made primarily upon the basis of the Massoretic accentuation, which in general provided a fairly reliable guideline. In addition, due consideration was also given to internal parallelism, especially with respect to parallel words. This was followed by division into strophes on the basis of external parallelism and markers of separation.[17] Justification of these divisions, accompanied by the relevant portion of the text, are presented according to the following scheme:
– Internal parallelism (int. par.)
– External parallelism (ext. par.)
– Separation upwards (sep. up)
– Separation downwards (sep. down)
The entire text is subsequently presented with divisions into canticles and sub–cantos, which in turn is followed by a discussion of the structure of the entire canto.

An additional, preliminary remark is necessary with respect to

---

14 In addition to the works cited in n.13 above, this division is found in Wolff: 1977:73f.; Van der Woude: 1978:15.

15 For a summary of the criticism and a response to it see Weimar: 1982:218f.

16 Cf. n.4 above.

17 P. v.d. Lugt, *Strophische structuren in de bijbels–hebreeuwse poëzie* (Kampen, 1980) 510–524; De Moor, *Or* 55 (1986) 45.

division of the text where direct discourse is introduced. The introduction of direct discourse should be considered an essential component of the entire unit,[18] and it is accordingly not treated as an independent verse. As a result, various derivatives of the root אמר are consistently viewed as forming parallelisms with derivatives of the roots קרא, דבר and פלל.

3.2 Jonah 1:1–16

1aA	ויהי דבר־יהוה
1aB	אל־יונה בן־אמתי לאמר
2aA	קום לך אל־נינוה
2aB	העיר הגדולה
2bA	וקרא עליה
2bB	כי־עלתה רעתם לפני

Int.par.: עלתה / עליה; (2b) assonance לאמר / דבר (1).
Ext.par.: לפני / יהוה ;ויקרא // לאמר / דבר.
Sep.up: ויהי.
Sep. down: imperative; כי.[19]

3aA	ויקם יונה
3aB	לברח תרשישה
3aC	מלפני יהוה
3bA	וירד יפו
3bB	וימצא אניה באה תרשיש
3cA	ויתן שכרה
3cB	וירד בה
3cC	לבוא עמהם תרשישה
3cD	מלפני יהוה

Int.par.: יפו / מלפני / תרשישה (3a,c) (to/from); (3b)
תרשיש ;-ה / -ה (3c).
Ext.par.: מלפני יהוה ;תרשישה / תרשיש / תרשישה
(antithetical); ויקם / וירד / וירד ;מלפני יהוה

---

18 Cf. De Moor, *Or* 53 (1984) 268: '.... it is important to note that the introduction of the direct oration is an integral part of a verse and that the principle of expansion and contraction is fully operative even in this case'.
19 The imperatives in vs. 2aA constitute indications to the contrary, but they are mitigated by the inclusions דבר, אמר with קרא and of יהוה with לפני.

לבוא / באה.

Sep.up:	tricolon.
Sep.down:	quadrocolon.

4aA	ויהוה הטיל רוח־גדולה אל־הים
4aB	ויהי סער־גדול בים
4aC	והאניה חשבה להשבר
5aA	וייראו המלחים
5aB	ויזעקו איש אל־אלהיו
5bA	ויטלו את־הכלים
5bB	אשר באניה אל־הים
5bC	להקל מעליהם

Int.par.:	וייראו (5a); בים / אל־הים (4); גדול / גדולה (4) / ויזעקו.
Ext.par.:	באניה / והאניה ;ויטלו אל־הים / הטיל אל־הים אלהיו / ויהוה.
Sep.up:	tricolon; ויהוה emphatic.
Sep.down:	tricolon.

5cA	ויונה ירד אל־ירכתי הספינה
5cB	וישכב וירדם
6aA	ויקרב אליו רב החבל
6aB	ויאמר לו
6bA	מה־לך נרדם
6bB	קום קרא אל־אלהיך
6bC	אולי יתעשת האלהים לנו
6bD	ולא נאבד

Int.par.:	וירדם / ירד (5c) assonance ;ויקרב אליו / (6a) האלהים / אלהיך (6b) ;לנו / לך (6b); ויאמר לו.
Ext.par.:	קרא / ויקרב assonance ;נרדם / וירדם; קום // וישכב / ירד ;לנו / לך // לו / אליו (antithetical); קרא / ויאמר.
Sep.up:	ויונה emphatic.
Sep.down:	quadrocolon; imperatives; מה.[20]

7aA	ויאמרו איש אל־רעהו
7aB	לכו ונפילה גורלות

---

20 Contrary indication: ויאמר (vs. 6aB); mitigated via inclusion of ירד, נרדם with וירדם of and קום with וישכב.

7aC	ונדעה
7aD	בשלמי הרעה הזאת לנו
7bA	ויפלו גורלות
7bB	ויפל הגורל על־יונה

Int.par.: (7a) assonance רעהו / הרעה;
           (7b) ויפלו גורלות / ויפל הגורל.
Ext.par.: ויפלו גורלות / ונפילה גורלות.
Sep.up: quadrocolon; cohortative; ויאמרו.
Sep.down: tautological par.

8aA	ויאמרו אליו
8aB	הגידה־נא לנו
8aC	באשר למי־הרעה הזאת לנו
8bA	מה־מלאכתך
8bB	ומאין תבוא
8bC	מה ארצך
8bD	ואי־מזה עם אתה

Int.par.: (8a) ויאמרו אליו / לנו ...הגידה; (8a) לנו / לנו;
           (8b) ומאין / מה / מה / ואי־מזה.
Ext.par.: מה / למי.
Sep.up: tricolon; imperative; ויאמרו.
Sep.down: quadrocolon; tautological par.; מה;אתה (2x).

9aA	ויאמר אליהם
9aB	עברי אנכי
9bA	ואת־יהוה אלהי השמים אני ירא
9bB	אשר־עשה את־הים ואת־היבשה

Int.par.: (9b) הים ... היבשה / השמים.
Ext.par.: אני / אנכי.
Sep.up: אנכי;ויאמר.
Sep.down: ואת־יהוה emphatic; אני; tautological par. (3x את־).

10aA	וייראו האנשים
10aB	יראה גדולה
10aC	ויאמרו אליו
10aD	מה־זאת עשית
10bA	כי־ידעו האנשים
10bB	כי־מלפני יהוה הוא ברח
10bC	כי הגיד להם

Int.par.:	כי / כי / כי (10b); ירראה / ויראו / וייראו (10a).
Ext.par.:	האנשים / האנשים.
Sep.up:	quadrocolon; מה; זאת; ויאמרו.
Sep.down:	tricolon; tautological par.; כי; הוא.

11aA	ויאמרו אליו
11aB	מה־נעשה לך
11aC	וישתק הים מעלינו
11b	כי הים הולך וסער

Int.par.:	מעלינו / לך / אליו (11a).
Ext.par.:	הים הולך וסער / וישתק הים (antithetical).
Sep.up:	tricolon; מה; ויאמרו.
Sep.down:	unicolon[21]; כי.

12aA	ויאמר אליהם
12aB	שאוני והטילני אל־הים
12aC	וישתק הים מעליכם
12bA	כי יודע אני
12bB	כי בשלי
12bC	הסער הגדול הזה עליכם

Int.par.:	כי / (12b); בשלי / אני (12b); הים / הים (12a) כי.
Ext.par.:	הים / הסער; עליכם / מעליכם.
Sep.up:	tricolon; imperatives; ויאמר.
Sep.down:	tricolon; כי; אני; הזה.

13aA	ויחתרו האנשים
13aB	להשיב אל־היבשה
13aC	ולא יכלו
13b	כי הים הולך וסער עליהם

Int.par.:	—
Ext.par.:	הים / היבשה.
Sep.up:	tricolon.
Sep.down:	unicolon;[21] כי.

---

21 Another possibility of division is to make a break after הים, thereby producing a bicolon, which at vs. 13 would be supported by the *zaqeph qaton*. With respect to internal parallelism that would produce the word-pair וסער / הים. A consistent division, whether as unicolon or as bicolon, is to be preferred.

14aA	ויקראו אל־יהוה
14aB	ויאמרו
14aC	אנה יהוה
14bA	אל־נא נאבדה
14bB	בנפש האיש הזה
14bC	ואל־תתן עלינו דם נקיא

Int.par.:   ;יהוה / יהוה (14a) ;ויאמרו / ויקראו (14a)
            .ואל / אל / אל (14b) ;דם נקיא / בנפש (14b)
Ext.par.:   assonance .אל / אל // אל
Sep.up: tricolon; vocative; ;ויאמרו .אנה
Sep.down: tricolon; cohortative; jussive; .הזה ;אל־נא

14cA	כי־אתה יהוה
14cB	כאשר חפצת עשית
15aA	וישאו את־יונה
15aB	ויטלהו אל־הים
15aC	ויעמד הים מזעפו

Int.par.:   .הים / הים (15a)
Ext.par.:   –
Sep.up: ;כי־אתה vocative.[22]
Sep.down: tricolon.

16aA	וייראו האנשים
16aB	יראה גדולה את־יהוה
16bA	ויזבחו־זבח ליהוה
16bB	וידרו נדרים

Int.par.:   / ויזבחו־זבח (16b) ;יראה / וייראו (16a)
            .וידרו נדרים
Ext.par.:   .יהוה / יהוה
Sep.up: tautological par.
Sep.down: tautologism (2x).

2.3 The higher units of Jonah 1:1–16

We now reproduce the text in its entirety:

---

22 For a possible interpretation of יהוה as predicate of a nominal clause
see Van der Woude: 1978:27f.; as a vocative see *inter alia* Wolff: 1977:96;
G.Ch. Aalders, *Obadja en Jona* (COT; Kampen, 1958) 82.

A.I.1	ויהי דבר־יהוה	1aA
	אל־יונה בן־אמתי לאמר	1aB
	קום לך אל־נינוה	2aA
	העיר הגדולה	2aB
	וקרא עליה	2bA
	כי־עלתה רעתם לפני	2bB
A.I.2	ויקם יונה	3aA
	לברח תרשישה	3aB
	מלפני יהוה	3aC
	וירד יפו	3bA
	וימצא אניה באה תרשיש	3bB
	ויתן שכרה	3cA
	וירד בה	3cB
	לבוא עמהם תרשישה	3cC
	מלפני יהוה	3cD

- -

A.II.1	ויהוה הטיל רוח־גדולה אל־הים	4aA
	ויהי סער־גדול בים	4aB
	והאניה חשבה להשבר	4aC
	וייראו המלחים	5aA
	ויזעקו איש אל־אלהיו	5aB
	ויטלו את־הכלים	5bA
	אשר באניה אל־הים	5bB
	להקל מעליהם	5bC
A.II.2	ויונה ירד אל־ירכתי הספינה	5cA
	וישכב וירדם	5cB
	ויקרב אליו רב החבל	6aA
	ויאמר לו	6aB
	מה־לך נרדם	6bA
	קום קרא אל־אלהיך	6bB
	אולי יתעשת האלהים לנו	6bC
	ולא נאבר	6bD

==

B.I.1	ויאמרו איש אל־רעהו	7aA
	לכו ונפילה גורלות	7aB
	ונדעה	7aC
	בשלמי הרעה הזאת לנו	7aD
	ויפלו גורלות	7bA
	ויפל הגורל על־יונה	7bB

8aA	ויאמרו אליו	B.I.2
8aB	הגידה־נא לנו	
8aC	באשר למי־הרעה הזאת לנו	
8bA	מה־מלאכתך	
8bB	ומאין תבוא	
8bC	מה ארצך	
8bD	ואי־מזה עם אתה	

9aA	ויאמר אליהם	B.II.1
9aB	עברי אנכי	
9bA	ואת־יהוה אלהי השמים אני ירא	
9bB	אשר־עשה את־הים ואת־היבשה	

10aA	וייראו האנשים	B.II.2
10aB	יראה גדולה	
10aC	ויאמרו אליו	
10aD	מה־זאת עשית	
10bA	כי־ידעו האנשים	
10bB	כי־מלפני יהוה הוא ברח	
10bC	כי הגיד להם	

===

11aA	ויאמרו אליו	C.I.1
11aB	מה־נעשה לך	
11aC	וישתק הים מעלינו	
11b	כי הים הולך וסער	

12aA	ויאמר אליהם	C.I.2
12aB	שאוני והטילני אל־הים	
12aC	וישתק הים מעליכם	
12bA	כי יודע אני	
12bB	כי בשלי	
12bC	הסער הגדול הזה עליכם	

13aA	ויחתרו האנשים	C.I.3
13aB	להשיב אל־היבשה	
13aC	ולא יכלו	
13b	כי הים הולך וסער עליהם	

14aA	ויקראו אל־יהוה	C.II.1
14aB	ויאמרו	
14aC	אנה יהוה	
14bA	אל־נא נאבדה	
14bB	בנפש האיש הזה	
14bC	ואל־תתן עלינו דם נקיא	

14cA	C.II.2 כי־אתה יהוה
14cB	כאשר חפצת עשית
15aA	וישאו את־יונה
15aB	ויטלהו אל־הים
15aC	ויעמד הים מזעפו

16aA	C.II.3 וייראו האנשים
16aB	יראה גדולה את־יהוה
16bA	ויזבחו־זבח ליהוה
16bB	וידרו נדרים

Canticle A.I is formed via the parallelism קום לך אל־נינוה (vs. 2aA) // ויקם יונה לברח תרשישה (vs. 3aA,B) and כי־ לברח תרשישה מלפני יהוה (vs. 2bB) // עלתה רעתם לפני (vss. 3aB,C); and the responsion of 2bB with 3cC,D.

Canticle A.II is formed via the inclusion ויהוה (vs. 4aA) and האלהים (vs. 6bC), the responsion והאניה (vs. 4aC) and הספינה (vs. 5cA), the responsion המלחים (vs. 5aA) and רב (vs. 6aA), and the parallelism of ויזעקו ... אל־אלהיו (vs. 5aB) with קרא אל־אלהיך (vs. 6bB).

Canticle A.I and A.II are connected together via the prophetic call קום ... וקרא עליה (vss. 2aA,bA) and the command from the captain קום קרא אל־אלהיך (vs. 6bB) (assonance in לך [imper. of הלך, vs. 2aA] and לך [prep. ל with the suffix, vs. 6bA]). Mention must also be made of the responsions of the subjects: דבר יהוה (vs. 1aA) and ויהוה (vs. 4aA) and of יונה (vs. 3aA) and ויונה (vs. 5cA). Note too the parallelism of הגדולה (vs. 2aB) and גדול(ה) (vs. 4aA,B). Furthermore, we detect a neat 'onion' structure of the sub–canto:

קום וקרא	(vs. 2aA/bA)
ויקם	(vs. 3aA)
וירד	(vs. 3bA)
וירד	(vs. 3cB)
ירד	(vs. 5cA)
וישכב	(vs. 5cB)
קום קרא	(vs. 6bB)

The entire sub–canto is bracketed by the injunction קום (ו)קרא. Within this framework we note that Jonah's faulty arisal to flee (vs. 3aA) corresponds with his lying down to sleep (vs. 5cB). At the centre of the entire unit we see the

characterization of Jonah's action, namely ירד (3x). The central
kernel וירד (vs. 3cB) forms an antithetical responsion with
עלתה (vs. 2bB), which helps to clarify the entire unit. Jonah
does not wish to go to the city where the evil had risen up
before God (לפני), in order to 'call out' against her, which
explains why vs. 3c states, וירד בה לבוא ... מלפני יהוה.

Canticle B.I is formed via the responsions ... ויאמרו
בשלמי (vs. 8aA) and of ויאמרו אליו (vs. 8aA) and of אל־רעהו
באשר למי־הרעה הזאת לנו (vs. 7aD) with הרעה הזאת לנו (vs. 7aA)
(vs. 8aC).[23]

Canticle B.II is formed via the inclusion ויאמר אליהם (vs.
9aA) and הגיד להם (vs. 10bC) the responsion יהוה (vs. 9bA) and
יהוה (vs. 10bB) and the parallelisms of ירא (vs. 9bA) with
ייראו ... יראה (vs. 10aA,B) and of עשה (vs. 9bB) with עשית
(vs. 10aD).

Canticles B.I and B.II are connected together via responsion
of ויאמרו (vs. 7aA) and ויאמרו (vs. 10aC). Responsion is also
formed by איש (vs. 7aA) and האנשים (vs. 10aA), and an
inclusion is established between איש (vs. 7aA) and האנשים (vs.
10bA). ונדעה (vs. 7aC) forms an inclusion with ידעו (vs.
10bA). חזאת (vs. 7aD and 8aC) forms a responsion with
מה־זאת (vs. 10aD). A responsion is also formed by ויאמרו
הגידה־נא לנו (vs. 9aA). ויאמר אליהם (vs. 9aA). אליו
(vs. 8aB) and הגיד להם (vs. 10bC) constitute an inclusion. An
additional inclusion is formed by מה־מלאכתך (vs. 8bA) and
מה ... עשית (vs. 10aD).

Canticle C.I is formed via the responsions כי הים הולך וסער
(vs. 11b), הסער הגדול הזה עליכם (vs. 12bC) and כי הים

---

23 Vs. 8aC is frequently viewed as a gloss prompted by vs. 7aD (cf. inter
alia Wolff: 1977:83; Van der Woude: 1978:24). However, the text—critical
arguments based upon divergencies in the LXX traditions are insufficient to
demonstrate a secondary character for this phrase. Moreover, the structure
detended here demonstrates that this colon is not superfluous but forms a
clear parallelism with vs. 7aD. The fact that the question is repeated even
though the answer has already been given by the lot (see W. Rudolph,
Joel-Amos-Obadja-Jona [KAT XIII/2; Gütersloh, 1971] 340) can be
explained as the sailors' demand for an explicit clarification that Jonah is
responsible, which heightens the literary drama by forcing him to explain his
own position.

(vs. מעלינו (vs. 13b), by the parallelism הולך וסער עליהם
11aC), עליכם (vs. 12aC), מעליכם (vs. 12bC) and עליהם (vs.
13b), as well as the repetition of הים (vs. 11aC and b, 12aB
and aC and 13b).

Canticle C.II is formed via the inclusion of אל־ייהוה (vs.
14aA) and ליהוה (vs. 16bA) and a responsion with את־יהוה
(vs. 16aB). There is a responsion established between אנה
יהוה (vs. 14aC) and כי־אתה יהוה (vs. 14cA). The designation
of Jonah as האיש הזה (vs. 14bB) forms a responsion with
יונה (vs. 15aA) and the expression דם נקיא (vs. 14bC) stands
in responsion with וידבחו־דבח (vs. 16bA).

Canticles C.I and C.II are connected together via the
responsion of ויאמרו אליו (vs. 11aA), ויאמר אליהם (vs.
12aA) and ויקראו אל־ייהוה ויאמרו (vs. 14aA,B), as well as
by the inclusion of שאוני והטילני אל־הים וישחק הים (vs. 12aB,C) with מעליכם
וישאו את־יונה ויטלהו אל־הים (vs. 12aB,C) with מעליכם
ויעמד הים מזעפו (vs. 15). There is a responsion between
האנשים (vs. 13aA) and האנשים (vs. 16aA), and an important
responsion of נעשה (vs. 11aB) with עשית (vs. 14cB). The
external parallelism of C.II.2 suggests that the actions of the
sailors, as wel as the calming of the storm, can be viewed as
Yahweh's doing. This is confirmed by the responsion based on
עשה (in this respect cf. the responsion formed by the question
מה־נעשה לך [vs. 11aB] with שאוני והטילני אל־הים [vs.
12aB]).

The sub–cantos are joined by means of the inclusion formed by
בשלמי הרעה הזאת לנו (vs. 7aD/8aC) with (באשר למי־)
כי בשלי הסער הגדול הזה עליכם (vs. 12bB,C), and ונדעה
with כי יודע אנו in the same verses respectively. An inclusion
is formed by ויקם יונה לברח ... מלפני יהוה (vs. 3a) and
כי־מלפני יהוה הוא ברח (vs. 10bB), and an additional
inclusion is formed by קרא אל־אלהיך (vs. 6bB) and ויקראו
אל־ייהוה (vs. 14aA; cf. the parallel ויזעקו ... אל־אלהיו in vs.
5aB). Furthermore, note וייראו המלחים (vs. 5aA), וייראו
וייראו האנשים (vs. 10aA,B) and האנשים יראה גדולה
גדולה את־ייהוה (vs. 16aA,B) and compare in this regard
Jonah's feeble אני ירא (verse 9bA) in contrast to וייראו
האנשים יראה גדולה (vs. 10aA,B). Consider too the more or
less antithetical responsion of vs. 4 with vs. 15.

There are also connections between the corresponding canticles.

Note the responsion formed by כי־עלתה רעתם לפני (vs. 2bB)
and ויזבחו־זבח ליהוה (16bA), as well as the inclusion ויקרא
(vs. 2bA) and ויקראו (vs. 14aA). By means of these links,
canticles A.I and C.II embrace the entire canto. The
first—mentioned responsion is indicative at the central concern of
the entire canto. The evil which rose up before God makes way
for offerings and vows to Yahweh. And it is Yahweh's hand
which regulates everything to this end. He throws (טול) a storm
onto the sea; the sailors struggle bravely but in vain to salvage
the ship by throwing (טול) the cargo overboard and are finally
driven to casting of lots (נפל). When the result indicates that
they must throw (טול) Jonah overboard they refuse at first but
ultimately are coerced to comply (as noted above this too
actually is described as part of Yahweh's action, see the
discussion of sub—canto C). When the storm appears to subside,
they are filled with fear of Yahweh and they offer sacrifices to
him. Thus, Jonah's descent (ירד) from Yahweh's presence finds
a counterpart in the ascending offerings.

Vs. 4, in addition to the responsion with vs. 15, establishes a
responsion (also antithetical) with vs. 12a. The captain's query
to Jonah .... מה־לך (vs. 6bA) forms an inclusion with ... מה־
לך (vs. 11aB). Moreover, ולא (vs. 6bD) and ולא (vs. 13aC)
constitute an inclusion. Accordingly, the central sub—canto is
embraced by the two canticles A.II and C.I. For the connections
between canticles B.I and B.II see the discussion of sub—canto
B above.

4 Conclusion

On the basis of a total overview of the parallelisms at the level
of the canto, it is possible to discern a concentric structure
spanning the entire canto. This also is apparent from the
strophic structure of the canto in its entirety:

sub—cantos	canticles		strophes	verses
A	2	I	2	6 (3+3)
		II	2	6 (3+3)
B	2	I	2	4 (2+2)
		II	2	4 (2+2)
C	2	I	3	6 (2+2+2)
		II	3	6 (2+2+2)

We see here a strong regularity in the formation of the canto and it is only in the number of strophes that there is some irregularity visible. The number of verses per literary unit forms a symmetric arrangement consistent with the structure of the canto. This concentric structure argues for viewing Jonah 1 as a unity. Contrary to the opinion of many[24] vss. 1–3 ought not to be severed from the rest of the chapter. The integral connection of vss. 1–3 to the bulk of the canto is evident in the 'onion' structure within sub–canto A. Consequently, we are forced to subject the traditional division of Jonah 1 and the concentric structure of vss. 4–16, to reconsideration.[25]

In the preceding analysis we have noted the employment of parallelism, responsion and inclusion in Jonah 1. These literary devices constitute three characteristic indicators of Hebrew poetry. Jonah 1:1–16 thus appears to constitute a carefully composed portion of the entire book. The results found here in the first chapter of Jonah suggest that the book in its entirety is similarly composed and accordingly belongs to the category of 'poetic narrative' and as such it is a literary artwork demonstrating much in common with the book of Ruth.[26] It presents a very refined description of the actions of Jonah and of Yahweh by employment of the stylistic devices indigenous to poetic narrative.

---

24 Cf. n. 13 and 14 above.

25 By accomodating vs. 16b within the structure of the entire chapter, we are able to do justice to one of the criticisms rightly raised by Rudolph: 1971:340 n.1 against the concentric structure of vss. 4–16.

26 Cf. n.4 and 5 above. Since the completion of this article the study by Christensen mentioned in n. 6 above has appeared under the title 'Narrative Poetics and the Interpretation of the Book of Jonah' in: Elaine R. Follis (ed.), *Directions in Biblical Hebrew Poetry* (Sheffield, 1987) 29–48. It does not cause me to change the conclusions reached in this study.

172

MICAH 1

A Structural Approach

Johannes C. de Moor

1 Introduction[1]

The scholarly debate on the composition and date of Micah 1 exemplifies how the literary and form critical approaches to the Old Testament may sometimes end up in dissent, distraction even.

Those who regard the chapter as a relatively complete literary unit are usually forced to accept a date before 722 B.C. for the whole chapter because verses 6 and 7 announce the fall of Samaria.[2] For these scholars the very clear references to military action in the Shephelah which we encounter in vss. 10—15 form a major problem. No historical events of this nature are known to have taken place shortly before 722.[3]

Others detach vss. 8—16 from vss. 2—7,[4] arguing that the data of the former agree perfectly with the events of 701 B.C. when Sennacherib marched against Jerusalem after having

---

1   Thanks are due to Paul Sanders and Herman de Vries for their assistence in preparing this paper.

2   Typical representatives of this point of view are W. Rudolph, *Micha. Nahum. Habakuk. Zephanja* (KAT; Gütersloh, 1975) 39 and A.S. van der Woude, *Micha* (POT; Nijkerk, 1976) 19ff. (as a matter of fact, Van der Woude discerns three distinct parts: 2—9, 10—12, 13—16); H.—W. Wolff, *Dodekapropheton: Micha* (BK; Neukirchen—Vluyn, 1980) 22f.

Recently, a date of 725 to 723 has been argued for the siege of Samaria, cf. B. Becking, *De ondergang van Samaria* (Meppel, 1985) 22—72.

3   This was one reason for G. Fohrer, 'Micha 1', in: *Das ferne und das nahe Wort*. Festschrift L. Rost (BZAW 105; Berlin, 1967) 65—80, to propose a date between 722 and 711.

4   So, with minor variations, J. Lindblom, *Micha literarisch untersucht* (Helsingfors, 1929) 17; E. Sellin, *Das Zwölfprophetenbuch* (KAT Bd. 1; Leipzig, 1929[2-3]) 309ff.; V. Fritz, 'Das Wort gegen Samaria Mi 1,2—7', *ZAW* 86 (1974) 316—331; B. Renaud, *La formation du livre de Michée* (Paris, 1977) 9ff.; L. Alonso Schökel—J.L. Sicre Diaz, *Profetas* (Nueva Biblia Española, t.2; Madrid, 1980) 1042ff.

subdued the plain of the Philistines. This, however, creates a number of other problems. An incision after vs. 7 means that the suffix of מכותיה 'her wounds' in vs. 9 lacks an antecedent. It is hardly convincing to eliminate this problem by emending MT.[5] Moreover, vs. 5 explicitly mentions the sins of Judah and Jerusalem. If vss. 8–16 is detached from vss. 2–7, only Samaria would have been punished for its sins. Of course this too can be remedied — by simple deletion of the offending cola vs. 5b–c.[6] Against the dating in 701 it is remarked that at that time Gath (vs. 10) was not even in the hands of Judah any longer,[7] and that vss. 13–15 speak of 'Israel' which is deemed impossible after the fall of Samaria in 722.

In general, it may be said that most modern commentators have to excise more or less substantial portions from the transmitted text in an attempt to solve the problems it poses.[8]

In the present study we want to investigate whether a careful structural analysis according to the method developed by the Kampen School may throw some light on this difficult chapter.

2 The Structured Text

Structure of Micah 1:2–16

A.I.1

‎– שמעו עמים כלם (2aA)
‎הקשיבי ארץ ומלאה (2aB)
‎– ויהי אדני יהוה בכם לעד (2bA)
‎אדני מהיכל קדשו (2bB)

---

5   Cf. J. Taylor, *The Massoretic Text and the Ancient Versions of the Book of Micah* (London, 1890) 18: 'At all events it is difficult to believe that the M.T., which is the harder reading, would have been introduced in place of the easier sing., and, on the other hand, the plu. is not contrary to Heb. Grammar.'

6   So a host of scholars, even Van der Woude: 1976:32f. See note 8.

7   Sargon II would have taken it in 712/711, cf. K. Galling, *Textbuch zur Geschichte Israels* (Tübingen, 1968[2]) 63f.

8   E.g., Sellin: 1929[2–3]:306ff.: 2b, 7a, 13b; Th. Lescow, 'Redaktions-geschichtliche Analyse von Micha 1–5', *ZAW* 84 (1972) 58ff.: 2, 5b–c, 6–7, 13b–c; Fritz: 1974: 2–7; Rudolph: 1975:33ff.: 5c, 13b–c; J.L. Mays, *Micah*, A Commentary (The O.T. Library; Philadelphia, 1976) 40ff.: 2, 5b–c, 6–7, 13b–c, 16; Renaud: 1977:9ff., 53ff.: 2, 5b–c, 13b–c; J. Vermeylen, *Du prophète Isaïe à l'apocalyptique* (t.2; Paris, 1978) 574ff.: 5b–c, 13b–c, 16; Wolff: 1980:19: 2–5, 7a, 13b–c.

A.I.2

כי הנה יהוה יצא ממקומו (3aA) –
וירד ודרך על במותי ארץ (3aB)
ונמסו ההרים תחתיו (4aA) –
והעמקים יתבקעו (4aB)
כדונג מפני האש (4bA) –
כמים מגרים במורד (4bB)

A.I.3

בפשע יעקב כל זאת (5aA) –
ובחטאות בית ישראל (5aB)
מי פשע יעקב (5bA) –
הלוא שמרון (5bB)
ומי במות יהודה (5cA) –
הלוא ירושלם (5cB)

– –

A.II.1

ושמתי שמרון לעי השדה (6aA) –
למטעי כרם (6aB)
והגרתי לגי אבניה (6bA) –
ויסדיה אגלה (6bB)

A.II.2

וכל פסיליה יכתו (7aA) –
וכל אתנניה ישרפו באש (7aB)
וכל עצביה אשים שממה (7aC)
כי מאתנן זונה קבצה (7bA) –
ועד אתנן זונה ישובו (7bB)

A.II.3

על זאת אספדה ואילילה (8aA) –
אילכה שילל וערום (8aB)
אעשה מספד כתנים (8bA) –
ואבל כבנות יענה (8bB)

A.II.4

כי אנושה מכותיה (9aA) –
כי באה עד יהודה (9aB)
נגע עד שער עמי (9bA) –
עד ירושלם (9bB)

= =

B.I.1

בגת אל תגידו (10aA) –
בכו אל תבכו (10aB)
בבית לעפרה (10bA) –
עפר התפלשתי (10bB)

B.I.2

עברי לכם (11aA) –
יושבת שפיר (11aB)
עריה (11bA) –
בשת (11bB)

B.I.3

לא יצאה (11cA) –
יושבת צאנן (11cB)
מספד בית האצל (11dA) –
יקח מכם עמדתו (11dB)

B.I.4

כי חלה לטוב (12aA) –
יושבת מרות (12aB)
כי ירד רע מאת יהוה (12bA) –
לשער ירושלם (12bB)

– – – – – – – – – – – – – – – – – – – –

B.II.1

רתם המרכבה לרכש (13aA) –
יושבת לכיש (13aB)
[(ראשית חטאת היא (13bA] –
[(לבת ציון (13bB]
כי בך נמצאו (13cA) –
פשעי ישראל (13cB)

B.II.2

לכן תתני שלוחים (14aA) –
על מורשת גת (14aB)
בתי אכזיב לאכזב (14bA) –
למלכי ישראל (14bB)

B.II.3

עד הירש אבי לך (15aA) –
יושבת מרשה (15aB)
עד עדלם יבוא (15bA) –
כבוד ישראל (15bB)

B.II.4

– קרחי וגדי (16aA)
על בני העוגיך (16aB)
– הרחבי קרחתך כנשר (16bA)
כי גלו ממך (16bB)

3 Motivation of the Structural Analysis

3.1 Strophes and Canticles

The Massoretic division of the text is in favour of a structural whole. The *setūmā* at the end of the chapter is the only ancient division and it is backed by Mur. 88, a manuscript of the second century A.D.

A.I.1 — Separation upwards: imperatives; vocatives.
Separation downwards: jussive יהי; tautology אדני / אדני.

Vs. 2a and 2b are also connected by content. Because the holy palace in vs. 2bB is a designation of the heavenly abode of God (cf. vs. 3a), this forms an external parallel with 'earth' in vs. 2aB. Moreover, שמע and עד form an attested pair.[9]

A.I.2 — Separation upwards: כי; הנה.
Separation downwards: tautology כ / כ.

The external parallelism binding the verses of this strophe together is evident: 'heights' / 'mountains', 'tread upon' / 'under him', 'melt' / 'wax', 'water' / 'wax' (cf. Ps. 22:15), ירד / מורד.

A.I.3 — Separation upwards: dominating position of the adjuncts; tautology ב / ב.
Separation downwards: מי; הלוא (the repetition neutralizes the separating effect of the same words in vs. 5b).

Again the external parallelism leaves no room for doubt: פשע / ירושלם, שמרון / שמרון, ישראל / יעקוב, יעקוב / פשע, יהודה / ישראל (inclusion). However, also במות and חטאות form such a pair (Hos. 10:8), and therefore it is not advisable to follow the early emendation of the LXX, Targum and Peshitta.

---

9 Isa. 43:9; 44:8; Prov. 21:28, cf. Jer. 6:10; 11:7; Am. 3:13; Ps. 50:7; 81:9; Job 29:11.

It is justified to regard the three strophes we have just identified as one canticle (stanza), because together they form the indictment which is followed by the verdict from vs. 6 onward. Moreover, the three strophes are connected by external parallelism: עמים (2aA) / יהודה (5cA) (inclusion); ארץ (2aB, 3aB); יהוה (2bA, 3aA); במותי / במות (3aB, 5cA). As we shall see, all other canticles of the canto consist of 8 verses. This should serve to make us weary of the proposals to delete two verses from vs. 5.

A.II.1 — Separation upwards: transition from one genre (indictment) to another (verdict).
        Separation downwards: tautological –יה.
External parallelism: אבניה / עי.

A.II.2 — Separation upwards: tricolon; tautology וכל / וכל.
        Separation downwards: כי; tautology דונה / דונה.
External parallelism: אתנן (7aB, 7bB).

A.II.3 — Separation upwards: emphatical על זאת;
        cohortatives; assonance.
        Separation downwards: tautology כ / כ.
External parallelism: מספד / אספדה.

A.II.4 — Separation upwards: two times כי.
        Separation downwards: tautology עד / עד.
External parallelism: ירושלם / יהודה, but also נגע / בוא [10].
The canticle A.II is embraced by the inclusion Samaria (6aA)/ Jerusalem (9bB). The laying 'bare' of Samaria (6bB) is imitated by the mourning prophet (8aB).

B.I.1 — Separation upwards: jussives; tautology אל / אל;
        paronomasia.[11]
        Separation downwards: imperative; assonance.

---

10 Cf. Ezek. 7:12; Job 4:5; Prov. 6:29; Eccl. 12:10.

11 In בכו no place name is hiding, in spite of the οἶ ἐν ᾽Ακιμ of the best LXX text. As observed by K. Elliger, 'Der Heimat des Propheten Michas', *ZDPV* 57 (1934) 84, only one place name per poetic (not Massoretic) verse is punned in vss. 10–15.

Therefore בכו has to be regarded as a masculine form of the absolute infinitive of בכה. Both in Hebrew (Bergsträsser, *HG*, 2, § 30a) and in Ugaritic (e.g., 'n from 'ny) such forms are attested. Since vs. 10aA is an obvious reference to 2 Sam. 1:20, vs. 10aB may be understood as countermanding 2 Sam. 1:24, where the daughters of Israel were invited to weep over Saul.

178   *Johannes C. de Moor*

External parallelism: place names; גת / החפלשתי.[12]

B.I.2 – Separation upwards: imperative; vocative.

Separation downwards: extremely short cola.[13]

External parallelism: probably antithetical parallelism between 'nakedness', 'shame' and שפיר.[14]

B.I.3 – Separation upwards: assonance.

Separation downwards: emphasized position of subject.

External parallelism: place names; יקח מכם עמדתו / לא יצאה (inclusion).[15]

---

12   Usually the Qere החפלשי is preferred. Some scholars follow Targum, Peshitta and Vulgate in reading the plural החפלשו / תגידו. However, it is very hard to explain the Ketib if it did not constitute the original reading. Whoever would insert a ת in a perfectly understandable החפלשי (cf. Jer. 6:26)? It is safer to accept the Ketib as being the *lectio difficilior.* In our opinion it is an *ad hoc* invention meaning 'behave like a Philistine' (compare התנבא, 'to behave like a prophet'), used as a transparent pun on החפלשי 'wallow in dust'. The unnamed subject is the same as that of עברי in the next verse, the יושבת שפיר. Finally, עפר is in the accusative of place (cf. GK § 118 d–g), or the preposition ב in בבית may be regarded as a so–called double–duty preposition (cf. F. Rosenthal, *Or* 8 (1939) 230f.; M. Dahood, *UF* 1 (1969) 27–29; *Psalms III* (Anchor Bible; Garden City, 1970) 435–437).

13   On the phenomenon of cola of only one word, see M.C.A. Korpel–J.C. de Moor, 'Fundamentals of Ugaritic and Hebrew Poetry', *UF* 18 (1986) 177f. (reprinted above, pp.7ff.). For the pair עריה / בשת see 1 Sam. 20:30.

14   The unidentified (*pace* W.G. Dever, *Qadmoniot* 4 (1971) 90) place name שפיר probably means 'fair, beautiful', as in Aramaic (*DISO*, 317). It is an invented name, a purposefully enigmatic designation of Jerusalem (see the tell–tale מכם in vs. 11), the daughter of Zion dwelling in 'large and beautiful houses' (Isa. 5:9). It balances the equally unidentified יושבת מרות, those who dwell in bitterness (vs. 12a), i.e., the country–dwellers who have to suffer for the sake of the capital (vs. 12b) – a major theme in Micah's prophecies.

The use of such invented names was common among the prophets, see Hos. 4:15; Ezek. 2:5–8; 3:9,26, etc.

15   The verb יצא doubtlessly has the military meaning of 'march out' here. Therefore the *hapax legomenon* עמדה should be explained with the help of the Akkadian *imittu* (from the same root), the 'standard' that was carried before the troops. When the officers from Jerusalem pass through the villages (עברי, vs. 11) to mobilize the army, they will find no one willing to do service.

B.I.4 — Separation upwards: כי.
     Separation downwards: כי.
External parallelism: ירושלם / מרות ;רע / טוב ;כי / כי.
  The canticle B.I. is marked by the puns on place names and the recurring ירושבת. Its literary form has a number of interesting parallels that merit further study: Num. 21:27−30; Isa. 10:28−32; 15:1−9; 17:1−3; Jer. 46:3−5; 48:1−5, 18−20; Hos. 5:8−9; Am. 5:5; Zeph. 2:4.

B.II.1 — Separation upwards: imperative;[16] vocative.
     Separation downwards: כי; emphatic position of בך.
External parallelism: ישראל / לכיש. At first sight one might be inclined to add the parallelism between חטאת and פשע. However, the indications that vs. 13b (not vs. 13c) should be regarded as a gloss[17] are too strong:

1) Vs. 13b disrupts the direct oration of vs. 13a and vs. 13c.
2) In vs. 13b the inhabitants of Zion are designated as בת, whereas the whole passage uses ירושבת.
3) The parenthetic clause 'this was the beginning (or: the most important) of the sin(s) of/for the daughter of Zion' would abruptly refer back to Jerusalem.
4) It is much more natural to regard it as a gloss explaining what the sins of Lachish were, namely reliance on military force, just like the capital (cf. Isa. 2:7−8; 30:16; 31:1−3; Hos. 14:4; Mic. 5:9,12).
5) The formula חטאת היא appears to be borrowed from the Priestly Code (cf. Lev. 5:11,12; Num. 19:9).

---

16 The *hapax legomenon* רתם might be an infinitive (for imperative, cf. König, *Syntax*, § 205c; GK § 110k) of a denominative verb derived from רתם (*rōtem*) 'broom'. The latter was used to make ropes, so that the meaning might be 'bind', cf. A. Caquot, *JANES* 5 (1973) 49; Z. Zevit, *IEJ* 27 (1977) 116. It is also possible to assume that a defectively written imperative os a verb רתה with enclitic *mem* is involved: רתם = *rattima*, cf. Akkad. *retû*, Arab. *ratā(w)* 'bind, attach.'
17 Mostly scholars delete both vs. 13b and vs. 13c. See in addition to the authors cited in n. 8, I. Willi−Plein, *Vorformen der Schriftexegese innerhalb des Alten Testaments* (BZAW 123; Berlin, 1971) 74. But Sellin: 1929$^{2-3}$:315 was right in observing that no objective arguments can be marshalled against the authenticity of vs. 13c.

In fact, the structural analysis of the whole chapter provides us with an extra argument; all canticles consist of eight verses.

B.II.2 — Separation upwards: לכן.

Separation downwards: none, but since the sentence runs on in vs. 14b, none was needed.

External parallelism: Mic. 1:10—16 contains some explicit references to episodes in the life of David, connected with this particular area (vss. 10, 15). The only time in the history of the Davidic dynasty that a town was presented as a שלוחים to a king of Israel was under Solomon, and significantly it was a town formerly occupied by the Philistines (1 Kgs. 9:16). So there is bitter irony in Micah's exhortation to burden his native town מורשת גת, 'the place inherited from Gath', with a town by way of שלוחים. Its fate will be the fate of Gezer, the שלוחים of Solomon, that had been taken from the Davidic dynasty only a few decades before by Tiglathpileser III.[18] Incidentally, this explains the enigmatic expression 'the kings of Israel'. If he wanted to allude to the time of Solomon, to the loss of Gezer ca. 733 under Ahaz, and to the policy of the present king of Judah (in our opinion Hezekiah, see below), Micah could do so only in using the comprehensive term 'kings of Israel' as a designation of the Davidic dynasty.

B.II.3 — Separation upwards: emphatic position of עד; vocative.

Separation downwards: emphatic position of the adjunct.

External parallelism: place names; assonance עד / עד.

B.II.4 — Separation upwards: imperatives.

Separation downwards: imperative; כי.

External parallelism: קרחתך / קרחי; suffixes.

The coherence of this canticle is indicated again by the play on names and words, as well as the responsions involving יושבת (vss. 13aB, 15aB) and ישראל (vss. 13cB, 14cB, 15bB).

3.2 *The Sub-cantos*

Our structural analysis shows that all four canticles count eight

---

18 Cf. M. Wäfler, *Nicht-Assyrer neuassyrischer Darstellungen* (AOAT 26; Neukirchen—Vluyn, 1975) 23f.

verses. As has been observed by several others, it is difficult to detach vss. 2–5 (A.I) from vss. 6–9 (A.II). שמרון (5bB and 6–9aA), יהודה (5cA and 9aB), and ירושלם (5cB and 9bB, responsion) are all mentioned in both canticles. It now appears that the two canticles are also enclosed by an inclusion: עמים (2aA) / עמי (9bA). If vs. 9 belongs to sub–canto A, there is no need whatsoever to delete vs. 5c, because vs. 9 announces that the impending fall of Samaria will be followed by an attack on Jerusalem. So both Samaria and Jerusalem are threatened with doom, just as they had both been indicted.

The equal number of verses of the two canticles, the concatenation מהיכל (2bB) / ממקומו (3aA), and the inclusion mentioned above strongly argue against the proposals to strike vs. 2. Mostly this is justified with the argument that the universalism expressed in vs. 2 would be incompatible with the authorship of an eighth century prophet. However, this is a prejudice based on certain theories about the development of the religion of Israel. It is time to reconsider these theories. Every scholar acquainted with the literature of Egypt and Mesopotamia knows that universalism was not a late phenomenon in the world of the Old Testament.

A similar conclusion may be drawn with regard to the canticles B.I (vss. 10–12) and B.II (vss. 13–16). Both are characterized by the play of words and the repetition of ישבת. Here too we find a strong inclusion marking the beginning and end; both in vs. 10 and vs. 16 a woman is exhorted to mourn. Both vs. 10 and vs. 15 refer to episodes in the life of David. B.I and B.II cannot be detached.

The conclusion must be that our structural analysis confirms the judgment of those scholars who divided Micah 1 into vss. 2–9 and vss. 10–16.[19]

3.3 *The Canto*

Can the sub–cantos A and B be viewed as independent compositions? The symmetry we discovered argues against this:

---

19   J.M.P. Smith *et al.*, *A Critical and Exegetical Commentary on Micah, Zephaniah, Nahum, Habakkuk, Obadiah and Joel* (Edinburgh, 1911) 32, 41; Fohrer: 1967; Willi–Plein: 1971:70ff.; L.C. Allen, *The Books of Joel, Obadiah, Jonah and Micah* (Grand Rapids, 1976) 241f., 266ff.

both consist of two canticles of eight verses each. Moreover, the rites of mourning described in vss. 8, 10—12 and 16 (responsion) argue against the hypothesis of totally independent compositions. The 'uncovering' of Samaria (6bB) is matched by the 'nakedness' of Judah (11bA) (responsion). The 'love—gifts' of Samaria (vs. 7) find a parallel in the 'bride—gift' for Moreseth—Gath (vs. 14aA) (responsion). The crucial phrase עד שער ... ירושלם (vs. 9b) is answered by לשער ירושלם (vs. 12b) (responsion). Also, יהוה ... ירד (vs. 3a) is echoed by ירד ... יהוה (vs. 12b) (inclusion). Finally, the phrases פשע יעקב / חטאות ... ישראל (vs. 5) correspond to פשעי ישראל in vs. 13cB (inclusion). It appears that the interrelations are too specific to attribute them to mere chance. The sub—cantos A and B belong together and so the result of our structural analysis seems to contradict the almost unanimous verdict of the historical—critical study of Micah 1.

4 The Date of the Sub—Cantos

4.1 The Date of Sub—Canto A

It would seem certain that verses 2—9 can only be dated shortly before the fall of Samaria. Its destruction is announced in the future tense (vss. 6—7). The city is 'weakened' by its 'wounds' (vs. 9aA), but apparently it did not yet succumb. The prophet expects that soon afterwards Jerusalem too will be attacked (vs. 9). Even though no raid by the troops of Shalmaneser V against Jerusalem is attested in historical records, it may well be that Micah, just like Isaiah, expected such an attack (cf. Isa. 10:5—11, 28—32). So sub—canto A is best dated in 722 or shortly before.

4.2 The Date of Sub—Canto B

Against the dating of the second sub—canto in 701 it has been argued that Gath, mentioned in vs. 10, was no longer a Judaean city after 712/711 B.C. However, it would seem likely that Hezekiah's rebellion against Assyria, to which the campaign of Sennacherib in 701 was the answer, was aimed, *inter alia*, at recapturing the cities of the Philistines (2 Kgs. 18:7—8). Several scholars believe that Hezekiah succeeded in re—taking Gath ca.

703 B.C.[20]

As a matter of fact, even if this hypothesis proves to be false, the objection is hardly decisive. The prophet wants to deny the inhabitants of Gath a malicious delight in the misery of Judah because now their arch—enemy, too, is defeated by the Assyrians. It is immaterial, then, whether Gath was an Assyrian city since 712/711, or only since a few days previously in 701.

A second objection involves the use of 'Israel' in vss. 13—15. As we have seen, it is stated that this is impossible after 722. Especially the term 'kings of Israel' in vs. 14 would only have been used before the fall of Samaria. As we have seen, however, the allusions the prophet wanted to make forced him to choose a most general term, which could include even king Solomon. Now that we have completed the structural analysis of the whole canto we may go a step further. If it is true that sub—canto A and sub—canto B cannot be separated, and if there is insufficient reason to strike vs. 13cB, Judah is called 'Israel' here for the very good reason that *the sins of Israel are found in Judah*. And just as Israel had to pay heavily for its sins, so Judah will find it impossible to extricate itself from the Assyrian occupation. The 'elite of Israel' will have to go into hiding (vs. 15b), as in the days of David (2 Sam. 22:1f.).[21]

What were the sins the prophet wanted to expose? Was not Hezekiah a pious king? Especially vs. 13 may be adduced in favour of the hypothesis that Micah criticized Hezekiah's trust in military power. In 5:9f., which was pronounced earlier than 1:13, Micah had already equated the trust in military power with idolatry. Isaiah criticized Hezekiah in more or less the same terms shortly before 701.[22] It appears that Hezekiah did a lot to fortify the cities of Judah (2 Chron. 32:5, 29). At least Jerusalem, Lachish, Achzib,[23] Adullam and Maresha[24] were fortified cities, and they are all mentioned in the second

---

20 N. Na'aman, 'Sennacherib's "Letter to God" on his Campaign to Judah', *BASOR* 214 (1974) 25—39; 'Sennacherib's Campaign to Judah and the Date of the *lmlk* Stamps', *VT* 29 (1979) 61—86; E. Vogt, *Der Aufstand Hiskias und die Belagerung Jerusalems 701 v. Chr.* (Rom, 1986) 8.

21 Cf. Isa. 5:13; 10:3; 17:3—4. Also in Mic. 3:1,8f. sinful Judah = 'Israel'.

22 Isa. 30:15f., cf. 20:1—6, and Vogt: 1986:6—9.

23 Lachish Letter No. 8.

24 2 Chron. 11:7f.

sub—canto.

The strongest arguments in favour of a dating in 701 are vs. 13, where Lachish is invited to mobilize, and vs. 16 where the deportation of the children of Lachish is announced. Lachish was captured early in the campaign of 701. The siege of the town is mentioned explicitly in 2 Chron. 32:9, and is presupposed by 2 Kgs. 19:8. The siege is depicted on Assyrian reliefs.[25] The annals of Sennacherib himself confirm that he first advanced against the cities of the Shephelah.[26] In the end Jerusalem narrowly escaped,[27] but a very large number of Judaeans from the countryside was deported.[28] Therefore we agree with F.J. Gonçalves in concluding: 'On the basis of what we know about Judah in the time of Micah, no other moment does fit the situation presupposed by our passage even remotely as well [as 701 B.C.].'[29]

5 Conclusion

How can our findings in paragraph 3 and 4 be reconciled? The structural analysis points in the direction of a well—balanced literary whole. The most likely dating of the sub—cantos, however, indicates that they were pronounced at different times, 722 and 701 B.C. respectively.

In our opinion the only possible explanation is that Micah

---

25 *ANEP*, No. 371—374; D. Ussishkin, *The Conquest of Lachish by Sennacherib* (Tel Aviv, 1982).

26 R. Borger, *BAL* I, 73; II, 60ff.

27 A. van der Kooij, *ZDPV* 102 (1986) 93—109.

28 The number of 200.150 mentioned by Sennacherib himself may be grossly exaggerated, but it is certain that many people were allotted to various armies and forced labour projects in Assyria. Cf. C. van Leeuwen, 'Sanchérib devant Jérusalem', *OTS* 14 (1965) 247; B. Oded, *Mass Deportations and Deportees in the Neo—Assyrian Empire* (Wiesbaden, 1979) 18f.; S. Stohlmann, 'The Judaean Exile after 701 B.C.E.' in: W.W. Hallo *et al.* (eds.), *Scripture in Context II*. More Essays on the Comparative Method (Winona Lake, 1983) 147—175; F.J. Gonçalves, *L'expédition de Sennachérib en Palestine dans la littérature hébraïque ancienne* (Louvain—la—Neuve, 1986) 115.

29 Gonçalves: 1986:283: 'D'après ce que nous savons de l'histoire de Juda au temps de Michée, aucun autre moment ne correspond aussi bien — ni même de loin — à la situation supposée par notre passage.'

himself later attached the second sub—canto to the first one, choosing a matching poetical structure. Shortly before 722 he had expected that the Assyrians would attack Jerusalem too (vss. 5c, 9). It was not the first time that he had announced doom over Jerusalem.[30] Then, ca. 734 B.C., nothing had happened. In 722 and during its aftermath,[31] Jerusalem was spared again. Glad as he may have been for the respite, all this must have been hard for Micah to understand. Is it not a natural reaction, then, that the prophet expected that YHWH would yet put him in the right when Sennacherib invaded his own region in 701? It was in that state of mind that he actualized his prophecy of 722 (vss. 2—9) by adding a second sub—canto (vss. 10—16).

We are happy to note we are not the first to envisage such a solution. More than twenty years ago H. Donner wrote:

'... the arguments in favour of an essential and temporal connectedness [of Mic. 1:10—16] with the preceding [1:2—9] merit serious consideration. It appears to be possible to regard the lamentation [1:10—16] as an explanation of vs. 9, the final colon of which forms a transition to what follows, also from a metrical point of view. The composition of the three speeches into a larger whole may well be the result of secondary, perhaps literary combinatory activity which in that case is best attributed to Micah himself, or to his followers.'[32]

---

30 We believe that Mic. 3:12 was pronounced under Jotham, shortly before Ahaz became king.

31 Becking: 1985:73ff.

32 H. Donner, *Israel unter den Völkern* (SVT 11; Leiden, 1964) 96f.: 'die Gründe, die für eine sachliche und zeitliche Zusammengehörigkeit mit dem Vorausgegangenen sprechen, wiegen schwer. Es erweist sich als möglich, das Klagelied als eine Explikation des V.9 zu verstehen, dessen zweite Halbzeile auch metrisch zum Folgenden überleitet. Die Komposition der drei Sprüche zu einem größeren Ganzen kann das Resultat sekundärer, vielleicht literarischer Zusammenfügung sein, die denn am ehesten Micha selbst oder seinen Anhängern zuzuschreiben wäre.'

CLASSICAL HEBREW METRICS AND ZEPHANIAH 2–3

Harm W.M. van Grol

In this essay I wish to present my theory of classical Hebrew versification and metrics, which is more elaborately delineated in my dissertation.[1] This theory will be illustrated with recourse to Zeph. 2:13–15, 3:1–5, 6–8, 14–17. These four poems are not analyzed in my dissertation, and their treatment here will also facilitate a test of the previous conclusions.[2] The fact that many scholars allege multiple 'historical layers' in this text adds to its interest here (see 1). In light of the nature of my thesis this study will concentrate primarily upon the question of metrics (3 and 4). Broader questions pertaining to versification can only be handled summarily (2).

1 Presentation of the text

1.1 Introduction

I designate four poems: 2:13–15, 3:1–5, 6–8, 14–17. Verbal repetitions confirm the internal unity of these poems (see 2). 3:14–17 is ordinarily split into 3:14–15 and 16–17, but there is no literary–stylistic reason for such a division. The external boundaries of the poems are satisfactorily established by thematic transitions and change of subject, and by the rhetorical indicators (*hoy* in 3:1 and the imperatives in 3:14). Zeph. 3:9–13 is not handled in this study; the three introductions (*ki–'az* in vss. 9 and 11b and *bayyom hahu'* in vs. 11a), along with the text–critical problem in vs. 10 obscure detection of the structure of these verses. Nor is 3:18a/b–20 handled; these verses are comprised of secondary prose, or prosaic poetry.

---

1   H.W.M. van Grol, *De versbouw in het klassieke hebreeuws*. Fundamentele verkenningen. Deel één: Metriek (Dutch; English summary; Amsterdam, 1986; Dissertation, Catholic Theological University of Amsterdam, under the supervision of Prof. dr. W.A.M. Beuken and Prof. dr. N.J. Tromp. This dissertation can be purchased from the author c/o K.T.U.A. [Keizersgracht 105], Postbus 19481, 1000 GL Amsterdam).

2   Twelve texts from various historical periods and genres are analyzed in my dissertation, i.e. Num. 23:7–10; 2 Sam. 1:19–27; Isa. 1:21–26; 5:1–7; 62; Joel 1:5–14; 4:9–17; Ps. 6; 121; 130; Prov. 8; 30:10–33.

1.2 The Text

SIGLA:

(1) The verse structure is presented under the column heading 'pattern':

    _____ = border of the strophe;
    ==== = border of the stanza.

(2) The Masoretic accentuation is given above the transcription:
    ´ = disjunctive accent;
    ` = conjunctive accent;
    .. = *metheg* (if significant).

(3) My own accentuation is given under the transcription:
    s = strongly stressed syllable, beat;
    w = weakly stressed syllable, (part of the) offbeat;
    – = deletion of auxiliary vowel, *hatep* or *shewa*.

(4) The analysis of rhythm. The rhythmic verse—line patterns are presented in the column 'pattern', the metrical themes in the column 'theme'.

Zephaniah 2:13–15; 3:1–5, 6–8, 14–17   pattern theme

13a *wᵉyéṭ yadó ʿal–ṣapón / wi'abbéd 'et–'aššúr*   3+2   3+2
   w s w s w w s   w w s w w s

13b *wᵉyaśém 'et–ninᵉwé lišmamá / ṣiyyá kammidbár* 3+2
   w w s   w w w s w w s   w s w w s _____

14a *wᵉrabᵉṣù bᵉtokàh ʿᵃdarím / kol–ḥayto–góy*   3+2
   w w s w w w s   w w s   w s w s

14b *gam–qa'át gam–qippód / bᵉkaptoréha yalínu*   2+2
   w   w s w   w s   w w w s w w s w

                                                 ====

14c *qól yᵉšorèr bahallón / ḥoreb bassáp /*
   s w w s   w w s   s – w s

                          kì 'arzá ʿérá[3]   (3+2+2)
                          w w s w s

                                            ====

---

3   The unintelligibility of 2:14c and the accompanying text—critical

15a *zót ha'ir ha'allizá / hayyošèbet labétaḥ*   3+2
     s   ws   wwws   w ws − ws −

15b *ha'om^erá bilbabáh / '^aní w^e'apsi 'ód*   2+3
     w w ws   w w s   s w ws w s

15c *'ék hay^età k^ešammá / marbéṣ lahayyá*   3+2
     s   wswww   s   ws   ww s

15d *kól 'obèr 'aléha yišróq / yaní^{a'} yadó*   3+2
     w   ws   wswws   ws− ws

1   *hòy mor^e'á w^enig'alá / ha'ir hayyoná*   3+2   3+2
     s   wws   ww ws   ws w w s
                                                        =========
2a   *lò šam^e'á b^eqól / lò laq^eḥá musár*   2+2   2+2
     w w s w w s   w w s w   w s

2b   *bayhwh lò batáḥa / 'el−'^elohèha lò qarèba*   2+2
     w w s w w s w   w ww s w w w s w

3a   *śarèha b^eqirbáh / '^arayót šo'^agím*   2+2
     w s w ww s   ww s   ww s

3b   *šop^eṭéha z^e'èbe 'éreb / lò gar^emú labbóqer* 2+2
     w ws w w−w s −   w ws w w s −
                                                        ====
4a   *n^ebi'éha poḥ^azím / 'anšé bog^edót*   2+2
     wws w w ws   w s wws

4b   *koh^anéha hill^elu−qódeš / ham^esú torá*   2+2
     w ws w wwww s −   w sw ws

5a   *yhwh ṣaddíq b^eqirbáh / lò ya'^aśé 'awlá*   3+2
     w s   w s   ww s   w w−s w s

---

problems of this verse make it methodically necessary to leave it beyond
purview in this study, but this does not impair the structure of the poem
(see 2).

5b   *babbòqer babbóqer* / *mišpató yittèn* /
    w s — w s —   w w s w s

                                 la'ór lò ne'dár   2+2+2
                                   w s w w s

5c   *wᵉlõ—yodèᵃ' 'awwál bóšet*[4]
    w s   w s— w   s   s —   (4)

6a   *hikràtti goyim* / *našámmu pinnotám*   2+2   2+2
    w s w w s   w s   w w w s

6b   *hehᵉràbti husotám* / *mibbᵉli 'obér*   2+2
    w — s w w w s   w s w w s

6c   *nisdù 'arehém* / *mibbᵉli—'iš*[5] *me'èn yošéb*   2+2
    w s w w s   w s   w s
                                       ———

7a   *'amárti 'ak—tirᵉ'i 'otí* / *tiqᵉhi musár*   3+2   3+3
    w s w w   w s w w s   w s w   w s

7b   *wᵉlõ—yikkarèt me'enéha*[6] / *kòl 'ašer—paqádti*
    w s   w w s   w w s w   s w w   w s w
                                         'aléha   3+3
                                         w s w

7c   *'akén hiškìmu hišhítu* / *kòl 'ᵃlilotám*   3+2
    w s   w s w w s w   s w w w s

8a   *lakèn hakku—lí nᵉ'um—yhwh*[7] / *kᵉyóm qumi*
    w s   s w s   w s   w s

---

4   3:5c gives away the point of the contrast between vv.2–4 and 5, and it creates a new antithesis (vs. 5a,c). The repetition '*awla* / '*awwal* disturbs the pattern of verbal repetitions in vss. 1–5 (see 2). This secondary verse weakens the conclusion formed by the tricolon in 5b.

5   3:6c *mibbᵉli—'iš* is probably a *lectio varia* (BHS). It is a unique, but stylistically weak, reduplication; the parallel (*mibbᵉli*) '*ober* is not followed by *'iš* but by (*me'en*) *yošeb*. The phrase disturbs the pattern of word repetitions in vss. 6–8 (see 2) and the pattern of parallelism in vs. 6 (with 3 elements which each occur twice: vs. 6a'."/b'."/c'.": A.B/A.C/B.C).

6   3:7b *me'eneha* (BHS) is not relevant to the verse structure and rhythm.

7   3:8a *nᵉ'um—yhwh* I view as a rhetorical (and thus authentic), or

| | | $le^{\epsilon}\acute{e}d^{8}$ | 3+3 | 3+2 |
| | | w s | | |

8b   *ki mišpaṭi le'ᵉṣòp goyím / lᵉqobṣi mamlakót*   3+2
      w   w   ws   wws   w s   ww s   w   ws

8c   *lišpòk 'ᵃlehèm za'mí / kól hᵃròn 'appí*   3+2
     w s   ww s   w s   w   ws   w   s

8d   *kí bᵉ'èš qin'atí / te'akél kol–ha'áreṣ⁹*   (2+2)
    w   ws   w   ws   ww s   w   ws –

14a   *ronní bat–ṣiyyón / harí̌u yiśra'él*   2+2   2+2
     s   w   w   w s   ws w   ww s

14b   *śimḥi wᵉ'olzí bᵉkol–léb / bát yᵉrušaláim*   3+2
    ws   w   wws w   ww   s   s   w w ws–

15a   *hesir yhẃh mišpaṭáyik / pinná 'oyᵉbék*   3+2   3+2
    ws   w s   w ws w   w   s   wws

15b   *mèlek yiśra'él yhẃh bᵉqirbék / lo–tirᵉ'i rá' 'ód*   3+2
    w–   ww s   w s   ww s   ww s w w   s

                                        =========

16a   *bayyòm hahú' / ye'amèr lirušaláim*   2+2   2+2
    w   s   w s   ww   s   ww ws–

16b   *'al–tirá'i ṣiyyón / 'al–yirpù yadáyik*   2+2
    w   ws w w   s   w   ws   w s   w

---

redactional interjection, which in either case does not function in the rhythm.
8   3:8a *lᵉ'ed* (BHS) is not relevant to the verse structure and rhythm.
9   3:8d is a redactional reference to 1:18. According to the commentators
the verse is either in contradiction to vs. 8a–c or a summary of what has
already been said in vs. 8a–c. In any case, vs. 8 is concluded in vs. 8c'',
prior to the unattractive doubling of *ki*. The noteworthy, chiastic alliteration
at the beginning of the cola in vs. 8a–c (*l–.l–/k–.l–/l–.k–*), the absence of
lᵉ + infinitive in vs. 8c'', and the pattern of word repetitions in vss. 6–8
(see 2) are indicative of this.

17a *yhwh* *'elaháyik* *b^eqirbék* / *gibbòr* *yošì*'   3+2   3+2
   w s   w w s w   w w s   w s   w s—

17b *yasìs* *'aláyik* *b^esimḥá* / *yah^aríš* *b^e'àh^abató* /
   w s   ws w   w w s   w —s   w w —w s
                             yagil *'aláyik* *b^erinná*[10]   3+2+3
                            w s   ws w   w w s

2. Versification

A theory of classical Hebrew versification ought to determine (1) of which textual units this poetry is made up, (2) which linguistic data constitute the versification. But such a theory does not exist. I shall sketch my opinion concerning the necessary development of such a theory, without entering into the innumerable areas of debate. Research into possible constitutive factors (metrics, syntax, parallelism, word–pairs, ...?) presupposes a working hypothesis regarding the various textual units (colon, verse, strophe, stanza, ...?). Therefore, this type of research necessitates a certain degree of circular reasoning, but in practice this can grow into a productive spiraling if characterized by a pluriform approach in which one constantly and rigorously re–evaluates the presuppositions (Van Grol: 1986:2–12).

Characteristic of a poetic text is its prosodic structure, i.e. the hierarchical ordering of textual units of various proportions. A working hypothesis ought to define these units along with their range and composition. I summarize the provisional conclusions of my study in the following *prosodic rules* (italics denote the frequent and very frequent realizations; Van Grol: 1986:239ff.):

(1) A metrical unit consists of one strongly stressed syllable (sometimes followed by a slightly stressed ultima) preceded by zero, *one*, *two*, three or four slightly stressed syllables.

(2) A colon consists of *two*, *three* or four metrical units.

(3) A line consists of one, *two* or *three* cola.

---

10 3:18a' can, with BHS, be read with vs. 17. The result is a well–balanced structure in vss. 14–18a (see notes 17 and 42).

(4) A strophe consists of one, *two* or *three* lines.

(5) A stanza consists of one, *two*, *three* of four strophes.

The first three rules of this definition of prosodic structure are in accord with the general European tradition which has determined the layout of BHK and BHS. The description of strophes and stanzas is based on the research of Van der Lugt which has demonstrated the probability of the existence of strophic structure.[11] For the sake of research the rules have been formulated as sharply as possible. The broader rule that a strophe consists of one, two, three, four or five verse—lines, for example, will never be proven false, but neither will it lead to interesting, optimally precise results.

A working hypothesis of this sort makes it possible to study the linguistic factors determinative of verse structure. Such research must be expected to produce rules complementary to the elementary prosodic rules. They restrict the possibilities implied by the elementary rules, and determine the internal and external coherence of the prosodic units. It is in this capacity that the *metrical rules* produced by my study function (see 4).

The research must also be focused on grammatical and semantic data. A comprehensive definition of a colon and a line must also reckon with syntax and (internal) parallelism.[12] Determination of the cola and verse—lines is in practice seldom problematic. My delineation of the lines in Zephaniah agrees with BHS (K. Elliger). At the level of the cola there are a few variances. In 2:15b I prefer a more syntactically obvious division. *'ani* is part of the citation. A similar case is found in 3:7b (note the Masoretic accentuation of *kol 'ašer*). Elliger's division of 3:5b is not clear. Viewed syntactically the line falls into two parts. The two elements of the first clause (specifier and predicate) are in fact doubled in comparison with the second clause, so that there is a reason, based on rhythm,

---

11 P. van der Lugt, *Strofische structuren in de bijbels—hebreeuwse poëzie* (Kampen, 1980).

12 Van Grol: 1986:13—18. At present I am preparing a publication concerning the role of morphology and syntax with respect to versification, based upon Isa. 5:1—7 as an example. This study is being conducted in conjunction with the *Isaiah workshop* (*inter alia* W. Beuken, A. van der Kooij and H. Leene) and in correspondence with E. Talstra of the *Werkgroep Informatica* of the Free University, Amsterdam.

for splitting the first clause into two cola. The sound pattern confirms the threefold division:[13]

babboqer babboqer	/	*mišpaṭo yitten*	/	*la'or lo ne'dar*
specifier		+ predicate	/	spec. + pred.
A + A	/	B + B	/	A + B
word repetition	/	*m--ṭ tt-n*	/	*l--r l----r*

Also at the levels of the strophe and the stanza we miss sharply defined rules, but at the same time an intuitive delineation of these units causes little difficulty.[14] Van der Lugt has developed a method of procedure which operates on three criteria: (1) thematic shifts, (2) strophic indicators, (3) external parallelism (especially word repetitions). But there is a long way to go from this provisional procedure to a definitive and satisfying theory of operative rules. In the meantime I prefer a broader scale of criteria. Thus, one might suggest that a strophe usually consists of two or three verse—lines which are connected by syntax or balance, or which constitute a rhetorical or semantic unit. Accordingly, my designation of units in Zephaniah is based, as far as that is possible, upon a complete inventory of the phonetic, grammatical and semantic data. An explication of these data would exceed the limits of this essay, but the reader can without much difficulty detect those data which serve to bind the verse—lines of a strophe together and distinguish the respective strophes from each other.[15] I will restrict myself here to a few interesting examples.

Following the chiastically structured and syntactically closed strophe of 2:15a—b, one finds two poetic lines which according

---

13 Cf. the tricolon in Isa. 1:23c: *yatom* (A) *lo yišpoṭu* (B) / *u'erib 'almana* (AA) / *lo-yabo' '³lehem* (BB); and the tricolon in Joel 4:9b: *ha'iru* (A) *haggibborim* (B) / *yigg'šu ya'³lu* (AA) / *kol 'anše hammilḥama* (BB).

14 Van Grol: 1986:18—25, 160—164. This is certainly valid for the strophe, as a comparison of the results attained by Van der Lugt and myself will demonstrate (see n. 20).

15 In addition to the macrosyntactic indicators, attention ought to be given to the interrelationship of the sentences, change of subject, anaphoric patterns, morphological and syntactic repetitions, external parallelism, word repetitions, sound patterns, rhetorical indicators and shifts (deixis), word—fields and themes.

to the prosodic rules surely form a strophe but upon first glance appear to show little unity (cf. the change in subject between vs. 15c and d). This sort of not very pronounced strophe occurs more frequently, especially in circumstances where the surrounding strophes are sufficient to demonstrate the prosodic structure. Nevertheless, this strophe contains the semantic link *marbeṣ / ʿober*, which is a variation of *wᵉrabᵉṣu / yalinu* in vs. 14. And this fourth strophe is almost entirely composed of words which occur already in the first two strophes (see below).

The lament cry (3:1) is not to be connected with vs. 2, which is itself a unit tightly knit by syntactic balance (4x *lo* + perfect + complement), and is also separated from the rest of the poem by the rhetorical alternation (2 fem sg / 3 fem sg).

The summary of leaders in 3:3—4 is not a strophe but falls into two parts. Vs. 3 concerns the political leaders, contains symbolic language, and employs only external parallelism (3a/3b); vs. 4 concerns the religious leaders, contains concrete language and employs internal parallelism (4a'/a''; 4b'/b'').

The documented judgment in 3:6—8 contains a threefold reasoning. YHWH appeals to his previous actions (vs. 6), emphasizes his justified expectation and the resulting disappointment in that regard (vs. 7: *'amarti 'ak ... 'aken*), and accordingly draws his conclusion (vs. 8: *laken ... ki*). The strophes contain a noteworthy alliteration pattern at the beginning of the cola: *h.nš/h.m/nṣ.m; '.—/—.kol/'.kol; l.l/k.l/l.k.*

Strophe 3:16 shows a self—evident continuity (introduction and beginning of salvation oracle) and a chiasm of *lirušalaim* and *ṣiyyon* (chiastic with regard to vs. 14). Nevertheless, this strophe is only slightly marked (see below).

Finally, the stanza division may briefly be indicated. The three strophes in 3:6—8 form one inseparable stanza. Two patterns of verbal repetition and wordplay confirm the beginning, middle and end of the chiastically structured poem. Vss. 6a.b.c/7a.b.c/8a.b.c = A.—.—/—.A.—/—.A.— en —.B.B/ —.BC.C/—.—.C. In pattern A the first colon, *hikratti goyim*, is taken up in the central verse—line of the second strophe, *yikkaret*, and the third strophe, *goyim*. In pattern BC the final line, *ᵃlehem ... kol*, is prepared for in the three part series *mibbᵉli, me'en* en *me'eneha* (B) and *kol ... 'aleha* and *kol ᵃlilotam* (C) which alternate in the central verse—line.[16]

In 3:14—17 the beginning of the second stanza is indicated by the introduction in vs. 16a. The second stanza (vss. 16—17) of this song which begins at vs. 14, is a salvation oracle giving the reason for the song. Numerous repetitions form a pattern—like connection between the salvation oracle and the song, e.g. the precise inclusion *ronni* / *berinna*.[17]

In 2:13—15 the beginning of the second stanza shows a thematic alternation (destruction and effect / taunt and complaint) and a renominalisation of Nineveh (vs. 13) as *ha'ir* (vs. 15a), in the midst of exclusively anaphoric references. Here too, the verbal repetitions respect the division—line between the stanzas. Vs. 15a—b has no repetitions, but semantically it contrasts with the context. Vs. 15c—d is composed of words from v.13 (*yado*, *'al*, *lišmama/lešamma*) and from vs. 14 (*werabesu/marbeṣ, kol, hayto/hayya*).[18]

In 3:1—5 as well, the repetitions (and themes) indicate a twofold division. Vs. 5 is composed of words taken from vs. 2 (4x and 2x *lo, yhwh*) and from vs. 3 (*beqirbah, šopeteha/mišpato, labboqer/babboqer* ... *la'or*). Just as in 2:15a—b, vs. 4 (in the same position!) lacks verbal repetitions. In addition to the evident correlation with vs. 3, there is a strong connection with vs. 2 (vss. 2a/4a: prophecy; vss. 2b/4b: cultus).[19]

The result of the analysis can be summarized as follows. The verse structure of 2:13,14a—b/15a—b.c—d = 2.2/2.2 verse—lines; two stanzas, each with two strophes, with each strophe in turn

---

16   These facts point to the central position of vs. 7b, indicate that the *ki*—clause in vs. 8 refers back to vs. 6, and confirm the MT *'alehem* in vs. 8c.

17   If one reads vs. 16a with BHS as an introductory monocolon, and takes vs. 18a' with vs. 17b''' as a bicolon, the strophe division in vss. 16—18a would fall between vs. 17a and b, and the word repetitions and themes would show a more obvious, chiastic pattern, vss. 14,15/16—17a,17b—18a = A,B/B,A; see n.42.

18   The pattern of word repetitions A,B/—,AB provides the basis for a simultaneously linear and chiastic strophic structure, A,B/A,B and A,B/B,A.

19   Just as in 2:13—15, the pattern of word repetitions X/A,B/—,AB forms the basis for a simultaneously linear and chiastic strophic structure, X/A,B/A,B and X/A,B/B,A. The border of the stanza interrupts the summary in vss. 3—4, and the most important semantic division, the contrast between the city and YHWH, falls precisely between vss. 2—4 and 5, in the middle of a stanza. Accordingly, prosodic structure and semantic/rhetorical structure may not simply be identified with each other. See the discussion in H.W.M. van Grol, 'De exegeet als restaurateur en

having two verse—lines. That of 3:1/2,3/4,5a—b = 1/2.2/2.2 verse—lines; an introductory strophe of one verse—line is followed by two stanzas, each with two strophes, with each strophe in turn made up of two verse—lines (final tricolon). That of 3:6,7,8 = 3.3.3 verse—lines; one stanza of three strophes, each consisting of three verse—lines. That of 3:14,15/16,17 = 2.2/2.2 verse—lines; two stanzas of two strophes with two verse—lines each (final tricolon). These are extremely conventional structures.[20]

3 Accentuation

The following metrical study is based on the thesis that classical Hebrew metrics — if it exists — will be based on a *pure stress metre*, determined by the word accents, i.e. beats, while the offbeats are of secondary importance. I hereby indicate my agreement with the theory of Ley (1875). He has been the formative influence behind the European research (Sievers, Gray), but subsequent to Alonso Schökel's *Estudios* (1963) there has scarcely been any research in this line of study.[21]

An important criticism of this type of research focuses upon the arbitrariness with which accentuation is usually determined. The metric theory of the researcher often appears to prejudice his rhythmic reading. But it is possible to avoid this arbitrariness (1) by strict separation of the accentuation of the text on the one hand and the rhythmic analysis of the text and the development of a theory of metrics on the other, (2) by describing the accentuation as much as possible in terms of

---

interpreet. Een verhandeling   over de bijbelse poëtica met Ps. 121 als exempel', *Bijdragen* 44 (1983) 234—261, 350—365.

20 As standards of conventionality, I take the conclusions in my own study: 91 strophes and 36 stanzas, and the results of Van der Lugt's study (L): 1056 strophes and 385 stanzas (see the overview in Van Grol: 1986:198f. and 223—227). 10% of the strophes count one verse—line (L 12%; especially introductory, as is the case here, or concluding lines), 64% two verse—lines (L 63%), 26% three verse—lines (L 23%). 75% of the stanzas consist of two strophes (L 38%), 11% three strophes (L 31%).

21 Van Grol: 1986:39—61 offers an evaluation of the various theories; in addition to the classical theories also that of word metrics and the theory of Kuryłowicz is treated (68f.).

reading rules, (3) by giving a detailed justification of the concrete accentuation, thereby making it verifiable.

The reading rules have been developed in three steps (Van Grol: 1986:63—86, 102—110 and 129—145). Based upon the Masoretic accentuation and the experience of other researchers of metre, a number of starting points have been established. On that basis it was possible to accentuate five brief texts and to develope a number of related and conclusive reading rules. [22] In a third phase I tested and corrected these rules on the basis of seven lengthier texts. The reading rules are determined by two factors, namely word length and syntax (see below).

In the course of the study of the accentuation it became apparent that it is necessary for the sake of theory to reconstruct the 'classical Hebrew' form of the MT. This reconstruction is restricted to the placement of the accent, and the number of syllables. Three types of emendation are necessary: (1) the deletion of *ḥatepim* and auxiliary vowels, (2) the partial replacement of the accent from the ultima to the penultima, and (3) a limited application of *shewa* deletion (Van Grol: 1986:86—93).

The concrete reconstruction of Zephaniah offers a good picture of the suggested rules. Under the first rule falls, (A) the so—called *pataḥ furtivum*; (B) the segolata: in our text only the nouns such as *ḥóreb* (2:14c: s—); (C) the separated diphthongs, such as *báyit* (s—);[23] (D) laryngal forms, such as *yaʿᵃśé* (3:5a: w—s); and furthermore *zᵉʾebé* (3:3b, w—s; originally *ze'b/zeb*).

Under the second rule falls, (A) pronouns, such as *'ᵃni* (2:15b, *'áni*, sw); (B) perfect forms, such as *hayᵉta* (2:15c, wsw) and *garᵉmu* (3:3b, wsw); (C) perfect consecutives, such as *wᵉqatálta* and *wᵉqatálti*; (D) imperfect forms, such as *tirᵉʾi* (3:7, wsw);[24] (E) imperatives, such as *rónni* (3:14a, sw); (F) a few

---

22 'Related' indicates that the reading rules match in theory, which is demonstrated by a generalization into one formalized reading rule (Van Grol: 1986:140—143); 'conclusive' signifies that the reading rules must be able to justify the accentuation entirely, which has been achieved to 96.5% (see below).

23 With forms such as *mišpatáyik* (3:15a) I do not apply this rule because I accept as the classical Hebrew form *mišpatáyki* or *mišpatéki* (wwsw).

24 A *l"yw*—form such as *yirpú* (3:16b) I read unchanged as (ws) because in this case there has been no late shifting of the accent.

nouns, such as *mibb^eli* (3:6b: *mibbály:* ws[w]); (G) certain forms
with the 2 m sg suffix, such as *láka* (preposition).

Under the third rule, that of *shewa* deletion after an open
syllable with a short vowel, in our text only the case of
b^e'ah^abató (3:17b: ww—ws) is relevant.

In only a few instances is the reconstruction essential. There
are two cases in Zephaniah. *z^e'èbe 'éreb* (MT 3:3b), with four
syllables up to and including the second accented syllable, calls
for two stresses, but in the reconstruction it contains only three
syllables (w—s s—), so that one stress suffices (w—w s—; see
below). *mèlek yiśra'él* (MT 3:15b), because of the absence of a
monosyllabic word, demands two stresses, but in the
reconstruction it counts only four syllables (s— wws), so that
one stress is sufficient (w— wws; see below). I wish to
emphasize that my accentuation is only partially dependent upon
reconstruction. The accentuation of the MT usually produces the
same results.

I combine the justification of the accentuation in Zephaniah
with a thorough overview of the various *reading rules* (Van
Grol: 1986:144f.):

(1) Base rule: Each word accent counts as a stress.
Each graphic unit in the MT counts as a word, and every word
has an accent.[25]

(2) Secondary—stress rule: The initial secondary accent in a
word with two secondary accents counts as a stress unless if it
collides with the stress of the preceding word.[26]

(3) Word—complex rule:

(a) Particle rule: A particle is counted along with the next
following noun, verb (or particle) as a word—complex if at
least one of the two is monosyllabic.

A word—complex is a group of words joined together and
bearing one accent. The following examples may be noted in
Zephaniah: 8x *lo* (e.g. *lo ne'dár*, 3:5b), 3x *ki* (*ki 'arzá:* 2:14c;
3:8b.d), 2x *'al* (3:16b), *'et* (2:13), *gam* (2:14b) and 1x *'ak* (3:7a),
'el (3:2b) and *'al* (2:13a).

---

25 A necessary generalization, cf. Van Grol: 1986:106f.
26 Cf. Van Grol: 1986:75f. The rule is seldom applicable; in my dissertation
it occurs twice, in Joel 4:10 *umázm^erotekém* and Prov. 8:21 *w^e'ôṣ^erotehém*
(wswẅws).

(b) Construction rule: a constructive or adjective word—group is viewed as a word—complex under the condition that the first word is monosyllabic and the word—group does not exceed four syllables, or under the condition that the second word is monosyllabic and the word—group does not exceed three syllables.

In the first category may be listed forms such as *kol 'obér* (w ws, 2:15d) and *bat—ṣiyyón* (w ws, 3:14a; further, 2:14a; 3:7b, 8c, 8d), and with maximal length *melek yiśra'él* (w—wws, 3:15b). In the second category, *zᵉ'ebe 'éreb* (w—w s—, 3:3b) and *bᵉkol—léb* (ww s, 3:14b).

(c) Complement rule: A verb is considered along with its following complement as a word—complex if at least one of the two words is monosyllabic and the resulting word—complex does not exceed three syllables.[27]

(d) Restriction regarding the word—complex rule: The word—complex rule may only be applied one time to a given word.

This restriction guarantees, among other things, that a word—group with three words, of which two are monosyllabic, e.g. *kol—hayto—goy* (2:14a), receives two stresses (Van Grol: 1986:108ff., 136f.). It is not possible to take *hayto* simultaneously with *kol* and with *goy*, as, incidentally, is done in the Masoretic accentuation.

(4) Emphasis rule: Emphasis can disrupt the working of the word—complex rule.

The particle rule is not applied to the emphatic particles *'ek* (2:15c) and *hoy* (3:1). They maintain their stress. Furthermore, contrary to the complement rule, the phrase *hakku—li* (3:8a) is given two accents (ws s) in light of the emphatic, threatening character of this verse.[28]

---

27 Two examples: *'ara—li* (ww s: Num. 23:7b) and *haṣeb bó* (Isa. 5:2b). As complement, all the various components of a clause are possible (cf. discussion in Van Grol: 1986:134).

28 Once in a while we apply *nesiga*, the withdrawal of the accent to avoid collision of two accents. Nesiga has no influence on the number of accents, but sometimes produces a more even, readable rhythm. E.g., the colon *'ᵃni wᵉ'apsi 'od* (2:15b) implies a collision between the accents of *wᵉ'apsi* and *'od* (wws s); nesiga shifts the accent from *si* to *'ap* (wsw s) and strengthens the alliteration, *'áni wᵉ'ápsi 'ód*. A collision, and thus a, not functional, rhythmic

An exception is twice made to the reading rules. In 3:4b, according to the rules one would read *hillēlu–qódeš* (wsw s–). Instead, along with the Masoretic accentuation, I read *hillᵉlu–qódeš* (www s–), a positive exception to the complement rule. This is motivated by the stringent syllable structures in vss. 2–4 with their repeated twofold rhythm, by the parallel reading of vs. 3b' and by the contrast with vs. 5a' which has evidently three stresses. Incidentally, there is no metric reason for this exception; a reading of 3+2 would also fit in vs. 4b.

According to the rules, in 3:15b one ought to accent both *raʿ* and *ʿod*. Instead, I take the two words together *raʿ ʿód* (w s); the double *ayin* strengthens the connection. Comparable cola are found elsewhere, e.g. *lo–yeʾamer lak ʿod* (w wws w s, Is.62:4a). Double accentuation seems undesirable in this case in light of the collision which would result, and in view of the necessity for a consistent treatment of this type of sequence (Van Grol: 1986:139). Here too my decision is not determined by metric considerations; a 3+3 reading would be equally appropriate in vs. 15b.

A statistical overview makes it possible to compare the conclusions here with the results of my dissertation.[29]

Total number of word			dissertation:		
accents	213	100 %	1385	100	%
base rule reading	179	84.05 %	1159	83.7	%
word–complex rule	29	13.6 %	176	12.7	%
= particle rule	20		120		
= construction rule	9		40		
= complement rule	–		16		
emphasis rule	3	1.4 %	25	1.8	%
exceptions	2	0.95 %	25	1.8	%

The statistics of the accentuation in Zephaniah differ only

pause, is found between *ḥakku* and *li* (3:8a). But in this case *nesiga* actually produces a new collision which does have a rhetorical function, *lakén ḥákku–lí* (ws sw s).

29 Van Grol: 1986:135; in the calculation of Zeph. 2:13–3:8, 14–17 the entire text is included, secondary passages as well.

marginally from the results attained in my dissertation. The comparison demonstrates that the result of the accentuation remains consistent. The reading rules guarantee a considerable degree of 'objectivity'. The accentuation is more than 95% predictable. It is only in the emphasis rule, and of course in the exceptions, that a degree of subjectivity is presupposed and various applications of the reading rules are possible.

4 Rhythmical analysis

Our text consists of 47 cola with two stresses (67%) and 23 cola with three stresses (33%). We encounter six rhythmic verse–line patterns: 3+2 stresses (16x), 2+2 (13x), 3+3 (2x), 2+2+2 (1x), 2+3 (1x) and 3+2+3 (1x). A first glance confirms the conclusion long held by scholars: little regularity is detectable in the distribution of the line patterns. Nothing is changed in this respect by a thoroughly consistent accentuation. It is true that the selection and use of verse–line patterns incline towards regularity and simplicity, but this can not be systematized, and certainly not with respect to sequences of lines.[30] We do discover a series of six verse–lines with a pattern of 2+2 (3:2–4), but in the analyzed text as a whole, a given verse pattern spans an average of merely 1.8 verse–lines.[31]

The classical Hebrew poetic rhythm – which does exist anyway! – is evidently not possibly described with our traditional norms or criteria. Accordingly, I am inclined to move beyond the relative irregularity at the level of the line, in order to pose the question whether rhythm can more properly be described at the level of the strophe. If, inspired by Margalit and generative metrics, we take the strophe instead of the verse–line as the domain of analysis, rhythm appears to be more easily described and metrically regular, much to our own surprise.

Margalit concludes that Ugaritic poetry demonstrates a

---

30   To this point I have found 3+3, 3+2 and 2+2 to be very frequent patterns; 2+2+2 and 3+3+3 are frequent, 4+3, 4+4, 3+4 and 2+3 are incidental, and 4+4+4, 3+2+2, 2+2+3, 3+2+3 and 2+3+3 are very rare patterns (cf. Van Grol: 1986:145–148 and 218ff.).

31   The average length in all texts analyzed in the dissertation is 1.55 verse–lines. Zephaniah is thus relatively regular. Cf. Van Grol: 1986:145–153.

variety of verse−line patterns comparable to the results sketched above.[32] But in each strophe he detects a 'strophic theme', an elementary verse−line pattern, which at the beginning or end of the strophe can be alternated with a different but related verse−line pattern. Rhythm is accordingly arranged per strophe, and variations have a describable function. I have taken Margalit's theory as starting point, and have further developed and systematized it.[33] Furthermore, I have sought a theoretical explanation and justification, something which Margalit deliberately avoided.

I have found a theoretical basis in generative metrics.[34] Generative metrics reveals, in the iambic pentameter (stress−syllable metre), that metrical deviations are often simply variations which conform to strict rules, and that the analysis can not be focused upon the deviating unit (the foot) but must focus on the next textual level (the verse−line). Similarly, I view the deviating unit (the verse−line) in light of the next textual level (the strophe), and I describe the extremely variable rhythmic patterns as regular realizations of a number of abstract metrical themes.

The provisional results of my studies of rhythm are formulated in a number of *metrical rules*, which I summarize here:[35]

---

32 B. Margalit, 'Studia Ugaritica I: Introduction to Ugaritic Prosody', *UF* 7 (1975) 289−313, and *A Matter of 'Life' and 'Death'. A Study of the Baal−Mot Epic (CTA 4-5-6)* (AOAT 206; Kevelaer und Neukirchen−Vluyn, 1980). I make no judgement on the value of Margalit's 'accentuation' and observations regarding rhythm for understanding *Ugaritic* poetry. And I certainly do not draw comparisons between Ugaritic and classical Hebrew poetry (Van Grol: 1986:60f.). However, Margalit's observations have provided an important inspiration for this work.

33 Cf. the detailed evaluation of Margalit's observations in Van Grol: 1986:158−164.

34 See especially M. Halle and S.J. Keyser, 'Chaucer and the Study of Prosody', *College English* 28 (1966) 187−219; 'The Iambic Pentameter', in: W.K. Wimsatt (ed.), *Versification: Major Language Types* (New York, 1972). Van Grol: 1986:25−33 provides an illustrative sketch of generative metrics.

35 The complete, more precisely formulated version is found in Van Grol: 1986:241f. A formalized version is also developed as a contribution to generative metrics (214−220).

(1) Classical Hebrew poetry has four metrical themes: 2+2, 3+2, 3+3 and 4+4 (metrical units).[36]

(2) The strophe contains line patterns which are all realizations of the same metrical theme.

(3) The following realizations of the metrical theme are distinguished:

    (a) the base pattern   e.g. 3+3   for theme 3+3

    (b) the tricolic pattern[37]   e.g. 3+3+3 for theme 3+3

    (c) and (limited to the first and/or the last line of the strophe!)

        the hypercatalectic pattern   e.g. 4+3   for theme 3+3

        the brachycatalectic pattern   e.g. 3+2   for theme 3+3

        the hypercatalectic combination pattern   e.g. 3+2+3 for theme 3+2

        the brachycatalectic combination pattern[38]   e.g. 3+3+2 for theme 3+3

    (d) in addition to these the stylistic pattern[39]   e.g. 2+2+2 for theme 3+3

(4) The regularity on a level higher than the strophe can be noticed in repetitive patterns of metrical themes and/or strophe forms.[40]

These metrical rules produce two types of strophes, pure strophes and marked strophes. Pure strophes consist of a base

---

36 A fifth theme, 4+3, is theoretically possible but not yet demonstrated.

37 The tricolic pattern consists of the base pattern plus a third colon with a number of metrical units equal to the second colon of the base pattern. For the frequency and complexity scale of this realization, as well as the following ones, see Van Grol: 1986:208f. and 218ff.

38 The hypercatalectic or brachycatalectic pattern consists of the base pattern either lengthened or shortened by one metrical unit in one of the two cola. The combination pattern consists of the tricolic pattern lengthened or shortened by one metrical unit in the first or last colon.

39 The stylistic pattern consists of the same number of metrical units as the base pattern, but grouped differently. For the stylistic pattern of Zeph. 2:15b cf. Van Grol: 1986:209. The employment of this unusual pattern in the strophe is difficult to account for in the rules (211).

40 Van Grol: 1986:229−239 offers an overview and analysis of these patterns of repetition.

pattern and/or a tricolic pattern. Marked strophes contain a hyper— or brachycatalectic marking. Some marked strophes are susceptible to multiple interpretations. A 3+3, 3+2 strophe can belong to a 3+3 metrical theme (with a brachycatalectic ending) or to a 3+2 metrical theme (with a hypercatalectic beginning). In such a situation only the context can be determinative.[41]

We turn now to an analysis of rhythm in Zephaniah. For each poem the metrical theme, rhythmic patterns, strophic forms, the regularity at the higher level, and the stylistic details will be described. In 2:13—15 we find one metrical theme, 3+2, which is the characteristic pattern of six of the eight verse—lines. Also present is a brachycatalectic 2+2 pattern and a stylistic 2+3 pattern. Vs. 14c, which is a debatable case, with its tricolic 3+2+2 pattern does, incidentally, fit well with the theme. The poem is thematically regular and contains a chiastic repetition of the strophic forms, vss. 13,14a—b/15a—b,c—d: pure, marked / marked, pure. The marking is found in both cases in the second line of the strophe. From a stylistic point of view the chiastic rhythm in strophe 15a—b is noteworthy in that it emphasizes the citation.

In 3:1—5 we encounter two metrical themes: 3+2 in v.1, and 2+2 in vss. 2—5. In these latter verses the base pattern of 2+2 occurs six times, along with one occurrence of the tricolic pattern 2+2+2 and a single hypercatalectic 3+2. The first four strophes are pure strophes, the fifth is marked (hypercatalectic beginning). Subsequent to the deviating introductory strophe there is thematic regularity. In the three central strophes the strophic pattern is repeated, while the first and last strophe demonstrate formal correlation. Stylistically striking is the regularity in the description (vss. 2—4), and the correspondence between the introductory verse and the 'kernel' verse (vss. 1

---

41   Van Grol: 1986:212ff. offers a panorama of all the strophic forms which have been found. The metrical rules generate 90% of the material analyzed. The 10% exceptions are usually explainable on the basis of stylistics (220ff.). In Zephaniah we find no exceptions, but we do encounter three new, well integratable strophe forms, 2:15a—b; 3:7,14.   Incidentally, the marking of a strophe of two verse—lines is of course restricted to one of the two (for a discussion of these short strophes see Van Grol: 1986:210f.). Furthermore, as a restriction upon strophe formation, the cola of a given strophe may not differ by more than one metrical unit.

and 5a), and the concluding, proclamational tricolon. Perhaps one can draw a connection between the rhythm of vs. 1 and the preceding poem about Nineveh with its 3+2 metrical theme.

In 3:6—8 we find three metrical themes: 2+2 in vs. 6, 3+3 in vs. 7 and 3+2 in vs. 8. Verse 6 is a pure strophe with a 2+2 base pattern. Verse 7 is a double marked strophe; the central line shows the 3+3 pattern, while the other lines have the brachycatalectic 3+2 pattern. In vs. 8 the situation is reversed. The base pattern is 3+2, and a 3+3 pattern gives the strophe a hypercatalectic marking. The poem, with its three metrical themes, contains no thematic regularity and no repetition of strophic form, which entails that the last mentioned metrical rule is not operative here. It is stylistically striking that the descriptive opening strophe is composed in the brief 2+2 form, the argumentative second and third strophes proceed to a 3+2 pattern, while the two contrasting climaxes (vss. 7b and 8a) expand to 3+3. Does vs. 6, with its 2+2 theme, make an association with the previous poem?

In 3:14—17 we find two metrical themes in linear alternation, i.e. 2+2 in vss. 14 and 16, 3+2 in vv.15 and 17. In vss. 14 and 16 the base pattern is 2+2, with a hypercatalectic 3+2 marking pattern. In vss. 15 and 17 the base pattern is 3+2, with a 3+2+3 hypercatalectic combination pattern in vs. 17. While the metrical themes alternate linearly, the strophe forms are chiastically arranged, vss. 14,15/16,17: marked, pure / pure, marked. In both cases the hypercatalectic marking is found in the second verse—line. Stylistically the festive, broad tricolon draws attention. Standing at the end of the book, it places the spotlight on the joy of YHWH.[42]

From this research it is the *strophe* which emerges as the level at which metrics is operative in classical Hebrew poetry. In extreme cases the regularity of the rhythm is restricted to the strophe. For example, in 3:6—8 the metrical theme varies per strophe. It is more common, however, for the regularity of the

---

42 If vss. 16—18a is divided according to BHS (see n.17), the following verse patterns are attained: 4, 2+2, 3+2 / 3+2, 3+2 (vss. 16a,b,17a / 17b,c—18a). In that case, in a manner comparable to 2:13—15, the poem contains one metrical theme, 3+2, and a linear alternation between two identical, brachycatalectically marked strophes and two identical, pure strophes (A,B/A,B).

rhythm to extend beyond the level of the strophe to the stanza and even the poem as a whole. Thus, in 2:13—15 we find a single metrical theme, in 3:1—5 a varying theme in the introductory strophe, and in 3:14—17 a linear parallelism between two metrical themes.

The description of classical Hebrew rhythm which has been presented, with new illustrations from portions of Zephaniah, demonstrates the systematic stylization of rhythm, and the possible existence of classical Hebrew metrics. Furthermore, my conclusions confirm the theory of strophic structure described by Van der Lugt, but approached from a different angle. Nevertheless, this metrical theory is not yet a full explanation of verse structure. New research will have to demonstrate the other linguistic data which constitute the basis of classical Hebrew versification, and their leading rules: grammatical, semantical and phonological structures of repetition, and balance.

PSALM 110: A PSALM OF REHABILITATION?

Willem van der Meer

1 Introduction

Psalm 110 has received a great deal of attention from both Old Testament[1] and New Testament[2] starting points. At the heart

---

1   See the literature mentioned in L.Dürr, *Psalm 110 im Lichte der neueren altorientalischen Forschung* (Münster, 1929); R. Tournay, 'Notes sur les Psaumes', *RB* 51 (1945) esp. 220–237; J. Coppens, 'La portée messianique du Ps. CX', *ETL* 32 (1956) 5–23; R. Tournay, 'Le Psaume CX', *RB* 67 (1960) 5–41 esp. 5 n. 1; H.–J. Kraus, *Die Psalmen*. 2. Teilband (BKAT XV/2; Neukirchen, 1978[5]) 925f; E. Beaucamp, *Le Psautier. Ps 73–150* (Paris, 1979) 185f. In addition to the commentaries on the book of Psalms mention may be made of a number of articles which have appeared since the list of literature found in Kraus: 1978[5]. See for example J. Coppens, 'Le Psaume CX', *ETL* 53 (1977) 191f.; S. Schreiner, 'Psalm CX und die Investitur des Hohenpriesters', *VT* 27 (1977) 216–222; M. Gilbert S. Pisano, 'Ps 110 (109), 5–7', *Bibl* 61 (1980) 343–356; H. Möller, 'Der Textzusammenhang in Ps. 110', *ZAW* 92 (1980) 287–289; J. Schildenberger, 'Der Königspsalm 110', *Erbe und Auftrag* 56 (1980) 53–59; G. Gerleman, 'Psalm CX', *VT* 31 (1981) 1–19; P. Auffret, 'Note sur la structure littéraire du Psaume CX', *Sem* 32 (1982) 83–88; L. Kunz, 'Psalm 110 in masoretischer Darbietung', *Theologie und Glaube* 72 (1982) 331–335; K.–H. Walkenhorst, 'Theologie der Psalmen', *ZKathT* 104 (1982) 25–47 esp. 30–37; A. Rebić, 'Psalm 110, 1; Zur Bedeutung von 'Sedet ad dexteram Patris' im AT', *IKZ Communio* 13 (1984) 14–17; S. Wagner, 'Das Reich des Messias. Zur Theologie der alttestamentlichen Königspsalmen', *TLZ* 109 (1984) 865–874.

2   Cf. D.M. Hay, *Glory at the Right Hand. Psalm 110 in Early Christianity* (SBLMS 18; Nashville–New York, 1973); W.R.G. Loader, 'Christ at the Right Hand – Ps. CX. 1 in the New Testament', *NTS* 24 (1978) 199–217; M. Gourgues, *A la droite de Dieu. Résurrection de Jésus et actualisation du psaume 110 : 1 dans le Nouveau Testament* (Paris, 1978, with extensive list of literature); G. Dautzenberg, 'Psalm 110 im Neuen Testament', in: R. Kaczynski (Hrsg.), *Liturgie und Dichtung. Ein interdisziplinäres Kompendium I. Historische Präsentation* (St.Ottilien, 1983) 141–171; J. Dupont, <<*Assis à la droite de Dieu*>> *L'interprétation du Ps 110. 1 dans le Nouveau Testament*. in: J. Dupont, *Nouvelles études sur les Actes des Apôtres* (Lectio Divina 118; Paris, 1984) 210–295.

of New Testament discussions has been the role of Ps. 110 in the formation of Christological conceptions in the New Testament.[3] With respect to the Old Testament studies it is also possible to distinguish a number of central concerns. Much attention has been paid to questions pertaining to the historical and religious background of this psalm, to theories of kingship in Israel and her *Umwelt*, and to questions of dating, etc. But little research has concentrated upon the structure of Ps. 110.[4] Although one encounters random observations regarding the structure of this psalm in various commentaries and articles,[5] in

---

3   Cf. Dupont: 1984:210: 'Il a certainement joué un rôle important dans la réflexion christologique de la première génération chrétienne, plus spécialement dans son interprétation mystère pascal'.

4   Cf. Auffret: 1982:83. He begins his article with the sentence: 'La texte, la traduction et l'interprétation du Ps. CX ont jusqu'ici donné tant de fil à retordre aux exégètes qu'ils ne sont guère penchés sur sa structure littéraire, laquelle pourtant peut apporter sa pierre à l'intelligence du psaume'.

5   With regard to commentaries see for example J. Olshausen, *Die Psalmen erklärt* (KEH; Leipzig, 1853) 420: 'Viell. hat man V. 1–3. und V. 4–6. als vollständige Strophen zu betrachten, V. 7. als Ueberrest einer dritten'.   Also in F. Delitzsch, *Biblischer Commentar über die Psalmen* (Leipzig, 1874) mention is made of division into three sections, cf. 201: 'Ps. 110 besteht aus drei Siebenten, indem dreimal ein Tetrastich nebst einem Tristich einander folgen'. This means that Delitzsch sees 1+2, 3+4 en 5–7 as belonging together.   E.G. Briggs, *The Book of Psalms*, Vol II (ICC; Edinburgh, 1907) 373, 375f. sees the psalm composed of 2 strophes, namely 1–3 and 4–7. A similar proposal is found in H. Schmidt, *Die Psalmen* (HAT; Tübingen, 1934) 202 en H. Lamparter, *Das Buch der Psalmen II. Psalm 73–150* (BAT; Stuttgart, 1959) 227. Even though he speaks in terms of stanzas, mention may also be made of M. Dahood, *Psalms III. 101–150* (AB; New York, 1970) 113 L. Jacquet, *Les Psaumes et le coeur de l'homme. Etude textuelle, littéraire et doctrinale* (Gembloux, 1979) 207 also indicates two sections 1–3 and 4–7, but he sub–divides each of these into three strophes, namely 1, 2–3a, 3b–d and 4, 5–6b, 6c–7. In opposition to these views B. Gemser, *De Psalmen III* (TU; Groningen–Batavia, 1949) 36f. suggest four strophes: 1, 2–3, 4–6 and 7.
With respect to articles etc. see Schreiner: 1977:218. This author suggests a parallelism in the structure of 1–3 and 4–7: 1bα // 4aα; 1bβc // 4aβb; 2ab // 5ab; 3abc // 6ab. The entirety is bracketed by the heading in 1a and the conclusion in 7ab. S. Springer, *Neuinterpretation im Alten Testament*.   Untersucht an den Themenkreisen des Herbstfestes und der

most cases these observation do not lead to an integrated study of the correlation between analysis of structure and interpretation of content.

Two recent articles, by *Auffret* (1982) and by *Kunz* (1982) respectively, have introduced a change in the present scene. Auffret suggests that a double structure is present in Ps. 110. In addition to a concentric structure (1aα, 1aβb, 2–3, 4aα, 4aβb, 5a, 5b–7) in which 4aα forms the midpoint, there is a parallel structure (1aα, 1aβb, 2–3; 4aα, 4aβb, 5–7). He allows both structures to stand side–by–side because in each structure certain emphases of the psalm are highlighted. One finds a different approach in the study by Kunz. By means of an assessment of the various stichoi, and their internal connections he comes to the conclusion that Ps. 110 has an 'outer' and an 'inner' structure. This 'outer' structure is formed by a 'symmetrische Reihe mit I + II + I + II + I Versen', that is vs. 1, 2+3, 4, 5+6, 7.[6] To find this 'inner' structure Kunz ties together the 'Kleinstichen' of vs. 1, 4 and 7. From this he argues that Ps. 110 has an 'inner' structure of 11 + 15 + 7 'Kleinstichen'[7], which can be seen as an 'arithmetrische Reihe'.

The results of the two studies are quite different, and they raise questions concerning methodology. One might question whether Auffret's method pays sufficient attention to the literary aspect. Especially with regard to the position attributed to vss. 5–7 one must ask whether the analysis of structure is not dominated by observations concerning content[8]. With respect to Kunz it must be asked whether he doesn't place too much emphasis upon the masoretic accents. The use of the 'Kleinstiche' for the 'inner' structure seems rather artificial.

Viewed both against the background of the articles by Auffret and Kunz and in light of the diversity of structural divisions in the commentaries,[9] a new study of the structure of Ps. 110 is

---

Königspsalmen Israels (Stuttgart, 1979) 139f. sees this psalm as composed of five strophes, namely 1, 2–3, 4, 5–6, 7.

6   Kunz: 1982:334.

7   A 'Kleinstiche' is a unit indicated by the masoretic accents. One finds 5 'Kleinstichen' in vs. 1, 11 in vss. 2+3, 6 in vs. 4, 7 in vss. 5+6, 4 in vs. 7.

8   Cf. Auffret: 1982:83 where he follows the suggestion of Gilbert–Pisano (1980) with respect to the 3rd person in 5bff.

9   Cf. note 5.

fully justified. Such a study must allow the structure of the psalm to be determined on the basis of formal criteria. Only subsequent to establishment of the structure can questions of content be treated. Due to the nature of this article it will not be possible to engage in an exhaustive treatment of questions concerning content. Priority is given to the problem of structure and to the subsequent implications entailed by this structure for exegesis.

2 The Structure of Psalm 110

2.0 *Introductory comments*

The Masoretic text serves as starting point for the analysis. In this first stage of analysis text—critical questions are kept to a minimum. A text—critical approach often obscures structure, and it allows the determination of literary structure to be too easily dominated by questions of content.[10] This frequently hinders the holding of structure and content in balance as two components of the methodology.

Detection of the structure is facilitated by first determining the respective verses. A verse can consist of one or more cola. Internal parallelism plays an important role in determining the boundaries of the verse. Once the respective verses have been established it is necessary to pursue the relationship between the verses. Are there indications that the verses are joined together to form strophes? Detection of external parallelism and markers of separation can be important in this respect. A following step involves analysis of the various strophes. Are there indications that the strophes are connected together to form canticles? If so, how are the canticles in turn related? Is it possible to determine a certain arrangement at the level of the canticle? In order to illustrate the entire process, each stage will be handled separately in the following analysis.

---

10   See for example H. Gunkel, *Die Psalmen* (HK II,2; Göttingen, 1926[4]) 481, with a transposition of 7b before verse 5 and 7a before the end of verse 6. Mention may also be made of O. Loretz, *Die Psalmen. Teil II. Beitrag der Ugarit—Texte zum Verständnis von Kolometrie und Textologie der Psalmen. Psalm 90–150* (AOAT 207/2; Neukirchen—Vluyn, 1979) 162ff. Cf. the manner in which he concludes that verses, or parts of verses, are secondary.

2.1 The Verse

The Masoretic accents, and comparison with other texts, makes it clear that נאם יהוה לאדני forms a colon.[11] The important question is whether it stands independently as a unicolon[12] or should be taken together with the following line as part of a larger verse. When one observes how נאם functions elsewhere, it is noteworthy that expansions of the colon containing נאם frequently give a more precise typification or description of a divine title. The content of the divine oracle generally constitutes a new poetic line of verse.[13] Since נאם in this case does not have a parallel counterpart in the following colon, we may conclude that we are dealing here with a unicolon as an independent line (1a).

The following line begins with the imperative שב, which along with לימני forms a colon. This colon is connected with the following two cola: הדם לרגליך and עד־אשית איביך. This connection is indicated by the presence of ימין and רגל. The word ימין can appear in parallelism with a variety of words. A frequently occurring parallelism is that of right and left.[14] ימין can also stand in parallelism with various body parts, among others with יד[15], with פה[16] and with פנים[17]. The combination of ימין and רגל also occurs.[18] This observation is reinforced by the words which occur in parallelisms with יד.

---

11 Cf. J.C. de Moor, 'The Art of Versification in Ugarit and Israel, II', *UF* 10 (1978) 189f.

12 In order to avoid possible confusion in the use of the word 'verse', in section 2.1 the word 'line' is used in reference to structural unit, and the word 'verse' is employed strictly in reference to the usual demarcation of the verses.

13 See the examples in De Moor: 1978:189f.

14 Cf. Y. Avishur, *Stylistic Studies of Word-Pairs in Biblical and Ancient Semitic Literature* (AOAT 210; Neukirchen−Vluyn, 1984) 588f.

15 Cf. L.R. Fisher, *Ras Shamra Parallels*. Vol I (AnOr 49; Roma, 1972) 195.

16 Fisher: 1972:206.

17 Fisher: 1972:313.

18 Prov. 4:27; Judg. 5:26f. (ימין...יד) and in verse 27: (רגל); cf. too Job 30:12: ארח...רגל...ימין.

Parallel body parts include, among others, fingers[19], knee[20], lip[21] and foot[22]. On the basis of these multiple examples it may be concluded that in Ps. 110 too the words ימין and רגל form a parallelism embracing the poetic line. As further support for the contention that the three cola stand parallel, one might also mention the 1 sg. suffix in למיני and the 1 sg. subject in אשית, the phonological wordplay upon שׁ in שׁב and אשׁית, the 2 sg. imperative in שׁב and the occurrence of the 2 sg. suffix in רגליך and איביך. Furthermore, the beginning of the line, by virtue of the concept of exaltation, forms a certain contrast with the end of the line which refers to humiliation. On the basis of these internal connections line 1b can be viewed as a tricolon, namely:

1bA שׁב לימיני /1bB עד־אשׁית איביך /1bC הדם לרגליך.

The commentaries differ in their analysis of the number of cola present in vs. 2. Are there three[23] or two cola[24]? In any event the verse may be divided into two poetic lines. Line 2a consists of מטה־עזך ישׁלח יהוה מציון and line 2b consists of רדה בקרב איביך. This is indicated by the absence of direct parallelism between 2a and 2b. The two lines are indirectly joined by the imagery of ruling, but this can also be attributed to the external connection between the two lines. Separation of the two lines is argued for by the fact that 2a speaks of an action of the Lord, while in 2b the party addressed is

---

19 אצבוע cf. Fisher: 1972:193.

20 ברך cf. Fisher: 1972:194.

21 שפה cf. Fisher: 1972:197.

22 רגל cf. 2 Sam. 3:34; Ezek. 25:6; Ps. 36:12; 115:7 (with respect to the structure of the verse see P. van de Lugt, *Strofische structuren in de bijbels-hebreeuwse poëzie. De geschiedenis van het onderzoek en een bijdrage tot de theorievorming omtrent de strofenbouw van de Psalmen* [Kampen, 1980] 390). The combination of יד and רגל occurs frequently, for example in Gen. 41:44: 'to raise hand or foot'; Ex. 21:24 and Deut. 19:21: 'hand for hand , foot for foot'; Ex. 29:20; Lev. 8:23v.; 14:14, 17, 25, 28 etc.: 'to smear blood on hands and feet'.

23 Delitzsch: 1874:199; F. Baethgen, *Die Psalmen* (HK II,2; Göttingen, 1904³) 336; Gunkel: 1926:481; Lamparter: 1953:224; Kraus: 1978:926; Jacquet: 1979:202. Cf. too the Masoretic accentation.

24 Schmidt: 1934:202; Gemser: 1949:37; J.P.M. van der Ploeg, *Psalmen* (BOT VIIb; Roermond, 1973–75) 246; Dahood: 1970:112.

summoned to rule. The imperative at the beginning of 2b may also indicate the beginning of a new line. This makes it clear that 2b is a unicolon. It is more difficult to decide in 2a. Those who divide the verse into three cola see this poetic line as a bicolon. The first section consists of מטה־עזך and the second colon is ישלח יהוה מציון. Although direct parallelism is absent between these cola, there are a number of indicators which suggest division into two cola. A more semantic parallel is present through mention in 2aA of the might of the one addressed, while 2aB speaks of Zion as the center of might. Furthermore, מטה and מציון form a phonological wordplay via the מ. And finally, the emphatic placement of מטה־עזך at the beginning of the line argues for a separate colon. On the basis of these considerations it appears that vs. 2 consists of 2 poetic lines, the bicolon 2a and the unicolon 2b.

Division of vs. 3 is complicated by the virtual absence of parallelism in particular and formal indicators in general. The problem is not resolved by the various textual emendations which have been proposed. Furthermore, the emendations alter the meaning of the text. In the first place one must begin with the Masoretic text. Vs. 3 then appears to consist of two lines. The first line, 3a, is formed by עמך נדבת ביום חילך, the second by the remainder of vs. 3. The delineation of 3a is marked by the presence of the 2 sg. suffix at the beginning, עמך and at the end, חילך. This indicates the borders of the line. The internal unity of 3b is indicated in the parallelism between שחר and טל.[25] Finally, the structure of 3a and 3b may be mentioned. The first begins with a noun clause, followed by a further explication prefaced with the preposition ב, while the second begins with ב and concludes with a noun clause. These indicators appear to distinguish two lines.[26] A subsequent question concerns the designation of the cola. Via Masoretic accentuation one can determine that 3a is a bicolon consisting

---

25 Cf. the external parallellism of these words in Hos.6: 3,4. In contrast to the reliability of God, described in the imagery of dawn, stands the love of the people, typified as being as fleeting as the dew.

26 Cf. Baethgen: 1904[3]: 337; R. Kittel, *Die Psalmen* (KAT XIII; Leipzig, 1929[5,6]) 355; Dahood: 1970:112. One also encounters division into two lines in the studies of Briggs: 1907:373 and Schmidt: 1934:202 but these authors incorrectly make a division after בהדרי־קדש.

of עמך נדבת and ביום חילך. Both parts contain the 2 sg. suffix. Line 3b can be scanned as a tricolon, namely:
3bA בהדרי־קדש /3bB מרחם משחר /3bC טל ילדתיך.[27]
This division is supported by a twofold connection between the cola. A parallelism between 3bB and 3bC is established by the words שחר and טל. And a correlation between 3bA and 3bB is made via the expressions ב and מן, both of which introduce a description of a situation, and function accordingly as modifiers of 3bC. Justice is done to these correlations by viewing 3b as a tricolon.

Two lines are distinguishable in vs. 4. In the first line, 4a, יהוה as subject constitutes the unifying element. The second line, 4b, begins with the personal pronoun אתה. In 4a we may also point out the positive—negative contrast, by means of which נשבע is emphasized. This entails that 4a is a bicolon. Both cola contain a verb, and both have יהוה as subject. Line 4b, by contrast, is a noun clause. On the basis of the *atnach* this line may be divided into two cola, namely אתה־כהן לעולם and על־דברתי מלכי־צדק.[28] Additional formal indicators do not appear to be present.

According to the Masoretic verse divider, vs. 5 consists of two cola. A number of connections between these cola are present. They have the subject אדני in common. This is referred back to by the 3 sg. suffix in אפו. Furthermore, there is a parallelism between אדני and מלכים.[29] This indicates that the cola in vs. 5 are parallel, and they together form one poetic line:
5aA מחץ ביום־אפו מלכים /5aB אדני על־ימינך.

Vs. 6 is composed of three cola, namely מלא גויות, ידין בגוים and מחץ ראש על־ארץ רבה. The first and third cola both have a 3 sg. subject. Furthermore, there is a coherence of imagery in the three cola by virtue of the depiction of war and its results. This imagery progresses in stages. In the first colon war takes place among the nations. The second colon speaks

---

27 See e.g. Gemser: 1947:37 and Dahood: 1970:112 for a division giving a bicolon in 3a and a tricolon in 3b.
28 See too Delitzsch: 1874:199; Baethgen: 1904[3]:338; Gemser: 1949:37; Lamparter: 1953:225; Van der Ploeg: 1973–75:246; Jacquet: 1979:202.
29 Cf. e.g. Isa. 19:4; Ps 45:12; 105:20f. See Fisher: 1972: 262f.; Avishur: 1984: 383f.

more generally of corpses, that is to say, from among the nations people will be judged. The third colon makes a more specific application to the individual ראש. From these connections the conclusion may be drawn that the three cola together form one poetic line (6aA / 6aB / 6aC).

The Masoretic accentuation clearly indicates that vs. 7 consists of two cola. The question is whether these two cola together form one of two poetic lines. The only element that they have in common is a 3rd sg. imperfect form of the verb, which could also be taken as an indicator of external parallelism. Additional indicators of parallelism are absent. Lack of further evidence makes it impossible at this stage to choose between the options of one or two poetic lines. Both possibilities will need to be evaluated upon the basis of the entire structure of the psalm.

The analysis of the individual lines offered above leads to the following overview of Psalm 110:

1aA נאם יהוה לאדני
1bA שב לימיני / 1bB עד־אשית איביך / 1bC הדם לרגליך
2aA מטה־עזך / 2aB ישלח יהוה מציון
2bA רדה בקרב איביך
3aA עמך נדבת / 3aB ביום חילך
3bA בהדרי־קדש / 3bB מרחם משחר / 3bC לך טל ילדתיך
4aA נשבע יהוה / 4aB ולא ינחם
4bA אתה־כהן לעולם / 4bB על־דברתי מלכי־צדק
5aA אדני על־ימינך / 5aB מחץ ביום־אפו מלכים
6aA ידין בגוים /6aBמלא גויות /6aCמחץ ראש על־ארץ רבה
7aA מנחל בדרך ישתה
7bA על־כן ירים ראש[30]

2.2 The Strophe

A strophe can consist of one or more verses.[31] To distinguish the boundaries of the strophes it is necessary to look for

---

30 Or should this line be taken as parallel to 7aA?
31 In the preceding section of the analysis of the lines of Ps. 110, the word 'verse' was used strictly as a reference to the ordinary verse divisions. In the following section the word 'verse' is used in reference to the structural units formed by one or more cola. In other words, verse 1a, 1b, 2a, 2b etc. See the overview above.

indicators of demarcation which signal the beginning and end of the strophe.[32] In Ps. 110 the following indicators of separation are present:

1a: the divine name יהוה; verse 1a is a unicolon.

1b: imperative שב; verse 1b is a tricolon; tautological presence of the 2nd sg. suffix (רגליך ... איביך).

2a: the divine name יהוה; change of grammatical subject (in 1bB, C 1 sg.; in 2aB 3rd sg.).

2b: imperative רדה.

3a: change of grammatical subject (in 3aA: עמך); tautological presence of 2nd sg. suffix (חילך ... עמך).

4a: the divine name יהוה; change of grammatical subject, namely יהוה in this verse.

4b: the personal pronoun אתה and the change of grammatical subject connected with it; the substantive לעולם.

5a: the divine name אדני; change of grammatical subject.

6a: verse 6a is a tricolon.

7a: special criteria are not recognizable here. This is altered, however, if 7a and 7b are seen as independent lines. In that case 7a and 7b are both unicola, which may be seen as evidence of separation.

When one views these results collectively, it is noteworthy that markers of separation are present in every verse. This indicates that consistently two verses belong together. By this means the division markers can be honoured in each case. This entails that 1a–1b, 2a–2b, 3a–3b, 4a–4b and 5a–6a in any event form strophes. And on the basis of regularity thus far present, one can go a step further. Since two verses consistently are joined to form strophes, one might expect this also to be the case at the end of Ps. 110. Therefore, one can presuppose that 7a and 7b both are verses, and that 7a and 7b together form the last strophe. The entire psalm therefore consists of 6 strophes, each containing 2 verses. However, before a definitive delineation of the strophes can take place it is necessary to determine whether there is external parallelism between the

---

32   For the various criteria consult Van der Lugt: 1980:502ff.; J.C. de Moor, 'The Poetry of the Book of Ruth' I, *Or* 53 (1984) 273; Idem, 'The Poetry of the Book of Ruth' II, *Or* 55 (1986) 45f.; M.C.A. Korpel–J.C. de Moor, 'Fundamentals of Ugaritic and Hebrew Poetry' *UF* 18 (1986) 173–212, esp. 191–198.

strophes, and if so, whether it confirms or counters the tentative divisions into strophes. With respect to the first strophe the following connections can be mentioned: the divine name יהוה in 1aA is picked up again in 1bA: לימיני and in 1bB: אשית. The 1 sg. suffix of 1aA (לאדני) reappears in the imperative שב in 1bA and in the 2nd sg. suffixes in 1bB (איביך) and 1bC (לרגליך). Furthermore, 1b may be characterized as the content of the נאם of 1a.[33]

The following relations are visible between 2a and 2b: the 2nd sg. suffix of עזך (2aA) also occurs at the end of 2bA, thereby framing the strophe. Also, the motif of 'ruling' forms a connection between the strophes. Compare the manner in which the words מטה and רדה also appear in Isa. 14:5–6. This strophe is also separated from the preceding one by the manner in which the relationship between the persons is described. In the first strophe the parties are designated by 'I' (=God) and 'you' (=addressee). In the second strophe the circle is expanded. It begins with 'He' (=God) to 'you' (=addressee), but goes further with respect to 'you' in relationship to the enemy.

Despite all the questions which exist concerning the interpretation of 3a and 3b, it is clear that these lines demonstrate external parallelism. To begin with, one can point to the repetition of the 2nd sg. suffix which occurs in 3aA (עמך), 3aB (חילך) and twice in 3bC (לך and ילדתיך). Furthermore, a parallelism is visible in the structure of both verses. In 3a a noun clause is followed by an explication with ב, while 3b begins with an explication with ב, and concludes with a noun reference. This appears to constitute a frame for the whole strophe. Finally, mention may be made of a parallelism which arises if one chooses for the reading of the LXX with respect to עמך. The LXX has μετα σου, which presupposes עמך in the Hebrew text, in which case one could speak of a framing parallelism established by עמך and לך. Furthermore, it would then also be possible to see a parallelism between נדבת of 3aA and ילדתיך of 3bC. Both words could

---

33 A unicolon containing נאם can stand alone as a strophe. See the examples in De Moor: 1978:189f. However, it can also be part of a larger strophe, e.g. in Isa. 56:8 (where a strophe is formed in conjunction with the content of נאם in 8b); Jer.2:22; Joel 2:12.

34 Cf. the examples with respect to עם and ל in Fisher: 1972:243, 295.

be used as designations of military units. Regardless of whether one opts for the reading of the LXX, it is clear that 3a and 3b constitute a strophe. These verses are distinguished from the previous ones by the fact that the description now focuses upon the relationship of 'you' (=addressee) and the people.

With respect to 4a and 4b it may be noted that here, as in the first strophe, 4a indicates a divine utterance and 4b explicates the content. Additional formal parallelisms are absent. Here, as in the second strophe, the relationship is that of 'He' (=God) to 'you' (=addressee).

Verses 5a and 6a show a parallelism in the presence of the verb מחץ in both. With respect to verbs, a connection is made via the grammatical person of the verbs in 5aB, 6aA and 6aC as a continuation of the subject אדני in 5aA. Mention may also be made of a sort of chiasmus between the two verses. In 5aA the delimitation of the verse is marked by אדני and מלכים. In other words, the beginning contains a singular form and the ending a plural noun. In 6a this is reversed. The line begins with a plural, בגוים and it ends with a singular form, ראש. These connections are reinforced by the fact that מלכים and גוים can form a parallelism.[35] The connection between 5a and 6a is also demonstrable by means of content. The emphasis of the Lord's presence in 5aA is expanded upon in what follows.[36]

With respect to the last two verses, 7a and 7b, it is scarcely possible to speak of external parallelism. One can only list the grammatical parallelism established by the 3rd sg. imperfect form of the verbs ישתה and ירים. However, since the preceding strophes all consist of two verses it is likely that that is also the case with the final strophe.

On the basis of markers of separation in the various verses, along with the analysis of external parallelism, it is possible to

---

35 Cf. Gen.17:6; 35:11; Isa.41:2 45:1; 52:15; 60:3; 62:2 etc., and the external parallellism in Isa. 10:7f.; 49:22f.

36 A similar thought is evident in Isa. 45:1 with respect to king Cyrus. Grasping by the right hand results in the smiting of the nations before him, ungirding of kings, and opening doors before him. Cf. Ps. 17:7, 13 (God rises to defend those who seek refuge at his right hand); 89:22f. (God's support implies that the enemy is crushed before him); Lam. 2:3 (because God has withdrawn his right hand, the enemy is able to trample Israel under foot).

conclude that Ps. 110 contains 6 strophes. Each strophe is
formed of 2 verses. The question which next arises is whether
connections between the strophes indicate that they are tied
together into units at a higher level than the strophe.

2.3 *The canticle*

As connections between the first and second strophes we
mention:
—the divine name יהוה in 1aA and 2aB.
—mention of the enemy איביך in 1bB and 2bA.
—the 2nd sg. suffix ך in 1bB, 1bC, 2aA, 2bA.
Strophes 1 and 2 are also connected with strophe 3. This is
evident in the 2nd sg. suffix ך in 3aA, 3aB and 3bC. In the
fourth and sixth strophes this suffix is not present. In the fifth
strophe it is only present in 5aA. Use of this suffix in the first
three strophes suggests that they form a unity. This is
supported by the coherence of imagery employed in strophes
1—3. Imagery of enemies, of ruling and of opposition entirely
dominate. In this unit a sort of indirect approach is taken with
respect to the persons. In the first strophe the relationhsip is
between 'I' (=God) and 'you' (=addressee). In the second
strophe this becomes 'He' (=God) in relation to 'you'
(=addressee), and 'you' (=addressee) in relation to the enemy.
And the final strophe concentrates upon the addressee and those
around him.
  The fourth strophe appears to mark a new beginning. As in
the first strophe, it begins with a divine utterance. Other than
the divine name and the 2nd person singular form of the
addressee there are no immediately evident connections with the
preceding section. And these connections which *are* present may
be operative at the level of the unity of the entire psalm. A
greater number of connections may be seen between strophe 4
and those which follow. מלכי in 4bB makes a connection with
מלכים in 5aB. Furthermore, אתה (4bA) finds a correspondence
in the 2nd sg. suffix of ימינך (5aA), and the divine names
יהוה (4aA) and אדני (5aA) also establish a connection. By
means of these literary ties the fourth strophe is interwoven
with the fifth strophe. And the fifth strophe is related to the
sixth strophe via the substantive ראש. Also significant is the
contrast established between the fifth and sixth strophes. While
6aC speaks of crushing the head, 7bA speaks of exalting the

head. By means of these various ties strophes 4—6 form a unity.

By virtue of the unity between strophes 1—3 and 4—6, the entire psalm can be divided into two canticles.[37] These canticles, in turn, do not stand loosely side—by—side, but they too are held together by a number of literary ties. Mention may be made of:

—the presence of the divine name יהוה in 1aA, 2aB, 4aA and אדני in 5aA.

—לאדני in 1aA and אדני in 5aA.

—לימיני in 1bA and ימינך in 5aA.

—ביום in 3aB and 5aB.

—mention of enemies in the first canticle and kings and nations in the second canticle.

On the basis of these connections the conclusion is warranted that the two canticles together form a canto. Schematically summarized:

Canticle I: strophe 1: 1a—1b   Canticle II: strophe 1: 4a—4b
            2: 2a—2b   2: 5a—6a
            3: 3a—3b   3: 7a—7b

The entire psalm shows structural regularity in its present form. It consists of two canticles, each containing three strophes, which in turn are all composed of two verses. Coherence of the entire canto is established via the contrast between lowering of the enemy in the first strophe and the exaltation in the final strophe. The parallel structure of the two canticles comes to expression via the initial divine utterance in each (cf. 1b and 4b), and the fact that the second and fifth strophes concentrate on the relationship to the enemy. Consequently, strophes 2—3 and 5—6 appear to be elaborations of the divine utterances.

Thus, the present form of the psalm appears to demonstrate a clear cohesion and structure. Nevertheless, there are indicators in the psalm which create doubts as to whether it is simply an original unit. It is noteworthy that a couple of keywords of verses 1a and 1b reappear in 5a (אדון and ימין), thereby forming a sort of frame. This is reinforced by the fact that the 2nd sg. suffix does not appear after 5a. It should be further noted that the position of the verb מחץ tends to create

---

37   For related positions see the literature mentioned in note 5 above.

a certain unity of 5aB—6a. And it is in this section that mention is made of the enemy. However, the word איביך, which is used twice in the first canticle, is not employed, but mention is made, rather, of kings and nations. It is noteworthy that this change in terminology is accompanied by a shift with respect to the word יום. In 3aB it is elaborated with חילך but in 5aB אפו is used. And finally, in 6aC and 7aB there is a wordplay on the concept ראש. The nature of these terminological connections gives the impression of elaboration and expansion. This impression is reinforced by careful attention to the matter of speaker and addressee. When one approaches the psalm from this perspective the following scheme becomes evident:

Strophe 1: A to B via C   Strophe 4: C to B concerning A
          2: C to B concerning A   5: C to B concerning A
          3: C to B   6: ?

In this scheme A = Lord; B = my lord; C = speaker.

This scheme demonstrates that the first strophe occupies a unique place in the psalm by virtue of its transmission of a direct divine utterance. This is not the case in the fourth strophe. With respect to person, strophe 4 appears to correspond with strophe 2.[38] The fifth strophe, or at least 5aA, shows similarity to the third strophe. The sixth strophe stands independently because it is not clear who functions in the position of the addressee. But it is clear that the end of the sixth strophe establishes a correspondence with the first via the contrast between humiliation and exaltation.

From these various relationships between the strophes one gets the impression that from a structural perspective two movements may be identified. In addition to the parallel structure of the canticles is another structure in which the first strophe dominates and the sixth strophe stands as conclusion. The intervening strophes are more or less an elaboration of the first strophe. These different movements appear to be especially evident in the second canticle. Consider how 5aA correlates back to the beginning of the first canticle and 5aB—6aC has its own

---

38 This position receives possible support from the mention of Zion in strophe 2 and priest in strophe 4.

coherence. For now we must simply indicate the problem and let the issue stand at that. The question of whether Ps. 110 is an original unity cannot be answered on the basis of structural analysis. At most one can say that the ambiguity to which attention has been called raises the possibility of editorial revisions in this psalm. This question must be dealt with from the perspective of content in the study which follows.

3 Exegetical Notes

A survey of research pertaining to Ps. 110 shows that the exegesis of this psalm is disputed. Especially vss. 3, 4, 6 and 7 have been central to the discussions. Questions of structure have scarcely played a role in these debates. Accordingly, an important point has been overlooked, namely, the relationship between the various parts of the psalm. Stated more concretely, we may ask what bearing canticles 1 and 2 have to each other. Do these canticles stand more or less independently beside each other, as the symmetric structure suggests, or is it necessary to emphasize the dependence of the second canticle upon the first, as is suggested by the more 'bracketing' structure? In order to answer this question it is crucial to determine the specific character of the fourth strophe. Can one speak here of a new oracle, as is generally concluded, or is this a reference to a promise previously made? In other words, what is the function of נשבע in 4aA? The verb שבע can function in the context of a new oracle, or of an utterance referring to a present or future situation.[39] It is concluded, without further discussion, that this function is also present in Ps. 110:4. But this is by no means the only manner in which this verb can be employed. Frequently it is used to remind of a promise from the past. The relationship to the past is indicated by means of a relative clause[40] or via a clause with כאשר.[41] However, even without employment of כאשר, the 'swearing' can refer back to an utterance from the past. As such it can serve to create or

---

39 Cf. Gen. 22:16; Num. 32:10; Jer. 40:9.
40 E.g. Gen. 26:3; Ex. 13:5; 33:1; Num. 11:12; 14:16, 23; 32:11; Deut. 1:35; 4:31; 6:10, 18, 23; 7:12, 13; 8:7, 18; 10:11 etc.
41 Ex. 13:11; Deut. 2:14; 13:18; 19:8; 26:15; 28:9; 29:12; Judg. 2:15; 2 Sam. 3:9 etc.

reinforce a background for a present action of word, etc.[42] In light of this function of שבע it is no longer possible to simply assume that Ps. 110:4 refers to a new oracle. A promise made in the past is also a possibility. To choose between these two options a comparison with Ps. 89 and 132 is of particular importance. These psalms speak of the irrevocability of the Davidic promise. Ps. 89:36 [35] emphasizes that the Lord does not lie to David. The promise stands unchanged. That entails for the present situation that the covenant is not absolved. A similar emphasis is present in Ps. 132. The Lord states in 132:11 that he does not turn back on the oath sworn to David. This same emphasis also seems to be present in Ps. 110:4, ולא ינחם. The promise is not, and will not be, taken back. Against this background it is possible to conclude that Ps. 110:4, like Ps. 89 and 132, makes reference to the past.[43] This conclusion is supported by 5aA, 'the Lord is at your right hand.' Structural reemployment of words from 1b makes the concept of protection evident here. Seen from the perspective of a promise already given, the emphatic reference to God's protecting right hand becomes understandable. This indicates a clear dependence with respect to the relationship between the two canticles. As to content, this entails that the canticles may not be interpreted as two relatively independent oracles standing side by side. It is necessary to look for a theme integral to both.

In order to trace the theme of this psalm it is advisable to begin with the verses least hampered by exegetical debate. From this starting point it is possible to construct an interpretive

---

42 Cf. Deut. 1:34 ('swearing' is mentioned in the context of a look at the past); Josh. 14:9 (the question of the land is posited with an appeal to the swearing of Moses); Judg. 21:1 (the actions of the men of Israel is explained by reference to an oath previously sworn); 1 Kgs. 1:17 (memory of David's swearing in the past constitutes the basis for the present situation; cf. vs. 30); Jer. 49:13 (כי constitutes the tie with what preceeds; the oath which has been sworn forms the basis for the oracle against Edom); Jer. 51:14; Isa. 62:8; Ps. 89:21−38 (cf. the reference to 2 Sam. 7 in 89:4f.; here the reference to swearing in the past functions as ground for what will happen in the future, cf. 89:36, 50); 132:11 (the Lord does not turn back from the oath sworn to David, in other words, the promise now given is not a new one but a reference to the promise already given).

43 This conclusion is reached by Olshausen: 1853:423; Briggs: 1907:373.

framework, which in turn provides a means of studying the
function of the more enigmatic verses. Important data for the
interpretation of this psalm is provided by 1b. Frequently the
greatest emphasis is placed upon the first section of the verse,
שב לימיני. This is conceived in a number of ways. Some view
it as an accession to a place of honour.[44] Others take this a
step further and claim that it includes participation in the
Lord's rule.[45] When one then attempts to envision a specific
context in which this must be viewed, the thought of a
ceremony[46], or more specifically of an enthronement ritual[47],
immediately looms large. The latter idea constitutes the context
in which the psalm is frequently handled. However, the
objection may be raised that in what follows in the psalm there
is no direct support for this theory. Futhermore, 1b mentions
not only sitting at the right hand, but also the subjection of
enemies. Both thoughts are bound together by the framing
structure of 1b. And the temporal aspect of עד also fits in this
framework. Therefore, the action of 1bA can no longer be
construed as an independent event. Rather, sitting at the right
hand of God is connected with His exertion against the enemy.
In this connection the phrase שב לימיני appears to emphasize
the protection which God provides.[48] A similar thought is also
present in Ps. 80:16, 18, in the Lord's protection of the man of
his right hand. This view of שב לימיני also gives an initial
clue to the background of this psalm. There is apparently a

---

44 E.g. Olshausen: 1853:422; Delitzsch: 1874:202f.; Baethgen: 1904³:337;
Briggs: 1907:376; Kittel: 1929⁵·⁶:356; Gunkel: 1926⁴:481; Beaucamp: 1979:191.
45 Cf. H. Herkenne, *Das Buch der Psalmen* (HSAT V,2; Bonn, 1936) 364;
Gemser: 1949:135; Lamparter: 1953:227; Jacquet: 1979:215.
46 Schmidt: 1934:202f.
47 So e.g. A.H. Edelkoort, 'Psalm 110', *Vox Theologica* 15 (1944) 86–90
esp. 87; Th.C. Vriezen, 'Psalm 110', *Vox Theologica* 15 (1944) 81–85; A.
Weiser, *Die Psalmen* (ATD 14/15; Göttingen, 1966⁷, 477; Dahood: 1970:114;
A.A. Anderson, *Psalms*, Vol 2 (NCeB; London, 1972) 767; Van der Ploeg:
1973–1975:251.
48 Cf. W.O.E. Oesterley, *The Psalms Translated with Text–critical and
Exegetical Notes* (London, 1953) 463: 'The picture is a poetical way of
expressing the truth that he is under divine protection, as well as being
honoured. But, further, he is to *sit*, an attitude which throughout the East
... implies inactivity'.

situation in which a king is in need of protection from the
enemies who have placed him in a difficult position.

The picture is elaborated in vs. 2a,b. In the first place there
is the extension of the sceptre from Zion. This could indicate
accession to kingship, but it can also be viewed as a
reinstatement to power. The latter option fits well with verse
1b. One may presume that the king was brought into difficulty
by his enemies, and thereby lost his rule. He can no longer rule
in and from Zion. His dominion is now בקרב איביך. The
combination of רדה and בקרב occurs only here. In other
instances רדה is always connected with ב. It is possible that
the striking combination used here was chosen deliberately to
emphasize that it is a ruling amidst the enemies. In other
words, the problem raised in the first and second strophe is
that of the king who receives protection under circumstances in
which he is no longer able to exercise his dominion in the
appropriate manner. It is in this situation that he receives
assurance of the Lord's protection.

The problem sketched above brings us ultimately to vs. 7,
and especially 7b. This verse provides a conclusion for the whole
psalm, e.g. with the combination רגל and ראש. Because of this
connection it may be expected that the problem delineated
above also plays a role in 7b. Of significance for the
interpretation of 7b is the meaning of the combination ירים
ראש. This combination occurs with the *Hiphil* form of the verb
in Ps. 3:4; 110:7, and with the *Qal* in Ps. 27:6. In the latter
psalm the concept of victory over the enemy is placed in the
foreground. 'My head raises itself up above my enemies.' This
victory is possible because God acts as protector. A similar
thought is present in Ps. 3:4. God provides protection against
the enemies[49] and 'raises my head.' In both of these psalms the
conviction is expressed that amidst enemies and opposition God
grants restoration. A similar notion of restoration is expressed in
the related but more frequently occurring phrase נשא ראש.[50]

---

49 The threat by Absalom may be seen as the context of this psalm.
50 In Gen. 40:13, 20 this expression is used to describe the restoration of
the butler to office. Similarly, it is used to describe the restoration of
Jehoiachin (2 Kgs. 25:27 = Jer. 52:31). A similar thought is present in Judg.
8:28. The Midianites are subdued; they bow down and do not raise their
heads. Here the concepts of subjugation and non—restoration stand parallel.

Consequently, ירים ראש may be assumed to mean restoration or rehabilitation. How this relates to 7a we momentarily leave aside. But it is clear in any event that this meaning fits well with the psalm as a whole. In contrast to the threat at the hands of the enemies with which the psalm begins, the conclusion indicated by על־כן deals with delivery. This rehabilitation is a result of the Lord's presence at the right hand (5aA).

From the introduction and conclusion of the psalm the main theme can be summarized. A king (consider אדני in 1aA) is entangled in a threatening situation. Apparently this threat results in loss of kingship; he must now exercise his authority in the midst of enemies. Therefore God himself extends to him the sceptre from Zion. But that is not yet the end of the matter. He will be restored.

This summary of the main theme of Ps. 110 suggests that a specific historical situation constitutes the background of the psalm. A concrete situation is hinted at in the opening נאם of 1aA and in the swearing of the Lord in 4a. This is directed at a specific addressee, אדני.[51] Apparently a word from the Lord comes to him in a situation in which he is threatened. It is not a simple matter to detect the precise background, but the proposal of an enthronement defended by many authors[52] does not seem probable. Why would 7b then speak of rehabilitation? This argument also opposes Dahood's view in which Ps. 110 is a song celebrating a military victory.[53] Dahood correctly emphasizes the military dimension of the entire psalm. But what purpose is served by this military emphasis? Does it indicate conflict concerning kingship in the Hasmonean period, as assumed by Gerleman?[54] Or is it more justifiable, in accord

---

Zech. 2:4 [1:21] expresses this with the statement that Judah is so scattered that no one can raise his head. Thus, they could not be restored. Finally, mention may be made of Job 10:15. Job's miserable situation precludes the possibility of raising his head. Restoration is no longer possible.

51   Cf. too Gunkel: 1926[4]:486.

52   Cf. Gemser: 1949:133; Van der Ploeg: 1973–1975:251; Kraus: 1978[5]:929 etc.

53   Dahood: 1970:112.

54   G. Gerleman, 'Psalm CX', *VT* 31 (1981) 1–19 esp. 17ff.

with most exegetes, to look for a pre—exilic kingship?[55] The
latter option is reinforced by the affinity between Ps. 110 and
Ps. 3. Both psalms speak of threat at the hand of enemies,
and exaltation of the head. In both instances the Lord rises
against the enemy. David's flight from Absolom, which is
described in 2 Sam. 15:13ff. and 16:5—14, is mentioned as the
background for Ps. 3. David's kingship is threatened and he
temporarily deserts Jerusalem. One can assume that this
situation is also reflected in the background of Ps. 110. In this
time of flight and threat comes the divine word promising
protection and restoration of kingship. The sceptre will be
extended to the king from Jerusalem, now that he is literally in
the midst of his enemies. And the enemies will not overcome
him because he is sustained by the Lord's promise.

On the basis of the major theme of this psalm and the
historical background which has been posited above, it is now
necessary to investigate how the verses not yet discussed fit into
the picture. Do these verses refute or confirm the theory thus
far proposed? Of the remaining verses, 3a,b first demands our
attention. This verse is translated and explained in a great
variety of ways.[56] However, it appears to be clear that 3aA
speaks of the presence of a people.[57] This people is prepared to
assist the king in his day of combat. The conclusion of 3b
reinforces this emphasis with לך ... ילדתיך. Viewed structurally
this forms an inclusion with 3aA. The young men are present.[58]
In 3bA,B mention is then made of the circumstances in which
these helpers of the king appear. What precisely is intended
here is not clear. One can debate whether 3bA refers to

---

55 A context in the Davidic period is defended by, among others, Delitzsch:
1874:201; Briggs: 1907:374; M.A. Beek, 'De exegetische moeilijkheden van
Psalm 110', *Vox Theologica* 15 (1944) 96; Vriezen: 1944:84; E.R. Hardy, 'The
Date of Psalm 110', *JBL* 64 (1945) 385—390; Gemser: 1949:133; cf. too J.W.
Bowker, 'Psalm CX', *VT* 17 (1967) 31—41 esp. 41. A more general,
pre—exilic reference is held by, e.g., Kittel: 1929[5,6]:357; Gunkel: 1929[4]:484;
Van der Ploeg: 1973—75: 248ff.

56 For a summary of various translations consult Jacquet: 1979:210f.

57 See the discussion of H.J. Stoebe, 'Erwägungen zu Psalm 110 auf dem
Hintergrund von 1 Sam. 21,' in: *Festschrift Friedrich Baumgärtel zum
70.Geburtstag 14.Januar 1958* (Erlangen, 1959) 175—191 esp. 184ff.

58 With respect to ילדות as young men see e.g. Stoebe: 1959:188f.

clothing. Or, with a textual emendation בהררי, a location could
be intended. For the latter option some support may be
adduced from the fact that if this is the case a certain affinity
of imagery is created in 3b namely הר, שחר and טל. The
combination of these terms is also found elsewhere.[59] However,
the proposal concerning clothing is also possible, as Stoebe has
demonstrated.[60] Regardless of which option is chosen, the major
emphasis of 3a,b is clear. It has to do with the help offered the
king. Consequently, this verse confirms the main emphasis
identified above.

Is that also the case in 4a,b? Structural research showed that
this verse does not refer to a new utterance but to the promise
previously granted. The promise places particular emphasis upon
the phrase לעולם. The primary reference here is not to an
unlimited time duration, but must be viewed relative to the
addressee. לעולם indicates that the addressee will continue to
function as כהן for the duration of his life.[61] This does not
deny that echoes of a broader reference pertaining to promised
dynastic succession may also be heard. But in the context of
this psalm it refers more immediately to the addressee. He
remains כהן forever. This כהן is described more precisely in
4bB via comparison[62] with Melchizedek, who is known from
Gen. 14:18 as king and priest. This connection with Melchizedek
suggests that the function as כהן here cannot be viewed as an
independent function as priest.   The king is addressed in his
function as priest. This in turn raises new questions. Can the
king be addressed as priest, and if so, why is he addressed here
in this manner?

A study of kingly functions significantly reveals that David
and Solomon are described as fulfilling priestly functions. David
is pictured in priestly attire during the return of the ark (2
Sam. 6:14). He made a tent for the ark (2 Sam. 6:17; 7:2). And

---

59   Cf. the combination הר and שחר in Joel 2:2; Am.4:13 and the
collocation of הר and טל in 2 Sam. 1:21; Hag. 1:10,11; Ps. 133:3.
60   Stoebe: 1959:187v.
61   Compare the expression in 1 Kgs. 1:31; Neh. 2:3; Ps. 61:7f. See, for
example, Olshausen: 1853:424; Schmidt: 1934:203.
62   Cf. Delitzsch: 1874:205; Baethgen 1904[3]:338; Briggs: 1907:378, 380;
Kittel: 1929[5,6]:355, 357f.; Gunkel: 1926[4]:481, 483; Schmidt: 1934:202;
Herkenne: 1936:365; Beek 1944:95; Tournay: 1960:18f.

David makes sacrifices (2 Sam. 6:17) and offers prayers to the Lord (2 Sam 7:18). Solomon too sacrifices in the tent (1 Kgs. 3:15). David and Solomon both bring offerings in a context which includes the presence of the congregation (2 Sam. 6:13, 17; 24:25; 1 Kgs. 3:15; 8:5, 63). Both bless the people (2 Sam. 6:18; 1 Kgs. 8:14, 56) and pray on their behalf (2 Sam. 24:17; 1 Kgs. 8:30ff.). And there are additional hints at a relationship between the functions of king and priest. Priests are mentioned in the list of his officebearers (2 Sam. 8:15—18; 20:23—26; regarding Solomon cf. 1 Kgs. 4:2). The sons of David are called priests (2 Sam. 8:18).[63] Solomon installed priests (1 Kgs. 2:35). And in a later period of the kingship it is possible to detect kings functioning as priests, as e.g. in 2 Kgs. 16:13 where king Ahaz makes the first sacrifice on the new altar. Is there a hint of something similar in Jer. 30:21 where the ruler may approach the Lord? Finally, mention may be made of the place occupied by the leader (נשיא) in Ez. 44:3; 45:17; 46:2ff., etc. This section of Ezekiel also emphasizes the priestly role of the leader.[64] Only in later times the priestly function of the king became problematical (cf. 2 Chron. 16ff.). These facts are sufficient to demonstrate that in any respect, in the offices of David and Solomon, a priestly, mediatorial role is present.[65] The king is able to function in this role because he is the head of a theocratic nation. Naturally this does not entail that the king becomes a priest in the ordinary sense of that word.[66] His function in this capacity must also be viewed against the background of the concept of kingship in the *Umwelt* of that time.[67]

---

63   Is this possibly related to David's provision of a tent for the ark?

64   Concerning נשיא cf. W. Zimmerli, *Ezechiel 2* (BKAT XIII/2; Neukirchen—Vluyn, 1962ff.) 1227ff.

65   Cf. Briggs: 1907:378,380; Kittel: 1929⁵,⁶:357f.; Beek: 1944:95; Jacquet: 1979:221f.

66   Cf. the description which Jacquet: 1979:223 gives: '....en Israël, le Roi, Chef d'une *Nation théocratique*, se trouve, du fait de son Onction sacrée, constitué dans un état privilégié, qui, sans faire de lui un Prêtre au sens propre et institutionnel du terme, l'habilite néanmoins à agir, dans des circonstances déterminés, comme Chef religieux du Peuple qu'il gouverne politiquement de la part de Yahvé.'

67   Cf. e.g Jacquet: 1979:221f.

If 4bA is viewed as a reference to a priestly *function* rather than to a priest as such, the reference to 'swearing' as an action of the past also becomes clearer. The emphasis then falls upon the continuation of his function. In this manner the Lord's oath can change the present situation in which the king is caught in the midst of his enemies. As 5aA states, 'the Lord is at your right hand.' Therefore restoration may be expected in accord with the promise of a continuing function in his office. But the question then remains, why is this function described by use of the term כהן? It may be possible to answer this question with reference to the entire structure of the psalm. The chart on p. 221 demonstrates that strophes 2 and 4 are more or less parallel. The reference to ציון in 2aB could have called for the term כהן in 4bA. Furthermore, employment of this term in 4b serves to include the entire kingly function (cf. כהן in 4bA and מלכי in 4bB). Taken together these references emphasize that the king continues to function, and that his kingship is maintained through the relationship to Zion, the religious symbol of the royal city. It was to that city that David brought the ark, and there he erected the tent.

With respect to 5aB and following, the discussion above of structure raised a number of questions. It appeared as if a shift in the whole structure of the psalm was detectable. On the basis of structure it was not possible to conclude more than that. Any further conclusions must also take content into consideration. When one concentrates on the content of 5aB and following, it is noteworthy that the imagery of judgement is far more extensive than the day of apposition in 3aB. The perspective here seems to be broader than in 3aB. It is not only enemies in the immediate vicinity who fall under judgement, but all peoples are included. And one gets the impression that 6aC intends a specific opponent, referred to as ראש על־ארץ רבה. The combination of ראש with על also has the meaning of 'head over' in Deut. 1:15.[68] The territory of which he is head is described somewhat secretively here as the whole earth. It is difficult to correlate this with the head of the enemies in vs. 1.

---

68 Cf. Josh. 11:10; Judg. 10:10; 11:8,9,11; 2 Sam. 22:44 = Ps. 18:44; Hos. 2:2; Isa. 7:8f.; Job 29:25 (ראש / מלך). Zie J. Bartlett, 'The Use of the Word *rōš* as a Title in the OT', *VT* 19 (1969) 1−10.

In light of vs. 6 he seems to be ruler of a world empire. If this is correct it breaks with the unified interpretation of the psalm to this point. Or is it necessary to conclude that the perspective is consciously expanded? Is this an actualisation within the psalm? There are a number of clues in these verses which suggest that this is the case. First, mention may be made of the structural coherence of 5aB–6aC via the verb מחץ. This causes 5aA to stand somewhat independent from what follows. The connection with על־כן in 7b is also problematic. Ordinarily this is viewed as a conclusion arising out of 7a. But this is not entirely satisfactory, as may be seen from the great variety of interpretation of 7a. Or, is it necessary to conclude from the somewhat awkward connection between 7a and 7b that this is evidence of actualisation? Is there an intentionally distorted connection? It is noteworthy that the word ראש is used in both 6aC and 7b. Via this concept a connection is executed between the second and third strophes of the second canticle. Additional links are absent. In light of all the tensions mentioned above it is possible to assume a deliberate connection here.

The approaches via structure and content produce the same picture. These verses do not seem to join simply and naturally with the surrounding verses. On the contrary, it is possible to detect a thematic expansion. And this thematic expansion leads to structural changes within the Psalm. In other words, 5aB–6a is an actualising expansion. This expansion probably also includes 7a. The phrase על־כן of 7b then joins directly to 5aA as the conclusion stemming from the presence of the Lord at the right hand. This help designates rehabilitation as has been sketched in the discussion of the major theme of this psalm.

The background and incentive for this actualisation becomes evident via a number of expressions in these verses. Mention may be made of יום־אפו (the judgement which will come upon the peoples), and ראש על־ארץ רבה. Taken together, these concepts remind one of the period of the exile. In this time period 'the day of the Lord' is mentioned numerous times. The king of the whole earth may be equated with the king of Babylon. He will be crushed. And in contrast, an enduring dynasty will remain in Israel. One can think specifically of king Jehoiachin who was taken into captivity. As was the case with David previously, he no longer rules in Jerusalem; his situation is comparable. David's return and the restoration of his rule, will find a similar counterpart in the case of Jehoiachin. The

Lord will defeat the enemy and create the opportunity for the restoration of the king to his office. By this means, the actualisation of 5aB and following continues the original expectation of the psalm. The same theme, namely expulsion from rulership and then subsequent restoration, continues to sound through.

This leaves only 7aA to be considered yet. Numerous emendations have been proposed for this verse,[69] but neither the Masoretic text or the other manuscripts support such changes. The interpretation will have to be based upon the Masoretic text. The subject of 7aA is debated. Is it the Lord? 7b counters this possibility. The Lord restores the king to his function. This can hardly be seen as the result of drinking of water. Furthermore, 7b appears to continue the line of 5aA, and the על־כן must be taken in that connection. Nor does it seem likely to take the defeated king as subject, since he is crushed. Furthermore, 5aB—6aC forms a self—contained unity. A third possibility as subject is the king who is being addressed. In this case one must not think of a king who has already been victorious, but rather of a king who enjoys God's protection and who will be restored. If it is correct that 7a must also be viewed as an actualisation, it speaks of a king in exile. With respect to this king is stated that he will drink water. The imagery of drinking water along the way reminds one of Isa. 41:17ff. Here too mention is made of people in search of water because they are traveling through the wilderness. From the manner in which reception of water functions in Isa. 41:17ff., it is possible to assume that the imagery in Ps. 110:7a refers to protection. Perhaps this can be stated even more concretely as an indication of a return from exile.

Following these exegetical notes we return to a consideration of the structure. The discussion above indicated that it was necessary to conclude that there is a double structure operative in Ps. 110. The question raised in that regard, as to whether the plurality of structure could be explained via a theory of actualisation, may be answered positively on the basis of our study of content. This correspondence between structure and content can be shown as follows:

---

69   Cf. Jacquet: 1979:213f.; Gilbert—Pisano: 1980:353f.

Original structure of Ps. 110:

Canticle I: strophe 1: 1a—1b
       2: 2a—2b   Canticle II: strophe   1:   4a—4b
       3: 3a—3b   2:   5aA+7b

This original structure is dominated by the first strophe, with the word בא׳ם, of which strophes 2 and 3 of the first canticle and strophes 1 and 2 of the second canticle are further elaborations. The line of thought focuses upon the king David who was driven out but will be restored to kingship again.

Subsequent to actualisation the following structure is present:

Canticle I: strophe 1: 1a—1b   Canticle II: strophe 1: 4a—4b
       2: 2a—2b   2: 5a—6a
       3: 3a—3b   3: 7a—7b

The two canticles now stand parallel. Accordingly, the divine oracle in 1b stands parallel to that in 4b. The main line of thought continues to focus upon the king who will be restored to kingship. However, now that the two canticles receive a more independent existence there is more freedom for a new elaboration of Ps. 110. Even in a time when there is no longer a king, this psalm can continue to reflect a tune of hope and expectation. Various aspects of the psalm can be emphasized. The motif of the priest, (as restoration of the past?) can play a role in the time of the Hasmonean kings. At that time king and priest once again appear to be closely correlated. They called themselves priests of the highest God.[70] A new interpretation is also present in the translation of the LXX of Ps. 110. This is especially present in the translation of vs. 3. By translating the end of vs. 3 with 'I have born you' a connection is made with Ps. 2:6ff.[71] The king is seen as the son of God, which shows a messianic anticipation.[72] It is noteworthy that vs. 3 is never

---

70   Assumptio Mosis 6:1. Consider too 1 Macc. 14:41.
71   Cf. Van der Ploeg: 1973—1975:255.
72   Tournay: 1960:12: 'L'interprétation alexandrine est directement messianique et doit être rapprochée de textes comme *Dan.*, VII,9—14 et *Hénoch*. XLVI, 1—5. Qu'elle soit considérée comme inspirée ou non, elle témoigne de conceptions évoluées sur l'origine céleste du Messie, dans le courant du IIe siècle avant J.—C.'

cited in the New Testament. In addition to the appeal to vs. 4 in Hebrew, and the emphasis upon Christ's highpriestly office, it is especially vs. 1 which plays a role in the New Testament. Via citation of this verse the entire focus is placed upon humiliation and exaltation. It is this theme which also constitutes the major emphasis of Ps. 110 in the interpretation defended above. The open interpretation of the psalm in this way shows how it plays a role in the formation of New Testament Christology.

STROPHES AND STANZAS IN THE BOOK OF JOB

A Historical Survey

Pieter van der Lugt

Modern researchers sometimes create the impression that serious study in the area of the structure of Hebrew poetry really only begins with them. Similarly, the impression is frequently given that it is hardly worthwhile to present the efforts of previous scholars when discussing the strophic arrangement which is fundamental to the structure of this poetry. These observations also pertain to studies of the poetic structures in the book of Job. Brief insight into earlier research is afforded by H. Möller, who discusses the theories of strophe expressed by Stevenson, Hölscher, Szczygiel, Ley and Hontheim.[1] And from R. Gordis we receive a cursory bibliography of relevant literature.[2] But to attain a good understanding of the problem of strophic structure in the poetic sections of the book of Job it is essential to engage in a more in—depth and systematic analysis of the history of interpretation in this area. This history now spans more than 150 years.[3]

A. The Masoretic verse as starting point

1   F.B. Köster

The history of strophic research begins, as far as the book of Job is concerned, with the scholar *F.B. Köster*, who is also known for his theory of strophic structure in the Psalms. In

---

1   H. Möller, *Sinn und Aufbau des Buches Hiob* (Berlin, 1955) 43—45. The order of treatment appears to be quite arbitrary.

2   R. Gordis, *The Book of Job* (Moreshet Series 2; New York, 1978) 507. See too C. Kuhl, 'Neuere Literarkritik des Buches Hiob', *ThR* 21 (1953) 183—185 (discusses among others Condamin, Hölscher, Peters, Irwin and Kissane); S.L. Terrien, *Job* (CAT 13; Neuchâtel, 1963) 33 n.2.

3   For a more complete review of the history of interpretation pertaining to strophic structure in Hebrew poetry see my *Strofische Structuren in de Bijbels—Hebreeuwse Poëzie* (Kampen, 1980) 1—120.

1831 he presented a study of Job and Ecclesiastes in which he offered translations printed in such a way as to clearly delineate strophic structure.[4] In Köster's estimation the phenomenon of strophic arrangement in Hebrew poetry was closely correlated with the presence of parallelism within the verse, described by Lowth in 1753 as the *parallelismus membrorum*. 'Wie die Verse aus einer Zusammenfassung paralleler Glieder entstehn, eben so bilden sich durch Zusammenfassung paralleler Verse gewisse Strophen'.[5] In contrast to parallelism within the verse, however, Köster viewed strophic structure as an effort towards external symmetry. Discernment of these strophes is particularly dependent upon the coherence of content and thought—progressions within the *Masoretic* verses. However, in the book of Job chapters are seldom found with all the strophes containing an identical number of verses. Some strophes seem to be short one verse, or there is an extra verse, or sometimes an isolated verse which does not appear to belong to a strophe is present. With this reservation Köster distinguishes four strophic structures in the book of Job: a) strophes with an equal number of verses, e.g. the strophic scheme of 4 x 5 (Job 4) or 7 x 3 (Job 8); b) strophes with progressively higher verse totals, for example 3.4.5.5.5 (Job 10); c) an antistrophic structure such as 4.3.2.3.4 (Job 17); d) a parallel strophic structure, e.g. 3.2.4/3.2.4 (Job 18).

As already stated, Köster was of the opinion that in the discernment of the strophes particular attention must be paid to the coherence of thought—content in the verses. Köster suggested that in contrast to the Psalms and the prophets, in the book of Job virtually no formal indications could be found to assist in recognition of the strophes. Thus, he sought here in vain for the clearest indicator of strophic structure, the refrain. It also lacked 'gewisse stehende Wörter und Ausrufungen, welche sonst den Anfang der Strophe zu bezeichnen pflegen'.[6] As an exception to this rule, however, Köster pointed to the

---

4   See F.B. Köster, *Das Buch Hiob und der Prediger Salomos nach ihrer strophischen Anordnung übersetzt*. Nebst Abhandlungen über den strophischen Charakter dieser Bücher (Schleswig, 1831) esp. VIII–XXIV.

5   Köster: 1831:VIII.

6   Köster: 1831:IX. The absence of these formal indicators was judged to be a result of the brevity 'der gnomischen Dichtkunst'.

frequent use in Job of the particle הן, which usually indicates
the beginning of a new strophe. Especially chapter 36 provides a
striking example of this (note vss. 5, 22, 26 and 30). On these
grounds we must conclude that the 'Sinn-Abschnitte' form the
most reliable indicators in the search for strophic structure in
the poetry of the book of Job.

2   *Further in the line of Köster*

Köster's insights into strophic structure have in the previous
century exercised considerable influence upon many scholars.
J.G. Stickel agreed in principle with his theory, though in its
practical implementation he made many corrections.[7] The
commentary on Job by *K. Schlottmann* also took Köster's
insights very seriously.[8] And in the Job commentary of 1869 *A.
Dillmann* in turn demonstrated his dependence upon
Schlottmann for his structural analysis of the speeches of Job
and his friends.[9] Dillmann already also expressed his conviction
that the exegete could no longer avoid a discussion of the
'logische und strophische Gliederung der Reden'.[10] Schlottmann
and Dillmann frequently bring greater precision to Köster's
strophic delineations. This is evident for example in the
respective strophic analyses offered for Job 8. While Dillmann
finds in this chapter a 3.3//3.3/6//3 pattern, Köster offers a
less precise 7 x 3 structure. So, Schlottmann's commentary
marked a step forward on the path of strophe research. Köster
had already detected that some of the debate portions of Job
could be divided into two or three parts. Chapter 3, for
example, he divided into the sub–units of vss. 3–10, 11–19 and
20–26. Schlottmann, however, distinguished various layers in
every poem. In other words, according to Schlottmann, the
development of the thought patterns within a given poem was
structured at various levels. As starting point he frequently
divided a poem into some major units, which in turn were

---

7   See J.G. Stickel, *Das Buch Hiob* (Leipzig, 1842) esp. 278–283.
8   See K. Schlottmann, *Das Buch Hiob* (Berlin, 1851) esp. 67–68.
9   See A. Dillmann, *Hiob* (KeH 2. Lief.; Leipzig, 1869[3]). Regarding the
4th edit. of this commentary from 1891 see below, section B, n.20.
10   Dillmann: 1869[3]:VII.

238 Pieter van der Lugt

further divided into strophes. And finally, in his opinion the strophes continually demonstrate a particular poetic structuring. Accordingly, for ch. 15 he suggested the following division: vss. 2—16 (first major unit), 17—19 ('Zwischenglied'), 20—35 (second major unit); the strophes he marked as vss. 2—6, 7—11, 12—16 / 17—19 / 20—24, 25—30, 31—35. As strophic scheme he thus suggests a 5.5.5/3/5.6.5 pattern. The poetic structuring of the strophes can then be presented as 2.2.1/2.2.1/2.2.1//3//3.2/ 2.2.2/3.2.

In this connection mention must also be made of the contribution of *H. Ewald* to the study of strophic structure in the book of Job.[11] In his opinion not one of the debate speeches consists of all uniform strophes; rather, various groups of uniform strophes follow each other within the progression of the speech.[12] The most noteworthy was that a single verse would frequently interrupt a regular series of strophes when the emotions could no longer be restrained. Ewald refers in this regard to 5:17, 27; 9:29; 13:13; 21:16; 24:13; 19:21—22. This variegated interchanging of strophic structure was credited to the 'dramatic' character of the book of Job.

In the twentieth century *H. Möller* made more or less explicit recourse to the strophic theories of Köster.[13] Typical of this author is a repeated assertion of antistrophic structure (Köster's third category of strophic structure) in the debate speeches of Job and his friends. Möller speaks here of chiastic strophic arrangement, for example 20.7.20 (chs. 4—5), 10.13.10 (chs. 9:25—10:22) or 10.9.10 (ch. 13). As these strophic schemes already depict, for Möller the strophes are frequently much lengthier than is the case with Köster.[14]

---

11 See H. Ewald, *Allgemeines über die hebräische Dichtung und über das Psalmenbuch* (Die Dichter des Alten Bundes I.1; Göttingen, 1866[2]) esp. 195—197. By the same author, *Das Buch Ijob* (Die Dichter des Alten Bundes III; Göttingen, 1854[2]).

12 That is why Stickel already reproached Ewald that the strophes presupposed were too long and that his strophic schemes did not show enough regularity (Stickel: 1842:279).

13 See Möller: 1955:45—47.

14 However, the length of Möller's strophes is somehow connected with the length of the poems in the book of Job. In shorter poems 2—line and 3—line strophes are also recognized, e.g. in ch. 26 (scheme: 2.1.3.3.3.1).

All of the authors mentioned thus far have in common the principle of measuring the length of the strophe in terms of the *Masoretic* verses constituent to the particular strophe.[15] Dillmann continued this practice through the 1869 edition of his commentary. In the edition of 1891, however, he broke a new trail in this respect! He then adopted what was at that time the most accessible conception of the delimitation of the Hebrew verse line. A new phase had dawned in the study of strophic structure.

B. The stich as the fundamental unit of the strophe

Shortly after publishing his ideas regarding strophic structure, Köster was indirectly attacked by J.G. Sommer. Sommer too was of the impression that strophic structure was recognizable in O.T. poetry. In a work published in 1846 he attempted to demonstrate, however, that the length of the strophe was determined by the sum total of the verse elements, called stichoi, of which the strophe is structered.[16] He thereby departed from the vision of Köster in which the Masoretic verse was treated as the most important building—block of the Hebrew strophe. Sommer's conclusions slowly gained increasing support amongst other researchers of O.T. poetry.

With regard to the study of poetic structure in the book of Job it was particularly *Franz Delitzsch*'s commentary that for the first time proceeded from the stichos as the fundamental unit of the strophe.[17] Especially the study of *A. Merx* gained a certain degree of fame in this regard.[18] In contrast to Delitzsch, he suggested that within a given pericope a certain amount of consistency must be seen in the length of the strophes, and furthermore, that any given strophe could not include more than

---

15   This is also done in the commentaries of Zöckler and Hitzig. See O. Zöckler, *Das Buch Job* (Bielefeld usw., 1872) and F. Hitzig, *Das Buch Hiob* (Leipzig und Heidelberg, 1874)

16   See J.G. Sommer, 'Die alphabetischen Lieder von Seiten ihrer Structur und Integrität', *Biblische Abhandlungen I* (Bonn, 1846) 93—182. Regarding Sommer see now Van der Lugt: 1980:8—13.

17   See Franz Delitzsch, *Das Buch Iob* (Keil—Delitzsch IV.2; Leipzig, 1876²) esp. 13—14.

18   A. Merx, *Das Gedicht von Hiob* (Jena, 1871) esp. LXXV—LXXXVIII.

8 stichoi.[19]   Consequently, we find with Merx a strophic scheme of 6.6.6/8.8.8 (ch. 8), or 4.4.4.4/4.6.6.4/4.6.4.6 (ch. 22), while Delitzsch proposed schemes such as the structural schematisation 6.7.6.10.8.6 (ch. 8). According to Merx, a shift to a new strophic structure within a given poem is always indicative of a shift in the debate 'so daß in den strophischen Systemen zugleich die ganze logische Anordnung der Reden ausgedrückt liegt'.[20]

Much affinity to the strophic analyses of Merx is encountered in *G.H.B. Wright*'s critical translation of the book of Job.[21] Wright emphasizes that a distinction must be made between what he terms 'cantos' and 'stanzas'. A canto always includes several stanzas; two or more cantos together constitute a complete poem. However, in relatively short poems, such as Job 8 and 11 for example, the cantos may not be present. 'There is not however the regularity in the formation of these that is required in modern poetry'.[22]

G. Bickell too used the total number of stichoi to measure the extent of a strophe.[23] In contrast to Delitzsch, Merx and Wright, however, Bickell[24] was of the opinion that the author of

---

19 Merx: 1871:LXXVI and LXXVIII. Cf. Delitzsch: 'Ueberhaupt ist es nicht unsere Meinung, das Buch bestehe durchweg aus liederartig strophischen Reden', 1876[2]:14.

20 Merx: 1871:LXXX. As an example Merx points to the structure of Job 15: 6.4.4.4/5x6/7.7.8. As noted above (see A.2), in 1891 Dillmann accepted the position of Delitzsch and Merx concerning the length of the Hebrew poetic line. According to Dillmann by counting the number of stichoi one receives a more precise picture of the length of the strophe (1891[4]:XXIV).

21 G.H.B. Wright, *The Book of Job* (London, 1883) esp. 23–25. In the foreword Wright states that his book 'is intended to follow in the wake of the Critical Edition of A. Merx'.

22 Wright: 1883:23. Merx is unjustly reproached here as not having had an eye for the 'cantos'. At times there is a high degree of conformity between the strophic analyses of Merx and Wright, e.g. regarding chs. 9–10: 6.6.6.6 /6.8.8.8.8 /6.8.8.8.8 /6.4.6 (Merx);   6.6.6.6 /6.8.8 /8.8.6 /8.8.8 /8.5.5.7 (Wright). But frequently their conclusions disagree, e.g. regarding ch. 22: 6.6.6/8.8.4/4.8.8 (Wright); for Merx see above.

23 Regarding Bickell see Van der Lugt: 1980:28–30 and 133 (!).

24 See G. Bickell, 'Kritische Bearbeitung des Iobdialogs', *WZKM* 6 (1892) 137–147, 241–257, 327–334; –––––, *WZKM* 7 (1893) 1–20, 153–168; esp. 6 (1892) 137. See from the same author: *Das Buch Job nach Anleitung der*

the book of Job utilized only one strophic form, namely the tetrastich strophe. *B. Duhm*, in his Job commentary, accepts Bickell's position[25], though in the concrete application of this starting point he is frequently more independent of Bickell's work than is *C.J. Ball*, who also purported that strophes in Job consisted singularly of tetrastichs[26]. Duhm combined the tetrastich strophes together into progressively higher unities, which represented the logically determined major units of debate (for example 11:2−12 and 13−20).

Although *M. Löhr* determined the extent of a strophe by the total of distichoi (bicola) rather than simply by the number of stichoi, his position should be mentioned in this context because in certain respects he went a step further than Duhm. Löhr attempted to prove that in a number of the debates in Job not only are the strophes of equal length, but also these uniformly structured strophes within the debates could be united to higher units, which in turn again produce 'Sinnesabschnitte' of uniform length.[27] This produces, for example, the structure 4x2/4x2/ 4x2/4x2/4x2/4x2 in chs. 6−7.

G. Beer already expressed his reservation regarding the strophic theories of Bickell and Duhm. In certain chapters the presence of 4−line strophes is evident. Beer hesitated, however, to conclude on this basis that the original poem was constructed entirely on the format of 4−line strophes.[28] *G. Hölscher* too was

---

Strophik und der Septuaginta (Wien, 1894) esp. 11.

25 B. Duhm, *Das Buch Hiob* (KHC 16; Freiburg i.Br., 1897). According to Duhm this very simple form of strophic structure was the most appropriate for the 'lange Reihen von Weisheitsreden' (at Job 3:2).

26 C.J. Ball, *The Book of Job* (Oxford, 1922). Ball speaks in this connection of 'quatrains'. Despite the numerous interpolations in the text this strophic form is not totally unrecognizable (Ball: 1922:34).

27 M. Löhr, 'Beobachtungen zur Strophik im Buche Hiob', *Abhandlungen zur semitischen Religionskunde und Sprachwissenschaft*, FS W.W. Graf von Baudissin (BZAW 33; Giessen, 1918) 303−321. We find here a strophic analysis of Job 3−7, 19, 29−31, 38−40:14 and 42:2−6. See from the same author: 'Die drei Bildad−Reden im Buche Hiob', *Beiträge zur alttestamentlichen Wissenschaft*, FS K. Budde (BZAW 34; Giessen, 1920) 107−112, and 'Job c. 28', *Oriental Studies Presented to Paul Haupt* (Leipzig, 1926) 67−70.

28 G. Beer, *Der Text des Buches Hiob* (Marburg, 1897) VIII.

of the opinion that strictly speaking it was not possible to produce conclusive evidence for exclusively 4–line strophes in the book of Job, though he did strongly incline to agree that the author had pursued some such structuring scheme.[29] More recently *A. de Wilde* has explicitly concurred with Hölscher's opinion.[30] He sees himself standing in a line of tradition which boasts Bickell as its first representative.[31] Nevertheless, De Wilde assumes that in certain places the structure of tetrastich strophes is broken by divergent structures: a) at the end of a debate or a substantial pericope the strophes can be lengthened, the so–called 'Fermatstrophen' (among others, 9:23–24 and 10:20–22); b) 2–line strophes sometimes serve somewhat as a heading (e.g. 24:1 and 37:1 and 14), or as a conclusion to, and emphasis of, what precedes (e.g. 5:27); c) in a few instances we find short series of hexastich strophes (3:11–19, 4:12–21 and 6:8–13).[32]

C. Formal indications of strophic structure

In A.1 above has already been noted that according to Köster in the book of Job formal criteria by which to discern strophic structure are virtually non–existent. Köster attempted to delineate an acceptable strophic structure of the speeches purely

---

29 G. Hölscher, *Das Buch Hiob* (HAT 17; Tübingen, 1952[2]) 8. In the commentary itself the layout of the translation of the debate speeches suggests that Hölscher, like Löhr, viewed the distichon as the Hebrew poetic line; repeatedly two components of the poetic verse (cola) are printed beside each other. Furthermore, consistently two (!) of these distichoi are combined together into a strophe. See further in this connection S. Mowinckel, *Real and Apparent Tricola in Hebrew Psalm Poetry* (ANVAO 2; Oslo, 1957) 102; here too is accepted that the poetic portions of Job are written in 'basic stanzas' of two distich (occasionally tristich) poetic lines.

30 A. de Wilde, *Das Buch Hiob* (OTS 22; Leiden, 1981) 63.

31 De Wilde: 1981:VIII. In approximately 40 instances De Wilde deems it necessary to resort to emendation of a damaged text (transposition, addition or deletion of poetic lines; 1981:64). Despite the circumspect manner in which these conjectures are introduced I note little difference between his approach and that of Bickell *cum suis*.

32 De Wilde: 1981:64–65. The tristichoi which appear in some instances are presumably later glosses (1981:65).

by means of consideration of contents. He did note, however, that the particle הן often served to mark the beginning or the end of a strophe. And Dillmann, in his commentary on chs. 3 and 33, noted the repetition of למה (3:11 and 20) and וצעה (30:1, 9, 16), by means of which the beginning of a strophe is repeatedly called to attention. Scholars in the 19th century were unable to discover many additional formal indicators of strophic structure in the book of Job. That is why there was a general consensus of agreement with Köster's most important presupposition. But that was not only so in the previous century, for as we shall see in the following discussion, the conclusion that in the book of Job research into the strophic structure of the debate speeches must be conducted essentially on the grounds of the progression of content and thought—development continues to be generally defended yet today.

1. The tristich as indicator of transition

Nevertheless, since the end of the previous century research into a more systematic manner of identifying formal markers of strophic structure in the book of Job has not been entirely lacking. *J. Ley*, in his metric analysis of the poetic line in Job, strongly opposed the opinions of his contemporaries who believed that the length of the Hebrew strophe could be determined by the total number of stichoi (cola) upon which it is built.[33] On the other hand he also considered it incorrect to view the Masoretic verse as the fundamental building—block of the strophe. In a number of instances we are confronted with 'Doppelverse'.[34] In his discussion of this question Ley noted the

---

[33] J. Ley, 'Die metrische Beschaffenheit des Buches Hiob', *ThStKr* 68 (1895) 635—692; esp. 635—638. Among other points Ley emphasizes that by counting the number of stichoi the 'Konformität der ... Strophen' can be disrupted when tristich verses occur in a strophe (cf. above, n.20). We must note, however, that Ley is not always consistent in this regard; see e.g. 1895:636—637.

[34] Ley: 1895:635. Ley mentions 7:20, 21; 11:6; 16:4; 31:35; 37:12; 42:3. Although an important decision is here at stake the results of this insight are not as important for strophic research in the book of Job as is the case, for example, in the Psalms or in the prophets. This is mainly due to the

appearance of many tristich lines at the end of the strophe; he
mentioned among others 4:16, 6:4, 10, 7:4, 9:24, 10:17, 11:20,
14:12. And sometimes such a tristich verse stands at the
beginning of a logical entity (e.g. 10:1, 14:7). 'Es liegt daher die
Vermutung nahe, daß diese Langverse als ein metrisches
Hilfsmittel zur Bezeichnung des Schlusses oder des Anfanges der
Abschnitte gebraucht wurden'.[35] By utilizing these metric
indicators, along with other things, Ley arrived at a reasonably
unified strophic structure for the debate speeches of Job and his
friends: e.g. 3.3.3.4.4.3.3.3.3 (ch. 6); 4.4.5.5.5 (ch. 10); 7x3 (ch.
11); 5.5.5/5.5.5 (ch. 15, where vss. 17—19 are considered to be
later additions).[36] He is unable, however, to find a similar
unified structure in the Elihu speeches.[37]

2. *Responsion and inclusion*

A completely different indication of strophic structure in Hebrew
poetry was concentrated upon at the end of the previous
century in the research of *D.H. Müller*. According to Müller the
strophes in Hebrew poetry may be recognized via their utility of
the stylistic devices of 'Responsion', 'Concatenatio' and 'Inclusio'.
The phenomenon of responsion had developed out of the
parallelismus membrorum. Responsion is for the structure of
the Hebrew poem what parallelism is for the structure of the
Hebrew verse. 'Bei streng durchgeführter Responsion

---

fact that the poetic lines delineated by Ley in the book of Job in a great
majority of instances concur with the Masoretic verses, which in turn are
ordinarily composed of two stichoi. Concerning the problem of the length of
the poetic line in Hebrew poetry see Van der Lugt: 1980:121—209.

35 Ley: 1895:636. This function is also ascribed by Ley to the 'fünftonige'
and the 'achttonige' poetic lines (1895:638). The first category appears
especially at the end of a strophe, e.g. 6:27, 11:9 and 15:6.

36 Regarding the debate speeches of Job in the first cycle, this author
presupposes that each chapter contains an independent strophic
schematization. This is also assumed for chs. 29—31; cf. Möller: 1955:47.

37 Ley: 1895:678. Also Ewald was of the opinion that regular strophic
structure was absent in chs. 32—37. Cf. too the layout of these chapters in
the translations of KBS. In his subsequent study in the book of Job Ley
made only minor corrections upon these results, for example in chs. 15,
16—17, 21—24, 30—31 and 33. See J. Ley, *Das Buch Hiob* (Halle, 1903).

correspondirt jede Zeile der einen Strophe mit der entsprechenden Zeile der zweiten Strophe entweder wörtlich genau oder gedanklich, parallel oder antithetisch'.[38] In concatenation the end of one strophe is logically or formally connected with the beginning of the following strophe. The stylistic device of inclusion serves to demarcate the borders of the strophe from the surrounding material, and to emphasize the particular character of the strophe. In Müller's opinion responsion had its origin in the manner by which the oldest prophecies in Israel were presented. These were intended to be sung responsively and were frequently structured with a strophe and an antistrophe (cf. 1 Sam. 10:5 and 19:19—24). Müller ultimately presupposed Punic influence in this regard.[39]

While Müller initially was of the impression that the artistic forms he had researched were primarily present in the prophetic texts of the O.T., two years later he detected the same principles operative in Psalms and in the wisdom literature.[40] In the studies which he then published we find, in addition to other material, an analysis of Job 14. This chapter falls into three sections, each consisting of a strophe and an antistrophe: vss. 1—3, 4—6 / 7—9, 10—12 / 13—17, 18—22 (structural scheme: 6.6/7.7/11.11). In the first section Müller indicates a number of notable responsions between the strophe (vss. 1—3) and the antistrophe (vss. 4—6): אדם ילוד אשה (vs. 1a) / טהור מטמא (vs. 4a); קצר ימים (vs. 1b) / חרוצים ימיו (vs. 5a); פקחת עינך (vs. 3a) / שעה מעליו (vs. 6a). The second strophe and its antistrophe relate to each other approximately as image and reflection. Vss. 7—9 speak about a 'dead' tree which could at anytime sprout again, while in vss. 10—12 Job says that man's death means their absolute end. In the third section the strophe suggests that there is a new life after

---

38 D.H. Müller, *Die Propheten in ihrer ursprünglichen Form* I (Wien, 1896) 191. A similar thought was in fact already suggested previously by Köster; see F. Köster, 'Die Strophen, oder der Parallelismus der Verse der hebräischen Poesie', *ThStKr* 4 (1831) 48—49 (cf. above, section A.1).
39 See Müller: 1896:ch. 5. Müller borrowed the term 'Responsion' from classical philology where it was used to designate the relationship between the strophes and the antistrophes in the chorus of the Greek drama (1896:1—2).
40 See D.H. Müller, *Strophenbau und Responsion* (Wien, 1898).

death (vss. 13–17), which is immediately denied in the
antistrophe (vss. 18–22).[41] In 1907 Müller turned once again to
the strophic structure of Job.[42] In the poems which he then
analysed (chs. 4 and 6), he was unable to indicate any
noteworthy responsions but he remained convinced that one
could not avoid the strophic structure of these chapters. The
strophic structure was closely related to the line of thought
development and it showed a certain degree of regularity:
10.10/11.11 (ch. 4) and 7.6/7.6/14.14/6 (ch. 6).

Müller's theory had a very significant influence upon research
into the strophic structure of Biblical–Hebrew poetry in the
beginning of the 20th century, and it was also applied to
research of the strophic structure in the debate speeches of Job
and his friends. *P. Vetter* already in 1897 came to the conclusion
that the strophic structures of these debates often are supported
by certain 'äußerliche Kennzeichen'. In this connection he
mentioned the refrain, responsion, anadiplosis and inclusion.[43]
For the rest, according to Vetter as well, the strophic structure
of a poem is primarily determined by 'die auf logischen
Gesichtspunkten ruhende regelmäßige Wiederkehr einer
bestimmten Gruppe von Versen'.[44] In chs. 3–27 and 29–31 the
strophes usually contain only two and never more than three
lines; in the Elihu speeches (chs. 32–37) the extent varies from
2–4 lines.[45]

Vetter's conclusion regarding the external literary form of the
strophes in the book of Job was in agreement with the
summary of *N. Schlögl*: 'Eines der wichtigsten Kennzeichen der

---

41 Müller: 1898:66–71. Strophic schematization is here made dependent
upon counting of the stichoi. However, in Proverbs and Ecclesiasticus he
defended distich poetic lines (for further discussion of Müller's position see
Van der Lugt: 1980:142–143). Job 14:4b and 14a were considered to be later
glosses, following Merx and Budde respectively.

42 D.H. Müller, *Komposition und Strophenbau* (Wien, 1907) 79–85.

43 P. Vetter, *Die Metrik des Buches Job* (Biblische Studien II.4; Freiburg
i.Br., 1897) 56 (cf. too 30–31). Instead of 'Concatenatio' (Müller) Vetter
employed the classic term 'anadiplosis' (1897:31 n.1).

44 Vetter: 1897:30. Thus, with 'verse' a combination of two or three stichoi
is understood (cf. 1897:1–2 and 27–28).

45 However, Müller was not always pleased with the analyses of Vetter; see
Müller: 1907:79 n.2 and 82 n.1.

hebräischen Strophik und in ihrem ausgedehnten Gebrauch für diese geradezu charakteristisch sind die Kunstfiguren der Responsio (Entsprechung), Concatenatio (Verkettung) und Inclusio (Einschließung, Umrahmung)'.[46] Strophic poems, according to Schlögl, can usually be dissected into uniform strophes, and the 'gemischtstrophige Lieder' usually show strophic pairs (strophe and antistrophe), or two fairly long, uniform 'Stollen' and a shorter 'Abgesang'.[47] In the book of Job that results in, among other schemes, the following patterns: 3x20 (ch. 6); 7x22 (chs. 12—14); 7x10 (ch. 15) and 14.14.4/ 10.10.2 (ch. 5); 18.18.6 (ch. 8); 20.20.10 (ch. 22).[48]

We also find recognition of the literary devices described by Müller in *N. Peters*' commentary on Job. According to Peters the 1—line, 2—line and 3—line strophes can be joined to form higher units, which within a given speech, however, do not constitute sections of a uniform length. As the most important criteria for designating both the strophes and the higher poetic units he listed among other things the 'Zusammengehörigkeit des Inhaltes, Wiederaufnahme (Anaphora), Entsprechung (Responsio), Einschließung (Inclusio) und Verkettung (Concatenatio)'.[49] Furthermore, tristich lines can indicate the beginning or the end of a logical unit. Peters thinks here, for example, of 10:22, 11:20, 19:29 and 26:14.[50]

---

46 N. Schlögl, *Die echte biblisch—hebräische Metrik* (Biblische Studien XVII.1; Freiburg i.Br., 1912) 101. In a discussion with Müller (OLZ 4 [1901] columns 417—418), Schlögl pointed out that E. Meier in 1856 had already recognized these stylistic devices in Hebrew poetry; see E. Meier, *Geschichte der poetischen National—Literatur der Hebräer* (Leipzig, 1856) 82—87, where a detailed analysis of strophic structure in the Song of Deborah (Judg. 5) is offered. As an indicator of strophic structure Schlögl also mentions 'anaphora' with reference to Ps. 96 (compare vss. 1—2a with 7—8a; 1912:98).
47 Schlögl: 1912:96—97.
48 See N.J. Schlögl, *Das Buch Ijjob* (Die heiligen Schriften des Alten Bundes III.2; Wien und Leipzig, 1916). Schlögl consistently determines the length of the strophe by a set number of stichoi.
49 N. Peters, *Das Buch Job* (EH 21; Münster in Westf., 1928) 74*. The length of the strophe is determined by Peters by the sum of the 'Langzeilen' (a 'Langzeile' is a distichon or a tristichon; 1928:69*).
50 Peters :1928:70*.

3. Strophe, antistrophe and 'Zwischenstrophe'

In *J. Hontheim*'s commentary the debate speeches of Job and
his partners—in—dialogue are subjected to the strophic system of
Zenner.[51] This system in turn displays clear affinity to the
methodology of Müller. The method, therefore, is not totally
unique.   Zenner distinguished in Psalms between songs which
could and could not be viewed as 'Chorlieder'. The uniqueness
of choir songs was that two uniform strophes (strophe and
antistrophe) were always followed by a strophe with an irregular
structure. This in turn was again followed by two uniform
strophes (the strophe and antistrophe). The uniform strophes
were sung respectively by two different temple choirs. The
middle strophe, however, was sung by the two choirs alternating
verse by verse. Zenner therefore terms it a 'Wechselstrophe'.[52]
Hontheim asserted that the strophic structure of the 'Chorlieder'
could also be found in the poetry of the book of Job. He
proceeded on the assumption that the 'poetische' and the
'logische Gliederung' of the debate speeches must totally
harmonize with each other. The term 'Wechselstrophe', however,
he replaced with the term 'Zwischenstrophe', which was more
appropriate in Job. The strophes of which the debates are
constructed always contain at least 3 lines.[53] Longer strophes
can always be divided into groups of lines ('Zeilengruppen');
sometimes an independent line can also be found here. These
'Zeilengruppen' are frequently marked by 'besondere
Kennzeichen'. Hontheim thinks for example of the repetition of
the word שם in 3:17—19 (see vss. 17a and 19a) and the
repetition of the root בוא in 3:24—26 (see 24a, 25b and 26b).[54]
In determining the strophic structure we must also be attentive
to a few frequently appearing 'Figuren'. In this connection the
stylistic features of concatenation, inclusion and responsion are

---

51   J. Hontheim, *Das Buch Job – als strophisches Kunstwerk nachgewiesen,
übersetzt und erklärt* (Biblische Studien IX.1–3; Freiburg i.Br., 1904) esp.
53–70.

52   See J.K. Zenner, *Die Chorgesänge im Buche der Psalmen* (Freiburg i.Br.,
1896) esp. 1–25.

53   With poetic line Hontheim thinks of ordinarily two and sometimes three
stichoi (1904:53–54).

54   Hontheim: 1904:90–91.

again mentioned. The beginning of a new strophe can be marked by a certain 'Stichwort' (e.g. by רעתה in ch. 30 or by הן אל in ch. 36) or by a certain particle (e.g. by אך in 13:20, 16:7, 30:24, 33:8 and 35:13 — always at the beginning of an antistrophe). Tristichoi can also be used to indicate the beginning or the end of a strophe (though this type of line is also used elsewhere), as can the use of divine names. Utilizing this system of analysis Hontheim attained schemes such as 4.4/3/8.8 (ch. 3), 3.3/6/4.4 (ch. 11), and 5.5/5/8.8 (ch. 15).

Although *A. Condamin* was not fully in agreement with the methodology of Hontheim, he too attempted to apply Zenner's system to the debate speeches in Job.[55] He does this in Job 3, 4—5 and 28. According to Condamin the correctness of the divisions suggested by Hontheim for Job 28 could not be refuted: vss. 1—5.6—11/12—20/21—24.25—28 (schematic structure: 6.6/9/4.4). But as far as external indicators are concerned, he thought that the 'répétitions verbales, destinées à souligner la distinction des strophes' in the book of Job are seldom encountered ('sont rares'); ch. 28 is an exception to this rule.[56]

D. Recent developments

We may turn now to an analysis of the more recent 'developments' in the research into strophic structure in the book of Job. We write the word developments in parenthesis here because in the last 50 years very few new perspectives have been advanced in this area. We therefore must recognize that at present not many Old Testament scholars are prepared to analyse the debates in Job according to a rigorously applied system of strophic structures. Of the few who have made such

---

55 A. Condamin, *Poèmes de la Bible* (Paris, 1933²) 192—205. For a critique of Hontheim see also Peters: 1928:75*—76*.

56 Condamin: 1933²:203. Like Hontheim he too rejected the term 'Wechselstrophe' (Zenner) and spoke of a 'strophe intermédiaire' (see 1933²:28—29). In the context of this section mention may also be made of F. Zorell, 'Ex disputatione Jobi cum amicis suis', *VD* 10 (1930) 265—268, 374—378; ------, *VD* 11 (1931) 33—37 and P. Szczygiel, *Das Buch Job* (HS V.1; Bonn, 1931). For a good discussion of the strophic system underlying Szczygiel's commentary see Möller: 1955:43—44 (see too Van der Lugt: 1980:61—63).

an attempt we mention Möller (1955) and De Wilde (1981), whose positions have already been reviewed above (in sections A.2, and B respectively). Nevertheless, in the last decades there have been other researchers who, whether in commentaries or in one or more articles, have attempted to discern the strophic structure of the debates in the book of Job, and their perspectives must also be brought to attention here.

1   E.J. Kissane

One exegete who in his commentaries continually attempted to solve the problem of strophic structure in Hebrew poetry is *E.J. Kissane*.[57] The problem of regular strophic structure is, according to Kissane, 'one of the most disputed questions' in the area of Hebrew poetry.[58] After briefly summarizing and rejecting the strophic theories of Bickell and Zenner, he defended his own system in his Job commentary as being much simpler and more natural. This system is only an application of the fundamental law that 'the strophe, like the paragraph in prose, consists of a group of verses which develop the same thought'.[59] As a result Kissane's strophes vary in length from 3 to 7 lines. These strophes can be arranged within the poem in two different ways: a) all the strophes can be of the same length; b) the strophes can have a length variation of one line within a given poem, in which case the strophes are arranged alternately. In this case the following sort of patterns emerge: 3.4.3.4 etc., 5.6.5.6 etc., or 6.7.6.7 etc. The most noteworthy aspect which Kissane believes can be demonstrated is the consistency which appears to characterize the strophic patterns utilized in the debates of Job and his partners—in—dialogue. Job's responses to Eliphaz always show the alternating strophic scheme 6.7.6.7 etc. His answers to

---

57   See E.J. Kissane, *The Book of Job* (Dublin, 1939; New York, 1946[2]); ——————, *The Book of Isaiah* I–II (Dublin, 1941–1943); ——————, *The Book of Psalms* I–II (Dublin, 1953–1954).

58   Kissane: 1939:lvi.

59   Kissane: 1939:lviii. According to Kissane the Hebrew poetic line is constructed of two, and sometimes three, stichoi. In general the Masoretic arrangement of the verses is trustworthy, but in some instances 2 consecutive tristichoi are grouped as 3 distichoi (e.g. in 29:15–17) and *vice versa* (1939:liv–lvi).

Zophar show the alternating 5.6.5.6 scheme, and Bildad is answered in strophes consisting of 6 lines. Eliphaz and Zophar speak in strophes of 5 lines each, while Bildad only uses the 3–line strophe. Somewhat more variation is found in the Elihu speeches and in the final chapters where God himself speaks.[60]

2   *W.A. Irwin*

In his strophic analysis of the book of Job, *W.A. Irwin*[61] built, in a certain sense, upon the results achieved by Ch.F. Kraft in his dissertation on strophic structure in the Psalms.[62] This study was appealed to in regard to the assertion that structural units in Hebrew poetry are only seldom indicated by formal markers. In fact, according to Irwin such markers are totally absent in the book of Job, and 'the logical separation of the contents' is the only criterion for strophic analysis.[63] Thanks to the relatively large scale of the poems in Job this material lends itself extremely well to research into the structure of Hebrew poetry. For that reason the phenomenon of strophes grouped together to form larger units, which in agreement with Kraft Irwin termed 'stanzas', particularly lends itself to such study. Studied for their structure were, in this order, Job 19, 20, 3–18, (21), 22, (23–24).

As a result of this research Irwin came to the following conclusions:

a) The occurrence of both 2–line and 3–line strophes throughout the dialogues is evident, but the 2–line strophes predominate.

b) Ordinarily the poetic line is a distich, but the tristich line must also be seriously considered, especially so when appearing in a more or less regular pattern.

c) In general the strophes are joined together in stanzas. These stanzas are 'of pure form'; in other words, the stanzas

---

60   See Kissane: 1939:lix–lx.

61   W.A. Irwin, 'Poetic Structure in the Dialogue of Job', *JNES* 5 (1946) 26–39.

62   Ch.F. Kraft, *The Strophic Structure of Hebrew Poetry as illustrated in the First Book of the Psalter* (Chicago, 1938). For a summary of this study see Van der Lugt: 1980:74–77.

63   Irwin: 1946:26a.

consist of either solely 2—line or 3—line strophes. Transition from one strophe form to another always coincides with a caesura between the stanzas.

d) Within a given debate—speech the stanzas are nearly without exception of equal length.[64] According to Irwin it is then noteworthy that in most cases a balance exists between stanzas composed of 'couplets' and stanzas composed of 'triads'; accordingly, in a given poem three 2—line strophes can occur along with two 3—line strophes. Irwin thus produces schematic patterns such as these examples: 2/4x2/4x2/4x2 (chs. 19 and 22); but also 3.3/3.3/2.2.2/3 (ch. 8).

e) 'A perplexing feature of the poem is the existence of a considerable number of isolated lines of excellent poetic form and not inappropriate content'.[65] In this category must be considered 3:6b—c, 23, 6:14, 15:6, 19:4, 22:12(?). This is probably a characteristic of the original author's style — 'a sort of artistic release from the regularity of his structure'.[66]

3 *J. Herz*

In an article entitled 'Formgeschichtliche Untersuchungen zum Problem des Hiobbuches' *J. Herz* was of the opinion that he could improve upon the conclusions of Kautzsch (1910), Volz (1921) and Hertzberg (1950) with regard to the strophic structure of the book of Job, by virtue of the results of his own research.[67] According to Herz, as a rule in Hebrew poetry a certain number of stichoi (usually 4 or 8, 3 or 6, less frequently 5 or 7) are connected to form uniform strophes. The strophic boundaries are always clearly recognizable because almost without exception they correspond 'mit den Sinnzäsuren des Textes'.[68] For the debate—speeches of Job and his friends Herz attempts for example to make the following schemes acceptable: 3x4/3x4/3x4 (ch. 3); 12x6 (chs. 4—5); 8x12 (chs. 6—7 and 9—10); 10x6 (ch. 15).

---

64 Cf. Löhr (see above, section B).
65 Irwin: 1946:38a.
66 Irwin: 1946:38b.
67 J. Herz, 'Formgeschichtliche Untersuchungen zum Problem des Hiobbuches', *WZ der Karl—Marx—Universität Leipzig* 3 (1953—1954) 157—162.
68 Herz: 1953—1954:157b.

4.   P.W. Skehan

In light of what has already been discussed in section C above,
it is noteworthy that the authors we have so far dealt with in
this section have said virtually nothing concerning use of formal
indications, stylistic devices, or poetic indicators which might
confirm or support an analysis of strophes in the poetry of the
book of Job. Irwin as much as flatly denied that such formal
devices exist in the poetry of Job. We find more attention paid
to this dimension of the strophic structure of the Job dialogues
in the articles written by *P.W. Skehan*.[69] Although this author
builds upon Kissane's commentary as a starting point, he also
attempts to combine Kissane's conclusions regarding strophe
with a new conception of the macro—stucture of the dialogues in
the first cycle (chs. 4—14), by means of which the formal
aspects of strophic structuring once again are allowed a function
in the analysis.

Skehan is of the opinion that the positive results of Kissane's
study of strophic structure in the dialogues have not nearly been
done justice by Old Testament scholars. He thinks in particular
of the conclusions regarding 3—line strophes in Bildad's speeches,
5—line strophes from Eliphaz, and the observation that the
responses of Job to Eliphaz always follow the same strophic
pattern.[70] However, one important principle in the first dialogue
cycle was missed by Kissane; the speeches of Eliphaz and Job
in chs. 4—14 are deliberately structured as alphabetic poems. In
other words, their structure is based upon the alphabetic
acrostic in which the poem can contain 22 or 23 lines. Thus,
according to Skehan, the first speech of Eliphaz has a
fundamental pattern of 22.23+1 (4:2—5:2/5:3—26+5:27), the
response of Job 22+4.3+23 (6:2—23+24—27/28—30+7:1—21;
6:24—30 forms the transition from the one poem to the next).

---

69   P.W. Skehan, 'Strophic Patterns in the Book of Job', *CBQ* 23 (1961)
125—142 (we find here a strophic analysis of Job 3—27); ——————, 'Job's
Final Plea (Job 29—31) and the Lord's Reply (Job 38—41)', *Biblica* 45
(1964) 51—61. Both studies reproduced in: *Studies in Israelite Poetry and
Wisdom* (CBQ Monograph Series 1; Washington, 1971) 96—113 and 114—123
respectively. The articles by Skehan form the basis for the strophic divisions
in NAB.
70   Skehan: 1971:96.

Job's response to Bildad has a basic pattern of 23.11.22
(9:2−24/9:25−10:1a/10:1b−22; the eleven lines in 9:25−10:1a
form exactly a 'half' poem). His response to Zophar shows a
pattern 22+2.3+22.23 (12:2−13:2/13:3−27/14:1−22; the first two
poems are connected by an 'extra, transitional, 5−line grouping'
in 13:1−5).[71]

The alphabetising character of these chapters is reinforced,
according to Skehan, by the poet's use of 'quasi−acrostic
devices', which to a certain extent serve as external markers of
the alphabetic units and strophes. Accordingly, the repetition of
a particular letter at the beginning of a series of lines can serve
to delineate a sense−unit; in the strophes 9:13−15, 22−24 and
29−31, for example, each line begins with an א. Some of the
letters of the Hebrew alphabet are more appropriate for this
purpose than are others. The first and the last letters of the
alphabet, the א and the ת respectively, were of course
particularly useful. The fact that the author of 5:8 allows
almost every word to begin with an א may then be seen as a
deliberate indication of the beginning of a new strophe; cf. too
5:17. It is of course no coincidence either that the last line of
the same poem (5:26) begins with a ת (in תבוא). But also the
ל (the first letter of the second half of the alphabet), the פ
(compare Ps. 25:22 and 34:23) and the ה appear to fill a
particular function in this connection. Such formal indicators of
strophic structure are according to Skehan, however, of a
supplementary nature and not really important. Once again he
too emphasizes, 'always, the sense must be the governing test,
for which the external devices can only be suggestive'.[72]

In Skehan's opinion, from ch. 15 onward the poet no longer
makes use of the alphabetising structure in the internal
arrangement of the dialogues. But Skehan does suggest the
presence in various places of the so−called 'quasi−acrostic
devices'. In the second cycle in the Eliphaz speech we once
again encounter primarily the 5−line strophe, with Bildad 3−line
strophes, and Zophar speaks, as was the case in ch. 11, in
6−line strophes. The responses of Job also continue the line
begun in the first cycle. The strophic analysis of the third cycle

---

71 Cf. Peters: 1928:74*: 'Auch die alphabetisierenden Abschnitte
(13,28−14,22 16,17−17,16 27,2−23 28,1−22) sind sicher kein Zufall'.
72 Skehan: 1971:98.

of the dialogues between Job and his friends is somewhat more problematic than was the case in the preceding chapters. Nevertheless, the debates in chs. 22—27, according to Skehan, still follow 'the conventions already established'.[73]

In his article treating the last chapters of Job Skehan defended the position that both chs. 29—31 ('Job's final plea') and chs. 38—41 ('the Lord's reply') consist of three major literary units, which is comparable to the tripartite structure of chs. 9—10 and 12—14. The fundamental structural scheme of Job 29—31 is 33.22.40, and God's answer has the foundational scheme of 36.34.50. The first two sections of this response (chs. 38—39) taken together total precisely 70 poetic lines. This total, according to Skehan, like the 40 poetic lines of Job 31 and the 50 poetic lines of Job 40:7—41:26, is deliberately intended by the poet.

5. *The commentaries: Terrien, Fohrer, Horst, Van Selms*

In this connection we also wish to call attention to a number of recent Job commentaries in which attempts are made to divide the debate—speeches into more or less uniform sections. What these commentaries all have in common is the fact that the authors now no longer attempt to lay a more or less crystallized strophic system upon the dialogues.

S.L. Terrien is convinced that the writer of the book of Job manifests exceptional skill in the area of strophic structure. Especially in the exchange between Job and Eliphaz can be seen the tightly—knit architectonic structure which he has provided.[74]

G. Fohrer, in his commentary, admits the presence of strophes as 'stilistische Abschnitte', but 'Strophen im metrischen Sinn' (in which the corresponding verses are continually similar to each other in a metrical sense) can seldom be proved. Nevertheless, these stylistic units are distinguishable not only in a logical sense, but there are frequently also 'äußere Merkmale' at play.[75]

---

73 Skehan: 1971:111.
74 S.L. Terrien, *Job* (CAT 13; Neuchâtel, 1963) esp. 33—34. Many of the divisions proposed in Terrien's commentary are accepted in TOB.
75 G. Fohrer, *Das Buch Hiob* (KAT 16; Gütersloh, 1963) esp. 55. For the rest, precisely what Fohrer intends with respect to these external indicators

Furthermore, it is striking that the units into which Fohrer divides the speeches very often consist of an equal number of poetic lines. This is true for example of Job 4—5 (schematic structure: 9x5), 6—7 (scheme: 5x3 and 8x4), 8 (scheme: 7x3), 10 (scheme: 4x5) and 13—14 (scheme: 17x3).[76]

Unfortunately *F. Horst* was not able to complete his commentary on the book of Job. So we do not know precisely what conclusions he would have drawn regarding the strophic schemes he had found.[77] It seems to me, though, that Horst would have been able to identify with Fohrer's distinction between strophes as 'stilistische Abschnitte' and 'Strophen im metrischen Sinn'.[78] With Horst too we often encounter series of 'strophes' with equal numbers of poetic lines; for example in Job 6 (scheme: 3.3/3.3/8/3.3.3), 7 (scheme: 4x3 and 3x4), 9 (scheme: 3.3.3.7.7.7.4), 10 (scheme: 7.5.5.5) and 11 (scheme: 4x3).

Finally, I wish to call attention here to the manner in which *Van Selms* approached the problem of strophic structure in the book of Job.[79] By virtue of observations first made in Job 3, Van Selms states that the component parts of the speeches in chs. 3—31 generally demonstrate a uniformity in length. But, according to Van Selms this does not mean that one can proceed to a division into regular strophes. The pericopes into which the speeches can be divided ordinarily contain from ten to twelve poetic lines.[80] But to support his divisions into pericopes Van Selms frequently points to certain grammatical

---

is not immediately evident. He does reject Skehan's starting points regarding strophic structure (1963:55 n.9).

76   Fohrer assumes the position that in the dialogues nearly exclusive use is made of the 'zweigliedrige Langvers'. Where this is not the case either a later gloss, or loss of a verse portion, must be assumed. Following precisely in Fohrer's path is F. Hesse, *Hiob* (ZBK AT 14; Zürich, 1978).

77   See F. Horst, *Hiob* (BK XVI.1; Neukirchen–Vluyn, 1968). The commentary ends at ch. 19.

78   Cf. also F. Horst, 'Die Kennzeichen der hebräischen Poesie', *ThR* 21 (1953) 97—121; esp. 119—121. In my opinion the positions of Fohrer and Horst were strongly influenced by the article by J. Begrich, 'Zur hebräischen Metrik', *ThR* 4 (1932) 67—89 (esp. 83—89; and see now Van der Lugt: 1980:90—91).

79   A. van Selms, *Job* I—II (POT; Nijkerk, 1982—1983).

80   Van Selms: 1982:82.

factors or to other considerations not strictly related to the thought—content. He sees his analysis of Job 4—5 in a certain sense confirmed by the fact that the first pericope begins with a question, the second (4:12) with the emphatic 'and to me', the third (5:1) with an imperative, the fourth (5:8) with a strong word for 'but', and the fifth (5:17) with an *anacrusis*.[81]

6. *E.C. Webster*

In the articles which *E.C. Webster* dedicated to the study of strophic structure in the book of Job[82] the author's purpose is not primarily to prove that the book contains a strophic structure; that it does is more or less assumed. Webster is much more interested in demonstrating that at the level of strophic structure there is a certain continuity in the speeches of each of Job's friends, and also that the overall structure of the dialogues and monologues bears testimony to a well—developed pattern. According to Webster a speech can consist of more than one poem. A poem is always constructed of a series of strophes which, with a few exceptions, contain 3, 4 or 5 poetic lines.[83] Particular attention is given to strophes which develop a specific thought by utilizing a concentric ordering of the poetic lines (e.g. 3:20—23). Webster's research proceeds on the basis of R.A.F. MacKenzie's strophic divisions in The Jerome Biblical Commentary (1968), which in turn draws upon Skehan's results. In this manner he comes to the conclusion that quantitative relationships exist between the speeches, which come to expression through the number of strophes present within a speech.[84]

---

81 Van Selms: 1982:60. In addition see 74 (for chs. 6—7), 82—83 (for chs. 9—10), 99 (for ch. 11).

82 E.C. Webster, 'Strophic Patterns in Job 3—28', *JSOT* 26 (1983) 33—60; —————, 'Strophic Patterns in Job 29—42', *JSOT* 30 (1984) 95—109.

83 Webster bases his judgment upon an analysis of Job 39 and 3. With the poetic line he thinks of a combination of two or three cola (a distich or tristich respectively; 1983:33—34).

84 Compare in this regard De Moor's assertion that the structure of Hebrew (and Ugaritic) poetry is determined more by the number of strophes within a formal unity (De Moor speaks here of a 'canticle') than by the total number of poetic lines of which the strophes and the 'canticles' are

These quantitative relationships can be described as follows:

a) In the first and third cycle Job's responses, as measured by the total number of strophes, are much longer than the accusational speeches to which they respond; in the second cycle accusation and response are of approximately the same length.

b) The speeches of Eliphaz in the first and the second cycles have an identical length (9 strophes); the same holds true for Bildad (6 strophes). The speeches of Job become continually longer in the first cycle (6, 15, 15 and 21 strophes); in the second cycle they show a concentric pattern (9, 7 and 9 strophes); in the third cycle they decline in length (12 and 8 strophes).

c) The progression of the poems in the dialogues shows a 'flowing pattern ... rising or falling from a base length of six strophes to a poem'.[85] The first half of the first cycle (chs. 3–7), for example has, according to Webster, a 6/4.5/6/4.5/6 scheme. For the second half of the cycle he assumes a 6/7.8/6/7.8/6 scheme.

d) In the monologues (chs. 29–41), which are handled in his second article, there is no longer any talk of a 'flowing pattern'. The monologue of Job (chs. 29–31), and the answer of God (chs. 38–41), with their parallel, rising patterns, encase 'the balanced speeches of Elihu's interjection': 6.9.12/6.4x9/3.6.9.12.

E. The criticism

If the description of the various theories of strophic structure, as they have been delineated in the preceding sections, has created the impression that researchers who have attempted to discern a certain strophic structure in the book of Job have never fully attained a consensus, then the impression created is in harmony with the facts. To be sure, we could indicate a number of chapters where the opinions regarding strophic structure do not vary significantly. But there is an equal number of speeches, or large segments of speeches, where any consensus among the scholars seems to be far down the road. Seen in that light it is

---

constructed; see J.C. de Moor, 'The Art of Versification in Ugarit and Israel II', *UF* 10 (1978) 200–217, and cf. by the same author in *Orientalia* 53 (1984) 283 and in *Orientalia* 55 (1986) 46.
85   Webster: 1983:58.

not so amazing that to this day commentaries and translations of the book of Job are published without the slightest attempt being made to present the speeches of Job and his partners—in—dialogue in a formal, poetic division in larger or smaller pericopes. Similarly, there have always been scholars who expressed their criticism of the attempts of their colleagues to discover a well—thought—out system in the macro—structure of Hebrew poetry.

F.W.C. *Umbreit*[86] was one of the first to openly express his doubts concerning the importance of Köster's discovery. He did not think it at all likely that a poet as great as the writer of Job would allow himself to be confined by precise, stiff, strophic patterns. In his estimation such poetry would drop to the level of a mass—produced alphabetic psalm. Köster could assert that the table of contents with which he began his treatment of the individual speeches was inextricably connected to the strophic divisions, but every commentator's description of the content would simply follow his own perspective anyway. And, where is then 'die eigentliche Entdeckung einer formellen Regel, deren der Verf. sich rühmt'?[87] With recourse to a discussion of Job 27—28 Umbreit attempted to demonstrate that Köster's discovery was more likely to obscure than to clarify the true meaning of these chapters. Köster's view of ch. 28 he considered to be particularly disappointing because it totally missed the significance of the repeated question in vss. 12 and 20 (where shall divine wisdom be found?), which is not only the theme of the whole chapter but of the entire book of Job.

At the 'oriëntalistencongres' of 1883 (Leiden), approximately 30 years after the appearance of his commentary on Job, Schlottmann systematically exposed his principles of strophic structure, which were dependent upon Köster's views.[88] Budde and Kautzsch took advantage of this opportunity to vent their scepticism regarding every attempt to discover precise rules

---

86   F.W.C. Umbreit, 'Die neuesten Beiträge zur Erklärung des Buches Hiob', *ThStKr* 13 (1840) 229—233.

87   Umbreit: 1840:230.

88   See K. Schlottmann, 'Über den Strophenbau in der hebräischen Poesie', *Actes du Sixième Congrès International des Orientalistes* II (Leiden, 1885) 473—492; regarding Schlottmann's Job commentary see A.2 above.

regarding strophes in Hebrew poetry.[89] In response to Schlottmann's speech, *E. Kautzsch* spoke explicitly regarding the alleged strophic structure of the book of Job. In Kautzsch's opinion the suggestion that the poets consciously attempted to incorporate an alternation between strophes of 2 and 3 poetic lines, for example, was not at all in accord with the loftiness of Hebrew poetry (compare Umbreit). 'Solche Strophenschemata aber, wie sie besonders den einzelnen Capiteln des Buches Hiob vorangestellt zu werden pflegen, wie etwa 6.6.8.8.7.6, halte ich für reine Selbsttäuschung'.[90] Almost every commentary which appears promises anew to finally solve the problem of strophic structure, but to this day no two are in harmony in counting strophes!

K. Budde also took this opportunity to express his opinion that these were unproven and unlikely theories.[91] He was of the same opinion in his Job commentary.[92] Since Köster the presence of strophes in Hebrew poetry was assumed by almost everyone as being virtually self—evident. That was the source of a puzzling mistake, namely that 'Sinnesabschnitte' and 'metrische Einheiten' were simply equated. Budde's reservation regarding the presupposed strophes then was aimed at the fact 'daß man eine neue, höhere Formeinheit behauptet oder unbefangen voraussetzt, ohne ein neues Formmittel — wie es sonst bei Strophen in regelmäßig wiederkehrender Abwechselung des Metrums, der Zeilenlänge, des Endreims usw. vorliegt — aufzuweisen oder auch nur zu begehren'.[93] Moreover, the search for strophes had lead to damaging of O.T. poetry (among others by Bickell) and also to a total overlooking of the parallelisms between members of a verse (for example by Delitzsch and Merx). And precisely this parallelism, which welds the poetic lines into cohesive units, inhibits, according to Budde, the formation of higher structural units. The parallel verse is already a sort of strophe. In fact, the higher units in the book of Job were 'nicht künstlich abgemessen', but rather they

---

89   See: *Actes du Sixième Congrès International des Orientalistes* I (Leiden, 1884) 91—95.

90   *Actes* .... I (Leiden, 1884) 93.

91   For a summary of Budde's position see Van der Lugt: 1980:36.

92   K. Budde, *Das Buch Hiob* (HK II.1; Göttingen, 1913[2]) VIII—IX.

93   Budde: 1913[2]:VIII.

developed in a totally free and natural way. The fact that in some cases (for example chs. 3 and 30) utility of rhetorical devices results in a clear division into approximately equal units, does not detract from this argument. In Budde's opinion it is simply an additional argument against continuously appearing strophes.

Budde may be considered one of the most outspoken critics of the defenders of strophic structure theories. But there appeared additional major Job commentaries in the beginning of this century in which the sole clue to the poetic nature of the dialogues was the fact that they were printed in the form of the poetic line. And such commentaries did not appear solely in German either. *P. Dhorme*, in his famous commentary, finally discussed the poetry of the book of Job without making any appeal to strophic division.[94] With regard to the problem which is our concern, Dhorme wished to distinguish two questions, namely the question of the presence of strophes and that of the internal relationship between the strophes. He does not wish to deny that the parallelism of Hebrew poetry also frequently unites two or three poetic lines into higher units. But it seldom occurs that by this means a whole row of uniform 'strophes' is produced. Repetitions of words, an argument sometimes appealed to as a criterion for strophic division, are frequently deceiving. In this connection Dhorme refered to a discussion that he had held with Condamin a few years prior to the appearance of his commentary. At that occasion he had called attention to texts such as Job 33:15–30. The poetic lines which make explicit the major motifs of the particular pericope (vss. 18, 22, 24, 28 and 30), appear with small variations at irregular intervals. The poet apparently felt no need to introduce any degree of uniformity into the length of the strophes.[95] Furthermore, a closer look suggests that the 'bâtisseurs de strophes' are difficult to make to agree with each other, to say nothing of the interference in the text by Bickell and Duhm for the sake of the construction of their tetrastich strophes. 'Au fond, la répartition qui se rapprocherait le plus de celle des vers et hémistiches de la

---

94   See P. Dhorme, *Le livre de Job* (Études bibliques, Paris, 1926) esp. CXLIX–CLI.
95   Cf. P. Dhorme, 'A propos d'une théorie strophique (2)', *RB* 33 (1924) 416.

poésie hébraïque, c'est la disposition en *laisses* ou *couplets* d'inégale longueur, telle qu'on la trouve dans les Chansons de Geste'.[96]

Another exegete from the beginning of this century who must be mentioned in this context is *E. König*. There is no doubt, says König, that in the poetic sections of Job 'Sinnabschnitte' can be distinguished.[97] Job's complaint in ch. 3, where the development of the thought clearly proceeds in three sections (vss. 3—10, 11—19, 20—26), is already immediately a good example of this. In the poetry of Job many more pericopes can be identified which 'wegen ihrer logischen Beziehung zu ihrer Umgebung und wegen ihres ungefähr gleichen Umfangs unter den Begriff der Sinnstrophen fallen: 14,1—6.7—12.13—17 usw.'.[98] But by their very nature the dialogues can only be divided into smaller units on the grounds of internal thought progression, and not into formal pericopes of equal length.[99] Also in his analysis of ch. 28 König saw no reason to support a strophic structure. The refrain—like questions of vss. 12 and 20 could scarcely be viewed as transition verses, contrary to the strophic divisions suggested by Duhm and Löhr for this chapter.[100]

In his discussion of recent literature pertaining to the book of Job it is primarily the great diversity of opinions regarding strophic structure which causes *C. Kuhl* to express his doubts as to the merit of the entire search for strophes.[101] And in the more recent commentaries by Pope, Gordis and Habel we encounter the same scepticism concerning the presupposition of regularly repeating combinations of poetic lines in Hebrew

---

96   Dhorme: 1926:CL. That Dhorme was not quickly finished with the problem of the strophe in Job is also evident from his discussion of the commentary by C.J. Ball (RB 32 [1923] 446—449), where this question receives ample attention. Here Dhorme compares the form of Hebrew poetry to the swinging of a cradle, 'dont les oscillations sont plus ou moins rapides suivant que la main de la mère intervient plus ou moins énergiquement' (1923:448).

97   See E. König, *Das Buch Hiob* (Gütersloh, 1929) esp. 14—16.

98   König: 1929:16.

99   König already came to these conclusions in his *Hebräisch Rhythmik* (Halle, 1914) 61.

100 König: 1929:283. For a discussion of Schlögl's theory see 1929:16.

101 Kuhl: 1953:185; cf. n.2 above.

poetry. To obtain a strictly executed, uniform strophic pattern in an O.T. poem of any length almost invariably demands, in *M.H. Pope*'s opinion, 'too much cutting and patching' to be convincing.[102] *R. Gordis* wishes only to speak of 'stanzas' in the relatively rare instances when a refrain is utilized in such a manner that it is repeated at regular intervals; Job 28, where the refrain of vss. 12 and 20 originally could have stood at the beginning of this 'Hymn to Wisdom' as well, provides one such example.[103] Where a comparable refrain cannot be identified, however, the strophic theory is doomed to failure. It is always foiled by the stubborn fact that the assumed units are not of the same length. Nor does Kissane's attempt to find a regular pattern in the 'irregular' strophes earn approval from Gordis; Kissane too is forced to make arbitrary divisions in the text, which leads to divorcing poetic lines which clearly belong together and the natural thought progression of the text must often be ignored. Gordis can finally do none other than concur with the judgment expressed by G.B. Gray already at the beginning of this century: 'If we use the term "strophe" it must mean simply a verse paragraph of indeterminate length uncontrolled by any formal artistic scheme'.[104]

Finally, the observation can be made that *N.C. Habel*'s conclusions are somewhat more complex than the criticisms mentioned thus far, and his position may rightly be seen to typify the most recent developments regarding the problem of strophic structure. On the one hand Habel has little confidence in traditional strophic research. He speaks of 'the futility of dividing the poetic passages of Job into stanzas or strophes of relatively equal length based on a common theme or structure'.[105] But it is noteworthy that Habel believes his point can be demonstrated with reference to Job 3. The usual division of this chapter into three pericopes of approximately equal length (vss. 3—10, 11—19, 20—26) is alleged to rest upon a

---

102 M.H. Pope, *Job* (AB 15; Garden City, New York, 1973[2]) LIII.
103 See R. Gordis, *The Book of Job* (Moreshet Series 2; New York, 1978) 506—507; cf. R. Gordis, 'The Structure of Biblical Poetry', *Poets, Prophets, and Sages* (Bloomington, Indiana, 1971) 83—85.
104 G.B. Gray, *The Forms of Hebrew Poetry* (London, 1915, 1972[2]) 192.
105 N.C. Habel, *The Book of Job* (Old Testament Library; London, 1985) 47.

'mechanical division' of the text. By virtue of a detailed study of formal (!) and thematic phenomena he concludes that only two 'major literary units' can be identified, vss. 3–10 and 11–26. So, on the other hand in the book of Job it clearly is justifiable to speak of 'distinctive literary structures and designs'.[106] And the structure of every major literary unit receives special attention in his commentary under the heading 'Design'. In general this structure is very clearly demonstrable and apparently it was used by the artist to focus attention upon certain themes and thoughts. At the same time, however, Habel is not always certain whether the structure he discusses was deliberately intended by the author!

Habel's analysis regularly points to what he calls the 'palistrophe'. A very important poetic line, or group of lines, is placed in the exact center of the A–B–C–D–C–B–A pattern typical of the 'palistrophe'. That is the case in 19:21–29, for example, where reference to the redeemer (vss. 25–26a) constitutes the precise center of the thematic palistrophe. Another frequently recurring stylistic device is inclusion. Here it is precisely the beginning and the end of a literary unit which have an important function in the explanation of a pericope.

Although Habel himself seems to suggest that his appraisal of Hebrew poetry and the traditional pursuit of strophic structure are more or less mutually exclusive, in my opinion that is not really the case, as may be seen already from the clarifying analysis of ch. 7 offered by Habel. In contrast to the predominant approaches he finds 'three balanced units' (vss. 1–8, 9–16, 17–21). The structures of these three units appear to a large measure to run parallel. Moreover, he concludes (in my opinion correctly) that within these major units, repeatedly two Masoretic verses form a minor sub–unit (with a few aberrations in the third section).[107] Accordingly, research into the strophic structure of the book of Job, precisely by means of one of the most recent commentaries on this book, has been confronted with new challenges.[108]

---

106 Habel: 1985:46.

107 For a further analysis of ch. 7 see P. van der Lugt, 'Stanza–Structure and Word–Repetition in Job 3–14', *JSOT* 40 (1988) 3–38; esp. 11–13.

108 Furthermore, in this context I wish to point once again to the commentary of Van Selms; see above, section D.5.

THE FORM AND FUNCTION OF THE REFRAINS IN JOB 28*

Some Comments Relating to the 'Strophic' Structure of Hebrew Poetry

Pieter van der Lugt

1. Introduction

In conjunction with the search by other scholars for strophic structures in the poetic part of the book of Job as outlined above, we will now attempt to illustrate the problems which the

---

* The following commentaries and articles will be referred to by the name of the author only: F.I. Andersen, *Job* (Tyndale OT Commentaries; London, 1976); K. Budde, *Das Buch Hiob* (HK II.1; Göttingen, 1913²); A. Condamin, *Poèmes de la Bible* (Paris, 1933²); D.J. Clark, 'In Search of Wisdom: Notes on Job 28', *BiTrans* 33 (1982) 401–405; F. Delitzsch, *Das Buch Iob* (Keil–Delitzsch IV.2; Leipzig, 1876²); A. Dillmann, *Hiob* (KeH 2. Lief.; Leipzig, 1891⁴); S.R. Driver–G.B. Gray, *The Book of Job* (ICC; Edinburgh, 1921); B. Duhm, *Das Buch Hiob* (KHC 16; Freiburg i.Br., 1897); C. Epping–J.T. Nelis, *Job* (BOT 7a; Roermond, 1968); H. Ewald, *Das Buch Ijob* (Die Dichter des Alten Bundes III; Göttingen, 1854²); G. Fohrer, *Das Buch Hiob* (KAT 16; Gütersloh, 1963); N.C. Habel, *The Book of Job* (Old Testament Library; London, 1985); G. Hölscher, *Das Buch Hiob* (HAT 17; Tübingen, 1952²); J. Hontheim, *Das Buch Job – als strophisches Kunstwerk nachgewiesen, übersetzt und erklärt* (Biblische Studien IX.1–3; Freiburg i.Br., 1904); E.J. Kissane, *The Book of Job* (Dublin, 1939; New York, 1946²); E. König, *Das Buch Hiob* (Gütersloh, 1929); F.B. Köster, *Das Buch Hiob und der Prediger Salomos nach ihrer strophischen Anordnung übersetzt* (Schleswig, 1831); J. Ley, 'Die metrische Beschaffenheit des Buches Hiob', *ThStKr* 68 (1895) 635–692; M. Löhr, 'Job c. 28', *Oriental Studies Presented to Paul Haupt* (Leipzig, 1926) 67–70; A. Merx, *Das Gedicht von Hiob* (Jena, 1871); H. Möller, *Sinn und Aufbau des Buches Hiob* (Berlin, 1955); A. Niccacci, 'Giobbe 28', *Studium Biblicum Franciscanum, Liber Annuus* 31 (1981) 29–58; N. Peters, *Das Buch Job* (EH 21; Münster in Westf., 1928); M. Rozelaar, *Job* (Kampen, 1984); N.J. Schlögl, *Das Buch Ijjob* (Die heiligen Schriften des Alten Bundes III.2; Wien und Leipzig, 1916); K. Schlottmann, *Das Buch Hiob* (Berlin, 1851); A. van Selms, *Job II* (POT; Nijkerk, 1983); C. Steuernagel, *Das Buch Hiob* (HSAT II; Tübingen, 1923⁴) 323–389; J.G. Stickel, *Das Buch Hiob* (Leipzig, 1842); S.L. Terrien, *Job*

student of the formal, poetic structure of a Hebrew poem encounters. For this purpose we have selected only one example, namely Job 28, the famous 'Hymn to Wisdom'.[1] This poem is well suited to demonstrate the problems which arise in a search for the formal structure of a Hebrew poem. At the same time the poetry of Job 28 gives us an opportunity to show the way in which the question of the poetic framework of Hebrew poetry, in our opinion, is to be answered. Thus, we hope to make a contribution to the insight in *the limitations and the possibilities* of the investigation of the *'strophic'* *structures* of Hebrew poetry in general and of the structure of Job 28 in particular.

2 Structural interpretations of Job 28

2.1 *General survey*

On first acquaintance with Job 28 the unsuspecting reader gets the impression that there will be no major obstacles to hinder detection of the poetic structure of this poem. Because vs. 20 (והחכמה מאין תבוא / ואי זה מקום בינה) is an almost literal repetition of vs. 12 (והחכמה מאין תמצא / ואי זה מקום בינה) the idea is obvious that the poet marked the borders of the main sections of his composition with a refrain. However, a general survey of the structural interpretations of this hymn since the days of Köster (1831) is sufficient to reveal that the repetition of the poetic line in vss. 12 and 20 did not make an important contribution to the understanding of the poetic structure of the poem. In some cases it even confused scholars in their search for the formal framework of this chapter.[2]

(CAT 13; Neuchâtel, 1963); P. Vetter, *Die Metrik des Buches Job* (Biblische Studien II.4; Freiburg i.Br., 1897); E.C. Webster, 'Strophic Patterns in Job 3−28', *JSOT* 26 (1983) 33−60; A. Weiser, *Das Buch Hiob* (ATD 13; Göttingen, 1968[5]); A. de Wilde, *Das Buch Hiob* (OTS 22; Leiden, 1981); G.H.B. Wright, *The book of Job* (London, 1883).

1 Modern scholars generally agree that this chapter is a quite self−contained literary unit within the speeches of Job in the 'third cycle' of the dialogues. Cf. e.g., R. Gordis, *The Book of Job* (Moreshet Series 2; New York, 1978) 298−299; De Wilde: 1981:9−11 and Habel: 1985:391−393.

2 After all, such a statement is also applicable to other Hebrew poems

Before we illustrate some main features in the search by other scholars for the structure of this poem, we will first present a general survey of the efforts to analyse this structure. This survey is a formalized description of the analyses by various authors, giving the name of the author or the translation, the year of the publication in brackets, the distribution of the Masoretic verses, and if applicable the structural scheme is added in brackets.

Köster (1831):
  .../1−3.4−6.7−8.9−11/12−14.15−17.18−19.20−22/23−24.25−26.27−28
  (.../3.3.2.3/3.3.2.3/2.2.2)
Stickel (1842):
  ...1−4.5−8.9−12.13−16.17−20.21−24.25−28
  (7x4)
Schlottmann (1851):
  .../1−3.4−8.9−11/12−14.15−19.20−22/23−24.25−26.27−28
  (.../3.5.3/3.5.3/2.2.2)
Ewald (1854):
  1−2.3−5.6−11/12−22/23−25.26−28
Merx (1871):
  ...1−2/3−4.5−6.7−9.10−11.12−14.15−16.17−19.20−21.22−24.25−26.27−28*
  (...4/6.4.6.4.6.4.6.4.6.4.6)
Delitzsch (1876):
  .../1−4.5−8.9−12.13−16.17−20.21−25.26−28
  (.../10.4x8.10.6)
Wright (1883):
  .../1−2+5−6.3−4+7−8.9−11/12−14.15−19/20−22.23−27/28
  (.../8.9.6/6.10/6.10/3)
Dillmann (1891):
  .../1−11.12−22.23−28 (11.11.6) or .../1−5.6−11.12−14+21−22.23−28
  (.../12.12.10.12)
Ley (1895):
  ...1−3.4−11.12−19.20−27.28
  (...3.8.8.8.1)

---

with a refrain. See P. van der Lugt, *Strofische Structuren in de bijbels-hebreeuwse Poëzie* (Kampen, 1980) 288−291 (on Ps. 62), 302−304 (on Ps. 67), 335−339 (on Ps. 80); cf. also J. Goldingay, 'Repetition and Variation in the Psalms', *JQR* 68 (1977−1978) 146−151 on Ps. 46 (see esp. 147−148 and 150).

Duhm (1897):
refrain.1−2.3−4*.5−6/refrain.7−8.9+10a+11a.10b+11b+24/
refrain.13−14.15−16.17−18/refrain.21−22.23+25.26−27
(refr.3x4/refr.3x4/refr.3x4/refr.3x4)
Vetter (1897):
.../1−12.13−20.21−28
(.../12.8.8)
Hontheim (1904):
1−3b.3c−5/6−8.9−11//12−14.15−17.18−20//21−22.23−24/25−26.27−28
(3.3/3.3//3.3.3//2.2/2.2)
Budde (1913):
1−4+7−11.12−14+21−22.23+25−28
Schlögl (1916):
1−11.12−22.23−28
(22.22.12)
Driver−Gray (1921):
1−11.12−19.20−27
Steuernagel (1923):
1−3+5−11.12−19.20−27
Löhr (1926):
1−2+5−8+12.13−18+20.21−25+27
(7.7.6)
Peters (1928):
...;1−2.3−4.5−6/7−8.9−11//12−14.15−17.18−19/20−22//23−24.25−26.
27−28
(...; 2.2.2/2.3//3.3.2/3//2.2.2)
König (1929):
1−14.15−19.20−28
Condamin (1933) 203−205:
1−3b.3c−5/6−8.9−11//12.13−14.15−17.18−19.20//21−22.23−24/25−26.
27−28
(3.3/3.3//1.2.3.2.1//2.2/2.2)
Kissane (1939):
1−4.5−6+9−11.12−13+7−8+14.15−19.20−24.25−28*
(6x5)
Hölscher (1952):
1−2.3*.4*.5−6.7−8.9−10.11−12.13−14.21−22.23+25.26−27
RSV (1952):
1−6.7−8.9−11.12−19.20−22.23−28
Möller (1955) 66:
1−11.12−22.23−28 (11.11.6) or 1−14.15−28 (14.14)
Fohrer (1963):
refrain+1−3b+4a+c+5−6.refrain+7−10+24.12−18.20−23+25−27
(4x7)

Terrien (1963):
  1−2.3−4.5−8.9−13/14−16.17−19.20−21/22−24.25−27.28
Epping (1968):
  1−2.3−4.5−8.9−12/13−20/21−28
Weiser (1968):
  1−11.12−19.20−28; similarly TOB (1978) and Niccacci (1981)
NAB (1970):
  1−2+5−6.12−13+15−18+20−21+7−8+14+22.23−24+3+9−11.25−28
Andersen (1976):
  1−11.12.13−19.20.21−27.28
KBS (1980):
  1−4.5−11.12.13−19.20−27.28
De Wilde (1981):
  5−6.7−8.9−10.11−12/13−14.15−16.17−18.19−20/21−22.23−24.25−26.
  27−28
  (4x4/4x4/4x4)
Van Selms (1983):
  refrain+1−11.12−19.20−27.28
Webster (1983):
  1−6.7−11/12−14.15−19/20−22.23−28
  (6.5/3.5/3.6)
Rozelaar (1984):
  1−11.12−19.20−22.23−28
Habel (1985):
  (1−2.3−4/5−6.7−8.9−11/12.13−14.15−19/20−22.23−27.28
  [A.B/A1.C.B1/A2.C1.B2/A3.ABC.D])

2.2 *Systematic approach*

Broadly outlined, with regard to the macro−strucure of Job 28
we can discern four opinions.

a. The denial of vss. 12 and 20 as a refrain

In the historical survey above, mention is made of Köster's view
'daß der Refrain, dieses leichteste Kennzeichen des
Strophenbaues, im Hiob nirgends vorkommt'.[3] At first sight this
utterance causes some surprise in light of Job 28. How does
Köster deal with the repeated poetic lines of vss. 12 and 20 in
this poem? According to Köster the Hymn to Wisdom forms an

---

3   Köster: 1831:IX; cf. our previous article A.1.

integral part of the book of Job. Accordingly, his denial of refrains must also be reflected in his interpretation of the macro—structure of this poem, which is, in fact, the case. Köster divides vss. 1—11, 12—22 and 23—28. In this interpretation the repeated lines are encapsulated in the second main part.

Up to present times Köster's division has found support. In the previous century Schlottmann, Ewald and Dillmann followed him in this respect; after 1900 Köster was followed by Budde, Schlögl, Peters and Möller, and upon closer analysis it is possible to be sympathetic to this view. A description of the thematic content creates the impression that Köster's three main parts are relatively self—contained sections. Ewald offers the following description of these sections: '1) der Mensch hat zwar eine wunderbare Kraft die verborgensten greifbaren Dinge aus ihren tiefsten Abgründen zu holen und sieht seine darauf gewandten Sorgen und Mühen endlich durch reichen Gewinn belohnt v. 1—11; aber 2) die Weisheit, kein greifbares und sichtbares, auf einen Ort beschränktes Ding, kann so mit aller Mühe nicht gefunden, auch mit allen äußern Schäzen nicht erworben werden v. 12—22, weil 3) bloß Gott sie besizt, der dem Menschen als seine Weisheit die Gottesfurcht bestimmt hat v. 23—28'.[4] Moreover, Schlottmann pointed to the 'kunstvolle strophische Ausführung' of chs. 27—28. That means with regard to ch. 28 that the two corresponding strophes (vss. 1—11 and 12—22) 'sich auch in der Untertheilung der Glieder genau entsprechen, während die das Ganze kräftig zusammenschließende Endstrophe kürzer gefaßt ist'.[5] However, Schlottmann does not elaborate the parallelism between vss. 1—11 and 12—22 on the basis of the 'Gliederbau' only, but upon the grounds of verbal repetitions and (parallel or) antithetic thought connections as well: 'Das מוצא in 12a entspricht dem

---

4   Ewald: 1854[2]:255.
5   Schlottmann: 1851:372; for the structure advocated by Schlottmann see above, 2.1 (cf. also Köster). Regarding vss. 23—28 we come across the same opinion defended by Ewald: 'aber der lezte von diesen Theilen, wo sich die höchsten Wahrheiten zusammendrängen, wird der nachdrücklich kürzeste, still und abgebrochen feierlichste, weil der Gedanke fast keine entsprechende Worte findet, in maßloser Höhe verschwimmend, aber für das weitere Nachdenken ein unendliches Feld eröffnend' (1854[2]:255).

מוצא in 1a; das מקום in 12b dem מקום in 1b; V. 13 entspricht in gewisser Weise dem V. 2, und noch genauer V. 14 dem V. 3, denn die Tiefe der Erde, welche der Mensch erleuchtet und wegen ihrer Schätze mit Erfolg durchspürt, steht im Gegensatze gegen die Tiefe der Fluth, bei welcher er eben so wie auf der bewohnten Erde vergeblich die Weisheit sucht. ... Das נעלמה מעיני כל חי V. 21 weis't offenbar absichtlich zurück auf das כל יקר ראתה עינו V. 10. Endlich liegt auch eine tiefe Ironie in dem Gegensatze der Schlußverse der beiden Strophen. V. 11 heißt es: das Verborgenste bringt der Mensch an's Licht, V. 22: der Unterwelt selbst ist die göttliche Weisheit verborgen'.[6] According to Schlottmann vs. 11b ('Das Ver—borgenste bringt man an's Licht') emphatically forms the end of the first strophe. So the central idea of vss. 1—11 sharply contrasts with the following section.

It is noteworthy that the above mentioned authors have nothing to say about the almost literal repetition of a whole poetic line within the second main part that they isolated (vss. 12—22). The significance of the repetition of vs. 12 in vs. 22 remains somewhat inexplicable. So, it is not astounding that other scholars in this structural tradition have sought alternative means to explain this enigma. Dillmann considers the whole passage of vss. 15—20 as suspect, 'da V. 12 nach dem Fundort der הכמה fragt, V. 15—19 aber von dem alle Schätze der Welt übertreffenden Werth derselben handeln, u. erst V. 20 den fallengelassenen Faden wieder aufnimmt'.[7] Like Schlottmann he calls attention to the connection between vss. 1 and 12, noting in the latter verse: 'Die Rückbeziehung auf V. 1 auch in den Ausdrücken תמצא u. מקום ist unverkennbar'.[8] But also in vss. 6—8 Dillmann discerns a return to the thought of vs. 1, the treasures which one finds in the earth.

Broadly speaking we come across the same ideas in Peters' commentary. The caesuras after vss. 11 and 22 'sind sachlich und durch das Stichwort מקום gefordert'.[9] Furthermore,

---

6   Schlottmann: 1851:382—383.
7   Dillmann: 1891[4]:242. So also Budde: 1913[2]:167 (cf. 2.1 above); however, it is possible, according to Budde, that originally the poetic line of vs. 12 also introduced the poem (see 164 and 167).
8   Dillmann: 1891[4]:242.
9   Peters: 1928:294 (note מקום in vss. 12b and 23b). Cf. Möller: 'Wenn

'Der Absatz V. 12—22 steht dem Absatz V. 1—11 parallel. V. 12 steht gegensätzlich zu V. 1'.[10]

b.   Vss. 12 and 20 as an introductory refrain

The second caesura in Köster's structural division needs only little shifting to arrive at the following framework for Job 28: vss. 1—11, 12—19, 20—27 (28). As far as we know G.H.B. Wright (1883) was the first to advocate this macro—structural division. The great difference compared to the interpretation of Köster is clear; vss. 12 and 20 are elevated now to a real refrain at the beginning of the second and the third main part. Especially in modern times the division of Wright has found many adherents, e.g. Weiser, TOB, Niccacci, Clark, Van Selms, Webster, Rozelaar, and Habel.

In Wright's opinion the second and the third main part show the same strophic structure: 6.10/6.10 (vss. 12—14.15—19/20—22.23—27).[11] Vs. 28 is an independent, closing verse. J. Ley builds on this idea when he disjoins vss. 1—3 from the first section. In his opinion it is easy to recognize that 'mit V. 4 die eigentliche Beschreibung des Bergbaues ... beginnt'.[12] The actual poem is introduced by 'eine allgemeine Einleitung', vss. 1—3. In this way Ley finds three uniform strophes of 8 verses.[13] Two years later Duhm went a step further by construing *four* uniform strophes (cf. 2.1 above). His reasoning was as follows: 'Jetzt heißt es v. 7f., daß Adler, Habicht und Löwe trotz ihres scharfen Blicks den Weg in die Bergwerke nicht kennen, das ist absurd; wie es sich v. 21 um die Weisheit handelt, deren Stätte den Vögeln verborgen ist, so muß auch v. 7 der Pfad der Weisheit gemeint sein. Dann muß aber ein Satz wie v. 20 vor v. 7 ausgefallen sein, und da dieser Satz ohnehin schon zweimal da ist (v. 12 20), so wird er in derselben Form vor v. 7

---

man nicht bloß auf den Kehrvers, sondern auf den sonstigen Inhalt und Zusammenhang sieht ...' (1955:66).

10 Peters: 1928:302. According to Peters, however, vss. 15—20 belong to the original poem.

11 Cf. Köster and Schlottmann above, who maintained that the *first* and the second main part showed the same structure.

12 Ley: 1895:672.

13 Cf. 2.1 above. For the structure vss. 1—11, 12—19, 20—27 see also Driver—Gray (1921) and Steuernagel (1923).

ergänzt werden dürfen. Damit ist auch die Schwierigkeit, die in v. 1 das כי macht, behoben: auch hier ist der Kehrvers wieder einzusetzen'.[14] Fohrer, following in the wake of Duhm, also discerns four uniform strophes. The refrain is to be supplied before vss. 1 and 7, and then 'umfassen die Strophen gleichmäßig je sieben Langverse'.[15]

At present the tendency to connect Wright's macro–division of this Hymn to Wisdom with a more or less rigid strophic interpretation is strongly diminished. At the same time this does not detract from the poetic value which is generally ascribed to the composition. We take Weiser's remark as an example: 'Das Kapitel ist ein kunstvoll aufgebautes Lehrgedicht in farbiger, bilderreicher Sprache, das durch einen Kehrvers (V. 12 und 20) in drei allerdings nicht gleichgebaute 'Strophen' aufgegliedert wird'.[16] The contents of the relevant sections are described as follows: the things which mankind researches by his own energy (the mining; vss. 1–11); the blocked way to wisdom (vss. 12–19); only God has access to wisdom (vss. 20–28) — cf. Weiser.

Habel finds himself in the same tradition as Weiser when he notes: 'Job 28 is a coherent structural unity. ... The intricacy of the integration techniques employed in the construction of this poem renders any ... efforts at rearrangement or *neat strophic division futile*'.[17] In each of the three main parts Habel discerns three motifs, namely 'the place or source of the precious item, the way or means of access to that item, and the process of discovering and acquiring the item'.[18] The first motif, according to Habel, is characterized by the key–word מקום (vss. 1, 6, 12, 20), the second motif by the key–words חקר (vss. 3, 27), ראה (vss. 10, 27) and עלם (vss. 11, 21), and the third motif by דרך / נתיב (vss. 7/8, 13*).

---

14   Duhm: 1897:134.
15   Fohrer: 1963:393; cf. above, 2.1.
16   Weiser: 1968⁵:198. Cf. also Hölscher and Van Selms among others.
17   Habel: 1985:393 (italics are mine [PvdL]). Cf. also: 'Examples of internal balance, symmetry, and recapitulation abound in this poem' (Habel: 1985:394).
18   Habel: 1985:393. On 394–395 Habel designates these motifs respectively as A, B, and C; cf. 2.1 above. For the three motifs in the main parts see also Niccacci: 1981.

Webster (1983) forms an exception to the rule. He maintains that each of the three main parts of Job 28 can be divided into two strophes (cf. 2.1 above). The first strophe — a description of mines — is 'ringed by vss. 1 and 6 (with the inclusion זהב)'.[19] We come across the same poetic device in the last strophe; with reference to בין / בינה in vss. 23 and 28 Webster supposes again 'a ring with an inclusion'. Furthermore, there is a correspondence between the first *strophes* of sections II and III (vss. 12—14 and 20—22 respectively); 'Each of the other two major divisions begins with a 3—period strophe asking the question, "Where can wisdom be found?". In vss. 12—14 the Deep and the Sea disclaim it; in vss. 20—22 Abaddon and Death claim only a rumour'.[20]

c. Vss. 12 and 20 as a closing refrain

It is instructive that already Stickel (1842) advocated a totally different strophic division of Job 28 than did Köster (cf. 2.1 above). When Stickel divides the poem into 7 strophes of four Masoretic verses, in two strophes the refrain of vss. 12 and 20 is a closing poetic line, namely in vss. 9—12 and 17—20 (the third and the fifth strophe). And Franz Delitzsch in his commentary made only a slight alteration to this strophic division at the end of the poem (vss. 21—25, 26—28; cf. 2.1 above).

This view of the strophic structure of Job 28 prepared the way for the opinion of Vetter, who involves vs. 28 as well as a refrain in the macro—structure of the composition, vss. 1—12, 13—20, 21—28. 'Diese Gliederung ist durch einen Kehrvers, der V. 12 und 20 als Frage, *V. 28 als Antwort* steht, sichergestellt'.[21]

---

19 Webster: 1983:54. See also Andersen: 1976:226, who points to vss. 1—6 as a 'well formed strophe', and Clark: 1982:402.
20 Webster: 1983:54—55. Cf. Möller, who defends his alternative division (vss. 1—14, 15—28) with the following words: 'Diese Teilung würde sich der Differenzierung des Kehrverses anpassen (*timmaṣe'* bzw. *tabho'*) und die Parallelität der auf den Kehrvers jeweils folgenden Vers 13f und 21f berücksichtigen' (1955:66). See also Terrien (1963:192 n.2 and 194—195) and Habel on vss. 14 and 22 (1985:393).
21 Vetter: 1897:47 (italics are mine [PvdL]). See also 75—78 where we find a translation of this chapter; in this translation vs. 28 is printed with spaces, just like vss. 12 and 20.

This conviction is shared by De Wilde. According to him the Hymn to Wisdom consists of three proportional sections; vss. 1–4 do not belong to the original poem. The refrain of vss. 12 and 20 *closes* an enumeration of results or precious things. But vs. 28 too plays a part in the formal framework: 'die ersten zwei Teile endigen mit dem Refrain in Frageform; *am Ende ist der Refrain in affirmativer Gestaltung transformiert*'.[22]

In the divisions of Löhr, Epping and Terrien too the refrain of vss. 12 and 20 has its place at the end of the main parts (see 2.1 above).

d.   The repetition in vss. 12 and 20 as inclusion

Lastly mention may be made of the strophic structure which is advocated by Hontheim and Condamin. According to these scholars the repetition in vss. 12 and 20 is not to be understood as a refrain, but as an inclusion. The almost identical lines embrace the 'Zwischenstrophe', vss. 12–20. This section forms a unity on the basis of its contents, 'sie variiert den einen Gedanken, daß die Weisheit bei den Geschöpfen nicht zu finden sei'.[23] The same uniformity is encountered 'in der festgeschlossenen symmetrischen Form'. This symmetrical structure is not only evident from vss. 12 and 20, but also from vs. 16a. This colon can be taken as the kernel of the 'Zwischenstrophe' because it is repeated almost verbatim in vs. 19b.

The first section of the poem (vss. 1–11), according to Hontheim, consists of two parallel strophes, a 'Vorstrophe' (vss. 1–5) and a 'Gegenstrophe' (vss. 6–11). The parallelism is especially founded on a similarity of the contents, 'die kostbaren Metalle weiß man auch an den verborgensten Verstecken zu finden' (vss. 1–3b); 'dasselbe gilt von den kostbaren Steinen' (vss. 6–8). Both vss. 3c–5 and 9–11 describe 'die Tätigkeit des Bergmanns'. The 'Vorstrophe' and the 'Gegenstrophe' of the third main part (vss. 21–28) also express a coherent notion, 'die Weisheit sei nur in Gott' (vss. 21–24); in vss. 25–28 it is claimed, 'daß wir trotzdem zu einer gewissen Teilnahme an der Weisheit gelangen können'.[24]

---

22   De Wilde: 1981:269 (italics are mine [PvdL]).
23   Hontheim: 1904:221.
24   See Hontheim: 1904:221.

Especially concerning poems of some length it seldom happens
that two scholars come to perfect agreement over the question
of strophic structure (cf. also 2.1 above). Therefore, it is
noteworthy that Condamin declares regarding Job 28: 'La
division du poème, établie par J. Hontheim, paraît
incontestable'.[25] This author has tried to consolidate the strophic
structure of Hontheim by means of pointing to the 'répétitions
verbales' which are woven into this poem. In the context of the
macro—structure Hontheim only mentioned the word מקום in
vss. 1, 6 and 12.[26] However, according to Condamin, in
distinction from the other poems in the book of Job, in ch. 28
these repetitions 'se présentent, parallèlles ou symétriques, très
nettement'.[27] On the basis of Condamin's translation we may
conclude that he was thinking of the following verbal repetitions
(responsions; they have been printed in heavy type): a) (between
the first strophe and the first antistrophe, vss. 1—5 and 6—11)
זהב in vss. 1 and 6, מקום in vss. 1 and 6 (cf. also vss. 12
and 20), אפר in vss. 2 and 6, אבן in vss. 2 and 6, יצא in vss.
5 and 11; b) (within the 'strophe intermédiaire', vss. 12—20) vs.
12 almost identical to vs. 20; c) (between the second strophe
and the second antistrophe, vss. 21—24 and 25—28) דרך in vss.
23 and 26, ראה in vss. 24 and 27; d) (within the composition
as a whole) חקר in vss. 3 and 27 —inclusion.[28]

2.3 *A provisional judgement of the divisions by other authors*

Before we present our own structural division of Job 28, an
attempt will be made to evaluate the strengths and weaknesses
of the above mentioned opinions concerning the framework of
this poem.

a) It is remarkable that one of the first opponents of strophic
theories, F.W.C. Umbreit, raised objections to the fact that
Köster's strophic division of Job 28 (cf. 2.2a above) did not
make due allowance for 'die sich wiederholende Frage V. 12 u.

---

25   Condamin: 1933²:203.

26   Hontheim: 1904:221.

27   Condamin: 1933²:203.

28   For the interpretation of חקר as inclusion see Condamin: 1933²:205 n.
on vs. 27.

20'.[29] Indeed, it would have been more justifiable in our opinion if Köster would have taken the repeated line of vss. 12 and 20 as a formal indicator to mark the macro—structure of this chapter. We have demonstrated that this lack of appreciation of vs. 20 lead to its elimination by Dillmann.

b) The parallelism between vss. 1—11 and 12—22 indicated by Schlottmann (cf. 2.2a above) partly rests on a selective use of the verbal repetitions woven into the poem (cf. already Condamin, 2.2d above), and to some extent is also due to a forced connection of their thought—contents (apart from that, judged on its own merits, the strophic scheme 11.11.6 is possible).

c) When the quest for structure is almost exclusively focused on the 'Gedankenzusammenhang' (cf. 2.2a above), it becomes impossible to detect the inner tension, which the poet may perhaps have employed deliberately in the separate parts of his composition. This criticism also applies to the division defended by König ('entspricht dem Gedankengange').[30]

d) Objections can be raised to the fact that by breaking off the first main part after vs. 11 (cf. 2.2a and 2.2b above), 'im ersten Hauptteile von dem Gegenstande, dem Kap. 28 gewidmet ist, der Weisheit, **gar nicht die Rede wäre**'.[31]

e) When Duhm (and Fohrer; cf. also Budde and Van Selms) inserts the refrain of vss. 12 and 20 before vss. 1 and 7, Löhr — in our opinion rightly — raised the objection that 'der Gedanke des Kehrverses doch erst als Ergebnis aus der ersten Strophe herauswächst'.[32]

f) The opinion described under 2.2b and 2.2d is not only supported by the refrain/inclusion of vss. 12 and 20, but by other verbal repetitions as well (cf. Habel and Webster under 2.2b and Condamin under 2.2d). However, we must ascertain again that the notion of the verbal repetitions given by the respective authors is incomplete, selective, and open to more than one explanation.

---

29 F.W.C. Umbreit, 'Die neuesten Beiträge zur Erklärung des Buches Hiob', *ThStKr* 13 (1840) 231.
30 König: 1929:282.
31 König: 1929:282.
32 Löhr: 1926:67; cf. König: 1929:283 and Andersen: 1976:224 n.1.

g) With regard to the division described under 2.2c above
(vss. 12 and 20 as a closing refrain) it is very strange that no
attempt is made to combine that division with a certain pattern
of verbal repetitions.

h) On the other hand, it is instructive that Vetter and De
Wilde (cf. 2.2c above) have tried to incorporate vs. 28 as a
refrain in the macro—structure of the poem.

3. The structure of Job 28 in the light of its refrains

In the following analysis an attempt will be made to prove that
the poetic structure of Job 28 shows to best advantage when
viewed within the framework described under 2.2c above. In
other words, the structural insights which have been put
forward on the grounds of connections of content and verbal
repetitions (cf. above, especially 2.2a, 2.2b and 2.2d) are
integrated most convincingly by taking as our starting point
that the refrain of vss. 12 and 20 was intended by the poet as
a closing verse at the end of the first and the second main part
of his composition.

Secondly, it will be argued that the strophic divisions
proposed by Stickel and Delitzsch (strophes of four Masoretic
verses) on the one hand, and Vetter and De Wilde on the other
hand (cf. 2.1 above) do not exclude each other, but must be
viewed as complementary. Accordingly, we do not agree with
Habel's statement that 'The intricacy of the integration
techniques employed in the construction of this poem renders
any ... efforts at ... neat strophic division futile'.[33] On the
contrary, it is our conviction that Job 28 shows a 'strophic'
structure which is very rigorously carried through. That is to
say, the poem is composed of three uniform stanzas of eight
lines (vss. 5—12, 13—20 and 21—28), introduced by an opening
'stanza' of half this length, four verse—lines (vss. 1—4). Next,
each of the eight—line stanzas falls into two uniform
sub—stanzas of four poetic lines. These in turn can be divided
into strophes of two lines like the introductory 'stanza' of vss.
1—4. Nearly all the lines of the poem consist of two cola, except
those of the last strophe of the introductory stanza (vss. 3—4);

---

33   Habel: 1985:393; cf. above, 2.2b.

the caesura between the introduction and the corpus of the poem is neatly marked by a strophe of two tricola (cf. also the last line of the whole poem, vs. 28).[34]

To establish the poetic structure of a Hebrew poem one must always rely upon arguments based on content, repetition of motifs, verbal repetitions and special words marking, in a more or less formal way, a transition from one stanza or strophe to another. It is always a combination of arguments which forms the basis of the poetic framework of a given composition. Nevertheless, in many cases it is one category of arguments in particular which shows the structure of a poem most clearly while the other arguments play only a supporting part in that framework. In Job 28 the transition markers are not represented very strongly. On the other hand, analysis of the verbal repetitions brings to light special patterns, which forms a basis sufficiently reliable to determine the poetic structure of this 'Hymn to Wisdom'.

Prior to some observations in support of this structure, the text of Job 28 is presented in a layout which attempts to visualize its structural stratification (A, I, II and III indicate the macro—structure of the poem, the stanzas; a and b indicate the sub—stanzas; the strophes are indicated by spacing alone):

A   ומקום לזהב יזקו   כי יש לכסף מוצא 1

      ואבן יצוק נחושה   ברזל מעפר יקח 2

---

34 For the function of tricola at the end of a structural unity see Van der Lugt: 1980:502—505. The tripartite structure of vss. 3—4 and 28 is indicated as such by the Masoretic accentuation. Although the translation of vs. 4 especially causes some difficulties, there are no compelling reasons for us to deviate from this tradition; cf. Job 4:16,19; 5:5; 6:4,10; 7:4; 9:24 etc., and M.B. Dick, 'Job xxviii 4: a new translation', *VT* 29 (1979) 216—221, esp. 219 n.3. Contra Kissane, M.H. Pope, *Job* (AB 15, Garden City [New York] 1973[2]) and Gordis: 1978 who take vss. 3—4 as three bicola; Fohrer deletes vss. 3c and 4b from the text. The first colon of vs. 28 is a projecting colon at the beginning of the second line in the two—line strophe of vss. 27—28. This combination of poetic lines within a strophe is quite rare; see Van der Lugt: 1980:495. The projecting colon ויאמר לאדם (vs. 28a) has its counterpart in the projecting colon אמר ליהוה in Ps. 91:1—2; see furthermore אמרו in Ps. 83:2—5 (note vs. 5a), but also ולציון יאמר in Ps. 87:5—6 and לאמר in Ps. 105:10—12 (note vs. 11a).

3 קץ שם לחשך   ולכל-תכלית הוא חוקר
אבן אפל וצלמות
4 פרץ נחל מעם-גר   הנשכחים מני-רגל
דלו מאנוש נעו

5 ארץ ממנה יצא-לחם   ותחתיה נהפך כמו-אש   Ia
6 מקום-ספיר אבניה   ועפרת זהב לו

7 נתיב לא-ידעו עיט   ולא שדפתו עין איה
8 לא-הדריכהו בני-שחץ   לא-עדה עליו שחל

9 בחלמיש שלח ידו   הפך משרש הרים   b
10 בצורות יארים בקע   וכל-יקר ראתה עינו

11 מבכי נהרות חבש   ותעלמה יצא אור
12 והחכמה מאין תמצא   ואי זה מקום בינה

13 לא-ידע אנוש ערכה   ולא תמצא בארץ החיים   IIa
14 תהום אמר לא בי-היא   וים אמר אין עמדי

15 לא-יתן סגור תחתיה   ולא ישקל כסף מחירה
16 לא-תסלה בכתם אופיר   בשהם יקר וספיר

17 לא-יערכנה זהב וזכוכית   ותמורתה כלי-פז   b
18 ראמות וגביש לא יזכר   ומשך חכמה מפנינים

19 לא-יערכנה פטדת-כוש   בכתם טהור לא תסלה
20 והחכמה מאין תבוא   ואי זה מקום בינה

21 ונעלמה מעיני כל-חי   ומעוף השמים נסתרה   IIIa
22 אבדון ומות אמרו   באזנינו שמענו שמעה

23 אלהים הבין דרכה   והוא ידע את-מקומה
24 כי-הוא לקצות-הארץ יביט   תחת כל-השמים יראה

25 לעשות לרוח משקל   ומים תכן במדה   b
26 בעשתו למטר חק   ודרך לחזיז קלות

27   אז ראה ויספרה
הכינה וגם-חקרה
28 ויאמר לאדם   הן יראת אדני היא חכמה
וסור מרע בינה

3.1 *Verbal repetitions in strophic perspective*

a. General survey

To obtain an objective picture of the patterns of verbal repetitions in a poem it is necessary to first detect all the verbal repetitions that occur. The following general survey lists all these repetitions in Job 28.

א: אבן, vs. 2 3 6; אי, vs. 12 20; אין, vs. 12 14 20; אמר, vs. 14 (2x) 22 28; אנוש, vs. 4 13; ארץ, vs. 5 13 24

ב: ‏ב‏-, vs. 9 10 13 14 16 (2x) 19 22 26; בין, vs. 12 20 23 28

ד: דרך, vs. 8 23 26

ה: ‏ה‏-, vs. 4 12 13 20 21 24 (2x); ‏-ה, vs. 5 (2x) 6 13 15 (2x) 17 (2x) 19 22 23 (2x) 27 (4x); הוא, vs. 3 23 24; היא, vs. 14 28; הפך, vs. 5 9

ו: ‏-ו, vs. 6 7 (2x) 8 9 10

ז: זה, vs. 12 20; זהב, vs. 1 6 17

ח: חיה, vs. 13 21; חכמה, vs. 12 18 20 28; חקר, vs. 3 27

י: ‏-י, vs. 14 (2x); ידע, vs. 7 13 23; יצא, vs. 1 5 11; יקר, vs. 10 16

כ: כון, vs. 25 27; כי, vs. 1 24; כל, vs. 3 10 21 24; כסף, vs. 1 15; כתם, vs. 16 19

ל: ‏-ל, vs. 1 (2x) 3 (2x) 6 24 25 (2x) 26 (2x) 28; לא, vs. 7 (2x) 8 (2x) 13 (2x) 14 15 (2x) 16 17 18 19 (2x)

מ: מן, vs. 2 4 (3x) 5 9 12 18 20 21 (2x) 28; מצא, vs. 12 13

ס: סלה, vs. 16 19; ספיר, vs. 6 16

ע: עין, vs. 7 10 21; עלם, vs. 11 21; עם, vs. 4 14; עפר, vs. 2 6; ערך, vs. 13 17 19; עשה, vs. 25 26

ק: קום, vs. 1 6 12 20 23; קץ, vs. 3 24

ר: ראה, vs. 10 24 27

ש: שמים, vs. 21 24; שמע, vs. 22 (2x); שקל, vs. 15 25

ת: תחת, vs. 5 15 24

b. Within the composition as a whole

Since the patterns of verbal repetitions which emerge on the level of the macro—structure of Job 28 provide the clearest evidence, it is advisable to begin an analysis with that dimension. Particular attention may be given here to the repetitions discerned at the beginning and at the end of the main parts, the stanzas (vss. 5—12, 13—20 and 21—28) and the introductory section (vss. 1—4). The results may be listed systematically as follows:

vss. 1—2/5—6: יצא, vss. 1a 5a (cf. too 3.1c)
                      מקום, vss. 1b 6a (cf. too 3.1a s.v. קום)
                      זהב, vss. 1b 6b (cf. too זהב in vs. 17a)
                      עפר, vss. 2a 6b
                      אבן, vss. 2b 6a (cf. too 3.1c)
vss. 5—6/13—14/21—22:
                      ארץ, vss. 5a 13b (see further below)
                      חיה, vss. 13b 21a
                      אמר, vss. 14a,b 22a (see too אמר in vs. 28a)
vss. 5—8/13—16/21—24 ('secondary responsions'):
                      ארץ, vss. 5a 13b 24a
                      תחת, vss. 5b 15a 24b
                      מקום, vss. 6a 23b (cf. too 3.1a s.v. קום)
                      ספיר, vss. 6a 16b
                      ידע, vss. 7a 13a 23b
                      עין, vss. 7b 21a (see too עין in vs. 10b)
                      דרך, vss. 8a 23a (see too דרך in vs. 26a)
vss. 12/20/28: והחכמה מאין תמצא/תבוא —
                      ואי זה מקום בינה , vss. 12 20
                      חכמה, vss. 12a 20a 28b (cf. too 3.1d below)
                      בינה, vss. 12b 20b 28c (linear!; cf. too בין in
                      vs. 23a)
vss. 5—12/13—20/21—18:
                      ה—, vss. 12a 13b (concatenation; cf. too 3.1a)
                      תמצא, vss. 12a 13b (concatenation)
                      ה—, vss. 20a 21b (concatenation; cf. too 3.1a)

Apart from the well—known refrain in vss. 12 and 20 there
appear to be other equally striking clusters of repetitions. These
clusters too can be designated as refrains.[35] Mention may first
be made of the repetitions that emerge in a comparison of vss.
1—2 and 5—6, the first strophes of the introductory section and
of the first stanza respectively. There are no less than five
repetitions. A close analysis reveals that the poet adheres to this
pattern throughout his composition, as is evident from the

---

35 Although we described such repetitions elsewhere as 'responsions' here
we stick to the definition of 'refrain' offered by Watson: 'A refrain is a
block of verse which recurs more than once within a poem. Such a block
can comprise a single word, a line of poetry or even a complete strophe'
(W.G.E. Watson, *Classical Hebrew Poetry* [JSOTS 26, Sheffield 1984] 295).

repetitions in the first strophes of stanzas II and III (note also
ארץ in vss. 5a and 13b):

ומקום לזהב יזקו	כי יש לכסף מוצא	1
ואבן יצוק נחושה	ברזל מעפר יקח	2

(first strophe of the introductory section)

ותחתיה נהפך כמו אש	ארץ ממנה יצא לחם	5
ועפרת זהב לו	מקום ספיר אבניה	6

(first strophe of stanza I)

ולא תמצא בארץ החיים	לא ידע אנוש ערכה	13
וים אמר אין עמדי	תהום אמר לא בי היא	14

(first strophe of stanza II)

ומעוף השמים נסתרה	ונעלמה מעיני כל חי	21
באזנינו שמענו שמעה	אבדון ומות אמרו	22

(first strophe of stanza III)

Obviously we are dealing here with 'refrain—strophes'. See in
this connection also the verbal repetitions in vss. 5—8, 13—16
and 21—24 as described above.

Regarding repetitions at the end of the stanzas it may be
noted that these are not restricted to the refrain of the first and
the second stanza, but that they are also demonstrable in the
last line of stanza III; see חכמה / בינה in vss. 12, 20 and 28.
It is especially noteworthy that each of the stanzas is closed by
the noun בינה (see vss. 12b, 20b and 28c).[36] Although the
combination of the nouns חכמה and בינה is virtually a fixed
pair in wisdom literature,[37] in Job 28 we come across that

---

36 Elsewhere we have demonstrated that the key word ואיננו has the
same function in Job 7: it is exactly the last word of stanza I and III; see
JSOT 40 (1988) 12—13.
37 For חכמה // בינה see Prov. 1:2 (אמרי בינה // חכמה); 4:5,7;
9:10; 16:16; Isa. 11:2 (רוח חכמה ובינה); cf. also חכמה // תבונה
in Prov. 3:13,19; 8:1; Job 12:12, and the parallelism of the roots חכם and
בין in Isa. 3:3 and Job 32:9.

word—pair only in the lines just mentioned, that is to say, each
time at regular intervals of eight lines counting back from the
end of the poem. The combination of this datum with the
pattern of repetitions described above (in vss. 1—2, 5—6, 13—14
and 21—22) firmly establishes the 8—line stanza—structure of
Job 28 in which the repeated lines of vss. 12 and 20 act as a
closing refrain.

c. Within the stanzas
Having formed a notion of the repetitions which establish the
macro—structure of the poem it is possible to analyse the
patterns of repetitions within the stanzas themselves. The
following picture is presented:

vss. 1—4:   ל—, vss. 1a,b 3a,b
              אבן, vss. 2b 3c (concatenation)
vss. 5—12:   הפך, vss. 5b 9b
              יצא, vss. 5a 11b   ⎫ inclusion
              מקום, vss. 6a 12b   ⎭
vss. 13—20:   לא, vss. 13—20!
              ערך, vss. 13a 17a, 19a
              ה—, vss. 13a 15a,b 17a,b 19a
              לא תסלה בכחם / בכתם ... לא תסלה, vss. 16a and
              19b respectively
vss. 21—28:   בין, vss. 23a 28b
              ראה, vss. 24b 27a

In the light of this analysis the second stanza (vss. 13—20)
shows a very solid inner framework. The repetition of the
negation לא is striking, also in the context of the poem as a
whole (cf. 3.1a above). To a lesser degree the same is true in
relation to the verb ערך.[38] The repetition of הפך in stanza I
(vss. 5b and 9b) is already an indication of division into
four—line sub—stanzas which can be discerned in each of the

_____

38 Ordinarily in vs. 13a דרכה is read instead of ערכה, in accordance
with LXX. Although the immediate context (vss. 13—14) indeed appears to
favour this reading, we prefer (with Delitzsch, Andersen, Van Selms, and
others) to give priority to MT. In our opinion the author has deliberately
employed the root ערך to emphasize the connection between sub—stanza IIa
and IIb.

stanzas; cf. ערך in stanza II and ראה / בין in stanza III.

d.   Within the sub-stanzas

A search for repetitions at the level of the sub—stanzas produces meager results:

vss. 17—20: לא יערכנה, vss. 17a 19a (exactly linear)
     חכמה, vss. 18b 20a
vss. 21—24: כל, vss. 21a 24b (inclusion)
     השמים, vss. 21b 24b (inclusion)
     ה—, vss. 22b 23a,b (concatenation)
vss. 25—28: כון, vss. 25b 27b

Regarding the strophes of the sub—stanzas IIb and IIIb (vss. 17—20 and 25—28) there are indications of a parallel construction. The strophes of sub—stanza IIIa, on the contrary, have a symmetric pattern; the sub—stanza as a whole shows a concentric framework.

e.   Within the strophes

The repetitions within sub—stanzas IIb and IIIb already supported the bipartite structure of these sections. There are further indications that this division into two 2—line strophes is intended by the poet in the other sub—stanzas as well:

vss. 5—6: ה—, vss. 5a,b 6a
vss. 7—8: לא, vss. 7a,b 8a,b
vss. 9—10: —ב, vss. 9a 10a (exactly linear)
vss. 13—14: —ב, vss. 13b 14a (chiastic)
vss. 23—24: הוא, vss. 23b 24a (chiastic)
vss. 25—26: עשות ל—, vss. 25a 26a (exactly linear)

'Man verachte nicht solche Kleinigkeiten'.[39]

f.   Remaining verbal repetitions

Naturally not every repetition of a word or a term within a Hebrew poem has a function in the context of its framework. We must also take into account the possibility that the poet

---

39   Hontheim: 1904:221.

repeated some words without any specific structural intention. A single repetition does not function structurally until there are other indications which complement the argument, e.g., another word or root of a verb which is reiterated in the same lines or strophes. In this case, from a total of 48 verbal repetitions we did not use eleven repetitions at all. We note the following words in the category 'no specific structural intention': אנוש, שקל, קץ, עם, עלם, מן, כסף, כי, יקר, חקר, ־ו.

3.2 *A description of motifs and contents in strophic perspective*

Having established the poetic structure of Job 28 on the basis of an analysis of the verbal repetitions, it is possible, in our opinion, to attain a rather coherent picture of the alternation of the motifs and the thematic progression as well.

With regard to content, we find the most coherent sections at the structural level of the 4—line sub—stanzas:

> A   Man presses forward into all the secret places on earth (vss. 1—4).
> Ia The earth contains treasures that remain hidden even to animals (vss. 5—8).
> Ib Mankind is able to reach these treasures, but fails to find wisdom (vss. 9—12).
> IIa Wisdom is not to be obtained by man on earth (vss. 13—16).
> IIb Nor can wisdom be compared with anything else on earth (vss. 17—20).
> IIIa Only God knows the place of wisdom (vss. 21—24).
> IIIb God himself gave wisdom a place in his creation (vss. 25—28).

In the introductory section two motifs can be discerned in the successive strophes. The first strophe (vss. 1—2) contains the motif of the *place* (where precious metals are found). The second strophe (vss. 3—4) formulates the motif of the *attempt at finding* (the precious metals).[40] The introductory character of

---

40   Another approach is defended by Niccacci and Habel, who try to show that the whole poem is governed by *three* motifs; see above, 2.2b.   The

these strophes finds expression in the fact that the successive motifs are elaborated in the first stanza, i.e., the motif of the *place* in sub–stanza Ia (vss. 5–8) and the motif of the *attempt at finding* in sub–stanza Ib (vss. 9–12). The first strophe of Ia (vss. 5–6) expresses the concern of vss. 1–2 in the same way: there is a place on earth (where a wealth of powers and riches is concealed), cf. 3.1b above! This positive statement is contrasted by the following strophe (vss. 7–8) which emphasizes that this place is very hard to reach. The strophe as a whole is dominated by the negation לא; it is used four times, once in every colon.

The first strophe of sub–stanza Ib (vss. 9–10) again expresses the motif of vss. 3–4 in a parallel way. Mankind attempts to find riches in the earth; cf. also כל (vss. 3b and 10b) and ראתה עינו / שם לחשך קץ (vss. 3a and 10b respectively).[41] In view of content alone, vs. 11 must be connected with vss. 9–10. Formally seen, however, vss. 11 and 12 belong together in the context of the poem. The root יצא precedes the noun מקום within the same strophe in vss. 1–2 and 5–6. When we unite vss. 11 and 12 as one strophe we come across the same pattern; note יצא in vs. 11b and מקום in vs. 12b. The two lines of vss. 9–10 formally belong together on the basis of the repetition of the preposition ב– (see 3.1e above). This preposition is lacking in vs. 11. Finally, in all the other sub–stanzas there is also an obvious tendency to form strophes of two lines (see also below). The formal indications detected within sub–stanza IIb fit this context perfectly. Thus, seen from the perspective of content, the poet created an enormous inner tension within the last strophe of the first stanza (vss. 11–12). Especially vs. 11b ('mankind brings to light what was hidden') forms a glaring contrast with the desperate

---

analysis of Habel has as defects, among other things, that the second and the third motif (the way of access to the precious item and the process of acquiring the item) are not clearly distinguished from each other within the poem, and that the 'key organizing term' עלם in vs. 11b coincides with the B–motif (Discovery/Acquisition) and עלם in vs. 21a with motif A (Place/Source).

41   Contra Andersen who connects vss. 9–10 with vss. 5–6 and 1–2; cf. also Clark: 1982:402 (vss. 10–11 repeat ideas and themes of vss. 5–6 and 1–2).

Pieter van der Lugt

question, 'where can wisdom be found' of vs. 12 (cf. the last strophe of stanza III, vss. 27—28). In this way the poet stresses the inability of mankind to press forward to the ultimate secrets of creation.   The strophe of vss. 11—12 as a whole has a negative sign; mankind is *not able* to reach (cf. vss. 7—8). We conclude that the beginning of this poem has a structure which is very well thought—out, as the following scheme tries to visualize:

introductory section	vss.	1—2	+ A
	vss.	3—4	+ B
sub—stanza Ia	vss.	5—6	+ A
	vss.	7—8	− A
sub—stanza Ib	vss.	9—10	+ B
	vss.	11—12	− B

In view of the contents the second stanza shows much less tension within its corpus. The whole section is governed by the negative idea that wisdom is unattainable for mankind; note לא // לא in the odd lines (except vs. 17) and לא in the first colon of the even lines (except in vs. 20, but see vs. 17 too; cf. 3.1b above). In this way the stanza obviously connects with the idea of the last strophe of stanza I (vss. 11—12). From the point of view of content we are dealing with some kind of 'enjambment'. This poetic device coincides with the concatenation between the first and the second stanza described above in 3.1b.

True, there is little suspence within the corpus of the second stanza, but we can point now to a sharp contrast between stanza II and III as a whole in view of the relationship of their thematic content. The negation of the second stanza, that wisdom is not to be found on earth, is balanced by the conviction of the third stanza that God is informed of the place of wisdom. Again, however, we are dealing with a kind of enjambment. The first strophe of stanza III (vss. 21—22) carries the theme of the second stanza to its climax; wisdom is *hidden*

---

42   See Webster in 2.2b above and n.20.

from the eyes of *all living.* See also ‏ה-‎ in vss. 20a and 21b (concatenation, cf. 3.1b). At the same time, the strophe contains an obvious allusion to the first strophe of stanza II, as has been noticed by other scholars too.[42] In vs. 22 the poet places on stage the divinities of death, just as in vs. 14 for a moment he let the divinities of the abyss speak. This fact coincides with the refrain of vss. 5—6, 13—14 and 21—22 as pointed out in 3.1b. This results in a rather strong tension within sub—stanza IIIa (vss. 21—24). The negative idea of vss. 21—22 again forms a glaring contrast with the statement of vss. 23—24 that God knows the place of wisdom; note ‏כי הוא..., והוא..., אלהים‎...

The ultimate turn in the thematic progression the poet reserved for the last strophe of his composition (vss. 27—28). In vs. 28 it finally appears that mankind in some way is able to share in wisdom so eagerly desired, 'the fear of the Lord'. As in vss. 11—12, the author concentrated the tension which can be discerned in the flow of the contents in the last strophe of the stanza. Especially the combination of ‏ראה‎ and ‏בין‎ in these verse—lines suggests that formally seen they belong together as one strophe (cf. 2.1c above).

On the basis of the preceding considerations we come to the following comprehensive design of Job 28:

stanza	description of contents[43]	pos./neg.	refrain
A	Introduction: man presses forward into all the secret places on earth. One can find all sorts of precious metals in the earth (vss. 1—2).	+	r. (1)
	Man explores all the remote corners of the world (vss. 3—4).	+	
I	Formulation of the problem (exposition): man presses forward to all the secret places of the		

---

43 For a description of especially the sub—stanzas, see p.286 above.

	earth but does not find wisdom there.		
Ia	The earth conceals a wealth of powers and riches (vss. 5—6); even the mighty animals are unable to attain these treasures (vss. 7—8).	+ —	r. (1)
Ib	Mankind digs tunnels in the earth in search of wealth (vss. 9—10); thereby he brings what was hidden to light, but wisdom remains concealed (vss. 11—12).	+ —	r. (2)
II	Deepening of the problem: wisdom is unattainable for mankind.		
IIa	Nowhere on earth is man able to find wisdom (vss. 13—14). Wisdom is not for sale for all the wealth in the world (vss. 15—16).	— —	r. (1)
IIb	Wisdom can not be compared with any earthly treasure (vss. 17—18). If wisdom can not be compared with any earthly wealth, where does wisdom come from? (vss. 19—20).	— —	r. (2)
III	Dénouement: Only God knows the place of wisdom.		
IIIa	The living are unable to discover wisdom; even death has only some understanding		

IIIb	of it (vss. 21–22).	–	r. (1)
	God only knows where wisdom can be found (vss. 23–24).	+	
	When God placed a 'boundary' on the forces of nature (vss. 25–26)	+	
	He also decided in which way human beings could share in wisdom: by fearing the Lord (vss. 27–28).	++	r. (2)

3.3 *Transition markers*

In the Psalms the turning–point from one strophe to another is frequently marked by special words and grammatical forms in the last line of the preceding and/or the first line of the following strophe.   There appear to be special words and grammatical forms which mark primarily the *beginning* of a strophe. The particle הן is a well–known example of this category. Other words to the contrary were used primarily in the *last line* of a strophe. Here the personal pronoun הוא is an obvious example.[44] Furthermore, it may be concluded from the analysis that the first category of transition markers also acted as ending–markers in larger poetic units (e.g. in sub–stanzas or stanzas).   The second category of transition markers in turn could indicate the beginning of such larger units. It now appears that in the book of Job all these markers play the same part as they do in the Psalms. As already indicated the analysis of these formal devices has only a supplementary meaning in the context of the strophic structure of Job 28.

a.   In the first line of a strophe
There is only one transition marker in the whole poem which plainly indicates the beginning of a new strophe, i.e., the

---

44 For complete lists of all these words and grammatical forms see Van der Lugt: 1980:510–524.

particle אז in vs. 27a.

b   In the last line of a strophe

Mention may first be made of the following words:

היא, vs. 14a

הוא, vs. 24a (externally parallel with הוא in vs. 23b)

היא, vs. 28b

In the second instance there appear to be some words in the poem that usually function in the first line of a strophe, but now are used to close a larger poetic unit (a stanza):

מאין, vs. 12a

אי, vs. 12b

מאין, vs. 20a

אי, vs. 20b

הן, vs. 28b

c   Contrary indications

Lastly, there are two words which ordinarily occur in the last line of a strophe, but now appear in the first line, namely הוא in vs. 3b and גם in vs. 27b. In both cases, however, we are not dealing with a 'head—strophe' in a larger poetic unit.

4 Conclusion

The 'Hymn to Wisdom' in Job 28 shows a very rigid poetic framework. It is constructed of three uniform stanzas of eight verse—lines, preceded by an introductory section of exactly half this length, four lines. Furthermore, each of the 8—line stanzas consists of two uniform sub—stanzas of four lines (cf. the introductory section). The sub—stanzas in turn, as well as the introduction, are all constructed of two uniform strophes of two lines. Lastly, nearly all the lines of the poem are bicola. The end of the introductory section is marked as such by a strophe consisting of two tricola; cf. vs. 28, the last line of the whole composition. From a stylistic point of view the poem as a whole makes a rather stiff impression.   It is reminiscent of the speeches of Bildad and Zophar in the first cycle of the dialogues, with *three uniform* stanzas subdivided into two uniform units and a concluding section.[45] But we can also

---

45 See P. van der Lugt, 'Stanza—Structure and Word—Repetition in Job

compare the lament of Job in ch. 30, with its structural scheme of 9.8.8.8; note ועתה at the beginning of stanza I, II and III (vss. 1a, 9a and 16a).   After all, long series of 4—line sub—stanzas consisting of 2—line strophes were already encountered in the speeches of Job in chs. 7 and 13.[46]

The borders of the 8—line stanzas are marked by refrains. As demonstrated, the well—known refrain in vss. 12 and 20 is only part of the structural repetitions which the poet wove into his composition to denote its framework. By including vs. 28 as a refrain in the macro—structure of the poem, Vetter and De Wilde contributed to a more definitive solution for the structure of Job 28. The analysis of the repetitions, however, demonstrated that in this poem there are *two refrains*, a refrain denoting the beginning of the main parts (vss. 1—2, 5—6, 13—14 and 21—22; refrain [1]) and a refrain denoting the end of these parts (vss. 11—12, 19—20 and 27—28; refrain [2]).

This formal framework sheds special light on the progress of the thought development within the stanzas and on the transitions from one stanza to another. A vivid flow in the sequence of ideas was detected. At the same time, the analysis of the motifs and themes of individual strophes more than once plainly supported the analysis of the verbal repetitions (note vss. 13—14 // vss. 21—22). The formal framework also elucidated the introductory function of the first four lines of the poem. As we noted (cf. 2.2b), only J. Ley had a vague suspicion of the true character of these lines.[47]

Finally, the analysis of the transition markers plays only a minor part in determining the poetic structure of Job 28.

3—14', *JSOT* 40 (1988) 3—38.

46   See note 45 above.

47   In this context we recall the remark by Andersen concerning vs. 1a ('There are mines for silver'): 'at once an intriguing riddle in the true Wisdom mode' (1976:224 n.1). In our opinion this remark applies to the introductory section as a whole (vss. 1—4).

THE LITERARY STRUCTURE OF LAMENTATIONS (I)[1]

Johan Renkema

Recently much scientific attention has been paid to structural analysis of Hebrew poetry.[2] For that reason it has become impossible for anyone who wishes to comment seriously upon the poetic texts of the OT to ignore such investigations. In our preliminary studies we wish to apply to the poetry of Lamentations the results of the studies mentioned in the preceding note.

Even without the impulse of modern research one can ask how poets in Israel wrote their songs. Subconsciously we usually assume that they wrote their songs in the same way as we read them: from the beginning to the end, that is linearly. Characteristic of a good literary piece is a transparent, logical and/or chronological arrangement of ideas and facts. However it is highly questionable whether such an idea of literature also fits ancient texts, especially when they were meant to be recited and heard in a liturgical context, as were the Psalms and probably also the songs of Lamentations. For example, by modern standards it is not acceptable when an author cites a main idea six times within one article, but the repetition 'there is no comforter' in Lam. 1 must have had a totally different effect on the audience. A similar observation might be made regarding the repetition of thought in vss. 5, 18, and 9, 11. These observations argue against linear writing. However, in the

---

1   I wish to express my gratitude to prof. dr. J.C. de Moor for his many inspiring and helpful remarks on the subject.
2   J.C. de Moor, 'The Art of Versification in Ugarit and Israel', I, in: Y. Avishur—J. Blau (eds.), *Studies in Bible and the Ancient Near East Presented to S.E. Loewenstamm* (Jerusalem, 1978) 119–139; II, *UF* 10 (1978) 187–217; III, *UF* 12 (1980) 311–315; 'The Poetry of the book of Ruth', I, *Or* 53 (1984) 262–283; II, *Or* 55 (1986) 2–32; M.C.A. Korpel—J.C. de Moor, 'Fundamentals of Ugaritic and Hebrew Poetry', *UF* 18 (1986) 173–212. P. van der Lugt, *Strofische structuren in de bijbels–hebreeuwse poëzie* (Kampen, 1980); W.G.E. Watson, *Classical Hebrew Poetry*. A Guide to its Techniques (Sheffield, 1984).

case of Lamentations the form of the alphabetic acrostic seems to be an argument pro. Is it possible that these poets wrote in a more loose linear way, combining their thoughts by association, like pearls on a chain? In regard to the Psalms this must be denied. In his commentary on the Psalms N.H. Ridderbos states that the Psalms are like buildings. Good building needs good architecture. Nobody will deny that the Psalms express deep felt emotions. However, these emotions are not expressed in an uncontrolled way. To the contrary. The Psalmists were skilled poets and one can say that their poetry bears a somewhat intellectual character. The composition of the Psalms is the output of a structuring intellect.[3] These statements of Ridderbos are confirmed by the results of recent investigations. Regarding the Psalms, one can point to the voluminous and thoroughgoing study of P. van der Lugt.

We speak deliberately of the Psalms because the investigations on their art of poetry are of direct importance to the study of the poetry of Lamentations. It was one of the main results of our study concerning the theological presuppostions of the poets of Lamentations that they belong to the circles of the pre−exilic temple−singers and it is amongst them we also find the poets of the Psalms.[4] Therefore we may assume that Lamentations was created by the same structuring intellect. That this is true we hope to prove by our analysis of the structure of each song of Lamentations and by our analysis of the composition of the booklet as a whole.

The structure of Lamentations 1

An important, and immediately visible, means of structuring is in the use of the alphabetic acrostic. Most commentators agree that this form has been chosen intentionally to express

---

3   N.H. Ridderbos, *De Psalmen I* (Kampen, 1962) 44; idem, *Die Psalmen. Stilistische Verfahren und Aufbau mit besonderer Berücksichtigung von Ps 1−41* (BZAW 117; Berlin, 1972) especially 112−115.
4   J. Renkema, '*Misschien is er hoop ...*'. (Franeker, 1983). Furthermore it is likely that the downfall of Judah and Jerusalem has been a matter of intense theological reflection in the circles of the temple−singers and we assume that more of them, at the same time, contributed to the major composition of Lamentation. For that reason we use in our essay the plural.

all—embracingly the sorrows of Jerusalem and Judah, from A to
Z.[5] As already noted, precisely this form might cause one to
suppose linear writing. However, that this is not the case
becomes clear when attention is drawn to another literary tool
of the poets, namely that of concentric structure. In modern
commentaries this literary technique is completely ignored. Yet
it is not very difficult to discover the concentric structure of
Lam. 1. It is indicated by some remarkable repetitions of
speech. We pointed already to vss. 5 and 18 with the repeated
phrase of the youth going into exile. Both verses are situated
the same distance from the centre of the poem, i.e. from verses
11 and 12. Here too we find a remarkable repetition of speech,
in this case the doublet of imperatives from ראה and נבט.
Looking on from this centre of the poem one finds the other
elements of the concentric structure. Which may be summarized
in this way:

1. א רבתי
22. ת רבות

2. ב אין מנחם...לאיבים
21. ש אין מנחם לי...איבי

3. ג המצרים
20. ר צר

4. ד כהניה
19. ק כהני

5. ה יהוה...הלכו שבי
18. צ יהוה...הלכו בשבי

6. ו ציון
17. פ ציון

7. ז אין עוזר //   צר //
16. ע רחק מנחם   אויב

8. ח מכבדיה // ?
15. ס אבירי

9. ט יהוה //
14. נ אדני

---

5   Watson: 1984:197f.

10. ‏פרש י‎
13. ‏פרש מ‎

11. ‏ראה...והביטה כ‎
12. ‏הביטו וראו ל‎

This exposure indicates very clearly that concentric structure constituted a major consideration in the structuring of this poem. However, the value of this concentric design is not limited to literary structuring, and it also surpasses poetical esthetics; it highlights the centre of the song — i.e. the kernel of this poem — where the main thought of the poets has been expressed, and that of course is of great importance for exegesis. The leading theme of the poets could be described as: 'beseeching God and men to pay attention to all their sorrows and griefs'. That central theme of misery is elaborated in the other strophes of this song. It offers a better clue to its understanding than the headings which Kraus and Kaiser use for their commentary on the first song, respectively 'Sion ist einsam und ohne Trost', and 'Die Verlassenheit der Tochter Sion'.[6] A heading like: 'God, men! Look at our misery', more aptly fits the content of the song.

Shortly after this discovery we noticed that already in 1933 the Frenchman Albert Condamin pointed out this literary technique in Lam. 1.[7] But in studies on Lamentations, as far as we know, no attention has been paid to his investigations.

Using the tools for analysing Hebrew poetry, as developed by the research team of the THUK, we may now proceed with a more detailed analysis of the literary structure of this song.[8] Looking for detailed structure entails looking for smaller units. It is possible to start with the smallest unit in Hebrew poetry, the foot, or the next higher structural units, the colon and the verse, but we prefer, because of the presence of a very clear strophe—division in Lam. 1, to look first at the unit following

---

6   H.J. Kraus, *Klagelieder* (BKAT XX; Neukirchen, 1968[3]) 21; O. Kaiser, *Klagelieder* (ATD 16; Göttingen, 1981[3]) 307.

7   A. Condamin, *Poèmes de la Bible* (Paris, 1933) 47—50.

8   We also use the same terminology as in 'Fundamentals of Ugaritic and Hebrew Poetry', see note 2.

the verse, that is, the strophe. The strophes are indicated by:
a) the alphabetic acrostic
b) the setumah at the end of each strophe
c) the strong uniting external parallelism in each strophe, compare for example:

v.1: שרתי // רבתי // רבתי

מדינות // גוים // עם

and the pairs:

כאלמנה // בדד

היתה // היתה

v.2: by the triplet of suffixes 3 fem. sing.

by the pairs אין לה מנחם // תבכה

and כל רעיה // כל אהביה

v.3: by the triplet: מצרים // לא...מנוח // עבדה

Strophe—division is no problem in the first song of Lamentations. But in which way are the strophes interconnected? Do they follow each other as relatively independent units, like pearls on a chain, or are they more integrally connected? In my opinion the latter view is correct. As demonstrated in the following analysis, the strophes in Lam. 1 belong together. They form higher units which we call canticles.[9] An argument for the unity of such a canticle is the phenomenon of inclusion, which is an external parallelism on the opposite level of the same literary unit, consisting of equal or synonym words and/or expressions, which mark the borders of the canticle and embrace it. Often such inclusions are recognized as a concentric design of the literary unit concerned. The inner coherence of the canticle is indicated by the literary techniques of responsion, which is an external parallelism on the same level in the strophes which together form a canticle, common external parallelisms, concatenation, alliteration, assonance, keywords etc. In addition to these formal points a material unity is also obvious. N.H. Ridderbos statement concerning the strophe, 'An actual strophe is a pericope that forms a unit not only from a material but also from a formal point of view' can be reversed and is valid for higher units too.[10] Now we will indicate and argue for the following canticle—division in Lam. 1.

---

9   See Korpel—De Moor 1986:200 n.61.
10   N.H. Ridderbos, *The Psalms: style figures and structure* (OTS 13; Leiden, 1963) 49.

Canticle I (Lam. 1:1—3)

Content/theme: *Jerusalem   and   Judah   are   lonesome,*
                    comfortless and oppressed widows

Literary arguments:
  inclusions:
  בגוים (1bB) // בגוים (3bA)[11]
  מס (1cB) // עבדה (3aB)
  אלמנה (1bA) // לא מצאה מנוח (3bB) cf. Ruth 1:9
  responsions:
  העיר (1aB) // יהודה (3aA)
  רבתי (1aB) // רב (3aB)
  לא מצאה מנוח (2bA) // אין־לה מנחם (2bA) // אלמנה (1bA)
  (3bB) (note also the alliteration between מנוח and מנחם)
  מדינות (1cA) // רעיה (2cA)
  אויבים (2cB) // רדפיה (3cA)
  ext. parallelism:
  ישבה (1aA) // ישבה (3bA)

Canticle II (Lam. 1:4—6)

Content/theme: *Zion without pilgrims* (the same theme as
                    in the first canticle, namely loneliness, but
                    the focus shifts from the city/cities to the
                    sanctuary)

Literary arguments:
  inclusions:
  בוא (4aB) \\ הלך (6cA)
  כהניה (4bB) // שריה (6bA)
  responsions:
  ציון (4aA) // ציון (6aA)
  עולליה (4cA) // בתולחיה (5cA)
  וילכו (6cA) // הלכו (5cA)
  לפני־רודף (5cB) // לפני־צר (6cB)

---

11   Notation: the successive bicola in a strophe are indicated by successive
small letters a,b,c,d; the first part of a bicolon is indicated by capital A and
the second by capital B. For an antithetic parallelism the sign \\ is used.

ext. parallelism:

(6bA) היו שריה כאילים \\ (5aA) היו צריה לראש

Canticle III (Lam. 1:7–9)[12]

Content/theme: *the bittter end of Jerusalem is caused by her sin*

Literary arguments:

inclusions:

(9cA) עניי // (7aB) עניה

(9aB) אחריתה // (7dB) משבתה

responsions:

(9aB) זכרה // (7aA) זכרה

(8cB) ותשב אחור \\ (7dA) שחקו

(9aA) טמאתה // (8aB) לנידה

(9cB) כי הגדיל אויב // (7dA) צרים שחקו

part. responsion:

(9cA) ראה יהוה // (7dA) ראוה צרים

ext. parallelism:

(9bB) אין מנחה לה // (7cB) אין עוזר לה

(9aB) אחריתה \\ (7bB) מימי קדם

Canticle IV (Lam. 1:10–11)

Content/theme: *A cry for YHWH to look at their dishonouring and hunger*

Literary arguments:

inclusion:

(11bB) כי הייתי זוללה // (10aA) ידו פרש צר...

responsions:

---

12 It is not necessary to delete a bicolon in vs. 7. See for argumentation p.18. Besides it appears from this canticle that is invalid to use a change of voice as an indication for the start of a new, independent literary unit within the song. The inclusion עניה (7aB) // עניי (9cA), the responsion צרים (7dA) // אויב (9cB) and ראוה (7dA) // ראה indicate that vs. 9c belongs to this canticle. In addition, setting apart vs. 9c damages the unity of the strophe involved and creates a large imbalance between the different parts of the song. A change of voice seems to be no more than a figure of speech, which enlivens the song. Contra R. Brandscheidt, *Gotteszorn und Menschenleid* (Trier, 1983) 82ff.

כל (10aB) // כל (11aA)
(11cB) כי הייתי זוללה (10bAB) גוים באו מקדשה
(11cA) ראה יהוה (10cA) // אשר צויתה
ext. parallelism:
(11cB) כי הייתי זוללה (10bA) // כי ראתה גוים..
keywords:
(11bA) מחמודיהם (10aB) // מחמדיה
(11cA) ראה (10bA) // ראתה

Canticle V (Lam. 1:12—13)

Content/theme: *A call for compassion*
Literary arguments:
  inclusion:
כל (12aA) // כל (13cB)
  responsions/inclusions:
(13bB) השיבני אחור (12bAB) // כמכאבי אשר עולל לי
(13aA) פרש רשת לרגלי (12bAB) // כמכאבי אשר עולל לי
  responsion:
(13cA) נתנני שממה (12cA) // הוגה יהוה
  part. responsion:
(13cB) כל היום דוה (12cB) // ביום חרון אפו

Canticle VI (Lam. 1:14—16)

Content/theme: *YHWH delivered them in the hands of their
                      enemies*
Literary arguments:
  inclusions:
(16bB) משיב נפשי \\ (14bB) הכשיל כחי
(15cA) אדני // (15aB) אדני
  responsions:
(15cA) אדני // (14cA) אדני
(15bA) עלי // (14bA) על־צוארי
(16cB) כי גבר אויב // (14cB) לא־אוכל קום
  concatenation: by means of suffixes 1 sing.

Canticle VII (Lam. 1:17—19)

Content/theme: *No comfort for Zion because of YHWH's
                      justified punishment*
Literary arguments:

inclusions
(19bA) בעיר // (17bA) ליעקב
(19aB) המה רמוני // (17cB) לנדה ביניהם
responsions:
(19aA) קראתי למאהבי // (17aA) פרשה ציון בידיה
(19aB) המה רמני // (17aB) אין מנחם לה
ext. parallelism:
(18aA) צדיק הוא יהוה // (17bA) צוה יהוה
(19bA) כהני וזקני // (18cA) בתולתי ובחורי
assonance:
(19cB) וישיבו // (18cB) בשבי

Canticle VIII (Lam. 1:20—22)

Content/theme:　　　　*A prayer for retribution of their enemies*
Literary arguments:
inclusions:
(22aA) כי רבות אנחתי // (20aA) כי־צר־לי
(22cB) ולבי דוי // (20aB) מעי חמרמרו
(22bB) על כל־פשעי // (20bB) כי מרו מריתי
responsions:
(22aA) תבא // (20aA) ראה
(22bA) כאשר עוללת לי // (21bB) כי אתה עשית
(21aB) כי נאנחה אני // (20aA) כי־צר־לי
ext. parallelism:
(22cA) אנחתי // (21aB) כי נאנחה אני
(22cB) לבי דוי // (20bA) נהפך לבי בקרבי

Our conclusion is that next to that of the strophes there also exists a canticle—division.

These divisions however, are not the only ones. As noted for example by Hillers, Kaiser and others, there is a main division which divides the song in two equal parts: vss. 1—11 and vss. 12—22.[13] We call these parts *Cantos*.[14] Hitherto such a major division was made on the sole basis of content. However,

---

13　D.R. Hillers, *Lamentations* (AB 7a; New York, 1979) 17; Kaiser: 1981³:310f.; B. Johnson, 'Form and Message in Lamentations', *ZAW* 97 (1985) 62f.
14　Korpel—De Moor: 1986:43.

there are literary arguments too. Note the inclusions in the first and the last canticle of the two parts.

Canto I (Lam. 1:1—11)

Content/theme: *Jerusalem remembers her days of misery*
Literary arguments:
  inclusions:

  (11cB) כי הייתי זוללה // (1bA) היתה כאלמנה
  (11aA) כל עמה // (1bB) רבתי עם
  (10bA) גוים // (1bB) גוים
  (8cA) נאנחה // (4bB) נאנחים
  (7dA) צרים // (5cB) צר

Canto II (Lam. 1:12—22)

Contents/theme: *A cry for help notwithstanding YHWH's justified punishment*
Literary arguments:
  inclusions:

  (22bB) כל // (12aA) כל
  (21bA) כל // (13cB) כל
  (22bA) כאשר עוללת לי // (12bB) אשר עולל לי
  (22cB) דוי // (13cB) דוה
  (21cA) הבאת יום־קראת // (12cB) ביום חרון אפו
  (20aA) יהוה // (12cA) יהוה
  ext. parallelism:
  (18bB) ראו...כמכאבי // (12aB—bA) וראו מכאבי...כמכאבי

On the same basis of literary arguments yet another subdivision can be made. Each canto consists of two *sub-cantos*,[15] A and B:

Subcanto A (Lam. 1:1—6)

Content/theme: *Depopulation and misery*
Literary arguments:
  inclusions:

  (6bA) היו // (1bA) היתה

---

15   See note 14.

(6aA) ויצא... // (1cB) היתה למס

part. inclusion:

(6bA) שריה // (1cA) שרתי

responsions:

(6bB) לא מצאו מרעה // (3bB) לא מצאה מנוח

(6cB) רודף // (3cA) רדפיה

(5cB) צר // (2cB) אויבים

Subcanto B (Lam. 1:7–11)

Content/theme: *Jerusalems humiliation and prayer to YHWH*

Literary arguments:

  inclusions:

(11cB) הייתי // (7bB) היו

(11aA) עמה // (7cA) עמה

(11aA) כל // (7bA) כל

(11bA) מחמודיהם // (7bA) מחמדיה

  responsions:

(10aA) ידו פרש צר // (7cA) ביד־צר

(11cA) ראה יהוה // (9cA) ראה יהוה

(10bA) ראתה // (7dA) ראוה

  concatenation:

(10bA) ראתה // (9cA) ראה // (8bB) ראו // (7dA) ראוה //

(11cA) ראה //

For the division of Canto II into two sub–cantos we have the following arguments.

Subcanto A (Lam. 1:12–16)

Content/theme: *The unparalleled punishment of Zion*

Literary arguments:

  inclusion:

(14cA) נתנני // (13cA) נתנני

  responsions:

(14cA) נתנני אדני בידי... // (12cA) הוגה יהוה

(16aB) ירדה // (13aB) וירדנה

(16bB) משיב נפשי // (13bB) השיבני אחור

(16cA) שממים // (13cA) שממה

Subcanto B (Lam. 1:17—22)

Content/theme: *Being   without   friends   Zion   turns   desperately to YHWH*

Literary arguments:

  inclusions:

  (22cA) כי־רבות אנחתי // (17aA) פרשה ציון בידיה

  (21bA) כל־איבי שמעו // (18bA) שמעו־נא כל־עמים

  (22bA) עוללת לי // (17bA) צוה יהוה

  responsions:

  (20aA) ראה יהוה // (17aA) פרשה ציון בידיה

  (22cB) לבי // (19cB) נפשם

  ext. parallelism:

  (20bB) מרו מריחי // (18aB) מריתי

  (21aB) אין מנחם לי // (17aB) אין מנחם לה

Now we can draw a very clear picture of the structure of the first song of Lamentations:

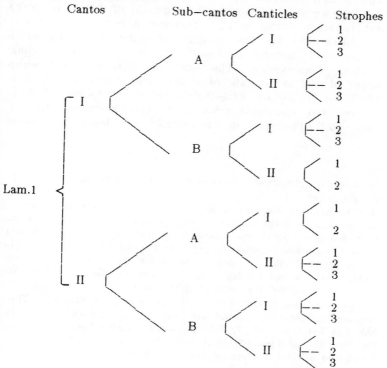

We conclude this section with some remarks on the value of this kind of structural analysis for exegesis. In most modern commentaries exegesis is done one verse after another, which shows a linear reading of the text. This means that most of the time the earlier verses/strophes do not play an important role in the exegesis of the following. We will illustrate this by the exegesis of Lam. 1:3. Kaiser and Boecker in their recent commentaries explain this verse on its own and do not really regard the context.[16] Kraus even states that there is no connection at all with the context.[17] The result is the following exegesis: Judah has gone into exile and has lost the מנוח, which is explained as the deuteronomic rest, the peace and security of the promised country.

If, however, the context of the first canticle is taken into account, the outcome is totally different. The metaphor of the widow used for Jerusalem appears to be used for Judah too. This is also indicated by the external parallelism between 1:3 and 1:20 we noted already at the beginning of this study: גלתה is balanced by שכלה in 1:20. Therefore it is not likely that in this place גלה has the meaning of going into exile, which anyhow was doubtful at best.[18] Far better fits the original meaning of uncovering. The widow Judah is uncovered, which means she is in a state of shame and oppression, cf. Nah. 3:5-7: Jer. 13:26; Jes. 47:2-9 and esp. Ez. 16:36 and 23:10. In the two last mentioned texts lovers became enemies too, cf. Lam. 1:2.[19] The state of un—covering and being unprotected

---

16   Kaiser: 1981[3]:316f.; H.J. Boecker, *Klagelieder* (ZB 21, Zürich, 1985) 27.

17   Kraus: 1968[3]:21.

18   The idea that Judah has gone into exile out of poverty and oppression only makes sense if one assumes a voluntary exile in Egypt, where one was really free from Babylonian oppression, cf. Jer. 44. But this is a very doubtful explanation, especially in regard to the last bicolon of this strophe and in regard to the last song of the booklet for there are connections between the first and the last song. We return to this subject later. We prefer to vocalize גלתה as pu'al pf. as in Nah. 2:8.

19   The expression אין מנחם found here, reminds of Nah. 3:7. There are more similarities cf. Nah. 3:5 and Lam. 1:8; Nah. 2:8 and Lam. 1:5,18; Nah. 3:18 and Lam. 1:6; 2:9; Nah. 2:10 and Lam. 1:10; Nah. 2:8 and Lam. 2:5; Nah. 3:7 and Lam. 1:2,9,17,21. The whole diction is the usual one to describe the downfall of a city, cf. Renkema: 1983:180ff.

becomes clear from the misery and slavery that overcomes Judah. That the metaphor of the widow is retained appears from the sentence לא מצאה מנוח. The same expression is used in Ruth 1:9 for the state of widowhood. No doubt here in Lamentations it also points to the depopulation and turmoil caused by enemies and hostile neighbours, who exploit the present weakness of Judah. So metaphor and reality are mixed. In short, this structural analysis affords a more contextual exegesis, because it indicates clearly the closer and wider context.

Finally, a closer look at smaller units exhibits common features. So, on the level of the canticles, a remarkable concatenation becomes visible if we look at the use of כל which appears very often in Lam.1.[20]: כל־רעיה (2cA) – כל־רדפיה (3cA) – כל־שעריה (4bA) – כל־הדרה (6aB) – כל מחמדי (7bA) – כל־מכבדיה (8bA) – כל־מחמדיה (10aB) – כל־עמה (11aA), כל־אברי דרך (12aA) – כל־היום (13cB) – כל־אבירי (15aA) – כל־עמים (18bA) – כל־איבי (21bA) – כל־רעתם (22aA) – כל־פשעי (22bB), which gives the impression of the completeness of the disaster.

Lamentations II

The Frenchman Condamin, already mentioned, also pointed out some peculiarities in this song.[21] First he drew attention to the circumstance that the same concentric structure is used as in Lam. 1. Indeed it is very clearly present, especially in the centre of the song:

1. ביום אפו א
22. ביום אף יהוה ת

2. לא חמל...לארץ ב
21. לארץ...לא חמלת ש

3. אכלה ג (verb אכל only in these verses)
20. תאכלנה ר

---

20 כל: Lam.1:2 (2x),3,4,6,7,8,10,11,12,13,15,18,21,22 (2x); compare the frequency in the other songs: 2:4,5,15 (2x),16,19; 3:3,14 (2x),34,46,51,60,61,62; 4:1,12.

21 Condamin: 1933:49f.

4. שפך ד
19. שפכי ק

5. אדני ה
18. אדני צ

6. יהוה ו
17. יהוה ע

7. אויב...כיום ז
16. איביך...היום פ

8. בת ח
15. בת ס

9. נביאיה...חזון ט
14. נביאיך חזו נ

10. בת ציון...בחולת י
13. בחולת בת ציון מ

11. נפשך...בעטף...ברחבות כ
12. בהתעטפם...ברחבות...בהשתפך ל

According to this structure the main theme may be expressed in the vss. 11,12: 'The breakdown of Judah and Jerusalem whose children starve to death'.

The second feature is the use of concatenation almost throughout the song. Condamin points to the following verses and words:

1 and 2 אדני
2 and 3 יעקב
3 and 4 כאש
4 and 5 כאויב
5 and 6 שחת
6 and 7 מועד
7 and 8 חומח
8 and 9 יהוה
9 and 10 ארץ
10 and 11 לארץ
11 and 12 ברחבות עטף שפך

12	and	13	?
13	and	14	?
14	and	15	?
15	and	16	עליך...שופי
16	and	17	עניך...אויב
17	and	18	יום
18	and	19	לילה
19	and	20	צוללים
20	and	21	הרג
21	and	22	ביום אף

Comparison with Lam. 1 reveals that concatenation is not as emphasized in the first song as in the second one (disregarding words either too general or too small to be of particular relevance). In Lam. 1. we find the following: vss. 4,5: יגה; vss. 5,6: פנים; vss. 7,8: ראה,ירושלם; vss. 8,9: ראה; vss. 9,10: ראה; vss. 10,11: מחמד ראה; vss. 11,12: יהוה נבט ראה; vss. 12,13: יום; vss. 13,14: נתן; vss. 14,15: אדני; vss. 16,17: נחם; vss. 17,18: יהוה; vss. 21,22: בוא אנח. However, note also what has been said before with regard to the concatenation on the level of the canticles through כל, see note 20.

What is the result of this literary technique? It has been described by D.H. Müller as follows: 'Die Verkettung ... verbindet das Ende der einen Strophe mit dem Anfang der zweiten und führt von der einen Gedankensphäre in die andere hinüber.'[22] In other words, concatenation shows the poet moving focus. However, a moving focus does not mean a lack of coherence in description as appears from the canticle—division for which we argue as follows:

Canticle I (Lam. 2:1–3)

Content/theme: *YHWH's anger hits Zion and Israel*
Literary arguments:
  inclusions:
    יעיב בשפו (1aA) // ויבער (3cA)
    ביום אפו (1cB) // בחרי-אף (3aA)

---

22 D.H. Müller, *Die Propheten in ihrer ursprünglichen Form* I (Wien, 1896) 200.

(3cA) יעקב // (1aB) ציון
responsions:
(3aB) קרן ישראל // 1aB) בת־ציון)
(3aB) כל קרן ישראל // (2aB) כל־נאות יעקב
(2bB) מבצרי בת־יהודה // (2aB) תפארת ישראל
ext.parallelism:
(3aB) ישראל // (2bB) מבצרי בת־יהודה
(2cA) לארץ // (1bA) ארץ
יעקב // (3aB) ישראל // (2aB) יעקב // (1bB) ישראל
(3cA) (note the regular alternation).

Maybe one is inclined to include vs. 4 because of the appearance of similar expressions like ימינו (3bA//4aB), ציון בת (1aB//4cA), כאש (3cA//4cB). Indeed these connections are not to be denied but they are caused by the macrostructure of the song (see below). The relative independence of the second canticle appears from limitation to Judah/Zion and the different theme.

Canticle II (Lam. 2:4—5)

Content/theme: *Like an enemy the Lord destroyed Zion and Judah*

Literary arguments:
  inclusions:
    (5bA) בלע // (4bA) ויהרג
    (5bA) כל // (4bB) כל
  responsions:
    (5aA) כאויב // (4aA) כאויב
    (5cA) בת־יהודה // (4cA) בת־ציון
  inclusion/responsion:
    (5bB) מבצריו // (5bA) ארמנותיה // (4bB) מחמדי־עין [23]

Canticle III (Lam. 2:6—7)

Content/theme: *YHWH destroyed his own temple and altar*
Literary arguments:
  inclusions:
    (7aA) בית־יהוה // (6aA) שכו

---

23   Mostly הרג (in 2:4bAB) is used for persons. Maybe here the buildings of the temple are involved; compare Ezek. 24:21 and Ps. 78:47.

(7cB) מוֹעֵד // (6aB) מוֹעֲדוֹ
responsions:
(7aA) מזבחו // (6aA) שכו
(7aB) מקדשו // (6aA) שכו
(7bB) מקדשו // (6aB) מוצדו
(7bB) חומת ארמנותיה // (6bA) בציון

Canticle IV (Lam. 2:8—10)

Content/theme: *Mourning city and inhabitants*
Literary arguments:
  inclusions:
  (10cB) בתולת ירושלם // (8aB) בת־ציון
  (10aA) ישבו לארץ // (8cB) אמללו
  responsions:
  (10aB) בת־ציון // (8aB) בת־ציון
  (10cA) הורידו לארץ // (8cB) יחדו אמללו
  (10aA)²⁴ ישבו לארץ // (9aA) טבעו בארץ

Canticle V (Lam. 2:11—13)

Content/theme: *The poets heartbreak over the dying children of Jerusalem*
Literary arguments:
  inclusions:
  (13cB)²⁵ מי ירפא־לך // (11aB) חמרמרו מעי
  (13bB) בתולת בת־ציון // (11bB) בת־עמי
  (13aB) ירושלם // (11cB) קריה
  (12cB) אמחם // (12aA) לאמחם
  responsions:
  (12cA) בהשתפך נפשם // (11cA) בצטף צולל ויונק
  (13bB) ציון // (12bB) עיר
  ext. parallelism:
  (13cA) שברך // (11bB) שבר

---

24 The responsion becomes more clear if one keeps in mind that the gate was pre—eminently the place of the elders.
25 Note the second inclusion of canticle VIII in the first song (Lam. 1: 20—22): חמר. So לבי דוי // מעי חמרמרו‎ .חמר can be parallel to רפא‎.

Canticle VI (Lam. 2:14–15)

Content/theme: *Because of the failure of the prophets the passers–by are appalled at the fate of Jerusalem*

Literary arguments:
  inclusions/responsion:
  על (14bA) // על (15bB)
  responsion:
  לך (14aA) // עליך (15aA)

Canticle VII (Lam. 2:16–17)[26]

Content/theme: *The enemies rejoice and YHWH cause them to do so*

Literary arguments:
  inclusions:
  עליך (16aA) // עליך (17cA)
  אויביך (16aB) // אויב (17cA)
  responsion:
  צוה מימי־קדם (17bA) // (16cA) היום שקוינהו
  ext.parallelism:
  אמרתו (17aB) // (16bB) אמרו

Canticle VIII (Lam. 2:18–19)

Content/theme: *Exhortation to the daughter of Zion to cry for the life of her children*

Literary arguments:
  ext.parallelism/inclusion:
  אל־אדני (18aA) // אליו (19cA)
  responsions:
  כנחל (18bA) // כמים (19bA)
  הורידי (18bA) // שפכי (19bA)
  ext. parallelism:
  לבם (18aA) // לבך (19bA)
  אדני (18aA) // אדני (19bB)
  ולילה (18bB) // בליל (19aA)

---

26 This canticle seems to be an expansion of Lam. 1:21 or otherwise this verse is a contraction of this canticle.

Canticle IX (Lam. 2:20−22)

Content/theme;   *Zions prayer*
Literary arguments:
  inclusion:
  (22aA) כיום מועד // (20cA) במקדש אדני
  responsions:
  (21cA) הרגת // (20cA) יהרג
  (22bAB) לא...פליט ושריד // (21bB) נפלו בחרב
  ext. parallelism:
  (22bA) ביום אף־יהוה // (21cA) ביום אפך
  (22bA) יהוה // (20aA) יהוה
  (22cA) טפחתי // (20bB) טפחים

Contrary to the situation in the first song, commentators
disagree about the outline of the second song. Internal divisions
are primarily designated on the basis of content.[27] Literary
indications are mostly neglected.   If we take them fully into
account, however, the macrostructure of the song becomes clear.

Canto I (Lam. 2:1−10)

Content/theme: *YHWH as enemy, destroyed land, city and
           temple*
Literary arguments:
  inclusions:
  (10aB) בת־ציון // (1aB) בת־ציון
  (9aA,10aA,cA) (ל/ב)ארץ // (1bA,2cA) (ל)ארץ
  (9bA) ממלכה ושריה // (2cB) מלכה ושריה // (8bB) לא־השיב ידו // (3bA) השיב אחור ימינו
  (7bA) ביד־אויב // (4aA) כאויב
  (7aB) מקדשו // (4cA) אהל בת־ציון
  responsions:
  (6cA) אפו // (4cB) חמתו
  (7aA) אדני // (5aA) אדני
  (7bB) ארמנותיה // (5bA) ארמנותיה

---

27   Kraus: 1968³:39: 1−10, 11−12, 13−17, 18−19, 20−22; Hillers: 1979:42:
1−9a, 9b−17, 8−19, 20−22; Kaiser: 1981³:329: 1−12, 13−19, 20−22;
Boecker: 1985:41: 18−19, 20−22.

Canto II (Lam. 2:11−22)

Content/theme: *Dying children, horror, jeers, prayer*
Literary arguments:
  inclusions:
  (22cB) כלם // (11aA) כלו
  (21bA) בתולחי ובחורי // (11cA) עולל ויונק
  (21aA) לארץ // (11bA) לארץ
  (21aA) חוצות // (11cB) ברחבות
  (20bA) נשים // (12aA,cB) אמחם
  (19dA) רעב // (12aB) איה דגן
  (19dA) העטפים // (12bA) החעטפם
  (19bA) שפכי...לבך // (12cA) בהשחפך נפשם
  (18aB) בח־ציון // (13bB) בח־ציון | (13aB) בח ירושלם
  (17aB) אמרתו \\ (14aA) נביאיך
  (16bA) שרקו // (15bA) שרקו

The main theme of the first canticle of canto II, starving and
dying children, returns clearly in the last one; so inclusion is
also evident from the content.

Together content and literary arguments indicate the subdivision
in cantos. Canto I can be divided into two subcantos A and B.

Subcanto A (Lam. 2:1−5)

Content/theme: *YHWH destroyed land and city*
Literary arguments:
  inclusions:
  (5cA) בח־יהודה // (1aB) בח־ציון
  (5bA) ארמנותיה // (1bB) חפארת ישראל
  (4cB) בח־ציון // (2bB) בח־יהודה
  (4aB) ימינו // (3bA) ימינו
  responsions:
  (5aB) בלע ישראל // (3aAB) גדע...ישראל
  (4cB) כאש // (3cA) כאש
  ext.parallelism:
  (5bB) מבצריו // (2bB) מבצרי

Subcanto B (Lam. 2:6−10)

Content/theme: *YHWH destroyed the sanctuary*
Literary arguments:
  inclusions:
  ציון (6bA) // ציון (10aB)
  אדני (7aA) // יהוה (9cB)
  ביד־אויב (6bA) // מלכה ושריה בגוים (9bA)
  יד (7bA) // ידו (8bB)
  חומת (7bB) // חומת (8aB,cA)
  responsion:
  שחת (6aB) // להשחית (8aA)

For the division of the second Canto of Lam. 2 we have the following arguments.

Subcanto A (Lam. 2:11−17)

This is a moving piece in the song. Rapidly the poets change subjects: the starving children, the incomparable fate of Jerusalem, the failure of the prophets, the horror of the passers−by, the sneers of the enemies. However, these different subjects do not mean a lack of coherence.   Concerning the context the connections between the single strophes are clear: the horrible fate of the children indicates the incomparable disaster which overcame Jerusalem and this was not to be avoided because of the failure of the prophets; now passers by are appalled, the enemies rejoice.   And all of this is fulfilment of YHWH's word! On literary grounds alone it is not easy to indicate the final border of this subcanto. It is more the clear starting point of the next subcanto that marks the end of the preceding one. Yet, some literary arguments can be given.

Literary arguments:
  inclusions:
  וישמח עליך אויב (17cA) \\ נשפך...על־שבר (11bAB)
  אמרו (16bB) // אמרו (12aA)
  הזאת העיר... (15cA) // מה־אעידך... (13aB)
  בת ירושלם (15bB) // בת ירושלם (13aB)

Subcanto B (Lam. 2:18—22)

Content/theme: *Cry for the children*
Literary arguments:
  inclusions:
    יהוה (22bA)²⁸ // אדני (18aA)
    אדני (20cA) // אדני (19bB)
    עללי (20bB) // עולליך (19cB)
    תאכלנה...פרים (20bA) // ברעב (19dA)
    חוצות (21aA) // חוצות (19dB)
  responsion:
    אשר־טפחתי ורביתי (22cA) // עולליך (19cB)

We close this section²⁹ with a few remarks on the value of our analysis for text—criticism.

By BHK, BHS and most commentators Lam. 2:19d is deleted as a gloss, because this strophe consists of four bicola instead of three and so it is not in harmony with the other strophes. The argument for deleting just this bicolon is that it contains the same words as in vss. 11,12, and 4:1. However, as we have seen, on the basis of this argumentation a lot more can be deleted in the songs. So the only real argument is the four instead of three bicola. Now it is hardly acceptable that the glossator did not notice the same regularity of three bicola. Yet, willingly he destroyed it by inserting his gloss. Are we to believe that this glossator was an untalented man of letters? In that case we may assume that this gloss not only fits badly in the ק־strophe, but that it also had no function in the macrostructure. A closer look shows that this is not true. On the level of the ק־strophe itself there is — as in many other strophes in the first two songs — a clear inclusion, including also the last bicolon, namely:

לראש (19aB) // בראש (19dB)

There is also assonance between the last words אשמרות and חוצות. Another including alliteration/assonance exists between שפכי (19bA) // שאי 19cA) and the bicola 19b and 19c have a fine chiastic structure by means of לבך // נפש and כפיך //

---

28 The same inclusion as in the ר־strophe.
29 See the next page for a picture of the second song of Lamentations.

The structure of the second song

Cantos	Sub–cantos	Canticles	Strophes

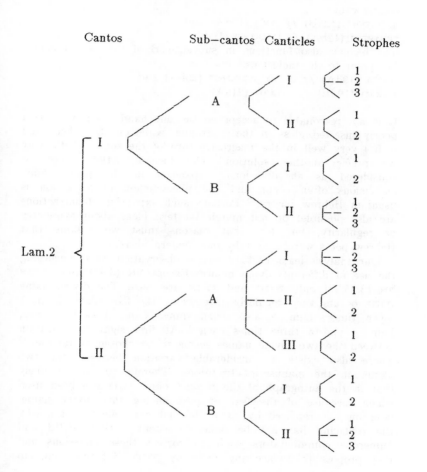

פני. So the quadrocolon is well—balanced. And vs. 19d fits very well into the macrostructure. We recall the inclusions in the second canto:

איה דגן (12aB) // רעב (19dA) and:
החמעטפם (12bA) // העטפים (19dA).

The bicolon also functions in subcanto B of the second canto. We point to the inclusions:

ברעב (19dA) // תאכלנה...פרים (20bA) and
חוצות (19dB) // חוצות (21aA)

It is not reasonable to accept on the one hand vs. 19d to be a poorly inserted gloss in the ק-strophe, while on the other hand it fits very well in the macrostructure of the song. That's why we prefer another solution. The bicolon 2:19d is to be considered as an occasional expansion in the poem. Such expansions often occur and the phenomenon of expansion is usual in Hebrew poetry.[30] Perhaps such expansions (contractions are also possible) do not match Western ideas about symmetry or regularity, but for what reasons must we assume that Hebrew poets were guided by our modern ideas?

Our analysis leads us to a second observation, now concerning the use of different divine names. Except אל (3:41) and עליון אל (3:35,38) only יהוה and אדני are used. The divine name יהוה occurs very regularly throughout the five songs: Lam. 1 seven times; Lam. 2 also seven times; Lam. 3 twelve times; Lam. 4 and 5 three times each.[31] At first sight the varation between the two divine names seems to be chosen at random.[32] There also exists a considerable variation between the two names in the manuscript traditions. Therefore it is not likely that in the autograph of the booklet only יהוה has been used which, because of the fear of pronouncing this divine name, later on was replaced by אדני. In that case one may ask why the replacing has not be done consistently. BHK, BHS and numerous commentators want to correct these omissions and they propose to replace any אדני by יהוה. But this seems to

---

30   Cf. De Moor: 1978:139.   Korpel—De Moor: 1986:9; Watson: 1984:349f.
31   יהוה in: 1:5,9,11,12,17,18,20; 2:6,7,8,9,17,20,22; 3:18,22,24,25,26,40,50,55, 59,61,64,66; 4:11,16,20,; 5:1,19,21. אדני in 1:14,15(2x); 2:1,2,5,7,18,19,20; 3:31,36,37,58.
32   See Hillers: 1979:12.

be forced.

Let us look at the distribution of divine names within the canticles:

Lam. 1:	1–3	יהוה	(1x, v. 5)
	1: 4–6	— —	
	1: 7–9	יהוה	(1x, v. 9)
	1: 10–11	יהוה	(1x, v.11)
	1: 12–13	יהוה	(1x, v. 12)
	1: 14–16	אדני	(3x, vv. 14,15)
	1: 17–19	יהוה	(2x, vv. 17,18)
	1: 20–22	יהוה	(1x, vv.20)
Lam. 2:	1–3	אדני	(2x, vv. 1,2)
	2: 4–5	אדני	(1x, v. 5)
	2: 6–7	יהוה	(2x, vv. 6,7) / אדני (1x, v.7)
	2: 8–10	יהוה	(2x, vv. 8,9)
	2: 11–13	— —	
	2: 14–15	— —	
	2: 16–17	יהוה	(1x, v.17)
	2: 18–19	אדני	(2x, vv.18,19)
	2: 20–22	יהוה	(2x, vv.20,22) / אדני (1x, v.20)

With regard to Lam. 1, of course, the sixth canticle is striking for אדני occurs only here, and three times at that! Furthermore one can observe a deliberate usage by the poets. In 1:15 there is a clear inclusion within the ס-strophe by the twofold אדני and responsion between 14cA and 15cA, also using the appelative אדני. The limitation to one canticle, as well as this deliberate usage, contradicts a haphazard occurrence of divine names in Lam. 1.

With regard to Lam. 2 we first observe that both divine names are spread almost equally over the two cantos. Moreover we notice that in five canticles the divine names are not mixed. Two show an exception: 2:6–7 and 2:20–22. There is a similarity in both canticles: the divine name אדני is bracketed by two references to יהוה. So one divine name is dominant. Maybe אדני in 2:20 has been chosen to establish the inclusion אדני (19bB) // אדני (20cB) in subcanto B (Lam. 2:18–22) and אדני in 2:7 to establish the responsion אדני (2:7aA) // אדני (2:5aA) within the first canto.

If we take also into account the canticles of the first song we may conclude that as a rule in these two songs the poets used only one divine name in a strophe or canticle and often these names were applied in inclusion and/or responsion. So their choice was not a haphazard one, but was inspired by the needs of their literary performance.

THE LITERARY STRUCTURE OF LAMENTATIONS (II)

Johan Renkema

Lamentations III

Coming from the first two songs of Lamentations one is inclined to look for some such concentric structure in the third song as well. Comparing the opposite strophes one finds the following words in common:

1 }	יד > א	{ 66 / ח65 / 64		19 }	על > ז	{ 48 / פ47 / 46
2				20		
3				21		
4 }	עלי > ב	{ 63 / ש62 / 61		22 }	לא > ח	{ 45 / ס44 / 43
5				23		
6				24		
7 }	עותחה // עוה > ג	{ 60 / ר59 / 58		25 }	יהוה > ט	{ 42 / נ41 / 40
8				26		
9				27		
10 }	יהוה // הוא > ד	{ 57 / ק56 / 55		28 }	פה > י	{ 39 / מ38 / 37
11				29		
12				30		
13 }	? > ה	{ 54 / צ53 / 52		31 }	לא | אדני > כ	{ 36 / ל35 / 34
14				32		
15				33		
16 }	מין|נפש|יהוה > ו	{ 51 / ע50 / 49				
17						
18						

However, not every connection is equally convincing, and in the centre of this elegy, in the neighbourhood of vss. 33 and 34, one cannot find such an accumulation of words as was the case in Lam. 1 and 2. The connection between the ו—strophe and the ע—strophe seems to be stronger. Besides, to indicate a kernel of this song in the כ— and ל— strophe seems to be difficult: if one translates vs. 36B as the 'The Lord did not see',[1] the ל—strophe breathes an atmosphere different from the

---

1   So correctly W. Rudolph, *Die Klagelieder* (KAT XVII/3; Gütersloh, 1962) 240f., with reference to Calvin's interpretation: 'Refert propheta impios

preceding כ—strophe. Furthermore, disagreement exists among
scholars regarding the outline of this song. Divisions are made
mostly on the basis of content and the outcome differs
considerably.[2] As far as I can see, literary indications are not
sufficiently taken into account. In our treatment we analyse
smaller and larger units and their interrelations on the basis of
both content and literary indications. As noted by everyone,
each bicolon in each strophe starts with the same letter of the
Hebrew alphabet. Furthermore, the end of each strophe is
marked by a *setumah.* So, as in the first two songs,
strophe—division is no problem. Therefore we now want to
argue for the canticle—division.

Canticle I (Lam. 3:1—6)

Content/theme: *YHWH struck the* גבר *with his anger and*
                    locked him up like the dead

Literary arguments:
  inclusion:
    (6A) במחשכים // (2B) חשך
  responsions:
    (4A) בלה בשרי ועורי // (1A) ראה עני
    (4B) שבר עצמותי // (1B) בשבט עברתו
    (5B) ראש ותלאה // (2B) חשך ולא־אור
    (6B) עולם // (3B) כל־היום
  alliteration:
    (6A) הושיבני // (3A) ישב

sermones'. Our structural analysis justifies this exegesis. Incorrect in his
analysis: B. Johnson, 'Form and Message in Lamentations', *ZAW* 97 (1985)
65ff.

2 W. Rudolph: 1962:234ff.: 1—20|21—24|25—33|34—36|37—41|42—47|48—51|
52—66. H.J. Kraus, *Klagelieder* (BKAT XX; Neukirchen, 1968[3]) 55f.: 1—19|
20—24|25—33|34—38|39—41|42—47|48—51|52—66. R. Gordis, *The Song of Songs
and Lamentations* (New York, 1974[3]) 174ff.: 1—20|21—30|31—38|39—47|
48—64?(66?). D.R. Hillers, *Lamentations* (AB 7A; New York, 1979) 65:
1—16|17—20|21—25|26—30|31—38|39|40—41|42—47|48—51|52—66. O. Kaiser,
Klagelieder (ATD 16; Göttingen, 1981[3]) 347ff.: 1—24|25—39|40—47|
48—51|52—58|59—66. R. Brandscheidt, *Gotteszorn und Menschenleid* (Trier,
1983) 40ff.: 1—16|17—20|21—24|25—33|34—39|40—47|48—51|52—66|. See also
p.34 about the disagreement over division. H.J. Boecker, *Klagelieder* (ZB 21;
Zürich, 1985) 59ff.: 1—24|25—39|40—47|48—51|52—66.

Canticle II (Lam. 3:7—12)

Content/theme: *YHWH lies in wait for the prisoner like a predacious animal*

Literary arguments:

  ext. parallelism:

  (11A) דרכי סורר // (9B) נתיבתי עוה

  alliteration:

  // (9A) דרכי // (9A) גדר // (7A) גדר

  (12A)³ דרך // (11A) דרכי

Canticle III (Lam. 3:13—21)

Content/theme: *YHWH struck the prisoner with mockery, bitterness, and made him peaceless and without hope*

Literary arguments:

  inclusions:

  (21A)⁴ לבי // (13A) בכליותי

  (19B) לענה // (15B) לענה

  (19A) מרודי // (15A) מרורים

  asson./ allit.:

  (16B) הכפישני // (15A) השביעני

  responsions:

  (21B) אוחיל // (18B) ותוחלתי

  (20B) נפשי // (17A) נפשי

Canticle IV (Lam. 3:22—27)

Content/theme: *Yet, the prisoner must speak of YHWH's proved loyalty⁵*

Literary arguments:

  inclusions:

  כי (22A) // כי (27A)

---

3   See W.G.E. Watson, *Classical Hebrew Poetry*. A Guide to its Techniques (Sheffield, 1984) 227.

4   Cf. Ps. 7:10; 26:2; 73:21; Jer. 11:20; 17:10; 20:12.

5   Note the frequent use of the divine name יהוה, which of course is chosen because of חסד.

‫אמונתך (23B) // תשועת יהוה (26B)‬
responsion:
‫חסדי יהוה (22A) // טוב יהוה (25A)‬
ext. parallelism:
‫אוחיל (24B) // ויחיל (26A)‬
concatenations:
‫אוחיל (24B) // לקוו (25A)‬
‫נפשי (24A) // לנפש (25B)‬

Canticle V (Lam. 3:28–33)

Content/theme: *May be there is hope, for YHWH does not
                        nurse his anger for all time; therefore man
                        must wait and endure*

Literary arguments:
  inclusions:
‫כי (28B) // כי (33A)‬
‫נטל עליו (28B) // ענה (33A)‬
  incl./resp.:
‫תקוה (29B) // חסדו (32B)‬
  responsions:
‫למכהו לחי (30A) // ענה (33A)‬
‫ישבע בחרפה (30B) // ויגה (33B)‬

Canticle VI (Lam. 3:34–39)

Content/theme: *A lament over evil, but this was not created by
                        the Lord*[6]

Literary arguments:
  inclusion:
‫פני אליון (35B) // מפי עליון (38A)‬
  responsion:
‫אדם (36A) // אדם (39A)‬
  ext. parallelism:
‫גבר (35A) // גבר (39B)‬
  concatenation:
‫אדני לא (36B) // אדני לא (37B)‬

---

6   See for this exegesis R. Gordis: 1974[3]:182f. and J. Renkema, *Misschien
is er hoop... (Franeker, 1983) 302–305. See also below p.395 n.11.

Canticle VII (Lam. 3:40–45)

Content/theme: *Indeed they sinned, but YHWH did not listen to their prayers. He did not forgive and so – He must know – they have to suffer*

Literary arguments:

  inclusions:

  בשמים (41B) // בעננך (44A)

  תפלה (41A) // נשא לבבנו אל־כפים (44B)

  inclusion/concatenation by means of suff. נו

  concatenation/assonance/alliteration:

  הרגת לא חמלת (42B) // אתה לא סלחת (43B)

Canticle VIII (Lam. 3:46–54)

Content/theme: *tormented by the enemies*

Literary arguments:

  including assonance/alliteration:

  פצו (46A) // צפו (54A)

  inclusions:

  עלינו (46A) // על (54A)

  עיני (49A) // עיני (51A)

  responsions:

  איבינו (46B) // איבי (52B)

  מים (48A) // מים (54A)

  עיני (48A) // עיני (51A)

  בנות עירי (51B) // בת־עמי (48B)

  נגזרתי (54B) // שבר בת־עמי (48B)

  על־ראשי (54A) // לנפשי (51A)

Canticle IX (Lam. 3:55–60)

Content/theme: *Prayer to YHWH*

Literary arguments:

  inclusion/responsion/concatenation by means of sf. 2 masc.sg.

  responsion/inclusion:

  שמעת (56A) // ראיתה (59A)

  ext. parallelism:

  יהוה (55A) // יהוה (59A)

  concatenation:

  גאלת חיי (57B) // אמרת אל־תירא (58B)

Canticle X (Lam. 3:61—66)

Content/theme: *a plea for retribution of the enemies*
Literary arguments:
  inclusion:
  יהוה (61A) // יהוה (66B)
  inclusion/responsion:
  קמי (62A) // לב (65A)[7]
  responsions:
  יהוה (61A) // יהוה (64A)
  כל-מחשבתם (61B) // כמעשה ידיהם (64B)
  alliterations:
  שבתם (63A) // תשיב (64A)
  מנגינחם (63B) // מגנת (65A)
  concatenation/inclusion/responsion by means of sf. 3 masc.pl.

There are indications that the poets designed the canticles to be parts of higher units in the song. As in the two preceding songs one can discern two cantos, each of which can be divided into two sub—cantos. First we want to argue for the canto division.

Canto I (Lam. 3:1—33)

Content: *YHWH made him suffer but the* גבר *can do*
             no other than to put his trust in Him

Literary arguments:
  inclusions:
  הגבר (1A) // ביני איש (33B)
  כל-היום (3B) // לעולם (31A)
  בלה (4A) // ישבע (30B)
  הושיבני (6A) // ישב (28A)
  נחשתי (7B) // על (27B)
  responsion:
  לא ענה (33A) \\ לא ידנח (31A) \\ לא-אור (2B)

---

7   In our opinion this is a very special inclusion/responsion. Together both words form an *atbash*, i.e. a cipher by which letters of one name, counted from the beginning of the alphabet are replaced by corresponding letters counted from the end. So לב קמי corresponds with כשדים, the Babylonians. To be understood, this *atbash* must have been well—known at the time. Cf. Jer. 51:1.

Canto II (Lam. 3:34–66)

Content: *Recognition that suffering was caused by themselves and now they renewed their trust in YHWH*

Literary arguments:

  inclusions:

  מתחת (34A) // מתחת (66B)

  ארץ (34B) \\ שמי (66B)

  אדני (36B) // יהוה (64A)

  אל־תעלם אזנך (44B) // מעבור תפלה (56AB)

  responsion:

  אדני (36B) // יהוה (66B)

  ext. parallelism:

  הביטה (36B) // אדני לא ראה (63A)

Inclusion is clear from the content too. What is complained about in the first two canticles (Lam. 3:34–45) returns in the pleas of the last two canticles, compare משפט (35A), בריבו (36A) and ריבי (58A), משפטי (59B). See also the construction of the second canto of Lam. 2.

Now we want to look at the division into sub–cantos. First the subdivision of Canto I.

Sub–canto A (Lam. 3:1–22)

Content: *A lament about suffering imposed by YHWH*

Literary arguments:

  inclusions:

  אותי (2A) // נפשי (20B)

  אבד נצחי (4A) // בלה בשרי ועורי (18A)

  הכפישני באפר (6B) // כמתי (16B)[8]

---

8 Here אפר undoubtedly points to the realm of dead, cf. Jer. 6:26, Ezek. 27:30. See also *THAT* II:355.

responsion:

(19A) עניי // (1A) עני

Sub–canto B (Lam. 3:22–33)

Content: *Yet, the* גבר *trusts in YHWH's mercy and*
                           waits for it

Literary arguments:
  inclusions:

(33A) כי לא // (22A) כי לא

(32B) כרב חסדו // (23B) רבה אמונתך

(31B) אדני // (24A) יהוה

(29B) יש תקוה // (26B) תשועת יהוה

responsion:

(31A) כי לא // (22A) כי לא

ext. parallelism:

(28A) וידם // (26A) ודומם

(32B) כרב חסדו // (22A) חסדי יהוה

The connection between the two sub–cantos becomes clear when
attention is paid to the bicola where the verb יחל appears;
compare:

(18AB) אבד ... תוחלתי מיהוה \\

(26AB) טוב ויחיל ... לתשועת יהוה

(24B) על־כן אוחיל לו // (21B) על־כן אוחיל

The same with the words טוב, אמר and the divine name יהוה:

(25A) טוב יהוה \\ (17B) נשיתי טובה

(18AB) ואמר אבד ... תוחלת מיהוה \\

(24A) חלקי יהוה אמרה נפשי

For distinguishing two sub–cantos in the second canto of this
song we have the following arguments.

Sub–canto A (Lam. 3:34–54)

Content: *Lament, confession of guilt, lament*

Literary arguments:
  inclusions:

(54A) על־ראשי \\ (34A) תחת רגליו

(50B) יהוה משמים // (38A) עליון

(49A) עיני נגרה // (39A) יחאונך
responsion:
(42A) פשענו // (39B) חטאו
ext. parallelism:
(53A) בבור // (34B) אסירי ארץ
(54B) אמרתי // (37A) אמר
(53A) חיי // (39A) חי

Sub—canto B (Lam. 3:55—66)

Content: *A plea for redemption*
Literary arguments:
  inclusions:
(66B) יהוה // (55A) יהוה
(66B) טחחת // (55B) מחתיות
  responsion:
(63A) הביטה // (60A) ראיתה
ext. parallelism:
(61A) שמעת // (56A) שמעת
(62B) היום // (57A) ביום

The connection between the two sub—cantos becomes clear when attention is paid to their common keywords. Often they are used in external parallelism and these are mostly antithetical. Compare:

1. ראה לא אדני (36B) // יהוה וירא עד־ישקיף (50AB) \\
(63A) ראיתה יהוה // (59A) ראיתה // (60A) הביטה

2. משפט להטות (35A) \\ משפטי שפטה (59B)

3. ראה לא אדני בריבו אדם לעות (36AB) \\
(58A) נפשי ריבי אדני רבת

4. לעות (36A) // עותתי (59A)

5. ותרדפנו באף (43A) \\ באף תרדף (66A)

6. חיי בבור צמתו (53A) \\ חיי גאלת (58B)

7. נגזרתי אמרתי (57B) \\ אל־תירא אמרת (54B)

The literary unity of the song cannot be doubted. It is evident from a) the alphabetic acrostic; b) the masoretic *petucha* after 2:22 and 3:66; c) further on the coherence between these ten canticles is indicated by concatenation on the level of the

canticles which cannot be overlooked; the concatenation כמתי
עולם (6B) // לא אצא (7A) combines the canticles I and II; the
concatenation חץ (12B) // ביני אשפתו (13B) combines the
canticles II and III; the concatenation על־כן אוחיל (21B) //
חסדי יהוה (22A) combines the canticles III and IV; the
concatenation ישא על (27AB) // נטל עליו (28B) combines the
canticles IV and V. Between the canticles V and VI there is a
concatenation by means of ויגה (33B) // לדכא (34A) and
between VI and VII by חטאו (39B) // נשובה (40B); between
VII and VIII by סחי ומאוס תשימנו (45A) // פצו ... איבינו
(46AB); between VIII and IX by צפו־מים על־ראשי (54A) //
בור תחתיות (55B); between IX and X by מחשבתם (60B) //
מחשבתם (61B); d) the many inclusions between the first and
the last canticle. Compare:

אני (1A) // אני (63B)
באף (1B) // בשבט עברתו (66A)
ישב (3A) // תשיב (64A)
ידו (3B) // ידיהם (64A)
כל־היום (3B) // כל־היום (62B)
עלי (5A) // עלי (62B)

These inclusions however are not limited to the first and the
last canticle but are also found in the next opposite canticles.
Between the second and the ninth canticle we noticed the
following inclusions:

ואשוע (8A) // לשועתי (56B)
עוה (9B) // עותתי (59A)
אל־תעלם אזנך (8B) // שמת תפלתי (56AB)

Between the third and the eighth canticle the following
inclusions are found:

פחד ופחת היה לנו (14A) // הייתי שחק (47A)
עמי (14A) // עמי (ם) (48B)
כל־איבינו (14A) // לכל־עמי (ם) (46B)
נפשי (17A) // נפשי (51A)
אמרתי נגזרתי (18A) // ואמר אבד נצחי (54B)
יהוה (18B) // יהוה (50B)

Between the fourth and the seventh canticle the following
inclusions are found:

יהוה (26B,22A,24A,25A) // יהוה (40B)
הרגת לא חמלת (22A) \\ כי לא־תמנו (43B)
נשא (27A) // ישא (41A)

Between the fifth and the sixth canticle we found these inclusions:

עליו (28B) // על (39B)

פיהו (29A) // מפי (38A)

אדני לא (36B) \\ לא ... אדני (31AB)

This observation indicates a concentric design of the song especially on the level of the canticles and this is much stronger than on the level of the strophes.[9] But in my opinion this is not the only concentric move of the poets. As indicated by the many inclusions a lot of canticles also show a concentric structure. Compare for example the third and the eighth one. But this was also found in the preceding songs. However, in the third song concentric design structured by the canticles does not lead us to a kernel. As already noticed, the atmosphere of the fifth and the sixth canticle is a different one. In Lam. 3:28−33 there is, despite suffering, trust in YHWH. In Lam. 3:34−39 we find a complaint that the Lord did not see oppression and injustice. Also יתאונן (39A) does not fit very well with וידם (28A). The second canto starts with a theme other than we find in the end of the first one. *It seems that the second starts with the same theme as the first canto.* Two times now the poets speak of גבר (35A, 39B). Moreover, there is a striking similarity, both in structure and in content, in the outline of the two cantos. So the first three canticles are complaints about suffering; in the last two canticles there is a turn to the Lord (note the frequent use of the divine name יהוה) and trust is put in Him. So the second canto seems to be a kind of repetition of the first one. The experience of suffering and being a prisoner and, in spite of this, refound confidence of the הגבר (1A) (note definite article !), seems to be meant as an example for others, i.e., the undetermined גבר (35A, 39B) // אדם (36A, 39A), who are also suffering and are prisoners. So it is not a continuous story, but a repeated one. For that reason both cantos must not be placed one after another, but *beside* each other, like a diptych. Outlining the song this way an amazing structure becomes visible:

---

9   See p. 321.

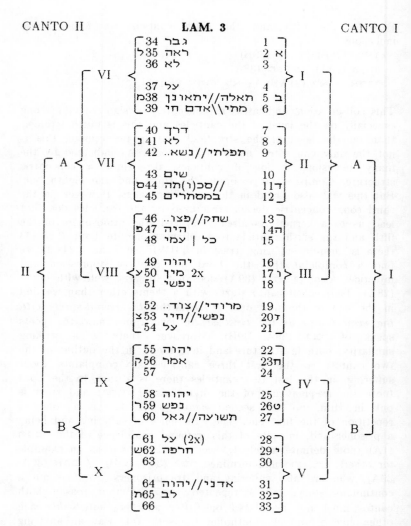

After outlining the structure of the song in this way we became aware of the many interconnections between the strophes on the same level in the cantos. We noted some keywords, synonyms and external parallellisms and placed them in the scheme between the corresponding strophes. Of course, on the level of the corresponding canticles the similarities increase according to the number of strophes they consist of. But when the content of the corresponding strophes is taken into account too, everybody can see the striking resemblance. Compare for example the ט—strophe with the ר—strophe with the theme of redemption by YHWH, and the י— strophe with the ש—strophe and their common theme of חרפה, etc. The similarities between the strophes on the same level in the two cantos are much stronger than the similarities between strophe 1 and 22; 2 and 21; 3 and 20, and so on. Therefore it is justified to consider Lam. 3 as a unity consisting of a diptych. The relative independence of the two cantos is indicated also by the inclusions we already mentioned. These inclusions indicate the concentric design of each canto. According to this structure the kernel of canto I must be vs. 17 and the kernel of canto II must be vs. 50. One has to read the two verses one after the other:

$$\text{ותזנח משלום נפשי נשיתי טובה}$$
$$\text{עד־ישקיף וירא יהוה משמים}$$

In my opinion this is the main theme of the booklet. The combination ראה and יהוה is found in the kernel of the first song (1:11) and at the start of the last song (5:1). Moreover it is found in the second song (2:20) and in the fourth song, now in a lament that YHWH did not see (not ראה but the synonym נבט is used, 4:16). We return to this subject when we treat the composition of the booklet as a whole. A final observation concerns the structure of the cantos of Lam. 3. The outline of each canto, if we take into account the division into sub—cantos and the canticles they consist of, is the same as the outline of the booklet as a whole: 3+2, which is a reflection of the *qinah*.[10] And, as in the booklet in the third song, so the kernel is to be found in the third canticle of the cantos.

According to our measures the structure of this song is rather complicated. But the fact that every strophe starts three times with the same letter indicates that the poets had a complicated structure in mind. And why should this be their only artistic

---

10   W.H. Shea, 'The *qinah* Structure of the Book of Lamentations', *Biblica* 60 (1979) 103—107.

ploy? The threefold macro—concentric design, one on the level of the canticles in the song as a whole, and two times on the level of the cantos, can be considered as an analogy.

We close our treatment of the third song of Lamentations with some exegetical remarks. Of course, methodically the point of departure for exegesis must be the text itself. But when such a text is not clear, (antithetic) external parallelism may be helpful. For example BHK, BHS and many commentators delete or change חי in vs. 39. From the opposite strophe it becomes clear that אדם חי contrasts כמתי עולם and therefore it is unwise to emend the text and delete חי. For the dead there is no hope, but for a living man things are different. He must not complain about the bad fate for which he has to blame himself, but he must repent and turn back to YHWH.

A second example is תמנו in vs. 22. BHK, BHS and the majority of commentators change it into תמו with חסדי יהוה as the subject. However, מבור תחתיות in the opposite strophe really points to the realm of death (cf. אמרתי נגזרתי in vs. 54 and גאלת חיי in vs. 58). Therefore it is likely that תמנו is the right reading: they did not die. They survived, and that bare fact is the theological basis for putting new hope in YHWH.

Lamentations IV

As in the preceding songs it is hardly necessary to indicate the strophe division. This is obvious from the alphabetic acrostic, the *setumahs* at the end of each strophe and the *petucha's* after 3:66 and 4:22. Therefore we want to analyze the next higher units, the canticles and sub—cantos. It will appear that our outline of this song differs a lot from that of others.[11]

---

11 Rudolph: 1962:250ff.: 1−2/3−6/7−11/12−16/17−20/21−22. Kraus: 1968[3]: 73: 1−16/17−20/21−22. Hillers: 1979:87: 1−17/18−20/21−22. Kaiser: 1981[3]: 366ff.: 1−2/3−6/7−11/12−16/17−20/21−22. Brandscheidt: 1983:167ff.: 1−16/ 17−20/21−22; subdivision: 1−2/3−4/5−6/7−8/9−10/11−12/13−14/15−16/ 17−18/19−20/21−22. This subdivision is made only on the basis of the clear pattern of the first strophe 1−2. Boecker: 1985:75ff.: 1−2/3−6/7−11/ 12−16/17−18/19−20/21−22.

Canticle I (Lam. 4:1−2)

Content/theme: *The fate of Zion and her inhabitants*
Literary arguments:
  inclusion:
  איכה (1aA) // איכה (2bA)
  responsions:
  היקרים ... בפז (2aAB) // זהב / הכתם (1aAB)
  לנבלי־חרש (2bA) // אבני־קדש (1bA)

Canticle II (Lam. 4:3−5)

Content/theme: *Thirsty and hungry children*
Literary arguments:
  inclusion:
  האמנים (5bA) // גורייהן (3aB)
  responsions:
  דבק לשון (4aA) \\ חלצו שד (3aA)
  יונק (4aA) // היניקו (3aB)
  פרש אין להם (4bB) // בת־עמי לאכזר (3aA)
  אשפתות (5bB) // מדבר (3bB)
  האמנים (5bA) // עוללים (4bA)
  concatenations:
  צמא (4aB) // מדבר (3bB)
  האכלים (5aA) // עוללים (4bA)
  למעדנים (5aA) // לחם (4bA)

Canticle III (Lam. 4:6)

Content/theme: *Worse than Sodom*
Literary argumentation:
As we have seen there were a lot of arguments for the
demarcation and the unity of the preceding canticle. However,
looking at Lam. 4:6 one may be inclined to reconsider the
marking out of the second canticle; the expression בת־עמי in
6:aA appears also in 3bA, and together they could form an
inclusion of a larger canticle 4:3−6. Yet, there are some
contra−indications for this solution.   Firstly, the verses 3−5
exhibit a strong coherence by many literary links. Vs. 6 shares
only one literary expression with the vss. 3−5. Secondly, the
vss. 3−5 and vs. 6 have a different content. In vs. 6 the theme
of hungry and thirsty children is clearly not present. Thirdly,

the expression בת־עמי occurs also in vs. 10bB, so there is a possibility that the expression functions on a higher level in the song. Fourthly, the following verses do not share their theme with vs. 6, nor are there literary correspondences. For these reasons Lam. 4:6 must be considered as a strophe which is at the same time a mini canticle. This phenomenon is not unknown in Hebrew poetry.[12]

Canticle IV (Lam. 4:7−9)

Content/theme: *The hunger struck nobles too*[13]
Literary arguments:
   inclusion:
     נזיריה (7aA) // שהם (9bA)
   responsions:
     זכו (7aA) \\ חשך (8aA)
     נזיריה (7aA) // מחללי רעב (9aB)
     שלג | חלב (7aAB) \\ שחור (8aA)
     עצם (7bA) // עצמם (8bA)
   concatenations:
     גזרתם (7bB) // תארם (8aA)
   by means of suff. 3.m.pl.
     צפד עורם ... יבש היה כעץ (8bAB) // מחללי רעב (9aB)
   assonance/alliteration:
     מחלב (7aB) // מחללי רעב (9aB)

Canticle V (Lam. 4:10−11)

Theme/content: *Consuming of children and Zion*
Literary argumentation:
At first sight these two strophes do not belong together because they seem to have a different theme. From the viewpoint of the content vs. 10 fits far better to the preceding verses which also speak about hunger. The theme of vs. 11 seems to be totally different, namely YHWH's anger.

---

12 M.C.A. Korpel−J.C. de Moor, 'Fundamentals of Ugaritic and Hebrew Poetry', *UF* 18 (1986) 173−212.
13 Cf. B. Albrektson, *Studies in the Text and Theology of the Book of Lamentations* (Lund, 1963) 180. KBL: 604b. The proposition of *HAL* appears to be incorrect.

However, a closer look shows another, more likely solution. In the first place there is a change of subject. In vss. 7–9 the nobles are involved, in vs. 10 the gentle mothers of Jerusalem. In the second place no clear external parallellism can be discerned between vss. 7–9 and vs. 10. The only literary connection consists of the concatenation חיר (9aA) // חיר (10bA). In the third place there are far more literary connections between vs. 10 and vs. 11, compare:

inclusion:

בשלו (10aB) // ויצת־אש (11aA)

responsions:

שבר בת־עמי (10bB) // ותאכל יסודתיה (11bB)

לברות (10bA) // ותאכל (11bB)

עמי (10bB) // ציון (11bA)

The coherence between vs. 10 and vs. 11 becomes clear if one pays attention to the verb אכל. Because of hunger the tender hearted women of Jerusalem must consume their own children. Vs. 11 contains an analogy and is thus a responsion to the preceding verse: YHWH's fire must consume his own Zion, which He loved so much (Ps. 78:68f.; 87:1f.).[14]

Canticle VI (Lam. 4:12–13)

Content/theme: *The downfall of Jerusalem is caused by the sins of prophets and priests*

Literary arguments:

inclusion:

צר ואויב (12bA) \\ כהניה ... נביאיה (13aAB)[15]

responsion:

בשערי ירולשם (12bB) // בקרבה (13bA)

As far as I can see there are no additional literary connections. But another argument to take together the ל— and the מ—strophe in one canticle can be found in the second song. In the sixth canticle (Lam. 2:14–15) the same connection is made: the failure of the prophets caused the downfall of Jerusalem

---

14 See for the influence of the theology of Zion on Lamentations, Renkema: 1983:280–294.

15 This inclusion is antithetical, viz. a change of guard.

(2:14), which appalled the passers—by; compare the אמינו לא
of 4:12aA.

Canticle VII (Lam. 4:14—16)

Content/theme: *The fate of priests, prophets and elders*[16]

Before arguing the demarcation and coherence of this canticle it
is necessary to focus on the text itself. Against the proposition
of BHK, BHS and others, the Masoretic reading of vs. 14b,
indicated by the דִקֵּף קטון, is preferable: יגעו בלבשיהם
(14bB). Vs. 15 is a longer strophe consisting of two tricola,
combined in a chiastic structure:

סורו טמא	קראו למו	סורו סורו אל־חגעו
	|	
כי נצו גם־נעו	אמרו בגוים	לא יוסיפו לגור

Deleting קראו למו damages this structure and the parallel with
אמרו בגוים. The poets used this longer strophe to formulate
the grievances against priests and prophets. Therefore it is not
necessary to delete one סורו. Such a duplication fits very well
in a public utterance. Concerning the demarcation one must
consider the possibility of a canticle consisting of the vss.
13—16. Some literary arguments can be given for this solution:
   inclusion:
   כהניה (13aB) // כהנים (16bA)
   concatenation:
   דם (13bB) // בדם (14aB)[17]

However, there are stronger arguments for the coherence of the
vss. 14—16 only. In the first place there is a clear switch of
theme: not the guilt of priests and prophets is at stake, as in
vs. 13, but their fate as the result of their sins. Secondly there
are more literary arguments. Compare:
   inclusion:
   בלא (14bA) // לא (16aB)

---

16   The appearance of the elders seems somewhat strange in this context.
However, they may also have played a cultic role. Compare Ezek. 8:11ff.
17   But concatenation is not always a reliable sign of connection. Because
it can also function on a higher level in the song. See the concatenation
between the canticles in the third song.

responsions:

בלא (14bA) // לא (15bB) // לא (16bAB)

עורים (14aA) // להביטם ... לא (16aB, as cause)

לגור ... לא (15bB) // לא נשאו (16bA)

ext. parallelism:

נעו (14aA) // נעו (15bA)

concatenations:

יגעו (14bA) // חגעו (15aB)

לא יוסיפו (15bB) // לא יוסיף (16aB)

לא (14bA) // לא (15bB) // לא (16aB)

Canticle VIII (Lam. 4:17)

Content/theme: *No human help*

Literary argumentation:

Because of the possible responsion גרי (17bB) // בגוים (20bB) one could argue for a canticle consisting of the vss. 17—20. But the occurrence of the same בגוים in vs. 15bA weakens this argument because it is possible that the expression functions on a higher level in the song. As for content, there is no clear connection with the theme of the preceding canticle, nor with the theme of the next one. For these reasons, as was already the case with Lam. 4:6, it seems advisable to consider the strophe of Lam. 4:17 to be a mini—canticle.[18]

Canticle IX (Lam. 4:18—20)[19]

Content/theme: *The chase and capture of the king*

Literary argumentation:

We can imagine one might contest the connection between the vss. 18—19 and vs. 20. The pursuing by enemies seems to be a theme different from the capture of the king. Yet this connection is indicated by the suffix of בשחיתותם (20aB). This suffix has to be related with the subjects of vss. 18—19, the pursuers. Without this connection the suffix remains inexplicable.

---

18   See note 12.

19   Vs. 18b is a tricolon: קרב קצינו | מלאו ימינו | כי־בא קצינו, and, with MT, בצלו belongs to the second part of the last bicolon of vs. 20.

We conclude that there are no different themes or events at stake, but the poets describe the consecutive phases of the same event, the flight out of the city, the pursuit in the desert, and at last, the capture of the king, cf. 2 Kings 25:5.

Clear literary arguments cannot be derived from identical words and expressions. However, in this canticle there is an abundant use of the suffix 3 masc. plur. (10x). Used in inclusion, responsion and concatenation, it lends a strong coherence to this canticle. To a lesser extent, the same is true of the preposition ב, which is used six times.

Canticle X (Lam. 4:21—22)

Theme/content: *Edom shall be punished as Zion was*
Literary arguments:
  inclusion:
    (22bA) בת־אדום // (21aA) בת־אדום
  responsions:
    (22bB) על // (21bA) עליך
    (22bA) פקד עונך // (21bA) גם ... כוס
    (22bB) גלה על־חטאתיך // (21bB) תשכרי ותתערי
  concatenation:
    (22aB)[20] להגלותך // (21bB) ותתערי
  responsion/concatenation by means of suffix 2 fem.sg.

Now we want to look at the macrostructure. In my opinion this song consists of two sub—cantos, A: 4:1—11, and B: 4:12—22. The unity of these sub—cantos is indicated by a very strong concentric design, especially on the level of the canticles. Compare:

---

20 On the basis of this concatenation and the concentric design of this canticle להגלותך must be considered as a synonym of ותתערי (21bB). If הגלות is vocalized as inf. nifal (to be uncovered) instead of inf. hifil (to exile) the synonymity becomes more clear and it gives a better sense. Because YHWH's anger has been completed (כלה 11aA), there will be no more shame for Zion. Compare also Lam. 1:3 and n.17 in my first article on the subject.

Sub–canto A (Lam. 4:1–11)

Content/theme: *A worse fate than Sodom*
Connections between the canticles I and V:
  inclusions:
    תשחפכנה (1bA) // שפך (11aB)
    אבני־קדש (1bA) // ציון (11bA)
    בני ציון (2aA) // ילדיהן (10aB)
    ידי (2bB) // ידי (10aA)

Also content clearly indicates the correspondence between vs. 1 and vs. 11, and vs. 2 and vs. 10.

Between canticles II and IV:
  inclusions:
    מדבר (3bB) // רעב (9aB)[21]
    דבק לשון (4aA) // צפד עורם (8bA)
    בצמא (4aB) // יבש היה כעץ (8bB)
    בחוצות (5aB) // בחוצות (8aB)
    האכלים למעדנים (5aA) // אדמו עצם מפנינים (7bA), sc.
    the former prosperity of children and nobles
    האמנים (5bA) // נזיריה (7aA)
    שלג | חלב | חולע (7aAB) // (5bA) חולע

From content it is also evident that both canticles have the same theme: hunger. In the second canticle however, the focus is on the hungry children, in the fourth canticle on the nobles. These inclusions confirm the central position of Lam. 4:6 within the first sub–canto. It is also confirmed by the fact that there are no clear subdivisions on a level between canticles and sub–canto. Maybe, vss. 1–5 belong together (incl. חוצות (1bB // 5aB), and the incl. בני ציון (2aA) // עוללים (4bA)) and vss. 7–11 (incl. היה (8bB) // היו (10bA) and concat. שדי מתנובת (9bB) \\ בשלו (10aB))[22] but even then it remains unclear whether 4:6 belongs to the preceding verses or to the next ones, since it shares expressions with both parts. On the other hand, in addition to the obvious inclusions, there are other strong indications for the unity of this sub–canto:

---

21 Cf. Lam. 5:9+10.
22 With regard to this concatenation, see note 16.

Literary arguments:

responsions:

   (6bA) ההפוכה // (1bA) משתפכנה אבני־קדש

   (11bA) ציון // (1bA) קדש

   (10bB) // 6aA // (3bA) בת־עמי

   (10aA) ידי // (6bB) ידים // (2bB) ידי

   (7aB) חלב // (3aAB) חלצו שד היניקו ...

   (10aB) ילדיהן // (3aB) גוריהן

   (9aB) חללי רעב // (5aB) נשמו

   (9bB) מתנובת שדי // (5bB) חבקו אשפתות

   (11bA)[23] ויצת־אש // (6bA) ההפוכה

   (11bAB) אש ...ותאכל ... // (6bB) ולא־חלו בה ידים

   ext. parallelism:

   (1bB // 5aB // 8aB) חוצות

Especially these inclusions and responsions show poetic skill.
They also make clear how the single strophe/canticle Lam. 4:6
is connected in a clever way with the surrounding canticles for
which it is the leading thought.

Sub–canto B (Lam. 4:12—22)

Theme/content: *No help*

Mainly because of different themes in the seventh and ninth
canticle inclusions and responsions are not so abundant as in
the first sub—canto. However,

Literary arguments:

  inclusions:

   (22bA) cf. Obad. 13 בת־אדום // (12bA) יבא צר ואויב

   (22bA) בת־אדום // (12aA) מלכי־ארץ

   (22aB) לא יוסיף להגלותך \\ (12bA) יבא צר ואויב

   (22aA) ציון // (12bB) ירושלם

   (19aA) רדפינו // (15bB) לא יוסיפו לגור

   (16aAB) // יהוה ... לא יוסיף להביטם

   (18bAB)קרב קצינו ...כי־בא קצינו

---

23   Of course this is a clear reminiscence of the Sodom—tradition, see Gen.
19:24.

responsions:

מלכי־ארץ (12aA) // עזרתנו (17aB)[24]

ישבי תבל (12aB) // ישבתי בארץ (21aB)

מחטאת | ענות (13aAB) // (double and chiastic)

עונך| חטאתיך (22bAB)

עורים (14aA) // תכלינה עינינו (17aA)

יהוה (16aA) // יהוה (20aA)

לא יוסיף (16aB) // לא יוסיף (22aB)

גוי (17bB) // בת־אדום (22bA)

גוי (17bB) // בגוים (20bB)

ext. parallelism:

בגוים (15bB) // גוי (17bB)

אמרו (15bA) // אמרנו (20bA)

Also in this sub—canto there are no clear indications for a division on a level between canticles and sub—canto. Only a few connections exist between the sixth and seventh canticle. Compare: incl. לא (12aA // 16aB); resp. כהניה (13aB) // כהנים (16bA); concat. דם (13bB) // בדם (14aB).[25] Between the ninth and tenth canticle there is a resp. בגוים (20bB) // בת־אדום (22bA). These few connections are not very convincing in view of the numerous inclusions and responsions which witness the unity of sub—canto B. And, as in the first sub—canto, the position of the middle strophe/canticle (Lam. 4:17) remains unclear.

Our next problem is the inter—relation of the two sub—cantos. As in the first and the second song it is possible to read them one after another. The fourth song too shows some concentric design, particularly on the level of the canticles (understandable, because of the shorter strophes). Compare:

24 Cf. Lam. 1:2.
25 See note 21.

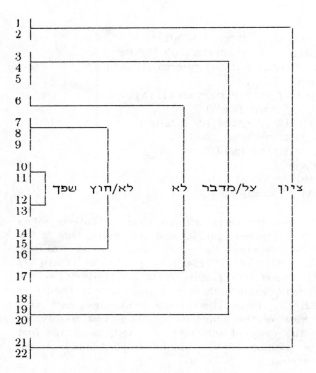

However, it is not very convincing to find the main theme of
the song expressed somewhere in the fifth and sixth canticle.
The vss. 10–12 seem to be an exposition of the disaster, and
vs. 13 explains it but does not exceed vs. 6 in content, which
appears to be the centre of the first sub–canto. Further on, if
we compare the concentric design of the song with the
concentric design of the sub–cantos, it becomes clear, that the
latter are far more elaborated. This is indicative of a relative
independence of both sub–cantos within the song.

We made another observation. If the canticles are connected
otherwise than according to the concentric design of the song,
they show a lot more similarities, both in words and content,
and it becomes very obvious that the poets structured this song
in the same way as Lam. 3 and composed it as a diptych.
Accordingly, we outline the song:

Subcanto B   Lam.4   Subcanto A

	VI — —	12 ⎱ 13 ⎰	שפך | כל ירושלם//ציון	1 ⎰ — — I 2
	VII — —	14 ⎱ 15 ⎰ 16	גם חוצות	3 ⎰ 4 — — II 5
B	VIII — —	17 ⎯⎱	לא	⎰⎯ 6 — — III	A
	IX — —	18 ⎱ 19 ⎰ 20	על|מין|ון|היה // חוצות ברחבתינו	7 ⎰ 8 — — IV 9
	X — —	21 ⎱ 22 ⎰	ציון | בת כלה//תמם	10 ⎰ — — V 11

In this scheme we noted already the words in common of the
opposite canticles. Maybe, one is not very impressed by some
general words which are shared by the canticles. Yet it is
justified to connect the canticles in this way. This will appear
when also the content of the canticles is taken into account:

Zion's fate and its cause	12 ⎱ 13 ⎰	— — —	1 ⎰ 2	fate of Zion
fate of prophets and priests	14 ⎱ 15 ⎰ 16	— — —	3 ⎰ 4 5	fate of children
and without help	17 ⎯⎱	— — —	⎰⎯ 6	(sin/fate)worse than Sodom
fate of the king	18 ⎱ 19 ⎰ 20	— — —	7 ⎰ 8 9	fate of the nobles
Edom's punishment (Zion's penance) תמם	21 ⎱ 22 ⎰	— — —	10 ⎰ 11	Zion's punishment (YHWH's anger) כלה

Some explanatory notes on this scheme are in order. Very often
the correlation between the second and the fourth song has been
noted. The diptych—structure of Lam. 4 shows connections
identical to those made in a single strophe or canticle of Lam.
2. For example, the fate of the starving children is connected
with the sin and fate of prophets and priests, cf. Lam. 2:11−14;
2:20. The same is true of the fate of king and nobles, cf. Lam.

2:9, where instead of שרים נדיר is used. However, in view of
the booklet as a whole, the use of נדיר shows the consistency
of the poets, because the שרים were hunted (1:5), exiled (2:9)
or hanged (5:12). Furthermore, as in the diptych of Lam. 3, the
leading thought is expressed in the kernel verses of both
sub—cantos, vss. 6 and 17: *Zion's sin (fate) is worse than
Sodom's and she is without help*. The dominant position of these
kernel verses appears also from other cross—connections, which
are definitely planned. So the עון and חטאת of 4:6 include
sub—canto B (cf. 4:12,22 with also עון and חטאת).

On the other hand the verb כלה of 4:17 appears only in
4:11. A literary connection between 4:17 and 4:1 does not exist.
However, in our investigation of the relation between the
canonical prophetic message and Lamentations, we discovered
striking similarities between Lam. 4:17 and Isa. 30:7ff. Compare:

מצרים הבל וריק יעזרו   (Isa. 30:7a)

אל־עזרתנו הבל   (Lam. 4:17aA)[26]

To rely on Egypt instead of YHWH is called עון (Isa. 30:13a,
cf. Lam. 4:6), which includes punishment. In the description of
this punishment we find same words like שבר, חרש, נבל, יוצר,
cf. Isa. 30:13f. and Lam. 4:1,27.[27] So, though literary connection
is absent, in my opinion the association of thought is
undeniable, and our conclusion can be: vs. 17 includes
sub—canto A in the same way as vs. 6 includes sub—canto B.

Maybe to the modern reader's taste this way of writing
poetry is too artificial.[28] But taste is always a subjective matter
and it changes with time. From an objective point of view it
can be stated: knowing the structure of these songs will be of
great value for their exegesis.

---

26 J. Renkema: 1983:265.

27 Cf. H. Wildberger, *Jesaja 28—39* (BKAT X3; Neukirchen, 1982) 1177f.

28 For example H. Jahnow,'Das hebräische Leichenlied', *BZAW* 36 (Giessen,
1923) 169: 'Freilich ist es keine Literatur hohen Ranges, die sich das Gesetz
durch den Buchstaben, statt durch den Geist geben läßt ...'. In the same
sense S. Bergler, 'Threni V — nur ein alphabetisierendes Lied ? Versuch einer
Deutung', *VT* 27 (1977) 305.   However, this is said only in view of the
alphabetic acrostic, the other structures have never been noted in modern
times.

THE LITERARY STRUCTURE OF LAMENTATIONS (III)

Johan Renkema

Lamentations V

A major difference between the closing song of Lamentations
and the preceding ones is that it does not contain the form of
the alphabetic acrostic. Accordingly, one of the main markers
for distinguishing strophic divisions is also absent. Therefore, in
this case it is necessary to investigate whether strophic divisions
are present in this song.

In previous works on the subject there are different opinions.
Wiesmann indicates the following strophic divisions: 1—5/6—10/
11—14/15—18/19—22.[1] But Kraus correctly objects 'Eindrückliche
Formkriterien vermag Wiesmann nicht zu nennen. Und vom
Inhalt ausgehend eine strophische Gliederung vorzunehmen, das
bleibt immer ein gewagtes und letzlich unbegründetes
Unternehmen'.[2] For that reason Kraus himself forgoes
attempting division into strophes. However, his warning was
neglected by R. Brandscheidt. She distinguishes the following
strophes in Lam. 5: 1/2—3/4—5/6—7/8—9/10—11/12—13/14—15/
16—17/18—19/20—21/22. She argues on the basis of content,
that especially vss. 6—7, 10—11, 12—13 and 16—17 belong
together. 'Diese Verknüpfungen von Strophen läßt die
Vermutung aufkommen, daß, wie im vierten Klagelied, auch in
Klgl 5 jeweils zwei Strophen eine gemeinsame Aussage
formulieren'.[3] However, it is a risky undertaking to define
strophes only on the basis of content. For example, a strophic
coherence of vss. 16—17 is very contestable. On the basis of
literary arguments one can prove a coherence between verses 17
and 18, which together form a strophe. So על-זה (17A),
paralleled by על-אלה (17B), does not point backward but
foreward. This is indicated by the repetition of על in 18A. The
sickness at heart is caused by the desolate Mount Zion. Exactly

---

1   H. Wiesmann, *Die Klagelieder* (Frankfurt, 1954) 271.

2   H.J. Kraus, *Klagelieder* (BKAT XX; Neukirchen, 1968[3]) 86.

3   R. Brandscheidt, *Gotteszorn und Menschenleid* (TTS 41; Trier, 1983)
192.

the same connection between sickness (דוה) and desolation (שממה) is made in Lam. 1:13cAB. Moreover, in the booklet the eyes are never touched by sin, but always by seeing downfall and destruction. Compare Lam. 1:16; 2:4; 3:48,49,51. Of course now the preceding and following strophe — vss. 16—17 and 18—19 respectively according to Brandscheidt — must be reconsidered.   And, as for the other strophes, it is necessary to determine whether their delimitation on the basis of alleged content is sustained by literary arguments. When we now argue for strophic division on the basis of literary arguments, it will become clear that the division suggested by Brandscheidt cannot maintained. Because of some difficulties in interpretation, we wish to argue in the first place mainly on the basis of literary considerations and secondarily we consider the accordance between form and content.

The Strophic Division

In my opinion one can indeed discern strophes in Lam. 5. As in Lam. 4 each strophe consists of two successive Masoretic verses. Though it is not directly visible in the first six verses, the scheme is clearly present from vss. 7—8 onwards. Compare:

Strophe	*Connecting literary elements*
IV (5:7—8)	אינם (7A) // אין (8B); the antithetic parallelism עבדים (8A) \\ אבחינו (7A)
V (5:9—10)	מפני זלעפות // (9B) מפני חרב המדבר רעב (10B); see also the inclusion מדבר (4:3bB) // רעב (4:9aB) between the second and the fourth canticle in Lam. 4. Moreover, there is a chiastic parallelism between לחמנו (9A) and רעב (10B).
VI (5:11—12)	There is asson. /allit. and formal parallelism between נשים ב (11A) // שרים ב (12A). For the parallelism between בתלת (11B) // זקנים (12B), Lam. 2:10,21 can be pointed to.
VII (5:13—14)	A chiastic parallelism exists between בחורים (13A) // בחורים (14B); also between נערים (13B) // זקנים (14A), cf.Lam. 2:21.
VIII (5:15—16)	A linear parallelism exists between לבנו אורי־נא // אבל (15A) // ראשנו (16A); also

	לנו (16B).
IX (5:17—18)	Linear parallelism between על (17A) // על (18A). See the remarks in our introduction. Besides, there is a closing *petucha* after vs. 18.
X (5:19—20)	Linear parallelism between לעולם (19A) // לנצח (20A) and between לדור ודור (19B) // לארך ימים (20B). Compare also the vocative יהוה at the beginning of vs. 19. In the Psalms this vocative often indicates the beginning of a strophe.[4] The same is true of the first word of vs. 19, the personal pronoun אתה.[5] In vs. 20 the expression לנצח and the parallel לארך ימים indicates the end of this strophe.[6]
XI (5:21—22)	In 21A there is also the vocative יהוה. Furthermore a formal parallelism exists between מאסתנו השיבנו...נשוב (21A) // מאס (22A). Antithetic parallelism between חדש ימינו כקדם (21B) \\ כי אם ... קצפת (21B) עלינו עד־מאד (22B)

In view of the regularity of these strophes consisting of two Masoretic verses it seems reasonable to also divide the first six verses into three strophes: 1—2/3—4/5—6. Comparison with the other strophes provides us with some literary arguments for this division. Compare:

Strophe	*Literary arguments.*
I (5:1—2)	The beginning of the first strophe is marked by the vocative יהוה which corresponds to a similar use in the last two strophes. An argument for the end of this strophe, in addition to the fact that each strophe consist of two verses, is the consideration that the

---

4 Cf. P. van der Lugt, *Strofische structuren in de bijbels-hebreeuwse poëzie* (Kampen, 1980) 515f.
5 See for this and other *markers* which (often) indicate the beginning of a strophe van der Lugt: 1980:510—517.
6 See for these and for other *markers* which (often) indicate the end of a strophe van der Lugt: 1980:519—524.

II (5:3—4)	second strophe clearly begins at vs. 3. For an additional argument see below. Here can be mentioned the similar beginning of the fourth strophe, which starts with the same words אין and אב. See below for the signs of the termination of this strophe.
III (5:5—6)	The end of this strophe is most clearly discerned by determining the beginning of the following strophe. In vs. 6 we find a parallelism אשור // מצרים. This parallelism shows an analogy with a parallelism in vs. 2, the end of the first strophe: זרים // נכרים. לחם (6B) at the end of this strophe is paralleled by מימינו and עצינו in vs. 4. So we may assume vs. 4 to be the end of the second strophe.

Canticle—division

Are strophes connected together in this song? In our search for possible canticle divisions we made the following observations. In each strophe in vss. 1—10 and 15—22, the suffix נו is used, but it is missing in the two strophes of vss. 11—12 and 13—14. A closer examination shows that these strophes share much external parallelism. Compare:

Literary arguments:

inclusions:

בערי (11B) // משער (14A)

במלח (11B) // בחורים (14B)[7]

זקנים (12B) // נערים (13B)[8]

responsions:

נישם (11A) // בחורים (13A)[9]

במלח (11B) // נערים (13B)

זקנים (12B) // זקנים (14A)

זקנים (12B) // בחורים (14B)

---

7   Cf. 1:15.

8   Cf. 2:21.

9   This responsion becomes clear when one keeps in mind that taking up the millstone and grinding meal was women's work, cf. Isa. 47:2.

Besides, there is a strong concatenation by means of assonance/alliteration: נישם (11A) // שרים (12A) // דקנים (12B) // בחורים (13A) // נערים (13B) // דקנים (14A) // בחורים (14B). This abundance of literary arguments indicates the coherence between these two strophes. And the inclusions, as well as the difference in content in the following strophes, justify their designation as a canticle. As for content, it is evident that a total loss of security in the cities of Judah is pictured.

Next, taking into account the *petucha* as a greater divider, it is natural to examine the possibility of a canticle consisting of the two strophes vss. 15−16 and vss. 17−18. Indeed, more uniting, external parallelism is present. Compare:

Literary arguments:

inclusions:

הר־ציון (18A)[10] // משוש לבנו (15A)

לבנו (17A)[11] // ראשנו (16A)

responsions:

לבנו (17A) // לבנו (15A)

חשכו עינינו (17B) // נהפך לאבל מחלנו (15B)

הר־ציון (18A)[12] // עטרת (16A)

Furthermore, mention may be made of the concatenation by means of the suffix נו. In view of these literary arguments it can be assumed that the two strophes together form a canticle. With respect to content it focuses especially on the downfall of Zion and its effect on the people.

After having defined vss. 11−14 and 15−18 as canticles, we now must examine whether the last two strophes of Lam. 5 also belong together. Content strongly indicates coherence; it is a closing prayer for restoration. In addition, many literary arguments can also be given. Compare:

Literary arguments:

inclusion:

ליעולם (19A) // עד־מאד (22B)[13]

inclusion/concatenation:

---

10 Cf. Lam. 2:15. Although not mentioned, Zion is of course included in the joy of כל־הארץ.

11 Cf. Ps. 40:13.

12 Cf. Isa. 63:2. This connection also becomes clear from the first inclusion.

13 Cf. Ps. 111:8; 119:44; 145:1,2,21; 148:6.

ימים (20B) // ימינו (21B)
responsions:
יהוה (19A) // יהוה (21A) (two vocatives)
לדר ודור (19B) // קדם (21B)
חשכחנו (20A) // מאסתנו (22A)
תעזבנו (20B) // מאסתנו (22A)[14]
תעזבנו (20B) // קצפת עלינו (22B)
לארך ימים (20B) // עד־מאד (22B)[15]
alliteration:
חשב (19A) // ונשוב and השיבנו (21A)

As in the preceding canticle there is also concatenation by means of the suffix נו.

Is it also possible to divide the five strophes of Lam. 5:1—10 into canticles? To answer this question one must look for connections between these strophes. We examined possible connections between the first and the second strophe, where we found the following external parallelism:

Literary arguments:

responsions:
מה־היה לנו (1A) // היינו (3A)
נחלנו (2A) // מימינו (4A)[16]
בתינו (2B) // עצינו (4B)[17]

In studying the coherence between these two strophes it became clear that in the history of exegesis Lam. 5:3 has been largely misunderstood. The majority of exegetes give a literal explanation: the men have been killed or captured in the war and now there is a lack of protection for the remaining mothers and their children.[18]

---

14 Cf. Isa. 54:6.
15 Cf. Ps. 119:8.
16 With the turnover of the land into the hands of foreigners the waterrights have also been lost. For that reason they must now buy their own water.
17 Cf. n.16. The same is true for the wood they used for their houses and for cooking.
18 Cf. Kraus: 1968[3]:88; R. Gordis, *The Song of Songs and Lamentations* (New York, 1974[3]) 195; O. Kaiser, *Klagelieder* (ATD 16; Göttingen, 1981[3]) 379f.; Brandscheidt: 1983:196; H.J. Boecker, *Klagelieder* (ZB 21; Zürich, 1985) 90. Not literal but still incorrect: D.R. Hillers *Lamentations* (AB; New York, 1979) 103.

However this explanation is very doubtful. Firstly, none of the commentators discuss how it is possible to speak of orphans who still have their mother. Secondly, as far as we know the number of killed, executed and captured men and/or soldiers was low,[19] and we may assume that a larger part of the population remained in the towns and villages of Judah. Thirdly, almost every commentator neglects the obvious, long–range, external parallelism between 1:1 and 5:3:

היתה כאלמנה (1:1bA) // כאלמנות (אמחינו) (...היינו) (5:3B)

As far as I know only Rudolph drew attention to 1:1 in this regard,[20] but he takes over the metaphor of Jerusalem as a widow too literally; he changes the plural of 5:3 into a singular and is of opinion that here too Jerusalem is involved. However, we have seen in the first canticle of Lam. 1 (1:1−3) that the metaphor of the widow is retained also for Judah.[21] For that reason it is very likely that the poets did not focus on the human mothers in Judah, but on the *cities of Judah* which have become like a widow. Moreover, *cities are elsewhere considered to be mothers*, cf. 2 Sam. 20:19. As a consequence also the fathers in 5:3A must not be interpreted literally but metaphorically as the fathers of the inhabitants of the cities, i.e. their leaders — the king, the rulers, the prophets and the priests.[22] They are

---

19   Cf. E. Janssen, *Juda in der Exilszeit* (Göttingen, 1956) 25; M. Noth *Geschichte Israels* (Göttingen, 1969[7]) 264; S. Herrman, *Geschichte Israels* (München, 1973) 353; P.R. Ackroyd, *Exile and Restoration* (London, 1968) 25; B. Oded, 'Judah and the Exile' in: J.H. Hayes−J.M. Miller, *Israelite & Judean History* (London, 1977) 479; J. Renkema, *Misschien is er hoop...* (Franeker, 1983) 148−151.

20   W. Rudolph, *Die Klagelieder* (KAT XVII/3; Gütersloh, 1962) 260.

21   Cf. page 306.

22   See for this metaphorical meaning of אב: Gen. 45:8; Judg. 17:10; 18:19; 1 Sam. 24:12; 2 Kgs 2:12; 6:21; 13:14. That these leaders are no longer present is stated many times in Lamentations. Priests and prophets have been killed (2:19) or exiled (4:15). The king has been captured (4:20) and exiled (2:9). The rulers too were exiled (1:6; 2:9) or hanged (5:12).As far as we know it was Babylonian policy to deport especially the upperclass. Our exegesis of 5:3 is confirmed by 5:6 where the same expression is found: אבתינו...אינם by which are meant not former generations, but above all the prophets and the priests. Because of their sins this disaster overcame Judah and Jerusalem, cf. 2:14; 4:13. See also n.34.

gone, leaving the mothers behind and these became like widows.
The children of the cities of Judah (also metaphorical for the
inhabitants) lost their fathers (leaders) and their mothers (their
own cities) and became (metaphorically) orphans. They have lost
their former rights and are now without protection because
strangers have taken over power. This interpretation reveals the
strong coherence of the first and the second strophe of Lam. 5.

It is possible to see an inclusion between חרפתנו of 1B and
the bicolon of 4B. Their shame is that they now have to buy
their own water and wood. However, it is also possible that the
content of this חרפה is pictured not only in vss. 2—4, but also
in the following strophe(s). For that reason we cannot yet
conclude that the first two strophes alone of Lam. 5 form a
canticle. First we must investigate whether there are connections
with the following strophes. As far as I can see only one
literary connection exists between vss. 1—4 and the next
strophe: לנו (1A) // לנו (5B), which could be a responsion.
However, in view of the abundant use of the suffix נו, this is
not very convincing. Besides, there is a change of theme in the
following verses. It is not the loss of rights and protection which
is at stake, but oppression and hunger. What are the
connections between the third and the fourth strophe? Here can
be mentioned the following external parallelisms:

responsions:

על צוארנו (5A) // סבלנו (7B)

ידם (6A) // יד (8B)

עבדים (8A) // אשור / מצרים (6AB)

Between the fourth and the fifth strophe there are at first sight
no clear connections. Nor is it possible to connect the fifth
strophe with the next one. However, a closer look shows a
connection between the third and the fifth strophe. Both
strophes speak about hunger. But there are also some literary
arguments. Compare:

Literary arguments:

inclusion:

לחמנו (9A) // לחם (6B)

responsion:

רעב (10B) // לשבע לחם 6B)

and also:

inclusion:

עורנו (10A) // צוארנו (5A)

responsion:

צוארנו (5A) // נפשנו (9A)[23]

According to these arguments the third and the fifth strophe frame the fourth one, which indicates the cause of the misery of oppression and hunger.

We may conclude that the poets composed the first five strophes of Lam. 5 as two canticles, consisting of respectively two and three strophes (2+2 and 2+2+2), and the last six strophes as three canticles, each consisting of two strophes.[24]

Subcanto division[25]

We must now deal with the question of the connection of the canticles. In tracing the canticles we already became aware of external parallelism beyond their borders, which provides further unifying factors. We found indications for the existence of two sub—cantos.

Subcanto A

Content: *Loss of property, oppression, hunger*
Literary arguments:
  inclusions:
    זרים/נכרים (2AB) // חרב המדבר (9B)[26]

---

23   The poets of Lamentations like to use the names of parts of the body and they often do so in concentration, cf. 1:13,16,20; 2:11,16,18; 3:4, 29—30,49—51; 4:3—4,7—8; 5:15—17.

24   Such canticles are quite typical, cf. the canticles of Lam. 4.

25   Our division of the song differs considerably from that of others. Most commentators divide this song as follows: 1/2—18/19—22. However, this division is made only on the basis of content.

26   In my opinion this is a clear reminiscence of the hostile behaviour of the Edomites who after 587 wanted to appropriate Judah, Ezek. 35:10, cf. W. Zimmerli, *Ezechiel 2* (BKAT XIII/2; Neukirchen, 1969) 861f.; also after the downfall of Jerusalem the Edomites were a constant threat for the remaining people of Judah, cf. Ezek. 35:5 (also with חרב) and Amos 1:11. Besides, far more allusions to the behaviour of the Edomites are present in the book of Lamentations than only in 4:21. For example the joy of the enemies (1:5,21; 2:16) was certainly also the joy of the Edomites. The same with the big mouth of the enemies (2:16; 3:46) which is, as is their joy, attested in Obad. 12. They have also been among the enemies that came in the gates of Jerusalem (4:12); cf. Obad. 13. See further on the subject: J.M.

Johan Renkema

אין אב (3A) // פרק אין מידם (8B)²⁷
כאלמנות (3B) // לא הונח־לנו (5B)²⁸
responsions:
זרים/נכרים (2AB) // מצרים / אשור (6AB)
זרים/נכרים (2AB) // עבדים משלו בנו (8A)
אין אב (3A) // אבתנו...אינם (7A)
אמחינו (3B) // אבתנו (7A)
...יבאו (4AB) // ...נביא... (9A)

Subcanto B

Content: *Violence, mourning about Zion, prayer*
Literary argumentation: the third (vss. 11—14) and fourth (vss. 15—18) canticle are connected by concatenation and an inclusion:
concatenations:
שבחו (14A) // שבח (15A)
מנגינתם (14B) // מחלנו (15B)
inclusion:
ציון (11A) // ציון (18A)
But in the same way the fourth (vss. 15—18) and the closing canticle (vss. 19—22) are connected. Compare:
concatenation:
הר־ציון (18A) // כסאך (19B)
inclusions:
/תעזבנו תשכחנו // (17AB) חשכו עינינו /דוה לבנו (20AB)²⁹
חדש ימינו כקדם \\ (16A) נפלה עטרת ראשנו (21B)
ונשוב \\ (16B) חטאנו (21A)
שבת משוש /נהפך לאבל מחלנו (15AB) // קצפת (22B)³⁰
responsions:
ששמם (18A) // קצפת (22B)³¹

Myers, 'Edom and Judah in the Sixth—Fifth Centuries BC', in: *Near Eastern Studies in honor of W.F. Albright* (Baltimore, 1971) 379—392 and U. Kellerman, *Israel and Edom. Studien zum Edomhaß im 6.–4. Jahrhundert v. Chr.* (Münster, 1975).

27 Cf. n.22.
28 Cf. the inclusion in the first canticle of Lam. 1. between כאלמנה (1:1bA) and לא מצאה מנוח (3bB).
29 Cf. Ps. 22:2, 15ff.; 42:10f.; Jer. 14:19.
30 Cf. Hos. 2:13; Amos 8:10.
31 Cf. Jer. 50:13; Zech. 7:12f.

ששמם (18A) // מאס מאסתנו מאס (22A)[32]

Regarding content it is clear that in prophetic preaching of divine judgement YHWH's anger is related to the violence and oppression of enemies. Therefore, also from the point of view of content, in the second subcanto there is inclusion between the fate of women, rulers and elders (vss. 11—14) and YHWH who, in his anger, forsakes, forgets and rejects them (vss. 20 and 22)[33] So the coherence of this subcanto is indicated by a strong interweaving of words and thoughts.

The Unity of Lamentation V[34]

There are also arguments for the unity of this song. Both subcantos show literary connections. They are bound together by external parallelism in the same way as the smaller literary units they consist of. Compare:
Literary arguments:

---

32 Cf. Jer. 14:19.

33 The same, however, is true of the taking over of the properties by strangers, cf. Jer. 6:11f.; 12:7—11. So there is also an inclusion between vs. 2 and vs. 22.

34 As will appear from the many arguments below, this unity is unquestionable. For that reason we cannot find ourselves in agreement with G. Brunet, 'La Cinquième Lamentation', *VT* XXXIII (1983) 149—170, who is of the opinion that the last song of Lamentations consists of two independent poems: vss. 1—14 and vss. 15—22. The incision is made on the basis of an alleged difference in style and content. His main reason is a supposed contradiction between vs. 7: *the fathers have sinned.* and vs. 16: *we have sinned.* According to Brunet it is possible to reconcile both utterances. But he finds it more likely to suppose two different poets. This solution is unacceptable. Only a strange logic finds a contradiction between both verses. One's sins do not exclude the sins of others. The key for a better interpretation is found in Lam. 2:14 and 4:13. The prophets (the fathers) have sinned. They did not reveal the guilt of their people and so they take away their chance to repent and to avoid judgement. So, the people sinned, and YHWH's judgement was justified, cf. 1:18.

According to Brunet the צרים in Lam. were Babylonians and the איובים were pro—Babylonian Judeans (i.e. Jeremiah), cf. his *Les Lamentationes contre Jérémie* (Paris, 1968). See for the rejection of this suggestive proposition Renkema: 1983:140f, Brandscheidt: 1983:217f.

358   *Johan Renkema*

inclusions:

זכר (1A) // חשכחנו (20A)[35]

יהוה (1A) // יהוה (19A, 21A)

חרפתנו (1B) // קצפת (22B)[36]

לעולם חשב \\ (2B) בתינו לנרכרים (19B)

שועלים // (2A) נחלתנו נהפכה לזרים (18B)[37]

אמחינו כאלמנות (3B) // הד־ציון ששמם (18A)[38]

על (5A) // על (17A, 18A)

חטאו (7A) // חטאנו (16B)

שרים בידם נתלו (7A) // אבתינו...אינם (12A)

בידם (8B) // מידם (12A)

נחלו (9A) // בנפשנו (12A)

לבנו (9A) // בנפשנו (15A)

פני (9B, 10B) // מפנו (12B)

responsions:

נהפך (2A) // נהפכה (15B)

נערים / בחורים / בחלת (3A) // יתומים (11B,13AB)

בחלת / נשים (3B) // אמחינו (11AB)

שרים בידם נתלו (3A) // אין אב (12A)

בעץ (4B) // עצינו (13B)

ראשנו (5A) // צוארנו (16A)

לבנו (9A) // בנפשנו (17A)[39]

These literary connections are found mainly on the level of the canticles. The many inclusions indicate a concentric design of this song. In the centre, the third canticle (vss. 11–14) pictures very concisely the general misery of the people left behind in Judah,[40] which is elaborated in the other canticles. The merismus נערים ־ זקנים indicates the male population, the hanging of the שרים the absence of the leaders (אבתנו) while the elders cannot take over because they have no longer authority and the raping of girls and women indicates the total loss of protection. The inadequate food supply appears from the boys who have to do the cooking. That miserable state of

---

35 This is an antithetical inclusion.

36 Cf. Jer. 49:13; 24:9; Ezek. 5:15 etc.

37 Cf. Ps. 44:20; Jer. 9:11; 10:22.

38 Cf. Lam. 2:6–8; 2 Kgs. 25:8ff.

39 Cf. Lam. 2:19; 3:20–21.

40 Note the absence of the suffix נו in this canticle. It is not only 'us', but all people in Judah.

affairs is the reason for the prayer, which this song is intended to be.

Outlining the structure of the last song results in the following scheme:

Subcantos	Canticles	Strophes	Verses
	I	1 --- 1 - 2	
A		2 --- 3 - 4	
	II	1 --- 5 - 6	
		2 --- 7 - 8	
Lam.5		3 --- 9 -10	
	I	1 --- 11-12	
		2 --- 13-14	
B	II	1 --- 15-16	
		2 --- 17-18	
	III	1 --- 19-20	
		2 --- 21-22	

At first sight this structure does not seem to be very regular. However, a closer look shows that for the outline of the song the poets choose a variant of a well known pattern in Lamentations, namely a reversed *qinah–metre*, 2+3. The structure of the qinah–metre (3+2) constituted a fundamental form for the poets designing their songs. They used it on the level of the colon, the subcanto, the canto, but also on the level of the whole book of Lamentations. Accordingly the first three songs each have three bicola in their strophes and the last two songs each two bicola. This 3+2 was recognized as a reflection of the *qinah–metre* by W.H. Shea.[41]

---

41   W.H. Shea, 'The *qinah* Structure of the Book of Lamentations', *Biblica* 60 (1979) 103–107.

In the last song the reversed variant is present two times, at the level of subcanto and canto.[42] Compare:

$$\frac{2 + 3}{2} \Big| \frac{2 + 2 + 2}{3}$$

But we must also notice an additional qinah—pattern, this time operative at the level of the five songs taken together. As we have seen, Lam. 1, 2 and 5 have the same structure. We have also noted that Lam. 3 and 4 both have a dyptych structure. So another 3+2 pattern is present.

---

42 It is possible that this variant has been chosen because of the different character of the last song, which is not meant to be a qinah but a prayer.

THE LITERARY STRUCTURE OF LAMENTATIONS (IV)

The Literary Structure of the Booklet

Johan Renkema

In our treatment of the literary structure of Lam. 5 we already mentioned the concise but illuminating essay of W.H. Shea treating the qinah—pattern which was used by the poets of Lamentations to outline their songs at different levels as well as the booklet as a whole.[1] But in my opinion this was not the only structuring principle used by the poets. In this section of our essay we will point out some other figures of speech which were applied by the poets not only in smaller units but also to outline the songs and the booklet.

Lam. 1 and 5

Our exegesis of Lam. 5:3 reveals the same metaphor as used in Lam. 1:3:

(1:1bA) ‫היתה כאלמנה // כאלמנות (אמתינו) (...היינו)‬ (5:3B)

Two other observations can be added. Firstly, this metaphor is used only in the first and the last song. Secondly, this literary connection is placed approximately on the same level in both songs. This may be a coincidence. Of course one becomes curious whether additional literary connections of this kind are present. This can be checked by means of a concordance of the booklet. We looked for similarities and when found approximately on the same level we marked them with an asterisk. Besides the already mentioned metaphor we found for Lam. 1 and 5 the following exclusive similar words or expressions:

*(1:8aA)   ‫חטא חטאה // חטאו‬ (5:7A)
 (1:8aA)   ‫חטא חטאה // חטאנו‬ (5:16B)
*(1:11aB,bB) ‫נפש / לחם // לחמנו... בנפשנו‬ (5:9a)

---

1   Cf. W.H. Shea, 'The *qinah* Structure of the Book of Lamentations', *Biblica* 60 (1979), 103–107.

(1:13cB)	(5:17A) דוה // דוה
*(1:14bB)	(5:13B) כשלו // הכשיל
(1:14bA)	(5:5A) על צוארנו // על־צוארי
*(1:16aA)	(5:17B) על־אלה // על־אלה
(1:18bA)	(5:16B) ־נא // ־נא
(1:22cB)	(5:17A) דוה לבני // לבי דוי

A closer look shows, if one takes into account their context, that most of these similarities concern main themes of the booklet: 1. sin of the people (1:8; 5:7,16); 2. hunger (1:11; 5:9); 3. sickness at heart (1:13,22; 5:17); 4. oppression by the enemies (1:4ff.; 5:5); 5. the destruction of Zion (1:13; 5:17f.) and 6. the loss of protection and leaders[2] (1:14ff.; 5:5). Therefore one cannot consider these similarities as coincidental. Besides, they sharpen the eye to see more.[3]

*(1:2bA)	(5:3A) אין אב // אין מנחם
(1:2bA)	(5:7A) אבחינו אינם // אין מנחם
*(1:3cA)	(5:5A) נרדפנו // רדפיה
*(1:3bB)	(5:5b) לא הונח־לנו // לא מצאה מנוח

---

2 See our exegesis of Lam. 5:3.

3 M. Löhr, 'Der Sprachgebrauch des Buches der Klagelieder', *ZAW* 14 (1894) 31−50, did not investigate the interrelations between the five songs but rather the connections with other Old Testament literature. Moreover, he restricted himself primarily to single words, many of which are too general to be of particular significance. His judgement concerning the relationship between the songs within Lamentations itself is indirect. For example, he concludes that the second and the fourth song have much in common because they both are dependent upon Ezekiel. However, this method of measuring relationship on the basis of (general) single words is not very useful, cf. J. Renkema, *Misschien is er hoop...* (Franeker, 1983) 217−239. For tracing literary similarities we applied the following method. A concordance of the booklet provides us with the words which only occur in both songs of which the relation is investigated. They indicate exclusive similarities. In the case of non−exclusive similarities, the same word also occurs in one or more of the other songs. However, if such words are used in a similar semantic context, we reckoned them as a literary similarity. Methodologically it is not the most helpful to look only for parallels simply or primarily at the level of individual words which appear in both songs being compared. A more appropriate methodology is to determine if various parallels − whether synonymous, synthetical or antithetical − are present. Such parallels must be considered as literary similarities.

(1:4aAB)	// דרכי ציון אבלות מבלי באי מועד
	שבת משוש לבנו נהפך לאבל מחלנו (5:15AB)
(1:4bA)	על הר-ציון ששמם // כל-שעריה שוממין (5:18A)
(1:4cA)	בתלח // בתוליה (5:11B)
(1:5aAB)	זרים / נכרים // צרוה / איבוה (5:2AB)
(1:6aA)	לא נהדרו // ויצא ... כל-הדרה (5:12B)
(1:6bA,cA)	שריה ... בלא-כח לפני רודף //
	שרים בידם נתלו (5:12A)
*(1:6cB)	נרדפנו // רודף (5:5A)
(1:7bB)	ימינו כקדם // מימי קדם (5:21B)
*(1:7cA)	פרק אין מידם // נפל... יד-צר (5:8B)
(1:7cB)	אין אב // אין עוזר (5:3A)
*(1:7cB)	אבחינו אינם // אין עוזר (5:7A)
*(1:7cB)	פרק אין מידם // אין עוזר לה (5:8B)
(1:8aB)	היה ל // היה ל (5:1A)
(1:9bB)	אין אב // אין מנחם (5:3A)
(1:9bB)	אבחינו אינם // אין מנחם (5:7A)
(1:9cA)	// ראה יהוה את-עניי
	יהוה ... הביט וראה את-חרפתנו (5:1B)
(1:9cB)	// כי הגדיל אויב
	נחלנו נהפכה לזרים בתנו לנכרים (5:2AB)
(1:10aAB)	// ידו פרש צר כל-מחמדיה
	נחלנו נהפכה לזרים בתנו לנכרים (5:2AB)
(1:11bA)	// נתנו מחמודיחם באכל
	מימינו בכסף שתנו (5:4A)
(1:11bA)	// נתנו מחמודיהם באכל
	נתנו ... לשבע לחם (5:6AB)
(1:11cA)	יהוה ... הביט וראה // ראה יהוה והביטה (5:1B)
(1:12aB)	הביט וראה // הביטו וראו (5:1b)
(1:13cAB)	ששמם / דוה // שממה / דוה (5:17A,18A)
(1:14aA)	אנחנו עונתיהם סבלנו // על פשעי (5:7B)
*(1:15bB)	שבתו בחורים מנגינתם // לשבר בחורי (5:14AB)
*(1:16aB)	חשכו עיני // עיני עיני ירדה מים (5:17B)
*(1:16cA)	ששמם // שוממים (5:18A)
(1:16cB)	// כי גבר אויב
	נחלתנו נהפכה לזרים בתנו לנכרים (5:2AB)
(1:17aB)	אין אב // אין מנחם (5:3A)
(1:17aB)	אבחינו אינם // אין מנחם (5:7A)
(1:17cAB)	היה ל // היה ל (5:1A)
(1:18aB)	חטאו // כי פיהו מריתי (5:7A)
*(1:18aB)	חטאנו // כי פיהו מריתי (5:16B)

(1:19bA)   בצרי // בערי (5:11B)

(1:19bA,cA)   זקני בעיר...בקשו אכל // (5:14A) זקנים משער שבתו

(1:20aA)   ראה יהוה את־ענייַ //
(5:1B) יהוה...הביט וראה את־חרפתנו

(1:20aA)   כי־צר־לי // cf. 5:11,12

(1:20aB)   (5:17A) דוה לבנו // מעי חמרמרו

(1:20bA)   (5:15AB) נהפך / לבנו // נהפך / לבי

(1:20aB)   (5:7A) חטאו // כי מרו מריתי

(1:20aB)   (5:16B) חטאנו // כי מרו מריתי

(1:20cA)   (5:9B) מפני חרב המדבר // מחוץ שכלה־חרב

(1:21aB)   (5:3A) אין אב // אין מנחם

(1:21aB)   (5:7A) אבחינו אינם // אין מנחם

*(1:21cA)   (5:20B) עזבנו לארך ימים //הבאת יום־קראת[4]

*(1:21cA)   (5:22B) קצפת עלינו עד־מאד // הבאת יום־קראת

(1:22bB)   (5:7A) חטאו // על כל־פשעי

(1:22bB)   (5:16B) חטאנו // על כל־פשעי

In view of the exclusive similarities and the abundance of these other connections, both as regards content and in a literary respect, it seems more than justified to consider the first and the last song of Lamentations as one great inclusion. Furthermore, it is impossible — as is often done in a literary—critical approach — to consider these two songs as independent ones versified by different poets in different times.[5] Nor is it likely correct to assume that these independent songs were adapted to each other by reworking. The close resemblance indicates that at least one of the songs must have been composed in view of the other. Often the absence of the form of the alphabetic acrostic was the reason commentators hesitated to include the last song as originally part of the collection of Lamentations. It has been said the poet of this song was less talented and not able to apply the form of the alphabetic

---

4   Cf. for the appropriation of the יום יהוה—preaching of the pre—exilic prophets by the poets of Lamentations: Renkema: 1983:274—279, where also other literature is mentioned.

5   So recently O. Kaiser *Klagelieder* (ATD 16; Göttingen, 1981[3]) and R. Brandscheidt, *Gotteszorn und Menschenleid* (Trier, 1983). Kaiser assumes five, Brandscheidt four different poets as did already Löhr in 1906.

acrostic.[6] However, in view of the outline of the last song, the use of the same literary technique as in the others and the many connections with the first song, this is a very unconvincing argument. Therefore, it is more likely that the poets deliberately did not use the form of the alphabetic acrostic. In my opinion they had a good reason. The A – Z scheme in Lam. 1–4 has been used because they wanted to picture total misery, in every aspect from A – Z.[7] However, this was not their intention with the last song, which gives, compared to the other songs, a very condensed account at this point. Furthermore, the poets left the qinah–metre, started the song with זכר יהוה and ended it with אתה יהוה. So they intended it to be a closing prayer. Now, in the situation of the poets and their people, the form of the alphabetic acrostic ill befits prayer. In that state of misery one cannot pray from A – Z and then stop. To the contrary, praying and shedding of tears must go on, restlessly, day and night, until the Lord in heaven looks down, watches their affliction and renews their days.[8]

It is very well possible that the poets foresaw questions about the absence of the form of the alphabetic acrostic in the last song, and that they hinted at this in a play on words. Again we call attention to Lam. 5:3A. As we have seen the word אב is not to be understood literally but metaphorically.[9] However, the formulation is somewhat strange. In view of the plurals יתומים and אמתינו, a plural אבות, as used in 5:7A, would have fitted better. But the first time the poets used this metaphor they avoided the plural and chose the singular:

אין אב

6   Cf. M. Löhr, *Die Klagelieder des Jeremias* (HAT; Göttingen, 1894) XIX; S. Bergler, 'Threni V – nur ein alphabetisierendes Lied? Versuch einer Deutung', *VT* 27 (1977) 319; G. Brunet, 'La cinquième Lamentation', *VT* 33 (1983) 150.
7   So for example, among others, W. Rudolph *Die Klagelieder* (KAT XVII/3; Gütersloh, 1962) 191; O. Plöger, *Die Klagelieder* (HAT I/18; Tübingen, 1969²) 128; R. Gordis, *The Song of Songs and Lamentations* (New York, 1974³) 124.
8   Cf. Lam. 2:18,19; 3:50; 5:21.
9   See page 353.

It can be read as a collective: no fathers/leaders. But it can also be read as an abbreviation of the alphabet: no aleph, no beth, etc. Of course the first meaning prevails, but the other may well be intended too. This somewhat hidden meaning can be considered as an indication that the poets deliberately abandoned the form of the alphabetic acrostic for the last song.

Lam. 2 and 4

We now want to investigate the literary connections between the second and the fourth song, for it has often been stated that these songs show a large resemblance to each other.[10] If a literary resemblance exists, this would prove that the technique of concentric structuring was not only used for smaller literary units, but applied by the poets also on the level of the booklet as well. Our search for exclusive similarities produced the following results:

(2:2cA)	הגיע // יגצו[11](4:14bA)
(2:2cA)	הגיע // תגצו (4:15bA)
*(2:3cB)	אכלה (אש) // האכלים (4:5aA)
(2:3cB)	אכלה (אש) // ותאכל (אש) (4:11bB)[12]
(2:4cB)	שפך // תשתפכנה (4:1bA)
(2:4cB)	שפך // שפך (4:11aB)
(2:4cB)	שפך // השפכים (4:13bA)[13]
(2:4cB)	חמתו // חמתו (4:11aA)
(2:6cB)	מלך // מלכי (4:12aA)
(2:8aA)	חשב // נחשבו (4:12bA)
(2:9bA)	מלכה // מלכי (4:12aA)

---

10 Cf. M. Löhr, *Die Klagelieder des Jeremias* (HAT III.2.2; Göttingen, 1906²) XIV–XV; Th.J. Meek, *The Book of Lamentations* (IB VI; New York, 1956) 4f.; H.J. Kraus, *Klagelieder* (BKAT XX; Neukirchen, 1968³) 15; H.J. Boecker, *Klagelieder* (ZB 21; Zürich, 1985) 14. Different: Brandscheidt: 1983:224–226.

11 In all three texts נגע implies ritual impurity, cf. also חלל and the expressions נידה (1:8aB,17cB) and טמאה (1:9aA).

12 Cf. the demarcation of the fifth canticle in Lam. 4.

13 The root שפך appears to be a keyword for both songs (2:4,11,12,19; 4:1,11,3). It is found in the kernel of the second song and the poets used it in their division of the fourth one.

(2:9cA)	נביאיה // נביאיה (4:13aA)
(2:11bA)	תשחפכנה // נשפך (4:1bA)
*(2:11bA)	שפך // נשפך (4:11aB)
*(2:11bA)	השפכים // נשפך (4:13bA)
(2:11cA)	עוללים /יונק // עולל ויונק (4:4aA,bA)
(2:11cB)	ברחבתינו // ברחבות (4:18aB)
(2:12bA)	מחללי ראב // כחלל (4:9aAB)
(2:12bB)	ברחבתינו // ברחבות (4:18aB)
(2:12cA)	תשחפכנה // בהשתפך (4:1bA)
*(2:12cA)	שפך // בהשתפך (4:11aB)
*(2:12cA)	השפכים // נהשתפך (4:13bA)
*(2:14aA)	נביאיה // נביאיך (4:13aA)
(2:14bA)	גלו על-(עונך) //
	גלה על-(חטאחיך) (4:22bB)
*(2:15bA)	נעו // וינעו (4:15bA)
(2:17cA)	וישמח (עליך אויב) //
	ושמחי (בת-אדום) (4:21A)
(2:19bA)	תשמפכנה // שפכי (4:1bA)
(2:19bA)	שפך // שפכי (4:11aB)
(2:19bA)	השפכים // שפכי (4:13bA)
(2:19dB)	בראש כל-חוצות // בראש כל-חוצות (4:1bB)
(2:20bA)	האכלים // תאכלנה (4:5aA) / ותאכל (4:11bB)[12]
(2:20bA)	נשים // נשים (4:10aA)
(2:20cB)	נביאיה // נביא (4:13aA)

In comparison with Lam. 1 and 5, these exclusive similarities already show peculiar themes shared by Lam. 2 and 4. These are, 1. the destructive anger of YHWH (2:3; 4:11); 2. the revealing of sin(2:14; 4:22); 3. the sin and fate of the prophets (2:14; 4:13ff.); 4. the hunger of the children (2:11ff.; 4:3ff.) and the horrible fate of the women who have to consume their own children[14] (2:20; 4:10). However, far more connections are present. Compare:

*(2:1aB)	ביני ציון // בת-ציון (4:2aA)
(2:1aB)	בת-ציון // בת-ציון (4:22aA)

---

14 For R. Brandscheidt Lam. 2 focus on the fate of Zion and Lam. 4 on the fate of individuals, as in Lam. 3. Therefore she assumes the same poet for Lam. 3 and 4. Lam. 2 is versified by another one. However, her distinction is not correct. The fate of the children and women is more fully elaborated in Lam. 2 than in Lam. 4.

(2:1aB)	בת־אדום \\ בת־ציון (4:21aA)
(2:1aB)	בת־אדום \\ בת־ציון (4:22bA)
(2:1aAB)	יציב באפו ... את־בת־ציון //
	ויצת־אש בציון (4:11bA)
*(2:1cA)	אבני־קדש // הדם־רגליו (4:1bA)
(2:1cB)	שפך חרון אפו // ביום אפו (4:11aB)
(2:2cAB)	הגיע...ממלכה ושריה // cf. 4:7,8,20
(2:3bA)	פני יהוה חלקם // השיב אחור ימינו (4:16aA)
(2:3cA)	ויצת־אש בציון // ויבער ביעקב (4:11bA)
(2:4bAB)	ויהרג כל מחמדי־עין //
	ויצת־אש בציון (4:11bA)
(2:4cB)	שפך חרון אפו // שפך כאש חמתו (4:11aB)
(2:5cA)	בת־אדים // בת־יהודה (4:21aA)
(2:5cA)	בת־אדים // בת־יהודה (4:22bA)
(2:5cAB)	חיו לברות // וירב...מאניה ואניה (4:10bA)
(2:6cAB)	וינאץ ... מלך //
	משיח יהוה נלכד בשחיתותם (4:20aAB)
(2:6cAB)	כהניה // וינאץ...וכהן (4:13aB) cf. vss. 14—15
(2:7bA)	יבא צר ואויב // הסגיר ביד־אויב (4:12bA)
(2:8cB)	חל וחומה יחדו אמללו //
	תאכל יסודתיה (4:11bB)
*(2:9aA)	תאכל יסודתיה // טבעו בארץ שעריה (4:11bB)
(2:9aB)	אבד ושבר בריחיה //
	יבא צר ואויב בשערי (4:12bAB)
(2:9bA)	מלכה ... בגוים //
	משיח יהוה נלכד בשחיתותם (4:20aAB)
(2:9bB)	כיניה // אין תורה (4:13aB) cf. vss. 14—15
(2:9cA)	נביאיה // נביאיה (4:13aA)
(2:9cAB)	עורים // לא־מצאו חזון (4:14aA)
(2:10aAB)	זקנים לא חננו // ידמו זקני ... (4:16bB)
*(2:11aA)	כלה // כלו (4:11aA)
(2:11aA)	תכלינה עינינו // כלו ... עיני (4:17aA)
*(2:11bB)	שבר בת־עמי // שבר בת־עמי (4:10bB)
(2:12aAB)	לאמם יאמרו איה דגן //
	עוללים שאלו לחם (4:4bA)
*(2:13aB)	ירושלם // ירושלם (4:12bB)
*(2:13cA)	לא האמינו ... // כי־גדול כים שברך (4:12ab)
*(2:14aAB)	נביאיך חזו לך שוא ותפל //
	מחטאת נבירייה (4:13aA)

*(2:14aAB)	עורים (4:14aA)[15] // נביאיך חזו לך שוא ותפל
*(2:15cA)	אמרו בגוים (4:15bA) // שיאמרו
(2:15cB)	כלילת יפי //
	יועם זהב ישנא הכתם הטוב (4:1aAB)
*(2:16aAB)	פצו פיהם כל-אויביך //
	כהנים לא נשאו זקנים לא חננו (4:16bAB)
*(2:17aB)	אל-גוי לא יושע (4:17bB)[16] // בצע אמרתו
(2:17cA)	שמחי בת-אדום (4:21aA) // וישמח עליך אויב
(2:17cAB)	צר ואיוב (4:12bA) // אויב ...צריך
*(2:18aB)	ברחבתינו (4:18aB) // חומת
*(2:18aB)	צדו צעדינו \\ חומת בת-ציון (4:18aA)[17]
*(2:18bB)	ימינו (4:18bA) // יומם
(2:19aB)	בראש (4:1bB) // לראש
*(2:19cB)	רוח אפינו (4:20aA) // על-נפש
*(2:19dB)	ברחבתינו (4:18aB) // חוצות
(2:19dAB)	נשמו בחוצות (4:5aB) // העטופים...חוצות
(2:20bB)	האכלים למעדנים (4:5aA) // עללי טפחים
(2:20bB)	האמנים עלי תולע (4:5bA) // עללי טפחים
(2:20cA)	אבני-קדש (4:1bA) // במקדש
(2:20cB)	נביאיה ...כהניה (4:13aAB) // כהן ונביא
(2:20cB)	משיח יהוה (4:20aA)[18] // כהן ונביא
(2:21aA)	שכבו לארץ חוצות //
	תשחפכנה ...חוצות (4:1bA)[19]

---

15   Cf. Isa. 29:9,10.

16   Cf. Isa. 30:7. There are other striking resemblances between Lam. 2 and 4 and Isa. 30. In Isa. 30:10 false prophecies are at stake, cf. Lam. 2:14; in Isa. 30:16 the swift pursuers remind us of the swift pursuers of Lam. 4:19.

17   Mostly 2:18 is considered to be corrupt and therefore emended. In my opinion MT is correct, but the poet's metaphor of the חומת בת-ציון has not been understood. In the theology of Zion יהוה is like a protecting wall, cf. Zech. 2:9. See also Ps. 46:8,12; 48:4 and Pss.9:10; 18:3 59:10,17f.; 62:3,7; 94:22: 144:2. In dire misery, their hearts cry for YHWH's protection and now they are exhorted to utter this fondest wish as a prayer. Cf. for the influence of this theology in Lamentations: B. Albrektson, *Studies in the Text and Theology of the Book of Lamentations* (Lund, 1963) 219–330, and Renkema: 1983:32–42; 90–139; 280– 294.

18   Cf. for the pair of king and priest Lam. 2:6cB.

19   In the songs the fate of Zion is identical with the fate of the inhabitants of the city. Cf. for example the use of the root שמם in 1:13,16; 3:11; 4:5.

(2:21bB)	(4:9aA) חללי־חרב // נפלו בחרב
(2:21cA)	(4:11aB) אפו // שפך
(2:22bAB)	(4:18bB) כי־בא קצינו // ולא היה ...פליט ושריד
(2:22bA)	(4:11aB) אפו // אף־יהוה
(2:22cA)	(4:5aA) האכלים למעדנים // טפחתי
(2:22cA)	(4:5bA) האמנים עלי תולע // טפחתי
(2:22cB)	(4:11aA)[20] כלה יהוה את־חמתו // איבי כלם

To sum up: the first and the closing song do have their own themes in common and there exists between these two songs a great number of connections, both in language and content, many of which are found on the same level. The same is true of the second and the fourth song. However, as we can see, the connections between these two songs are more elaborated than the connections between Lam. 1 and 5.[21] There is a good reason for this; in the booklet the second and the fourth song do not only form an inclusion, as do the first and the fifth song, but they also form a responsion. The poets versified Lam. 2 & 4 to fulfill this double function, as appears from the great number of similarities and connections in language. As for content, the similarities between both songs has always struck the commentators and even in the hey—day of literary—critical approaches no reasons were found to divorce both songs. Yet it can be tentatively concluded that *a concentric design of the booklet is intended and that its kernel is to be found in the third song.* Concerning the concentric design this cannot be the final word. For the moment it is necessary to refer back to the diptych—structure of Lam. 3, from which both cantos have their own themes in common: the experience of suffering by the גבר, of being a prisoner, of being left by YHWH who refuses prayer and despite all these experiences, of new—born confidence. It is important to analyze in which way both cantos are literarily

---

20 Cf. Lam. 2:5aA.
21 This can be expressed in figures. To do so it is necessary to take into account the size of the songs. For measuring the size we take as unit of account a bicolon; for the similarities we do not distinguish between exclusive, non—exclusive and repeated ones. The last song has 22 bicola, the first song 67. Together these 89 bicola share 58 similarities, i.e. a ratio of 1.5 to 1. The 111 bicola of the second and the fourth song share 91 similarities, i.e. a ratio of 1.2 to 1.

connected. In the first place, both cantos can be considered as the most inner inclusion in the concentric design of the booklet. Secondly, in accordance with the alphabetic acrostic, the strophes from ל - ת are also responsions to the strophes א - ב.[22] From these two points of view both cantos are as strongly connected as are Lam. 2 and 4. But there is an important difference. The second and the fourth song are separated by the third song, but both cantos of Lam. 3 are not separated by anything. Furthermore, we have noted that the opposite strophes of this dyptich share at least two or more words or expressions.[23] For that reason it is justified to speak of *concatenation* between the opposite strophes. So Lam. 2 and 4 are bound together by the two literary ropes of inclusion and responsion, but both cantos of Lam. 3 are bound together by three ropes. Besides inclusion and responsion, concatenation is also present. This strongest coherence between both cantos must have been essential to the poets[24] and the dyptich—structure provides them with the literary possibilities to express this coherence.[25] Now a more detailed description of the concentric structure of Lamentations can be given. In this concentric structure, the two cantos of Lam. 3 appear to be the very tightly—knit kernel. This kernel is framed by Lam. 2 and 4 and these songs also function as a responsion. Lam. 1 and 5 bracket the booklet.

But as already said, this conclusion is tentative. To be sure, all connections between the five songs must be investigated, because it is possible that even stronger ones are present, which would indicate another layout of the booklet.

---

22 The kernel verses 3:17 and 3:50 are even double inclusions. They form an inclusion for the song but also for the booklet. For that reason they include the main theme of song and booklet. Cf. page 333.

23 Cf. the interconnections in the outline of Lam. 3, page 332.

24 Of course this is of important exegetical and theological interest. That others, who experience the same deepest suffering of the גבר, come to share his renewed trust in YHWH must be considered as the main purpose of the poets.

25 For Lam. 4 the diptych—structure indicates the strong coherence between the themes in this song and just that is confirmed by Lam. 2. Cf. for the fate of the children and the prophets Lam. 2:13f., and for the fate of the king and the nobles Lam. 2:9.

Connections between the other songs

Lam. 1 and 2

We began with an investigation of the relationship between Lam. 1 and 2. First we looked for exclusive similarities. The following were found:

(1:2aA)	(2:18bB) בלילה // ולילה
(1:2aA)	(2:19aA) בלילה // בליל
(1:2aB)	(2:11aA) ודמעתה // בדמעות
(1:2aB)	(2:18bA) ודמעתה // דמעה
(1:2bA)	(2:13bA) מה ...אנחמך // אין לה מנחם
(1:3bB)	// לא מצאה
	(2:16cB) לא מצאה \\ (2:9cA) מצאנו //
*(1:4aB)	(2:6bB) מועד // (2:6aB) מועדו // מועדו // מועד (4x)
	(2:22aA) מועד // (2:7cB) מועד //
(1:4aA)	(2:8cA) ויאבל־חל וחומה // דרכי ציון אבלות
(1:6bB)	(2:9cA) לא מצאה // לא מצאו
(1:6bB)	(2:16cB) מצאנו // לא מצאו
(1:7bA)	(2:4bB) כל מחמדי־עין // כל־מחמדיה
(1:8cB)	(2:3bA) השיב אחור // ותשב אחור
(1:9bB)	(2:13bA) מה ...אנחמך // אין לה מנחם
(1:10aB)	(2:4bB) כל מחמדי־עין // כל־מחמדיה
(1:10bB)	(2:7aB) מקדשו // במקדשה
(1:10bB)	(2:20cA) במקדש אדני // במקדשה
(1:11bA)	(2:4bB) כל מחמדי־עין // מחמודיהם
(1:12aA)	(2:15aB) כל־עברי דרך // כל־עברי דרך
(1:12bB)	(2:20aB)[26] למי עוללת כה // עולל לי
(1:13bB)	(2:3bA) השיב אחור // השיבני אחור
(1:14bA)	(2:10bA) העלו // עלו
(1:15bA)	(2:6bB) // (2:6aB) מועדו // מועדו // מועד (4x)
	מועד // (2:7cB) מועד // (2:22aA)
(1:16bA)	(2:13bA) מה ...אנחמך // כי־רחק ממני מנחם
(1:17aB)	(2:13bA) מה ...אנחמך // אין לה מנחם
(1:17bA)	(2:2aB,3cA) יעקב // יעקב
(1:17bB)	(2:3cB) סביב // סביביו
(1:17bB)	(2:22aB) מסביב // סביביו
(1:20aB)	(2:11aB) חמרמרו מעי // מעי חמרמרו
*(1:20cA)	(2:21cA) נפלו בחרב // שכלה־חרב
(1:21aB)	(2:13bA) מה ...אנחמך // אין מנחם לי
(1:21bB)	(2:17aA) עשה יהוה // כי אתה עשית

*(1:22aB)   ועולל // למי עוללת כה (2:20aB)²⁶
*(1:22bA)   עוללת // למי עוללת כה (2:20aB)

Together these exclusive similarities point to the main themes which both songs have in common: 1) the tears of Zion at night (1:2; 2:11,18f.); 2) nobody can comfort Zion (1:2,9,16,17,21; 2:13); 3) no sacred feast for Zion, but for her enemies (1:4,15; 2:6f.,22); 4) Jacob's enemies coming from every side (1:17; 2:3,22); 5) their treasures into the hand of the enemies (1:7,10,11; 2:40); YHWH gave them into the hand of their enemies (1:21,22; 2:17,20).

Besides these similarities, additional literary resemblances are present. Compare:

*(1:1aA)   איכה // איכה (2:1aA)
 (1:1aA)   ישבה // ישבו (2:10aA)
 (1:1aA)   הדאת העיר... // העיר רבתי עם (2:15cAB)
*(1:2aA)   בלילה // יעיב (2:1aA)
 (1:2cB)   לאיבים ... היו // כאויב ... היה (2:5aA)²⁷
*(1:3aA)   יהודה // יהודה (2:2bB)
*(1:3aA)   ישראל // יהודה (2:3aB)
*(1:4bA)   כל-שעריה שוממין // טבעו בארץ שעריה (2:9aA)
 (1:4bB)   כהניה נאנחים // ויגאץ...כהן (2:6cAB)
 (1:4cA)   // בתולתיה נוגות
     בתולת ירושלם ... הורידו (2:10cA)²⁸
 (1:5aA)   לראש // לראש (2:19aB)
 (1:5aAB)   איביה ... צריה // צריך...אויב (2:17cAB)
*(1:5cB)   לפני-צר // מפני אויב (2:3bB)
 (1:6aA)   // בת-ציון (6x)
     בת-ציון (2:1aB,4cA,8aB,10aB,13bB,18aB)
 (1:6bA)   שריה // ושריה (2:2cB,9bA)
 (1:6cB)   לפני רודף // מפני אויב (2:3bB)
 (1:7aA)   ירושלם // ירושלם (3) (2:10cB,13aB,15bB)²⁹
 (1:7bB)   מימי-קדם // מימי קדם (2:17bA)

---

26 The root עלל occurs also in 3:51, but only in 1:12,22 and 2:20 is YHWH subject.

27 א(ו)יב appears most in the first two songs, cf. 1:2,5,9,16,21; 2:3,4,5,6,16,22; 3:46,52; 4:12.

28 Besides 5:11 בתולה is only found in 1:4,15,18 and 2:10,13,21.

*(1:7cA)   ביד-אויב // ביד-צר (2:7bA)
(1:8aA)   ירושלם // ירושלם(2:10cB,13aB,15bB)[29]
(1:8bB)   ...ראינו // כי-ראו ערותה(2:16cB)
(1:9aB)   ולא-זכר // לא זכרה (2:1cA)
*(1:9bA)   הורידו לארץ // ותרד פלאים (2:10cA)
(1:10cA)   צוה // צויתה (2:17bA)
(1:11bB)   ... על-נפש ... // להשיב נפש (2:19cB)
(1:11cA)   // ראה יהוה והביטה
         ראה יהוה והביטה (2:20aA)
(1:12aB)   ראה ... והביטה // הביטו וראו (2:20aA)
(1:12cB)   ביום אפו // ביום חרון אפו (2:1cB)
(1:12cB)   בחרי-אף // חרון אפו (2:3aA)
(1:12cB)   בזעם-אפו // חרון אפו (2:6cA)
(1:12cB)   ביום אפך // ביום חרון אפו (2:21cA)
(1:12cB)   ביום אף-יהוה // ביום חרון אפו (2:22bA)
(1:13aA)   שפך כאש // ממרום שלח-אש (2:4cB)
(1:14cA)   ביד-אויב // נתנני אדני בידי (2:7bA)
(1:15bA)   תקרא כיום מועד // קרא עלי מועד (2:22aA)
(1:15bB)   בחורי נפלו בחרב // לשבר בחורי (2:21bB)
(1:16aB)   // עיני עיני ירדה מים
         הורידו כנחל דמעה (2:18bA)
(1:16bB)   ... על-נפש ... // משיב נפשי (2:19cB)
*(1:17bA)   צוה // צוה יהוה (2:17bA)
(1:17cA)   ירושלם // ירושלם (3x) (2:10cB,13aB,15bB)[29]
*(1:19bA)   כהן // כהני (2:20cB)
*(1:19cB)   ... על-נפש ... // ושיבו את-נפשם (2:19cB)
*(1:20cA)   שכבו לארץ חוצות // מחוץ שכלה-חרב (2:21aA)
*(1:20cA)   נפלו בחרב // שכלה-חרב (2:21bB)
*(1:20cB)   יהרג מקדש // בבות כמות (2:20cA)
(1:21bB)   עשה יהוה // כי עשית (2:17aA)
(1:22aA)   פני אדני // לפניך (2:19bB)

According to our criteria indicated in note 21, Lam. 1 and 2 show the same strong relationship as Lam. 1 and 5: the 134 bicola share 93 similarities, i.e. a ratio of 1.4 bicola per similarity. Any further conclusions cannot be drawn before we know how strongly the other songs are interconnected.

---

29 Besides 4:12 ירושלם is only found in 1:7,8,17 and 2:10,13,15.

Lam. 1 and 3

As for exclusive similarities between these two songs we found the following:

(1:1aA)	ישב בדד // ישבה בדד (3:28A)
(1:1aB)	רבה // רבתי (3:23B)
(1:1bB)	רבה // רבתי (3:23B)
(1:2aB)	לחי // לחיה (3:30A)
(1:3aB)	כרב // מרב (3:32B)
(1:4cA)	הוגה // בתולתיה נוגות (3:32A)
(1:4cA)	ויגה // בתולתיה נוגות (3:33A)
(1:5bA)	הוגה // כי־יהוה הוגה (3:32A)
(1:5bA)	ויגה // כי־יהוה הוגה (3:33A)
(1:5bA)	כרב // רב (3:32B)
(1:6aA)	אצא // ויצא (3:7A)
(1:6aA)	תצא // ויצא (3:38A)
*(1:7aAB)	זכרה ... עניה ומרודיה //
	זכר־עניי ומרודי (3:19A)
(1:8aA)	חטאו // חטא (3:38B)
*(1:8aB)	על־כן // על־כן (3:21B,24B)
(1:8bA)	הכביד // מכבדיה (3:7B)
(1:12bA)	יש // יש (3:29B)
*(1:12cA)	הוגה // הוגה יהוה (3:32A)
*(1:12cA)	ויגה // הוגה יהוה (3:33A)
(1:14aA)	על // על (3:27B)
(1:16aA)	אני // אני (3:1A,63B)
(1:18A)	(יהוה) הוא //(יהוה) הוא (3:10A)
(1:18aB)	מרינו // מריתי (3:42A)
*(1:18bA)	שמעת // שמעו־נא (2x) (3:56A,61A)
(1:20bB)	ומרינו // כי מרו מריתי (3:42A)
(1:20cB)	כמתי // כמות (3:6B)
*(1:21aA)	שמעת // שמעו (2x) (3:56A,61A)
*(1:21aA)	אני // אני (2x) (3:1A,63B)
(1:21bA)	רצות // רעתי (3:38B)
(1:22aA)	רצות // רעתם (3:38B)
(1:22cA)	רבה // רבות (3:23B)

Other similarities in speech are:

(1:2bA)	מאין הפגות // אין־לה מנחם (3:49B)
*(1:4aA)	גדר דרכי // דרכי ציון אבלות (3:9A)
*(1:4aA)	דרכי ציון אהלות //
	דרכי סורר ויפשחני שמני שמם (3:11AB)

(1:5cAB)	(3:2AB) וילך חשך ולא־אור // הלכו שבי
(1:6cA)	(3:2AB) וילך חשך ולא־אור // וילכו בלא־כח
*(1:7aA)	(3:19A) זכר // זכרה ירושלם
*(1:7aA)	(3:20A) זכור תזכור // זכרה ירושלם
(1:7cB)	(3:49B) מאין הפגות // אין עוזר לה
(1:8cB)	(3:3AB) בי ישוב...ידו // וחשב אחור
(1:9bB)	(3:49B) מאין הפגות // אין מנחם לה
(1:9cA)	// (3:36B) אדני לא ראה \\ ראה יהוה(4x)
	/ (3:50AB) עד ... וירא יהוה
	(3:59A,60A) ראיתה יהוה
(1:9cA)	(3:55A) קראתי שפך יהוה // ראה יהוה
(1:10cA)	(3:37B) (יהוה) צוה // (יהוה) צויתה
(1:11cB)	(3:14A) הייתי שחק // כי הייתי זוללה
*(1:11cA)	// (3:36B) אדני לא ראה \\ ראה יהוה (4x)
	/ (3:50AB) עד...ויאר יהוה
	(3:59A,60A) ראיתה יהוה
(1:11cA)	(3:55A) קראתי שמך יהוה // ראה יהוה
(1:11cA)	(3:63A) הביטה // הביטה
(1:11cB)	(3:14A) הייתי שחק // כי הייתי זוללה
(1:11cB)	(3:47A) פחד ופחת היה לנו // כי הייתי זוללה
(1:13aB)	(3:4B) עצמתי // בעצמתי
(1:13bB)	(3:3AB) בי ישוב...ידו // השיבני אחור
(1:13cA)	(3:11B) שמני שמם // נתנני שממה
(1:13cB)	(3:3B,14B,62B) כל־היום // כל־היום (3x)
(1:14aB)	(3:3B) ידו // בידי
(1:15aAB)	(3:31AB) לא יזנח...אדני \\ סלה...אדני
(1:15bB)	(3:4B) שבר עצמתי // לשבר בחוני
*(1:16aB)	// עיני עיני ירדה מים
	(3:48A) פלגי־מים תרד עיני
*(1:16bA)	(3:49B) מאין הפגות // כי־רהק ממני מנחם
(1:16cA)	(3:11B) שמני שמם // היו בני שוממים
*(1:17aB)	(3:49B) מאין הפגות // אין מנחם לה
(1:17bA)	(3:37B) אדני לא צוה \\ צוה יהוה
(1:17cAB)	(3:14A) הייתי שחק // היתה ...לנידה
(1:18cB)	(3:2AB) וילך חשך ולא־אור // הלכו בבי
*(1:20aA)	/ (3:36B) אדני לא ראה \\ ראה יהוה (4x)
	/ (3:50AB) עד...וירא יהוה
	(3:59A,60A) ראיתה יהוה
*(1:20aA)	(3:55A) קראתי שמך יהוה // ראה יהוה
(1:20bA)	(3:21A) לבי // לבי
(1:20bA)	(3:3AB) בי...נהפך ידי // נחפך לבי בקרבי
(1:21aB)	(3:49B) מאין הפגות // אין מנחם לי

(1:21bA)	ששו...איבי-כל // איבינו-כל פיהם...פצו (3:46AB)
(1:21bB)	אחה (יהוה) // אתה (יהוה) (3:42B)
*(1:22aA)	חבא כל-רעתם לפניך // חשיב להם גמול יהוה (3:64A)
(1:22aA)	נגד פני נליון // לפניך (3:35B)
*(1:22cB)	מגנת-לב // לבי דוי (3:65A)

Especially the exclusive similarities indicate the themes shared by Lam. 1 and 3: 1) loneliness (1:1; 3:28); 2) being oppressed by YHWH (1:4,5,12; 3:32,33); 3) the remembering of misery and wandering (1:7; 3:3:19,20); 4) the rebellion against his commands (1:18,20; 3:42). The 133 bicola of both songs share 83 similarities, i.e. a ratio of 1.6 bicola per similarity.

Lam. 1 and 4

The following exclusive similarities between these two songs are found:

(1:3aA)	גלחה // גלה (4:22bB)
(1:10aA)	פרש // פרש (4:4bB)
*(1:12cB)	חרון אפו // חרון אפו (4:11aB)
(1:13bA)	פרש // פרש (4:4bB)
*(1:14cB)	לא-אוכל // בלא יוכלו (4:14bA)
(1:17aA)	פרשה // פרש (4:4bB)
(1:18aA)	צדיק // צדיקים (4:13bB)
*(1:21bA)	ששו // שישי (4:21aA)
(1:21cB)	כמוני // כמו (4:6bA)

Other similarities are:

*(1:1aA)	איכה // איכה (2x) (4:1aA,2bA)
(1:1bB)	בגוים // בגוים (2x) (4:15bB,20bB)
(1:2bA)	אין-לה מנחם // אין פרש להם (4:4bB)
(1:3bA)	בגוים // בגוים (2x) (4:15bB,20bB)
(1:3cA)	כל-רדפיה השיגוה // קלים היו רדפינו (4:19aA)
(1:4bA)	כל-שעריה שוממין // צר ואויב בשערי (4:12bAB)
(1:4bB)	כהניה // כהניה (4:13aB)
(1:5aA)	הין צריה לראש // צר ... בשערי ירושלם (4:12bAB)
(1:5aA)	הין צריה לראש // קלים היו רדפינו (4:19aA)
(1:5aB)	אויב בשערי ירושלם // איביה שלו (4:12bAB)
*(1:5cA)	עוללים // עולליה (4:4bA)
(1:5cA)	מלכת // הכלו שבי (4:18aB)

(1:6aA)	בת־ציון // בת־ציון (4:22aA)
(1:6bA)	(4:19aA) קלים היו רדפינו // היו שריה כאילים
(1:6cA)	(4:18aB) מלכח // וילכו בלא־כח
(1:6cA)	(4:19aA) קלים היו רדפינו // וילכו בלא־כח
(1:7cA)	// בנפל עמה ביד־צר
	(4:12bAB) צר ... בשערי ירושלם
(1:7cB)	(4:4B) אין פרש להם // אין עוזר לה
(1:9bB)	(4:4bB) אין פרש להם // אין מנחם לה
(1:9cB)	// כי הגדיל אויב
	(4:12bAB) אויב בשערי ירושלם
*(1:10bB)	(4:12bAB) יבא ...בשערי ירושלם // באו במקדשה
(1:11aB)	(4:4bA) שאלו לחם // מבקשים לחם
(1:11cA)	(4:16aB) לא יוסיף להביטם // יהוה הביטה
*(1:13aA)	(4:11bA) ויצת־אש בציון // שלח־אש
(1:13aB)	(4:7bA) עצם // בעצמתי
(1:13aB)	(4:8bA) עצמם // בעצמתי
(1:13cA)	(4:5aB) נשמו בחוצות // נתנני שממה
*(1:15aB)	(4:13bA) בקרבה // בקרבי
*(1:16aB)	(4:17aA) עינינו // עיני עיני
(1:16bB)	(4:4bB) אין פרש להם // כי־רחק ממני מנחם
(1:16cA)	(4:2aB) בני ציון...נבלי־חרש // היו בני שממים
(1:16cA)	(4:5aB) נשמו בחוצות // היו בני שממים
(1:16cB)	(4:12bAB) אויב בשערי ירושלם // כי גבר אויב
(1:17aB)	(4:4bB) אין פדש להם // אין מנחם לה
(1:17cAB)	// ירושלם לנידה
	(4:12bAB)³⁰ אויב בשערי ירושלם
*(1:18cB)	(4:18aB) מלכח // הלכו בשבי
(1:19bA)	(4:13aB) כהניה כהני
(1:19bA)	(4:16bB) זקנים לא חננו // ודקני...
(1:20bA)	(4:6bA) ההפוכה // נהפך לבי
(1:20bA)	(4:13bA) בקרבה // בקרבי
(1:20cA)	(4:5aB) בחוצות // מחוץ
(1:20cA)	(4:9aA) חללי־חרב // שכלה־חרב
(1:21aB)	(4:4bB) אין פרש להם // אין מנחם לי
(1:21bA)	// כל־איבי שמעו רעתי ששו
	(4:12aA) לא האמינו מלכי־ארץ
(1:21cA)	(4:18bB)³¹ כי־בא קצינו // הבאת יום־קראת
(1:21cA)	(4:18bB)³¹ מלאו ימינו // יום־קראת

---

30 Cf. 1:10.
31 Cf. n.4.

(4:16aA) פני יהוה // לפניך   (1:22aA)

The exclusive similarities reveal some common themes of these two songs: 1) uncovering (because of sin) (1:3; 4:22); 2) the burning anger of the Lord (1:12; 4:11); 3) the joy of the enemies (1:21; 4:21). The 111 bicola share 55 similarities, i.e. a 2 to 1 ratio.

Lam. 2 and 3

The following exclusive similarities between these two songs were found:

(2:2aA)	(3:43B) לא חמלת // לא חמל
*(2:2bA)	(3:1B) עברתו // בעברתו
*(2:4aA)	(3:12A) דרך קשתו // דרך קשתו
*(2:4aB)	(3:12A) ויציהני // נצב
(2:4bA)	(3:43B) הרגת // ויהרג
(2:7aA)	(3:17A) \\ ותזנח // זנח אדני (2x)
	(3:31A) לא יזנח אדני
(2:7aA)	(3:56A) קולי שמעת \\ קול נתנו בבית-יהוה
(2:8bA)	(3:35A) להטות // נטה
*(2:10aA)	(3:28A) וידם // וידמו
*(2:10bA)	(3:29A) עפר // עפר
*(2:15aA)	(3:41A) כפים // כפים
(2:15cA)	(3:21A) זאת / הזאת
*(2:16aAB)	(3:46AB) // פצו עליך פיהם כל-אויביך
	פצו עלינו פיהם כל-אויבינו
(2:16bA)	(3:16A) שני // שן
(2:16cA)	(3:3A) אך // אך
(2:16cA)	(3:25A) לקוו \\ שקוינהו
(2:17bB)	(3:43B) לא חמלת // לא המל
*(2:18cB)	(3:49A) לא תדמה // אל-תדם
(2:18cB)	(3:28A) וידם \\ אל-תדם
(2:19cA)	(3:41A) כפים // כפיך
(2:20cA)	(3:43B) הרגת // יהרג

Other similarities are:

(2:1bA)	(3:50B) משמים // משמים
(2:1aA)	(3:43A) // סכתה באף // יעיב באפו (2x)
	(3:66A) באף
(2:3aA)	(3:43A) // סכתה באף // בחרי-אף (2x)
	(3:66A) באף

(2:5cB)	(3:47A) פחד ופחת // תאניה ואניה
(2:6cA)	(3:43A) / סכתה באף // בזעם-אפו (2x) / (3:66A) באף
(2:7bA)	(3:64B) מעשה ידיהם // ביד-אויב
(2:8bB)	(3:3B) ידו // ידו
(2:8bA)	(3:3A) אך בי ישב // לא-השיב
(2:9aB)	(3:4B) שבר // שבר
(2:10bA)	(3:54A) על-ראשי // על-ראשם
(2:11aA)	(3:49A) כלו בדמעות עיני // עיני נגרה ולא תדמה
(2:11bB)	(3:47B,48B) על-שבר // על-שבר (2x)
(2:11bB)	(3:48B) בת-עמי // בת-עמי
(2:12bB)	(3:51B)[32] כל בנות עירי // ... עיר
*(2:13aA,bA)	(3:39A) ... מה יתאונן // מה
(2:13cA)	(3:47B,48B) על-שבר // שברך (2x)
*(2:14bA)	(3:39B) על-חטאו // על-עונך
*(2:15cAB)	(3:45AB) \\ כלילת יפי משוש לכל-הארץ סחי ומאוס תשימנו בקרב העמים
(2:15cB)	(3:18A) ואמר אבד נצחי // שיאמרו כלילת יפי
(2:16aA)	(3:61A) שמעת הרפתם יהוה // פצו עליך פיהם
(2:16bB)	(3:54B) אמרתי נגזרתי // אמרו בלענו
(2:16bc)	(3:61B) כל מחשבתם עלי // אמרו...
(2:17cA)	(3:14A) הייתי שחק // וישמח עליך אויב
(2:17cA)	(3:14B) / נגינתם // וישמח עליך אויב (3:63B) אני מנגינתם
(2:18aA)	(3:41A) לבבנו // לבם
(2:18bA)	(3:48A) תרד עיני // הורידי כנחל
(2:18bA)	(3:48A) פלגי-מים // כנהל דמעה
(2:18cB)	(3:48A) אל-תדם בת-עינך // פלגי-מים תרד עיני
(2:19bA)	(3:41A) לבבנו // לבך
(2:19bB)	(3:35B) נגד פני עליון // נכח פני אדני
(2:19cA)	(3:41A) נשא // שאי
*(2:20aA)	(3:36B) / אדני לא ראה \\ ראה יהוה (4x) / (3:50AB) עד ... וירא יהוה (3:59A,60A) ראיתה יהוה
*(2:20aA)	(3:58A) רבת אדני // ראה יהוה
*(2:20aA)	(3:63A) הביטה // והביטה

---

32 Cf. אל-חיק אמחם, 2:12cB.

(2:20bA)	אם־תאכלנה נשים פרים //
	כל בנות עירי (3:51B)
(2:21cA)	הרגת // הרגת (3:43B)
*(2:21cA)	סכמה באף // ביום אפך (2x) (3:43A) //
	באף (3:66A)
(2:21cB)	לא חמלת // לא חמלת (3:43B)
(2:22aB)	צוד צדוני כצפור // מגורי מסביב (3:52A)
*(2:22bA)	סכמה באף // אף־יהוה (2x) (3:43A) /
	באף (3:66A)
(2:22bAB)	צמתו בבור חי // לא...פליט ושריד (3:53A)

Already the exclusive similarities indicate the themes shared by both songs: 1) the Lord in his anger was without pity (2:2; 3:43); 2) YHWH as a fighting and killing warrior (2:4; 3:12,43) 3) rejection by the Lord (2:7; 3:17,31); 4) the jeers of the enemy (2:16; 3:46); 5) raising the hands in prayer (2:19; 3:41). Together the 133 bicola share 74 similarities, i.e. a 1.8 to 1 ratio.

Lam. 2 and 5

These two songs share only a few exclusive similarities. Compare:

(2:6bA)	למה לנצח תשכחנו // שכח יהוה (5:20A)
(2:12aA,cB)	אמחם // אמתינו (5:3B)
*(2:15cB)	שבת משוש לבנו // משוש לכל־הארץ (5:15A)
(2:21aB)	נערים // נער (5:13B)

However, they reveal two essential themes of the booklet: 1. being forgotten by YHWH, and 2. the loss of joy. Both themes remind of the kernel verse 3:17.[33] But more similarities are present:

*(2:1cA)	זכר יהוה // (אדני) ולא־זכר (5:1A)
(2:2cB)	שרים...נתלו // ...שריה (5:12A)
(2:3bB)	מפני חרב // מפני אויב (5:9B)
(2:4bB)	חשכו עינינו // ויהרג כל מחמדי־עין (5:17B)
(2:3aA)	קצפת עד־מאד // בחרי־אף (5:22B)

---

33 שכח can be read as a synonym of נשה, cf. Deut. 32:18, GK § 75s and *HAL* 688.

(2:6bA)	בציון // בציון (5:11A)
(2:6cA)	קצפת עד־מאד // זעם־אפו (5:22B)
*(2:7bA)	פרק אין מידם // ביד־אויב (5:8B)
(2:7bA)	שרים בידם נתלו // ביד־אויב (5:12A)
(2:7cA)	הר־ציון // בית־יהוה (5:18A)
(2:9aA)	זקנים משער // טבעו ...שעריה (5:14A)
(2:9bB)	אין אב // אין תורה (5:3A)
*(2:9bB)	אבחינו ...אינם // אין תורה (5:7A)
*(2:10aAB)	זקנים // ...ידמו זקני (5:12B)
(2:10aAB)	זקנים // ...ידמו זקני (5:14A)
(2:10bA)	// העלו עפר על־ראשם
	נפלה עטרת ראשנו (5:16A)
(2:10cA)	// הורידו לארץ ראשן
	נפלה עטרת ראשנו (5:16A)
*(2:10cB)	בחלח // בתולח (5:11B)
(2:11aA)	חשכו עינינו // כלו ... עיני (5:17B)
(2:14bA)	חטאו // עונך (5:7A)
(2:14bA)	עונתיהם // עונך (5:7B)
*(2:14bA)	חטאנו // עונך (5:16B)
(2:13ab)	מה היה לנו // מה... (5:1A)
(2:15cA)	ששמם // שיאמרו (5:18A)
(2:17bA)	ימינו כקדם // מימי־קדם (5:21B)
*(2:18aA)	דוה לבנו // צעק לבם (5:17A)
(2:18aA)	אליך // אל־אדני (5:21A)
*(2:18cB)	חשכו עינינו // אל־חדם בת־עיניך (5:17B)
*(2:19cA)	אליך // אלו (5:21A)
(2:19dA)	רעב // ברעב (5:10B)
(2:20aA)	יהוה...וראה // ראה יהוה (5:1AB)
(2:20aA)	הביט // הביטה (5:1B)
(2:20bA)	נשים // נשים (5:11A)
(2:21aAB)	זקנים // שכבו לארץ...זקן (2x) (5:12B,14A)
(2:21bA)	בחלח // בתולחי (5:11B)
(2:21bA)	בחורים // בחורי (2x) (5:13A,14B)
(2:21bB)	חרב // חרב (5:9B)
*(2:21cA)	קצפת // שפך (5:22B)
*(2:21bA)	קצפת // אף־יהוה (5:22B)

The 88 bicola of both songs share 45 similarities, i.e. a ratio of 2 to 1.

Lam. 3 and 4

The following exclusive similarities between both songs were found:

(3:10A)	במדבר ארבו לנו // דב ארב הוא לי	(4:19bB)
(3:11A)	סורו // סורר (3x)	(4:15aAB)
(3:17B)	ישנא הכחם הטוב // נשיתי טובה	(4:1aAB)
(3:22A)	חם עונך בת־ציון // כי לא־תמנו	(4:22aA)
*(3:52A)	צדו // צוד צדוני	(4:18aA)
(3:53B)	חשתפכנה אבני־קדש // וידו־אבן בי	(4:1bA)
(3:57A)	קרב קצנו \\ קרבת	(4:18bA)
(3:64B)	מעשה ידי // מעשה ידיהם	(4:2bB)
(3:64A,65A)	להם // להם	(4:4bB)

Themes in common are: 1. the enemy lies in wait (3:10; 4:19); and 2. the loss of the good things (3:17; 4:1).

Other similarities are:

(3:2A)	מלכח // וילך	(4:18aB)
*(3:2B)	יועם זהב ישנא // חשך ולא־אוד	(4:1aA)
(3:2B)	חשך // חשך	(4:8aA)
(3:3A)	ההפוכה // יהפך	(4:6bA)
*(3:4B)	לנבלי־חרש // שבר	(4:2bA)
(3:4B)	עצמם // (4:7bA) עצם // עצמותי (2x)	(4:8bA)
(3:4A)	צפד עורם // בלה ...עורי	(4:8bA)
*(3:11B)	נשמו בחוצות // שמני שמם	(4:5aB)
(3:13AB)	הביא בכליותי בני אשפתו // יבא צר ואויב	(4:12bA)
(3:13AB)	הביא בכליותי בני אשפתו // כי בא קצנו	(4:18bB)
*(3:15A)	האכלים למעדנים \\ השביעני במרורים	(4:5aA)
*(3:15B)	דבק לשון // הרוני לענה	(4:4aA)
*(3:16A)	הבקו אשפתות // ויגרס בהצץ שני	(4:5bB)
*(3:16B)	הבקו אשפתות // הכפישני באפר	(4:5bB)
(3:18A)	חשך משחור // אבד נצחי	(4:8aA)
(3:18A)	צפד עורם // אבד נצחי	(4:8bA)
(3:22B)	כלה יהוה את־חמתו // לא־כלו רחמיו	(4:11aA)
*(3:31A)	כלה יהוה את־חמתו // לא ידנח לעולם	(4:11aA)
(3:33B)	בני ציון // בני־איש	(4:2aA)
*(3:34B)	ארץ / כל...חבל // כל...ארץ	(4:12aAB)
(3:35B)	פני יהוה // פני עליון	(4:16aA)
*(3:42A)	בלא יוכלו... // נחנו פשענו ומרינו	(4:14bA)

(3:43A)	(4:11aB) שפך חרון אפו // סכחה באף
(3:43A)	(4:19aA) רדפינו // תרדפנו
*(3:45A)	// סחי ומאוט תשימנו
	(4:16bAB) פני כהנים לא נשאו זקנים לא חננו
(3:46B)	(4:12bA) צר ואויב // כל־איבינו
(3:47B)	(4:10bB) שבר // השבר
(3:48B)	(4:3bA,6aA) בת־עמי // בת־עמי (2x)
(3:48B)	(4:10bB) בשבר בת־עמי // על־שבר בת־עמי
*(3:49A)	(4:17aA) תכלינה עינינו // עיני ...לא תדמה
*(3:49B)	(4:17aA) עודינה // מאין הפגות
*(3:51A)	(4:17aA) תכלינה עינינו // עיני עוללה לנפשי
(3:51B)	(4:10aA) נשים // בנות עירי
*(3:52A)	(4:19aB) מנשרי שמים // כצפור
(3:52B)	(4:12bA) צר ואויב // איבי
*(3:53A)	(4:18bA) קרב קצנו // צמחו בבור חיי
*(3:54B)	(4:18bB) מלאו ימינו // אמרתי נגזרתי
*(3:61A)	(4:21aA) שישי ושמחי בת־אדום // שמעת חרפתם
(3:63A)	(4:16aB) לא יוסיף להביטם \\ הביטה
*(3:63B)	(4:21aA) שישי ושמחי בת־אדום // אני מנגינתם
*(3:64A)	(4:21bA) גם־עליך תעבר־כוס // תשיב להם גמול
(3:64B)	(4:6bB) ידים // ידיהם
*(3:65A)	// תתן להם מגנת־לב
	(4:21bAB) תעבר־כוס תשכרי ותתערי
*(3:65B)	(4:22bA) פקד עונך // תאלחך להם
(3:66A)	(4:19aA) רדפינו // תרדף
(3:66A)	(4:11aB) שפך חרון אפו // באף
(3:66B)	(4:19aAB) (רדפינו)...שמים // (תרדף)...שמי

Together the 110 bicola share 58 similarities, i.e. a ratio of 1.9 to 1.

Lam. 3 and 5

The following exclusive similarities are present:

(3:6B)	(5:19A) עולם // עולם
(3:14B)	(5:14B) מגונתם // (מ) נגינתם
*(3:15A)	(5:6B) לשבע // השביעני
(3:18A)	(5:20A) לנצח // נצחי
(3:30B)	(5:6B) לשבע // ישבע
(3:30B)	(5:1B) חרפתנו // חרפה
(3:31A)	(5:19A) עולם // עולם
*(3:33A)	(5:11A) ענו // ענה

(3:40B)	עד // עד (5:22B)
(3:50A)	עד // עד (5:22B)
(3:61A)	חרפתנו // חרפתם (5:1B)
(3:63B)	מנגינתם // מנגינתם (5:14B)

The themes in common are: 1) doom for ever? (3:6; 5:19); 2) being scorned (3:61; 5:1).

Other similarities are:

*(3:1A)	ראה את־חרפתנו // ראה עני (5:1B)
*(3:3A)	נהפכה // נהפך (5:2A)
(3:3A)	נהפך // נהפך (5:15B)
(3:4A)	עורנו ...נכמרו // בלה עורי (5:10A)
(3:6B)	תעזבנו לארך ימים // כמתי עולם (5:20B)
(3:6B)	קצפת עלינו עד־מאד // כמתי עולם (5:22B)
(3:14A)	חרפתנו // שחק (5:1B)
(3:18AB)	אבד...תוחלתי מיהוה // קצפת עלינו עד־מאד (5:22B)
(3:21A)	לבנו // לבי (2x) (5:15A,17A)
(3:26B)	חדש ימינו כקדם // לתשועת יהוה (5:21B)
(3:27B)	טהוך נשאו // ישא על (5:13A)
(3:27B)	נערים // בנעוריו (5:13B)
(3:29B)	אולי יש תקוה // כי אם ... קצפת עלינו עד־מאד (5:22B)
(3:36B)	ראה את־חרפתנו // אדני לא ראה (5:1B)
(3:39A)	מה היה לנו // מה יתאונן (5:1A)
(3:39B)	חטאנו / (5:7A) חטאו // על־חטאו (2x) (5:16B)
(3:40B)	השיבנו יהוה אליך // נשובה עד־יהוה (5:21A)
(3:40B)	ונשוב // נשובה עד־יהוה (5:21A)
(3:41A)	לבנו // לבבנו (2x) (5:15A,17A)
(3:42A)	נחנו פשענו ומרינו // חטאנו / (5:7A) חטאו (2x) (5:16B)
(3:42B)	אתה // אתה (5:19A)
(3:45A)	מאס מאסתנו // מאוס (5:22A)
(3:45A)	חרפתנו // סחי ומאוס (5:1B)
(3:43A)	נרדפנו // תרדפנו (5:5A)
(3:47A)	אין אב // פחד ופחת (2x) (5:3A) // אבותנו...אינם (5:7A)
(3:47A)	היה לנו // היה לנו (5:1A)
*(3:48A)	חשכו עינינו // ...תרד עיני (5:17B)
*(3:49A)	חשכו עינינו // עיני נגרה (5:17B)
(3:50A)	עד־מאד // עד־ישקיף (5:22B)
(3:50AB)	יהוה ...וראה // עד...וירא יהוה (5:1AB)

*(3:51A)   (5:17B) עיניני // עיני
(3:51B)   (5:11B) בערי // עירי
(3:54A)   (5:16A) נפלה עטרת ראשנו // צפו־מים על־ראשי
(3:55A)   (5:1A) זכר יהוה // קראתי שמך יהוה
*(3:55A)   (5:19A) אתה יהוה // קראתי שמך יהוה
(3:58A)   (5:9A) בנפשנו // נפשי
(3:59A)   (5:1AB) יהוה ...וראה // ראיתה יהוה
(3:60A)   (5:1AB) יהוה ...וראה // ראיתה
(3:60A)   (5:8B) פרק אין מידם // נקמחם
(3:62A)   (5:1B) חרפתנו // הגיונם
(3:63A)   (5:1B) הביט // הביטה
(3:63B)   (5:1B) חרפתנו // מנגינחם
(3:64B)   (5:8B) פרק אין מידם // מעשה ידיהם
(3:64B)   (5:12A) שרים בידם נתלו // מעשה ידיהם

Together the 88 bicola share 61 similarities, i.e. a ratio of 1.4 to 1.

Lam. 4 and 5

These songs share the following exclusive similarities:

(4:3bB)   (5:9B) מדבר // מדבר
(4:8aA)   (5:17B) חשכו // חשך
(4:8bB)   (5:13B) עץ / (5:4B) עצינו // עץ (2x)
*(4:19bA)   (5:18A) הר // הרים
(4:19bB)   (5:9B) מדבר // מדבר

On the basis of these similarities it is not possible to indicate themes in common. הר seems to be a keyword. Nevertheless both songs do have a lot of similarities. Compare:

Other similarities:

*(4:1bA)   (5:2A) נהפכה // תשחפכנה
*(4:1bA)   (5:1B) חרפתנו // תשחפכנה אבני־קדש
(4:2aA)   (5:11A) // נשים בציון // בני ציון (2x)
        (5:18A) הר־ציון
*(4:2bA)   (5:1B) חרפתנו // נחשבו לנבלי־חרש
*(4:3aB)   (5:3A) יתומים \\ גורייהן
*(4:4aA)   (5:4A) מימינו // דבק לשון
(4:4bA)   (5:9A) לחמו // לחם (5:6B) // לחם (2x)
*(4:4bB)   (5:3A) // אין אב // פרש אין להם (2x)
        (5:7A) אבותנו ... אינם

*(4:5bB)	(5:4B) עצינו // אשפתות
*(4:6aA)	(5:7B) עון בת-עמי // עונתיהם
*(4:6aA)	(5:7A) // עון בת-עמי // חטאו (2x) // (5:16B) חטאנו
(4:6bA)	(5:15B) ההפוכה // נהפכה (5:2A) // נהפך (2x)
(4:6bB)	(5:8B) ולא-חלו בה ידים \\ פרק אין מידם
(4:6bB)	(5:12A) ולא-חלו בה ידים \\ שרים בידם נתלו
(4:8bA)	(5:10A) צפד עורם // נכמרו ... עורנו
*(4:9aA)	(5:9B) חללי-חרב // מפני חרב
*(4:9aB)	(5:10B) רעב // רעב
*(4:10aA)	(5:11A) נשים // נשים
(4:10aA)	(5:6A) ידי נשים ... // ... נתנו יד
*(4:10aB)	(5:10B) בשלו ילדיהן // מפני זלעפות רעב
(4:10bA)	(5:1A) היה ל // היה ל
*(4:11bA)	(5:10B) אש ... מאכל // זלעפות רעב
(4:11bA)	(5:18A) בציון // בציון (5:11A) // הר-ציון (2x)
*(4:12bB)	(5:14A) בשערי // משער
(4:13aA)	(5:16B) מחטאת // חטאו (5:7A) // חטאנו (2x)
(4:13aB)	(5:7B) עונות // עונתיהם
(4:13aB)	(5:16B) עונות // חטאו (5:7A) // חטאנו (2x)
*(4:14bA)	(5:16B) בלא יוכלו // חטאנו
(4:16bB)	(5:12B) זקנים לא חננו // פני זקנים לא נהדרו
*(4:16bB)	(5:14A) זקנים לא חננו // זקנים משער שבתו
(4:16aB)	(5:1B) לא יוסיף להביטם // הביט
(4:16bAB)	(5:12B) פני ... זקנים // פני זקנים
(4:16bA)	(5:13A) נשאו // נשאו
*(4:17aA)	(5:17B) תכלינה עינינו // חשכו עינינו
(4:18bB)	(5:17B) מלאו ימינו \\ חדש ימינו
(4:19aA)	(5:5A) רדפינו // נרדפנו
(4:22aA)	(5:7B) עונך // עונתיהם
(4:22aA)	(5:16B) עונך // חטאו (5:7A) // חטאנו (2x)
(4:22aA)	(5:18A) בת-ציון // הר-ציון

The 66 bicola of both songs share 53 similarities, i.e. a ratio of
1.3. to 1.

The following outline makes it possible to take in everything at
a glance:

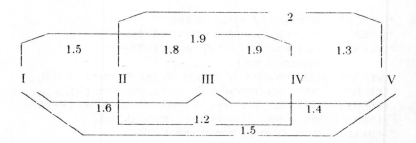

Conclusions

1. Our tentative conclusion concerning the concentric structure of the book of Lamentations can be confirmed. It appears that the second and the fourth song are most strongly connected. In view of the other connections the inclusion between the first and the last song is also a strong one. The central position of the third song appears from the almost equal distances between 3 and 2 and 3 and 4, which is about the same as the distance between 1 and 4 and 2 and 5. Besides 1 and 2 are also strongly connected, as are 4 and 5. So one could say that Lam. 3 is included by two blocks, i.e. Lam. 1+2 and Lam. 4+5. But aside from this concentric structure, a subdivision seems to be present. According to the figures a stronger coherence also exists between 3 and 5 (the two songs which bracket the fourth song) than exists between 3 and 1. In view of the strong coherence between 1 and 2, and between 4 and 5, it seems justified to consider 1 and 2 as a unity and 3—5 as another unity. There is another argument for such a division. Lam. 1 and 2 have 134 bicola. The sum of the bicola of Lam. 3—5 is 132. So this division balances the content of the booklet well and it reveals a reversed qinah—pattern.

2. It must be stressed that the figures obtained above are relative. They by no means justify an assumption that some of these poems have once been independent. To the contrary, in fact, the proportion of at least one similarity to two bicola indicates already a very close relationship, which never would have been obtained if these songs were versified by different poets in different times. The figures point to some centers in an already very coherent unity. This relationship appears of course

also from other peculiar features they share, such as the alphabetic acrostic, the qinah—metre, the other variations on its 3+2 structure, the same structure of cantos and subcantos and the repetition of themes and speech.[34]

It has been assumed that the final unity of the book of Lamentations must be ascribed to the editorial work of a deuteronomistic redaction. For various reasons this is not likely. The alphabetic acrostics are very unsuitable for reworking. Besides, our structure—analysis shows well—balanced literary units. Reworking would have certainly destroyed such balance. Furthermore, the coherence in theme and speech is clear and another, redactional theme would be striking. Clear literary incisions are not present. If these poems were adapted, the redactors must be considered as their poets. In that case it is not likely they were from the deuteronomistic school since language and themes of deuteronomistic theology are absent.[35]

---

34 Of course these repetitions are deliberate; people who mourn reiterate their lament.

35 Because of literary similarities Albrektson: 1963:231—237, assumes deuteronomic influence in Lamentations. A closer examination of the parallels he cites reveals, however, that his proof for a relationship between Lamentations and the deuteronomic school is far from convincing. Many of the literary parallels Albrekston adduces are not exclusive. They are also found in other parts of the Old Testament. Moreover, the majority of his parallels is taken from Deut. 28, a chapter which underwent a drastic deuteronomistic redaction. Most of the texts cited by Albrekston are precisely from these redactionally expanded passages. Uncritically Brandscheidt: 1983:210f., takes over this result of Albrektson, adding an argument of her own. Correctly she points to the influence of prophetic traditions in Lamentations. But, because these traditions are reworked by the deuteronomistic school, she concludes Lamentations must also have undergone deuteronomistic influence. This is too simple. In fact one clear literary parallel between Deuteronomy and Lamentations is present: Deut. 23:2—4 is cited in Lam. 1:10. But note that G. von Rad *Das fünfte Buch Mose* (ATD 8; Göttingen, 1968[2]) 104, regarding Deut. 23:2 ff., speaks of 'ein prächtiges Stück altjahwistischen Sakralrechtes' that is preserved here. He also points to the cultic—ritual context. This is in accordance with the upbringing of the poets of Lamentations, who like to speak, in view of sin, in terms of ritual impurity and that is not at all deuteronomistic. Even the dtr. main sin of idolatry is not clearly mentioned in Lamentations. More on the subject in Renkema: 1983:20—31; 201—213; 260—261.

3. However, another, far more important argument is present for the coherence of all five songs. We started this part of our investigation with the question whether additional similarities such as the metaphor of the widow, which 1:1 and 5:3 have in common, are present. Not all the similarities we found have such a close relationship. Similarities also arose in the diction used by the poets to describe downfall. But not every similarity can be explained in this way. Some similarities are certainly placed deliberately at special places in the songs. So we found a cross—connection between Lam. 1 and 2. The start of the second canto of Lam. 1 has the root עלל (1:12bB) and this is also found at the end of the second canto in the second song (1:20aB). The same cross—connection is found between the start of the second canto of Lam. 2 and the end of the second canto of Lam. 1 by means of חמרמרו מעי // חמרמרו מעי (1:20aB) // מעי חמרמרו (2:11aB).[36] But there seems to be something more important. During our investigation we noted a lot of traverse connections on the same level in the compared songs, as was already the case with the metaphor of the widow and we marked them with an asterisk. However, if we look at the same level of all songs in Lam. 1—5 *it appears that often more than two and sometimes all the songs, show interconnections,* indicated by words and thought. In fact this is the same phenomenon as noted in our analysis of Lam. 3, where the opposite strophes of the dyptich show the same relationship. In my opinion this technique is used by the poets on the level of all the songs. We will indicate some of this in an appendix. See below. All these interconnections permit the conclusion that the poets versified the strophes of each song with an eye to the strophes on the same or the nearest level in the other songs. For that reason again it becomes highly unlikely that in the case of Lamentations we are dealing with, to a certain amount, independent songs, versified in different times by different poets. It is far more likely that we are dealing with a well—thought—out composition. Because theology depends on

---

36 The same is found in the first cantos of Lam. 1 and 2: ישבה (1:1aA) // ישבו (2:10aA) and תפארת (2:1bB) // מחמודיהם (1:11bA). See also the use of the root שפך in Lam. 2 and 4 and the embracing function of the kernel verses in Lam. 4. Certainly there will be more of this.

dialogue it is possible that numerous poets contributed to the composition of Lamentations. In that case they have done so at the same time, in careful teamwork.

4. These interconnections reveal another feature. The outline of both cantos in Lam. 3 has been used as a model to outline the other songs, with complaints in the first, larger part, followed by confessions of confidence and prayers with pleas at the end.

5. A final conclusion can be drawn. It appears that the literary techniques such as concentric structuring by means of inclusions, responsions, common external parallelism, or concatenation are applied by the poets on the level of a small unit like a strophe, but also on the level of all higher units, including the booklet itself.

This is in accordance with the character of Hebrew poetry, which has been typified as a breathing universe, expanding and contracting according to the mood of the singers.[37]

In view of Lamentations one could say that these temple—singers in their ruined city, broken as wide as the sea (2:13), have taken a very deep breath and expanded their deepest feeling, that all good things of former times have been forgotten until the Lord looks again after them (Lam. 3:17,50), to one of the biggest songs of the Old Testament, as an everlasting monument of all their real sorrows, pain and fear, pleas, prayers and patience and despite this all, of their renewed trust in YHWH.

---

37 M.C.A. Korpel—J.C. de Moor, 'Fundamentals of Ugaritic and Hebrew Poetry', *UF* 18 (1986) 173ff.

Appendix[1]

Lam. 1 1–3	Lam. 2 1–3	Lam. 3 1–3	Lam. 4 1–3	Lam. 5 1–3
עיר רבתי עם	בת־ציון ---	אני ----	בני־ציון --	לנו -----
		ראה עני		ראה..חרפתנו
לילה	יעיב ----	חשך ----	יועם ----	נהפכה ---
שרתי מדינות	השליך משמים	יהפך ----	תשתפכנה	כסף מחיר\\
	תפארת ישראל	גבר ----	היקרים ---	זכר -----
	לא־זכר	------	------	
	הדם־רגלו	------	אני־קדש --	
	עברתו	עברתו ---	------	
היה ל	------	------	------	היה ל ---
כאלמנה	------	------	------	כאלמנות--
אין מנחם	לא חמל ---	לא־אור ---	------	אין אב --
גלתה יהודה	גדע...ישראל־	²שבר עצמותי	לנבלי־חדש־	
	ימינו	ידו-----		

Lam. 1 4–6	Lam. 2 4–6	Lam. 3 10–18	Lam. 4 4–6	Lam. 5 4–6
שעריה שממין	ויחרג...עין –	שמני שמם –	נשמו חוצות־	(3)יתומים –
דרכי ציון	אהל...ציון –	³שחם תפלתי		
איביה שלו	דרך...כאויב	דרך קשתו –	שאלו..אין.. –	לשבע ----
		השביעני	עוללים ---	מימינו ---
עולליה	------	------	דבק לשון –	
		הרוני לענה	למעדנים\\ –	
וחיא מר־לח	תאניה ואניה	מרורים לענה	חבקו אשפתות	לחם ----
		⁴חצץ...אפר –	האמנים..תולע	
ויצא מציון..	שכח...בציון–	נשיתי טובה		
שריה	מלך וכהן--	אבד נצחי –		
רודף	------	------	------	נרדפנו ---

Lam. 1 7–9	Lam. 2 7–9	Lam. 3 19–27	Lam. 4 7–9	Lam. 5 7–9
חטא חטאה	------	------	(6)עון+הטאת	(7) חטא+עון
⁵זכרה	------	זכר עני... –	שחור< שלג ..	עון..סבלנו
ביד־צר	ביד־אויב-	..עלי נפשי –	אין מידם	...אין מידם
⁶ירושלם	בת־ציון ---			
	חשב יהוה...	חסדי יהוה־\\		לחמנו / חרב / רעב
			חרב / רעב	
אין מנחם	אין...תורה –	טוב...חדרשנו	טובים ----	
⁷ראה יהוה..	------	לתשועת יהוה		בנפשנו ---
		לנמש		

10–11	10–11	28–33	10–11	10–11
במקדשה	בת-ציון/קריה	-----------	בציון----	בציון ----
	ישבו ...ידמו	9ישב /וידם	...לברות---	דלעפות רעב
	עפר	בעפר פיהו -	כלה ---	נשים בציון
כלו	כלו	-----------	נשים רחמניות	
	בתולת ירושלם	-----------	שפך-----	
	נשפך	-----------	שבר בת-עמי	
	שבר בת-עמי	-----------	כלה יהוה...	
		לא זנח לעולם	תאכל/ילדיהן	רעב -----
השיב נפש	בעטף עולל.	בעטף עולל.		נשים...ענו
7ראה יהוה...	-----------	לא ענה מלבו	-----------	

12–13	12–13	34–39	12–13	12–13
ראו	-----------	אדני לא ראה		10זקנים לא
אם...כמכאבי	בעטף עולל..	מתחת רגליו -	9בשערי----	דקנים משער
לרגלי	-----------	לעוה/להטות	בשערי ----	שרים נחלו-
		מח-יתאונן	ירושלם ---	
	(3x)מח	-----------	נביה/כהניה	ציון-----
	ירושלם	11מי ...אמר -		
	נביאיך(14)	יתאונן-----		
12שממה	שברך-----			
כל-היום דוה	מי ירפא-לך-	אדם חי \\ -		

14–16	14–16	40–48	14–16	13–17
על..על-צוארי	-----------	-----------	-----------	..טחון נשאו
השכיל	-----------	-----------	-----------	כשלו----
	נביאיה חזו..	-----------	15נעו עורים	
	נחפשה דרכינו לא-גלו..עונך			
פשעי	עונך----	משענו ----	בלא יוכלו -	
גת דרך/לשבר	-----------	הרגת----	-----------	בחורים---
בחורי	-----------	-----------	-----------	
בת-יהודה	בת-ירושלם--	-----------		
	ספקו/ שרקו..	סחי ומאוס-	סורו טמא--	
	שאמרו	-----------	אמרו-----	
	משוש	-----------	-----------	משוש ----
אויב	(16) אויביך	(46) איבינו	ענינו(17) --	חשכו עינינו
עין ירדה מים	-----------	מים תרד עיני	-----------	נפלה עטרת-
על-אלה....	בלענו	השאת והשבר	-----------	על-אלה... --
	-----------	על-שבר ---		

17—19	17—19	49—57	17—19	17—19
אין מנחם	על...עינך --	עיני ..הפגות	עודינה ..עין	חשכו עינינו
צוה יהוה	[14]צוה(יהוה)	עד...יהוה --	עזרתנו הבל	
	[15]בצע אמרתו	------	------	ציון ----
ציון/ירושלם	------	עירי ----	------	
צריו	אויב/צריך -	איבי ----	------	דוה לבנו--
	צעק לבם	------	------	אחה יהוה -
צדיק..יהוה.	[16]צעק...אדני	------	------	
הלכו בשבי	------	------	מלכת/נלכד-	
		צוד צדוני	צדו צעדינו-	
		כצפור	מנשרי שמים	
\\קראתי	שפכי..לבך..	קראתי שמך-	------	אחה יהוה -
		קרבת	קרב קצנו\\-	
בקשו אכל....	עטף/רעב --	נגזרתי ---	כי-בא קצינו	
...את-נפשם	על-נפש ---	נפשי/חיי --		

20—22	20—22	55—66	20—22	19/20—22
ראה יהוה	ראה יהוה--	ראימה יהוה	[17]משיח יהוה	אחה יהוה -
	הביטה	הביטה---		
שכלה-חרב	נפלו בחרב-	גאלת חיי\\-	נחיה----	
בבית כמות	יהרג במקדש			
	כהו ונביא	------	משיח יהוה -	
שמעו	------	שמעת ---		
אני	------	אני---		
אין מנחם	לא חמלת --	חרפתם----		
אין מנחם	------	[18]יהוה ---	------	----
ששו	------	אני מנגינם	שישי ושמחי	
יום-קראת	ביום אפך--	כל-היום--	------	לארץ ימים
עולל למו	------	חתן להם --	פקד עונך--	
על כל-פשעי	------	כמעשה ידיהם	עונך/חטאתיך	קצפת
	אפך	------	------	קצפת
רבות	אף-יהוה	באף ----	------	
לבי דוי	רבתי----	מגנת-לב--	כוס ---	כי-אם

1   Because of limitations of layout it is not possible to give a full account of all interconnections. See also the similarities marked with an asterisk. The density of connections is even far greater if content is taken into account. In this survey we started from the canticles of the first song and looked in the other songs at the strophes at about the same level.

2   Cf. page 369 n.19.

3   Of course Zion is the place of prayer, cf. Ps. 65:1−2.

4   Kraus and Boecker in their exegesis e.g. choose the methapor of the Lord as landlord, who gives his guest stones instead of food. However, if one takes into account the connection between 3:16 and 4:5bB, a far more likely and realistic exegesis will be achieved. So one can think of the גבר as one of the precious and luxurious children of Zion, who now, thirsty, eats plants for their bitter juice and hungry, grovels on the dunghills of the city, hoping for pieces of food in the ashes. But when found, in the mouth it appears to be cinders.

5   Also with מרוד and עני.

6   From the connection between 1:8 and 2:8,9 one gets the impression that with her falling walls Jerusalem's nakedness becomes visible.

7   These calls in prayer are placed on the same level as the confessions of confidence at the end of both cantos of Lam. 3.

8   The same is said in 1:1aA of Jerusalem. Here in 3:8 it could be meant as an appeal to the population.

9   On the basis of the coherence in this string we assume the expression 'in the gates' to have a double meaning. Not only the conquering of Jerusalem, but also afterwards the administration of justice was taken over. Cf. Gen. 22:17; 24:60; Deut. 21:19; 22:15.

10   The elders, in their function to take care of legal affairs, are meant.

11   The coherence in this string is of great importance for exegesis. The difficult text 3:37 becomes clear if one takes into account the sins of prophets and priests. They were the spokesmen of YHWH. However, they did not speak good things, but bad things which YHWH did not command, such as false visions, (2:14) and they command the bloodshed of the righteous (4:13).

12   Cf. Jer. 4:6−8; 8:21; 14:17.

13   Cf. Isa. 29:9−10.

14   This interconnection gives no reason to change the places of the strophes. The different alphabetical order in Lam 1 and 2−4 seems to be original.

15   Cf. Isa. 30:7ff. and page 346.

16   A confession of guilt is a form of an argument in prayer for YHWH's intervention.

17   At first sight the mention of the King seems to be somewhat strange compared to the explicit prayer to YHWH which is found in the other four songs at this level. However, in the theology of Zion the king represents YHWH and so he is of help for the poor, cf. Ps 72. So the mention of the king is consistent with the concept of prayer in the other four songs. But

the king has been captured. For that reason the poets, logically, did not include a plea to the king as representative of YHWH. Here they can only express their disappointment in losing their משיח יהוה, while in Lam. 2 on the same level the exhortation to pray to YHWH is expanded cf. 2:18f. As a result in Lam. 4:21f. the confidence of the punishment of the Edomites appears a little bit abrupt. Besides, the fulfilment of Israel's penance for their sins does not mean necessarily a restoration of the old relation between YHWH and his people. Cf. אולי in 3:29 and כי־אם in 5:22 and why should they pray?

18   Cf. the reversal of thought in 3:21.

THE RECONSTRUCTION OF THE ARAMAIC ORIGINAL

OF THE LORD'S PRAYER

Johannes C. de Moor

1. Introduction

In this contribution the author wants to show how the insights gained in our work on the structural analysis of Hebrew poetry can be made profitable to New Testament studies as well. Although there is a consensus nowadays that it is important to reckon with the Semitic background of the New Testament, the lack of agreement between the scholars who tried their hand in the reconstruction of the presumed Hebrew or Aramaic original inspired a justifiable amount of scepticism. Clearly what is needed here is a more systematic approach in which every step can be accounted for.

Even with regard to the language Jesus spoke, opinions widely diverge. Of course nobody doubts that Jesus will have spoken the Palestinian—Aramaic vernacular in daily life. But did he also use this ordinary language in his teaching? It might well be that just like the learned scribes of his time he chose Hebrew when he was discoursing upon religious matters. Even though very few people still spoke and understood Hebrew, several religious works from the intertestamental period were written in Hebrew. The Qumran sect used it extensively, and the oral Torah which was later on to be codified in the Mishnah was formulated in Hebrew, including the sayings of the rabbis who were contemporaries of Jesus. It appears that Jesus himself was able to read Hebrew (Lk. 4:16—20).[1] According to Papias[2] (ca. 130) the gospel of Matthew would have been

---

1   It is certain that Jesus was not reading from an Aramaic translation, because reading from a Targum scroll was forbidden in the synagogue. Cf. jMeg., IV.1; Midr. Tanchuma on Gen. 18:17.
2   K. Bihlmeyer, *Die apostolischen Väter*, Teil 1 (Tübingen, 1970[8]) 136 (II.16): 'Ματθαῖος μὲν οὖν 'Εβραΐδι διαλέκτῳ τὰ λόγια συνετάξατο, ἡρμήνευσεν δ' αὐτά, ὡς ἦν δυνατὸς ἕκαστος.', i.e., 'Matthew compiled the *logia* in the Hebrew language, and every one translated them as best he could.'

written in Hebrew. It is possible, however, that he made the same error as the author of the gospel of John who calls 'Hebrew' what is evidently good Aramaic (Jn. 5:2; 19:13,17).

Yet it makes a lot of difference whether one addresses a circle of learned initiates, as was the case among the sectarians of Qumran and among the Tannaim (the teachers of the Mishnah), or whether one has a much larger audience in mind. When Jesus was arguing with the Pharisees and the scribes, he usually addressed the listening crowd over their heads. It is unlikely that he was using Hebrew then, because ordinary people would not have understood him. The Aramaic vernacular, however, would not have been suitable either, not only because it would have been offensive to the rabbis, but because Jesus was constantly explaining the Holy Scriptures. Here no other languages than Hebrew or *literary* Aramaic, the language of at least part of the Old Testament *and* the language of the Targums, would have been acceptable among pious Jews at the beginning of our era. Literary Aramaic was a good compromise when preaching to both commoners and scholars. It was apparently understood well enough to serve as the language in which the Bible was orally translated in the synagogue. Several prestigious religious works of the intertestamental period had been written in Literary Aramaic.[3]

If Jesus and his first disciples were engaged in a conscious process of establishing a tradition of teaching, whether oral, or written, or both,[4] Literary Aramaic was a natural choice. It is abundantly clear by now that at the beginning of our era it still held the position of a *lingua franca*, to some extent comparable to that of Standard Arabic in our days. In spite of the many local Arabic dialects, literary Standard Arabic is used as the language of books, newspapers, and official documents. It is understood fairly well throughout the Islamic world.

Can it be ascertained whether Jesus may have entertained literary aspirations and, more in particular, whether he was making use of literary Aramaic? The first question must be

---

3   See now especially K. Beyer, *Die aramäischen Texte vom Toten Meer* (Göttingen, 1984).

4   Cf. B. Gerhardsson, *Memory and Manuscript*. Oral Tradition and Written Transmission in Rabbinic Judaism and Early Christianity (Uppsala, 1961).

answered in the affirmative for the simple reason that Jesus often phrased his sayings, parables and sermons as poetry. Even the Greek text easily betrays the typical characteristics of the Semitic verse.[5] People regarded Jesus as an Old Testament prophet,[6] and for that reason alone it is likely that he spoke in the manner of the prophets, i.e. in poetry.

The second question is a more difficult one. However, in the recent past it has become increasingly clear that many sayings of Jesus can only be understood on the basis of the Targums.[7] For those who are not acquainted with this kind of research, we give a few examples. In Mk. 4:12 Jesus quotes Isa. 6:10 not after the Hebrew or the Septuagint, but after the Targum: καὶ ἀφεθῇ αὐτοῖς 'and be forgiven.' The Hebrew text has ורפא לו 'and be healed.' What is important in this case is the circumstance that the targumic וישתביק להון 'and be forgiven' is a *typical* rendering. In the Targum, the vehicle of a metaphor is usually replaced by its tenor.

The 26th edition of Nestle–Aland does not register an Old Testament source for the saying 'Be merciful, even as your Father is merciful' (Lk. 6:36). It is, however, clearly inspired by Targum Pseudo–Jonathan to Lev. 22:28: עמי בני ישראל 'My היכמא דאבונן רחמן בשמיא כן תהוון רחמנין בארעא people, children of Israel, even as our Father is merciful in heaven, be merciful on earth.'[8]

Similarly, Mt. 23:10 'Neither be called masters, for you have one master, the Christ' has its Old Testament roots not in the Hebrew text, but in the Targum to Ezek. 34:23 and 37:24. Here the Hebrew רעה אחד 'one shepherd' is rendered by the non–metaphorical חד פרנס 'one master.'

Now if Jesus needed a language suited for the making of

---

5   This was recognized long ago; see e.g., C.F. Burney, *The Poetry of our Lord* (Oxford, 1925).

6   Mk. 6:15; 8:28; Mt. 11:9; 14:5; 16:14; 21:11,46; etc.

7   See P. Billerbeck–H.L. Strack, *Kommentar zum Neuen Testament aus Talmud und Midrasch*, Bd.5: Rabbinischer Index, ed. J. Jeremias, K. Adolph (München, 1956) 58–60; M. McNamara, *Targum and Testament. Aramaic Paraphrases of the Hebrew Bible: A Light on the New Testament* (Grand Rapids, 1972); R. Le Déaut, *The Message of the New Testament and the Aramaic Bible (Targum)* (Rome, 1982).

8   See also jBer., V.3,9c; jMeg., IV.9,75c.

verses *and* for explaining the Holy Scriptures to common people, the obvious choice was Literary Aramaic. This was the language in which the Bible was understood by people who were no longer fluent in Hebrew. As we know from the Targum manuscripts found in Qumran, the Targums of that time were of the fairly literal type and were written in Literary Aramaic. Obviously Jesus made use of them. If we try to reconstruct his words, our best chances lie with Literary Aramaic.

2   Method

A sound method is an absolute prerequisite for a more or less reliable reconstruction of the Aramaic original. It is a fortuitous circumstance that, just like the sect of Qumran, Jesus and his early disciples were composing their message in the form of mosaics of quotations from the Old Testament. It is very hard for us, slaves of the printed word, to fully realize how often even simple phrases in the New Testament are derived from the Old Testament. We no longer know the Scriptures by heart, let alone the Aramaic translations. So we tend to overlook parallels,[9] and have to compensate for this shortcoming in the method we employ.

2.1 Selection of Passage

Since our best chances lie with the reconstruction of poetry, we select a promising passage on the basis of the presence of parallelism. Not only the *internal* parallelism that binds the cola of a verse together, but also *external* parallelism connecting the larger units (strophes, canticles) should be taken into consideration.[10] The latter is especially important when we are

---

9   We agree with Gerhardsson: 1961:325 who writes: 'Few factors have been so important for the formation of the gospel tradition as the belief that the words and works of Christ were the fulfilment of the Law and the prophets. If we modern scholars knew our Old Testament (the Hebrew text, the Aramaic targum and the Greek translations) off by heart, we would be able to see this in the correct perspective.'
10   See for an explanation of these concepts, M.C.A. Korpel–J.C. de Moor, 'Fundamentals of Ugaritic and Hebrew Poetry', *UF* 18 (1986) 173–212, reprinted in this volume.

dealing with *narrative* poetry, a form of poetry that often went unrecognized even in the study of the Old Testament itself.[11]

2.2 *From Greek to Hebrew*

Assuming that the original Aramaic wording was patterned after its Old Testament model, it is legitimate to consult the concordance of Hatch and Redpath to the Septuagint to find possible Hebrew equivalents as a first step.[12] Of course concordances to intertestamental works in Greek of which we know the Hebrew original, e.g. the Wisdom of Ben Sira, may be consulted as additional tools.

From the Hebrew possibilities we find, we select the most promising ones in the following way. It has been observed that all North—West Semitic poetry made use of a stock of standardized parallel pairs.[13] So it is legitimate to assume that from the often bewildering number of possibilities mentioned by Hatch and Redpath only those pairs or triplets are valid that occur in poetical parallelism in the Old Testament itself. Previously it was a tremendous task to establish such a fact and understandably enough scholars did not always bother to check this for every word of their reconstruction. The lists of word—pairs that have now been published are most welcome new tools, but they are still incomplete. Therefore our team makes use of a computer program that enables us to scan the entire Old Testament for matching pairs in a matter of seconds. Of course this lends an entirely new dimension to this branch of research.

---

11   Cf. J.C. de Moor, 'The Poetry of the Book of Ruth, I', *Or* 53 (1984) 262—283; II, *Or* 55 (1986) 2—32; also the contributions of R. de Hoop and W.Th. Koopmans, elsewhere in this volume.
12   E. Hatch—H.A. Redpath, *A Concordance to the Septuagint*, 2 vols. (Oxford, 1897, repr. Graz, 1954).
13   See e.g., M. Dahood, 'Ugaritic Parallel Pairs', in: L.R. Fisher (ed.), *Ras Shamra Parallels*, vol. 1 (Roma, 1972) 71—382; vol.2 (Roma, 1975) 1—39; Y. Avishur, *Stylistic Studies of Word—Pairs in Biblical and Ancient Semitic Literatures* (Neukirchen—Vluyn, 1984).

2.3 From Greek to Aramaic

Sometimes it is possible to locate an Aramaic parallel directly on the basis of previous research. Strack—Billerbeck[14] and the *Theologisches Wörterbuch zum Neuen Testament* edited by Kittel—Friedrich are our most precious tools in this respect. Of course it is also possible to consult the arguments brought forward by others who have tried to reconstruct the Aramaic original.[15] However, it is our experience that work with the great concordances on Rabbinic literature that appeared *after* Strack—Billerbeck and the *ThWNT* often yields a number of parallels not mentioned in earlier studies.[16]

2.4 From Hebrew to Aramaic

This is the most safe way back. Having located the places in the Hebrew Old Testament where the word—pair(s) do occur (2.2), we consult the Targums to find out what the corresponding Aramaic might be. However, this would not lead us to the places where the Targums have an extra or a different rendering. Therefore we also make use of a computerized Hebrew—Aramaic concordance to the Targums that is being prepared by a team of our university at Kampen. In some cases it may be helpful to consult the Syro—Palestinian and Syriac translations of the New Testament

---

14 P. Billerbeck—H.L. Strack, *Kommentar zum Neuen Testament aus Talmud und Midrasch,* 5 Bde (München, 1974[6]).

15 Most of these are cited by G. Schwarz, *'Und Jesus sprach.'* Untersuchungen zur aramäischen Urgestalt der Worte Jesu (Stuttgart, 1987[2]), with a Greek—Aramaic glossary 338–352. Unfortunately the author himself feels free to tamper with the transmitted text and exhibits a rather imperfect grasp of the laws of ancient Semitic poetry. As a result, his reconstructions are often far from convincing.

16 See e.g., C.J. Kasowski, אוצר לשון התלמוד (Jerusalem, 1954–1977); C.Y. Kasovsky, אוצר לשון המשנה (Jerusalem, 1956–1960); B. Kosovsky, אוצר לשון התנאים *Mechilta* (Jerusalem, 1965–1966); *Siphra* (Jerusalem, 1967–1969); *Siphre* (Jerusalem, 1970–1974); M. Kosowsky, אוצר לשון תלמוד ירושלמי (Jerusalem, 1979–); E.G. Clarke, *Targum Pseudo—Jonathan of the Pentateuch:* Text and Concordance (Hoboken, 1984).

to get an impression of what the Aramaic text might have looked like.

On the basis of the New Testament texts we have attempted to reconstruct up to this time, we have found strong evidence in favour of our working hypothesis that Jesus made use of Literary Aramaic in his teaching. We have found no convincing arguments in favour of an original wording in either Hebrew or the Palestinian—Aramaic vernacular.

2.5 *Structural Analysis*

Finally we establish the structure of the Aramaic poem along the lines developed by the Kampen School and explained in other contributions to this volume. Questions that arise at this stage are the inner structural coherence of the piece and eventually what can be gained for its exegesis by viewing it from the perspective of the presumed Aramaic original.

3 The Lord's Prayer

As an example of the approach we are advocating here, we shall attempt a reconstruction of the Lord's Prayer. Of course we are by no means the first to do so,[17] but we found it an interesting example because we think it illustrates how a number of fundamental problems can be resolved by making use of our method. Among these often hotly debated topics are the question which version of the Lord's Prayer is the more original, the longer one transmitted in Mt. 6:9—13, or the shorter one in Lk. 11:2—4, and the question whether the original was in Hebrew or Aramaic.[18]

---

17 The Aramaic translations are summed up by Schwarz: 1987:209—226, to which C.C. Torrey, *The Translations Made from the Original Aramaic Gospels* (New York, 1912) 309—317 must be added. See also A. Finkel, 'The Prayer of Jesus in Matthew', in: A. Finkel (ed.), *Standing before God. Studies ... in Honor of J.M. Oesterreicher*, New York 1981, 131—170.

18 For a discussion of the various Hebrew translations see J. Carmignac, 'Hebrew Translations of the Lord's Prayer: An Historical Survey', in: G.A. Tuttle (ed.), *Biblical and Near Eastern Studies*. Essays in Honor of W.S. LaSor (Grand Rapids, 1978) 18—79. Carmignac himself fervently defends an Hebrew original in: *Recherches sur le 'Notre Père'* (Paris, 1969).

3.1 The Invocation

Mt. 6:9   Πάτερ ἡμῶν ὁ ἐν τοῖς οὐρανοῖς
Lk. 11:2   Πάτερ

Neither the vocative אב (*'āb*)[19] nor the vocative אבינו (*'ābīnū*) is attested in the O.T. However, it might well be that, against the Massoretic accents, people understood אבינו in 1 Chron. 29:10 as a vocative in apposition to the entire construct chain יהוה אלהי ישראל, 'O LORD, God of Israel, our Father.' This is attractive in so far as it is the invocation of a prayer of *David* and because the doxology that is preserved in part of the tradition of the Lord's Prayer is clearly inspired by the next verse, 1 Chron. 29:11. So the more elaborate versions of the Prayer would have derived both the beginning and end from the same source. The Hebrew אבינו corresponds to אבונן (*'ᵃbūnan*) in the late Targum to Chronicles, but in the earlier Literary Aramaic the form was doubtlessly אבונא (*'ᵃbūnā*).

According to many scholars the shorter invocation in the gospel of Luke would be more authentic. It would point to an *Aramaic* original because in Mk. 14:36 Jesus himself invokes God in this manner: ἀββα ὁ πατήρ, which in Luke corresponds to a simple πάτερ (Lk. 22:42). In its Aramaic form this invocation found general acceptance in the early church (Rom. 8:15; Gal. 4:6). However, does this mean that the longer form would have been impossible in Aramaic? It is easy to prove that the formula 'your/our Father who is in heaven' was just as well used by the early church[20] and the Rabbis of the Tannaitic period.[21] As we saw above, Targum Pseudo—Jonathan on Lev. 22:28 contains almost the complete formula in Aramaic: אבונן בשמיא... The addition 'who is in heaven' rests on the common

---

19   In the transliterations of Hebrew and Aramaic we omit the spirantization of consonants for the sake of clarity.
20   Cf. Mk. 11:25; Mt. 5:16; 7:11; see also Mt. 5:48; 6:14, 26, 32; 15:13; 18:35; 23:9. The authenticity of the longer formula is vindicated by J. Jeremias, *Abba*. Studien zur neutestamentlichen Theologie und Zeitgeschichte (Göttingen, 1966) 41; Carmignac: 1969:74—77; W. Marchel, *Abba, Père: La prière du Christ et des chrétiens* (Rome, 1971) 179—197.
21   mSotah IX.14: אבינו שבשמים.

The Lord's Prayer 405

Israelite concept that God dwells in heaven.[22] The relative form of the phrase occurs in Ex. 20:4 and Deut. 5:8, אשר בשמים. If the Lord's Prayer was worded in Hebrew, one might wonder whether the relative particle should not be ש in Middle Hebrew. However, two manuscripts from Qumran prove that at least there the relative form was still אשר בשמים.[23] So in Hebrew the formula requires two words, whereas the Targum on Ex. 20:4 and Deut. 5:8 has one word: דבשמיא (*d*ᵉ*bišmayyā*). So the original invocation would have run אבינו אשר בשמים ('*ābīnū* *ʾašer baššāmayim*) in Hebrew. In Literary Aramaic:

אבונא דבשמיא   '*ᵃbūnā dᵉbišmayyā*.

3.2 The First Entreaty

Mt. 6:9 ἁγιασθήτω τὸ ὄνομά σου
Lk. 11:2 Idem

Nobody will doubt that τὸ ὄνομά σου corresponds to Hebrew שמך (*šimkā*, or in pausal form, *šᵉmēkā*) or Aramaic שמך (*šᵉmāk*). The verb ἁγιάζειν is the Septuagint's common rendering of Hebrew קדש (*qiddēš*). In Isa. 29:23 and Ezek. 36:23 this verb occurs with the 'name' of God as its object.[24] However, nowhere in the Old Testament is this construction transposed into a passive form.[25]

In this case the *Qaddīš*, a very old *Aramaic* doxology,[26] offers a solution. Here the entreaty has the following form: יתגדל ויתקדש שמה רבא (*yitgaddal yitqaddaš šᵉmēh rabbā*),[27] 'Let his great name be exalted, be hallowed.' The interesting circumstance is that in the same context the prayer speaks of

---

22 Cf. Deut.3:24; Josh. 2:11; Ps. 115:3; 2 Chron. 6:14; 20:6.
23 1QH, fragm. 1, line 1; 11QBer, fragm. 1, line 7.
24 See also Ps. 111:9.
25 A close, but not an exact match is the niphal in Lev. 22:23. Contrary to what is sometimes asserted, the hitpaal of קדש never has a passive meaning, not even in Ezek. 38:23 and 1 Chron. 31:18.
26 The antiquity of the prayer is recognized by all authorities. It is already cited by R. Jose b. Halaphta (ca. 150) in bBer., 3a; see also Siphre to Deut., §306 (132b).
27 Cited after *Siach Jitschak*, ed. J. Dasberg (Amsterdam, 1979²) 72.

the will of God ('according to his will', Aram. כרעותה,
kir'ūtēh), and his kingdom (or kingship, Aram. מלכותה,
malkūtēh), just like the Lord's Prayer.
So the first entreaty decidedly speaks in favour of an
Aramaic original. Of the Aramaic of the *Qaddīš* the well−known
specialist on Jewish liturgy Elbogen writes:

'The Kaddish was not written in the vernacular tongue, but
in the peculiar artificial idiom which was spoken in the
schools and which we know from the officially accepted
Targums.'[28]

So the nearest parallel to the Lord's Prayer in the Jewish world
furnishes us with an argument for our hypothesis that Jesus
taught his disciples in Literary Aramaic. Since also the
Syro−Palestinian version and the Peshitta translate ἁγιασθήτο
by יתקדש, it would seem justified to reconstruct the first
entreaty as follows:

יתקדש שמך   *yitqaddaš š^emāk.*

3.3 The Second Entreaty

Mt. 6:10 ἐλθέτο ἡ βασιλεία σου
Lk. 11:2 Idem

Judging from the LXX, both ἔρχεσθαι and βασιλεία can be
translated in many different ways.[29] However, a computer scan
indicates that only in Mic. 4:8 are the verbs בוא (*bō*) and אתה
(*'ātā*) 'to come' combined with ממלכת (*mamlèkèt*) 'kingdom' or
'kingship'. The Targum has a clearly eschatological rendering
here and translates both בוא and אתה by the Aramaic אתא
(*'ªtā*), ממלכת by the Aramaic equivalent מלכותא (*malkūtā*).
The *Qaddīš* prayer also has מלכותה 'his kingdom'. So we may
assume that if the original was in Hebrew, it would have read
תבא ממלכתך (*tābō' mamlakt^ekā*), whereas an Aramaic version,

---

28 I. Elbogen, *Der jüdische Gottesdienst in seiner geschichtlichen
Entwicklung* (Frankfurt/Main, 1931) 94: 'Das Kaddisch ist nicht in einem
Dialekt der Volkssprache abgefaßt, sondern in jenem künstlichen Idiom, das
in den Schulen gesprochen wurde, das aus den offiziell anerkannten
Targumim ... bekannt ist.'
29 Cf. Hatch−Redpath: 1954²:192, 548.

which is again favoured by the available evidence, would certainly be

תיתי מלכותך   *tētē malkūtāk.*

3.4 The Third Entreaty

Mt. 6:10   γενηθήτω τὸ θέλημά σου,
       ὡς ἐν οὐρανῷ καὶ ἐπὶ γῆς
Lk. 11:2   Missing in the best manuscripts.

As far as the will of God is concerned, the LXX allows us to choose between רצון (*rāṣōn*) and חפץ (*ḥēpeṣ*). In Hebrew both words are constructed with עשה (*'āśā*), one of the possible equivalents of γίνεσθαι in the LXX.[30] In Ps. 40:9; 103:21; 143:10 we have עשה רצון, in 1 Kgs. 5:22f.; Isa. 46:10; 48:14; 58:13 עשה חפץ. Because in Qumran the former expression is attested several times, a Hebrew original would probably have been יעשה רצונך (*yē'āśèh r°ṣōnkā*). In this connection it is important to note that Rabbi Eliezer once advised his disciples to pray עשה רצונך בשמים (*'a śē r°ṣōnkā baššāmayim*) 'Do thy will in heaven'[31] and that the complete phrase עשות רצונו בשמים ובארץ (*'a śōt r°ṣōnō baššāmayim ūbā'āreṣ*) is attested in the early Tannaitic midrash *Siphre* on Deut. 33:5.[32] In Ps. 40:9 the Targum translates לעשות רצונך 'to do thy will' as למעבד רעותך (*l°ma'a bad r°'ūtāk*). See also the Targum on 1 Sam. 2:35, Ps. 103:21 and 143:10. However, the Targum translates עשה חפץ in Isa. 46:10 and 48:14 in exactly the same way. Because also the *Qaddīš* speaks of רעותה (*r°'ūtēh*) 'his will' in the introductory lines, it would seem certain that the Aramaic was in any case

תתעביד רעותך   *tit'a bēd r°'ūtāk.*[33]

The addition ὡς ἐν οὐρανῷ καὶ ἐπὶ γῆς would seem to be

---

30   Hatch—Redpath: 1954[2], sub voce, no. 31a and 31b. See Gen. 42:25; 44:2; 50:20, etc.

31   bBer., 29b.

32   Ed. L. Finkelstein (Berlin, 1939, repr. New York, 1969) 403.

33   Schwarz: 1987[2]:224 proposes מהא צבותך, which must be rejected if only because the Aramaic צבותא is never used to describe the will of God.

inspired by Ps. 135:6 כל אשר חפץ יהוה עשה / עשה בשמים ובארץ
'Whatever the LORD pleases / he does in heaven and on earth'
(see also Ps. 115:3).[34] The Targum renders this כל די יתרעי
ובארעא בשמיא עבד יהוה (*kol dī yitrᵉʿē yhwh ᵃbad bišmayyā
ūbᵉʾarʿā*), so the Targum uses the verb רעא (*rᵉʿā*) here from
which our רעותא (*rᵉʿūtā*) was derived.

The most difficult problem is posed by the particle ὡς. It is
lacking in the Septuagint of Ps. 115:3 and 135:6. For that
reason it must be assumed to represent an original element of
the Prayer, even though it is omitted in the Codex Bezae.
Theodotion's translation of Dan. 11:29 would seem to suggest
that ὡς ... καὶ represents the Hebrew sequence כ ... כ (*kᵉ ... kᵉ*).
However, this is impossible because the preposition ב (*bᵉ*)
required by the following ἐν would drop out after כ.[35] Only in
relatively rare cases Hebrew combines כ and ב.[36] Clearly the
scribes preferred to replace this by the combination כאשר ב
(*ka'ᵃšèr bᵉ*).[37] So if the Prayer would have been phrased in
Hebrew, the most likely reconstruction would be כאשר בשמים
(*ka'ᵃšèr baššamayim*), which is indeed the choice of J.
Carmignac in his latest Hebrew translation of the Lord's
Prayer.[38] The corresponding Aramaic would be כד בשמיא (*kad
bišmayyā*) or, if כד were connected with בשמיא, כדבשמיא
(*kidbišmayyā*).[39]

Because καὶ never represents Hebrew כן (*kēn*) 'so' in the
Septuagint,[40] constructions like כן ... כאשר, or the
corresponding Aramaic constructions,[41] can also be ruled out.
With Carmignac, the Hebrew may be reconstructed as כאשר
בשמים ובארץ (*ka'ᵃšèr baššāmayim ūbā'ārès*), the Aramaic
would be כד בשמיא ובארעא (*kad bišmayyā ūbᵉʾarʿā*), or rather

---

34   See also 1 Chron. 29:11 בשמים ובארץ לך יהוה הממלכה.

35   E. König, *Historisch-kritisches Lehrgebäude der hebräischen Sprache*,
Bd.2,2: Syntax (Leipzig, 1897) §319 d–f.

36   Judg. 20:32; 1 Sam. 14:14; 1 Kgs. 13:6; Isa. 1:26; Jer. 33:7, 11.

37   Cf. Gen. 41:21; Ex. 5:13; Josh. 8:5f.; 14:11; 1 Sam. 2:35; 2 Sam. 7:10.

38   Carmignac: 1978:63.

39   Compare Targum Onkelos to Gen. 41:21 כידבקדמיתא.

40   E.C. Dos Santos, *An Expanded Hebrew Index for the Hatch–Redpath
Concordance of the Septuagint* (Jerusalem, n.d.) 92f.

41   Cf. Targum Ps. Jonathan Lev. 22:21 ... בשמיא כן ... היכמא
כמא ... בשמיא כן ... בארעא or jBer., 9c and jMeg., 75c בארעה.

כדבשמיא ובארעא   *kidbišmayyā ūbᵉ'arᶜā.*

3.5 The Fourth Entreaty

Mt. 6:11 τὸν ἄρτον ἡμῶν τὸν ἐπιούσιον δὸς ἡμῖν σήμερον
Lk. 11:3 τὸν ἄρτον ἡμῶν τὸν ἐπιούσιον δίδου ἡμῖν τὸ
          καθ' ἡμέραν

There is no reason to assume a different 'Vorlage' for the two
versions. Rather the slight differences can be accounted for, by
assuming a translation from what was basically the same
Semitic text.

In the LXX ἄρτος usually corresponds to Hebrew לחם
(*lèhèm*). 'Our bread' is לחמנו (*lahmēnū*), which the Targum
paraphrases as סעדנא (*saᶜdanna*) 'our sustenance' in Num. 14:9,
and as דילנא (*dīlannā*) 'our own (food)' in Isa. 4:1. The most
literal rendering, however, is found in Josh. 9:12, לחמנא
(*lahmannā*) 'our bread', which we prefer for the obvious reason
that a literal rendering of the Lord's own Prayer is likely.

The Greek τὸν ἐπιούσιον is a notorious *crux interpretum*. It
does not occur in the LXX. However, in Prov. 27:1 we
encounter ἡ ἐπιοῦσα (from the verb ἐπιέναι). It is the translation
of a simple Hebrew יום (*yom*) in the sense of 'the next day'. In
a much cited papyrus ἐπιουσι[ον] might mean 'daily (ration)'.[42]
With God as the subject, 'to give bread to' occurs fairly often
in the O.T.[43] The Targums usually render this by יהב לחמא ל
(*yᵉhab lahma lᵉ*), and the imperative 'give us' doubtlessly
corresponds to הב לנא (*hab lannā*).[44] The combination of יום
and נתן לחם occurs in Ex. 16, the chapter about the gift of
the manna. Especially interesting is Ex. 16:4 where we
encounter the expression לחם מן-השמים ... דבר-יום ביומו
(*lèhèm min haššamayim ... dᵉbar yōm bᵉyōmō*). The expression
דבר-יום ביומו occurs twelve times in the O.T. and invariably
the Targums translate פתגם יום ביומיה (*pitgām yōm
bᵉyōmēh*). This is also the case in Jer. 52:34 where the
expression designates the daily ration of king Jehoiachin.

---

42 See W. Foerster, *ThWNT*, Bd.2, 587–595; Jeremias: 1966:165–167;
E.M. Yamauchi, *WThJ* 28 (1965–66) 145–156; S.A. Falcone, in: *Fs.
J.P. Brennan*, Rochester 1976, 36–59.
43 Gen. 28:20; Ex. 16:8, 15, 29; Isa. 30:20, 23; Ps. 136:25; 146:7.
44 Targum Onkelos to Num. 11:13.

If we follow the order of the Greek words exactly, we obtain the following verse in Aramaic:

לחמנא פתגם יום   *lahmannā pitgām yōm*
הב לנא ביומיה   *hab lannā beyōmēh.*

3.6 *The Fifth Entreaty*

Mt. 6:12 καὶ ἄφες ἡμῖν τα ὀφειλήματα ἡμῶν,
          ὡς καὶ ἡμεῖς ἀφήκαμεν τοῖς ὀφειλέταις ἡμῶν
Lk. 11:4 καὶ ἄφες ἡμῖν τὰς ἁμαρτίας ἡμῶν,
          καὶ γὰρ αὐτοὶ ἀφίομεν παντὶ ὀφείλοντι ἡμῖν

Because both Matthew and Luke have essentially the same text, it is unlikely that the second colon of this verse would be a later addition, as asserted by Schwarz.[45]

Only in 1 Macc. 15:8 the Septuagint does use ἀφιέναι with the object ὀφείλημα. The latter always denotes a financial debt in the Septuagint (Deut. 24:10; 1 Ezra 3:20; 1 Macc. 15:8). However, if this were the meaning in the Fifth Entreaty, it would be very hard to understand how Luke could interpret it as ἁμαρτία. The latter represents many different Hebrew terms in the Septuagint.[46] What we are looking for is an original Semitic word satisfying the following conditions:

1) The doubtlessly more difficult text of Matthew justifies the assumption that the word allowed a verbal play between 'debt/sin' and 'debtor/sinner'.

2) Because of the rather specific meaning of the Greek ὀφείλημα, the term should in any case also denote a financial debt.

As far as we know, no Hebrew word meets both these conditions. Only several derivatives of the *Aramaic* root חוב (*ḥōb*)[47] would seem ideal candidates. In Targum Pseudo—Jonathan to Deut. 19:15 חובא (*ḥōbā*) occurs with the meaning of 'financial debt.' Yet it is the normal Aramaic equivalent of Hebrew words for 'sin' in the Targumim.

45 Schwarz: 1987²:218f.
46 Hatch—Redpath: 1954²:62.
47 Cf. *HAL*, 283.

Also, the feminine חובתא (ḥôbtā) may mean 'debt' as well as
'sin.'[48] The Aramaic חיבא (ḥayyābā) means both 'debtor' and
'sinner.'[49] Again this argues decidedly in favour of an Aramaic
original of the Lord's Prayer.
    As a matter of fact, חובא also occurs with the verb 'forgive'.
In Targum Onkelos to Ex. 34:9 we find ותשבוק לחובנא
(wᵉtišbōq ᵉḥōbannā) 'and forgive us our sins' (Hebr. וסלחת
לעוננו, wᵉsālaḥtā laᵃwōnēnū). Also in Num. 14:19 God is the
subject: שבוק ... לחובי עמא (šᵉbōq ... ᵉḥōbē ʿammā, Hebr.
סלח־נא לעון העם, dᵉlaḥ-nā laᵃwōn hāʿām). And the same verb
may occur with a human being as its subject: Gen. 50:17 שבוק
לחובי ... (šᵉbōq ... ᵉḥōbē ᵃhāk, Hebr. אחיך שא נא פשע אחיך,
šā nā pèšaʿ 'aḥèkā). There is no need to add an independent
personal pronoun to emphasize 'we', because in a Semitic
language the same effect is achieved by repetition. So we get:

ושבוק לנא לחובנא   ūšᵉbōq lannā ᵉḥōbannā
כד נשבוק לחיבנא   kad nišbōq ᵉḥayyābannā.

The play on words is immediately clear.

3.7 The Sixth and Seventh Entreaties

Mt. 6:13   καὶ μὴ εἰσενέγκῃς ἡμᾶς εἰς πειρασμόν
           ἀλλὰ ῥῦσαι ἡμᾶς ἀπὸ τοῦ πονηροῦ
Lk. 11:4   καὶ μὴ εἰσενέγκῃς ἡμᾶς εἰς πειρασμόν

εἰσφέρειν occurs in Dan. 6:18 (19) as the translation of the
Aramaic עלל (ᵃlal) and, very often, as the translation of the
Hebrew בוא (bō) in the hiphil.[50] πειρασμός is מסה (massā) or
עניך ('inyān) in Hebrew.[51] A combination of two of these words
is not found in the Old Testament however.
    In this situation a passage in the Babylonian Talmud proved
to be helpful: ואל תביאני ... לא לידי נסיון (wᵉ'al tᵉbī'ēnī ...

---

48   J. Levy, Wörterbuch über die Targumim, Bd. 1 (repr. Köln, 1959) 241.
49   Levy: 1959²:252f.; DISO, 83.
50   Hatch–Redpath: 1954²:415.
51   Hatch–Redpath: 1954²:1116.

lō līdē nissāyōn) 'do not bring me ... in the power of temptation.'[52]

The phrase occurs two times on fol. 60b[53] and in the second instance there follows: וחצילני מפגע רע (*wᵉtaṣṣīlēnī mippèga' ra'*) 'and deliver me from misfortune.' All this is Hebrew. It is not difficult, however, to translate the phrase into Aramaic, because in bBer., 56b we find ולא אחית לידי נסיון 'and you will not come in the power of temptation.' The second person of the imperfect aphel of the verb אתא (*'ᵃtā*) is תיתי (*taytē*), with a first person plural suffix תיתינא (*taytēnā*). But in view of the parallel verses of the Lord's Prayer it is more attractive to choose the imperative: איתינא (*'aytēnā*).[54] As in the Targums, the negation becomes לא (*lā*) where Hebrew would use אל (*'al*). The Hebrew נסיון (*nissāyōn*) becomes נסיונא (*nisyōnā*) in Aramaic, but since the article is missing in the Greek text we prefer the absolute state in this case: נסיון (*nisyōn*).

With regard to the Seventh Entreaty it has always been a disputed matter whether ὁ πονηρός should be translated 'the evil' or 'the evil one.'[55] It is likely that this ambiguity was already present in the original text. This would indeed be the case if this original was a *Semitic* text, regardless whether it was in Hebrew (הרע, *hāra'*) or in Aramaic (בישא, *bīšā*).

Of the Hebrew verbs the Septuagint translates with ῥύεσθαι[56], it is legitimate to choose נצל (*nāṣal*) in the hiphil on the strength of the parallel from bBer., 60b quoted above. The prayer הצילני (*haṣṣīlēnī*) 'deliver me!' is very frequent in the Book of Psalms. Also הצילנו (*haṣṣīlēnū*) 'deliver us!' is attested.[57] In Judg. 10:15 and 1 Sam. 12:10 the Targum has שיזבנא (*šēzēbnā*), in Ps. 79:9 ופרוק יתנא (*ūpᵉrōq yātnā*) and in 1 Chron. 16:35 ושיזב יתנא (*wᵉšēzēb yātnā*).

If we now look for the combination of נצל with רע in the

---

52 bBer., 60b.
53 Compare also bSanh., 107a: אל יביא אדם עצמו לידי נסיון 'Man should not bring himself in the power of temptation.'
54 See Dalman, *Grammatik*, 391.
55 Most modern, annotated translations offer both, e.g. the 1952 revision of the Revised Standard Version (New York, 1952) 761. Cf. G. Harder, *ThWNT*, Bd. 6, 560f.
56 Hatch–Redpath: 1954²:1254.
57 Judg. 10:15; 1 Sam. 12:10; Ps. 79:9; 1 Chron. 16:35.

Old Testament, we find Hab. 2:9 להנצל מכף־רע (*hinnāṣēl mikkap—rāʿ) 'to deliver oneself from the power of evil,' and Jer. 15:21 והצלתיך מיד רעים (wᵉhiṣṣaltīkā miyyad rāʿīm) 'and he will deliver you from the power of the evil ones.' In the first text the Targum has לאשתיזבא מיד ביש (*ʾištēzābā miyyad bīš), in the second one ואשיזבינך מיד מבאשין (waᵃšēzbīnāk miyyad mabᵃʾšīn). The expression שיזב מן יד (šēzēb min yad) also occurs in Biblical Aramaic (Dan. 3:15, 17; 6:28) and so it would seem justified to render ῥῦσαι ἡμᾶς by שיזבנא (šēzēbnā).[58]

The next question is whether we should translate ἀπό by מיד (miyyad) 'from the power of' or simply by מן (min) 'from'. Again the close parallel in bBer., 60b proves to be helpful − it has a simple מן. It may be added that the Septuagint gives a literal translation of מכף in Hab. 2:9 and of מיד in Jer. 15:21, so one would expect the same in the Greek version of the Lord's Prayer if the original would have had either of these. So our reconstruction may be מבישא (mibbīšā).

Finally we have to look after ἀλλά. Clearly this has a strong adversative flavour here. In such cases it corresponds to Hebrew כי אם (kī ʾim) in the Septuagint. The Targum has אלהין (ᵃlāhēn) then.[59] So the full reconstruction becomes:

ולא איתינא לנסיון   wᵉlā ʾaytēnā lᵉnisyōn
אלהין שיזבנא מבישא   ᵃlāhēn šēzēbnā mibbīšā.

3.8 The Doxology

The doxology is missing in Luke and in the best manuscripts of Matthew. Commonly it is assumed to be a free liturgical addition, based on 1 Chron. 29:11, and added not later than the second century.[60] This consensus is based on the Didache,

58 In the Targum on the Book of Psalms נצל hiph. is often rendered by פצא מן, but this is clearly a later development which was inspired by the Hebrew text of Ps. 144:7, 11.
59 Gen. 15:4; Deut. 12:14; Josh. 17:3; 1 Kgs. 8:19, etc.
60 See e.g., J. Schmid, Das Evangelium nach Matthäus (Regensburg, 1965⁵) 134; D. Hill, The Gospel of Matthew (London, 1972) 139; W. Grundmann, Das Evangelium nach Matthäus (Berlin, 1975⁴) 197ff.

composed at the end of the first century. It contains the Lord's
Prayer according to the version of Matthew, plus the following
doxology: ὅτι σοῦ ἐστιν ἡ δύναμις καὶ ἡ δόξα εἰς τοὺς αἰῶνας 'for
thine is the power and the glory, for ever.'[61] Other prayers in
the *Didache* appear to have similar endings: σοὶ ἡ δόξα εἰς τοὺς
αἰῶνας 'thine is the glory, for ever',[62] ὅτι σοῦ ἐστιν ἡ δύναμις καὶ
ἡ δόξα εἰς τοὺς αἰῶνας 'for thine is the power and the glory, for
ever,'[63] ὅτι σοῦ ἐστιν ἡ δόξα καὶ ἡ δύναμις διὰ 'Ιησοῦ Χριστοῦ εἰς
τοὺς αἰῶνας 'for thine is the glory and the power through Jesus
Christ, for ever'.[64] It is very unlikely that in the days of Jesus
Jews would have omitted such a doxology at the end of their
prayers. As a matter of fact, the New Testament preserves
several very similar doxologies.[65] Apparently it was customary to
end a prayer with a more or less freely formulated doxology.
Therefore it is far from peculiar that we find the doxology of
the Lord's Prayer in different forms. As we have demonstrated
over the past few years, it was a *characteristic* of this kind of
poetry to be expanded or contracted according to the mood and
skill of the singers.[66] It would be wrong, therefore, to exclude
the expanded form of the prayer from our attempts to
reconstruct its original wording.

As we saw earlier, the invocation as transmitted by Matthew
was probably inspired by 1 Chron. 29:10. The doxology was
clearly inspired by the following verses. ὅτι σοῦ ἐστιν ἡ βασιλεία
echoes 1 Chron. 29:11 לך ... הממלכה (*l*kā ... *hammamlākā*)
which the Targum renders as follows: דילך ... מלכותא (*dīlāk
... malkūtā*). From innumerable other cases we know for certain
that ὅτι is the translation of Hebrew כי (*kī*), Aramaic ארי
('*ªrī*). καὶ ἡ δύναμις would seem to have been derived from 1
Chron. 29:11 והגבורה (*w*hagg*ᵉbūrā*), Targum וגבורתא

---

61 *Didache*, VIII.2, Bihlmeyer: 1970³:5f.
62 *Didache*, IX.2,3; X.2,4, Bihlmeyer: 1970³:5f.
63 *Didache*, X.5.
64 *Didache*, IX.4,5.
65 Cf. Rom. 11:36; 16:27; Gal. 4:18; 1 Tim. 6:16; 2 Tim. 4:18; Hebr.
13:21; 1 Pet. 5:11; 2 Pet. 3:18; Jud. 25; Rev. 1:6.
66 J.C. de Moor, 'The Art of Versification in Ugarit and Israel, I' in: Y.
Avishur, J. Blau (eds.), *Studies in Bible and the Ancient Near East Presented
to S.E. Loewenstamm* (Jerusalem, 1978) 119–139; M.C.A. Korpel–J.C. de
Moor, *UF* 18 (1986) 174, 178–181, 187–189, 197f., 212.

(*ūg^ebūrtā*). Finally, καὶ ἡ δόξα might reflect 1 Chron. 29:11 והכבוד (*w^ehakkābōd*), Targum ויקרא (*wīqārā*), but since δόξα is also a rendering of Hebrew הוד (*hōd*)[67], we might just as well assume that the source was 1 Chron. 29:11 וההוד (*w^ehahōd*) which the Targum likewise renders by יקרא (*y^eqārā*).

It may be observed in this connection that the Targum of Ps. 145:11 exhorts the pious to bless the LORD in speaking of 'the glory of thy kingdom' (Aramaic איקר מלכותך, *'īqār malkūtāk*) and of 'thy power' (Aramaic גבורתך, *g^ebūrātāk*). The next verses of the Targum speak of the 'everlasting kingdom' (Aramaic מלכותא דכל עלמיא, *malkūtā d^ekāl 'āl^emayyā*). Here we have all the ingredients for the full doxology as transmitted in many manuscripts of Matthew.[68]

The closing words εἰς τοὺς αἰῶνας are evidently the Greek rendering of Hebrew לעולמים (*l^eōlāmīm*, Ps. 77:8), Aramaic לעלמין (*l^eāl^emīn*, Dan. 2:4, 44). So the full doxology ran like this in Aramaic:

ארי דילך מלכותא   *'^arī dīlāk malkūtā*
וגבורתא ויקרא לעלמין   *ūg^ebūrtā wīqārā l^eāl^emīn.*

3.9 Structural Analysis

When we tried to reconstruct the original text of the Lord's Prayer by applying a relatively objective method, we came across several cases where a Literary Aramaic original proved to be more likely than a Hebrew one (3.2, 3.3, 3.6). If we now enter upon the structural analysis of the poem, a simple comparison on the level of the cola shows that the Aramaic version is indeed preferable:[69]

HEBREW		ARAMAIC
אבינו אשר בשמים	1	אבונא דבשמיא
יקדש (?) שמך	2	יתקדש שמך
תבוא ממלכתך	3	תיתי מלכותך

---

67 Hatch–Redpath: 1954²:341.
68 See also the Targum on Ps. 72:19 and 104:31.
69 We start with the full form of the prayer and will return to the shorter versions later on.

תחעביד רעותך	4	יעשה רצונך
כדבשמיא ובארעא	5	כאשר בשמים ובארץ
לחמנא פתגם יום	6	לחמנו דבר יום
הב לנא בימיה	7	תן לנו ביומו
ושבוק לנא לחובנא	8	וסלח לנו לפשעינו (?)
כד נשבוק לחיבנא	9	כאשר נסלח לפושעינו (?)
ולא איתינא לנסיון	10	ואל תביאנו לנסיון
אלהין שידבנא מבישא	11	כי אם תצילנו מרע
ארי דילך מלכותא	12	כי לך הממלכה
וגבורתא ויקרא לעלמין	13	והגבורה וההוד לעולמים

In the Aramaic form, the first five cola all have two words, while in the Hebrew version the first and fifth cola take *three* words if we accept the philologically most plausible reconstruction. The cola 6–13 all have three words in Aramaic, but in Hebrew colon 11 takes *four* words. So, in addition to the earlier arguments in favour of a Literary Aramaic original we can now point to the greater structural regularity of the Aramaic version. Therefore we shall confine ourselves in the sequel to the Aramaic.

3.9.1 Division into Verses

In accordance with the principles laid down in our publications on the structural analysis of North–West Semitic poetry, we now set out to establish the division into verses.

Verse 1

אבונא דבשמיא
יתקדש שמך

One might debate whether or not to join colon 3 with 1–2. However, the formal parallelism between the feminine תיחי and תחעביד as compared to the masculine יתקדש in colon 2, as well as the rhyme between מלכותך and רעותך, argue against this possibility.

The cola of the first verse are interconnected by a chiastic internal parallelism: 'our Father' is 'your name', and the place where it is 'hallowed' is the 'heaven' where the angels continually call out 'holy!' (Isa. 6:3). Moreover, we note the assonance between שמיא and שמך.[70]

Verse 2

תיתי מלכותך
תתעביד רעותך
כדבשמיא ובארעא

As we saw, cola 3 and 4 are connected by formal parallelism and rhyme. Because colon 5 cannot exist independently, we have a tricolon here. This is confirmed by the internal parallelism between 'thy kingdom/kingship' and 'heaven and earth', cf. Ps. 103:19.

Verse 3

לחמנא פתגם יום
הב לנא בימיה

It is self—evident that these cola belong together. The internal parallelism between the personal suffixes –נא and יום//ימיה corroborate this conclusion. The latter is a convincing example of a typically Semitic poetic figure of style called the break—up of stereotyped phrases.[71]

Verse 4

ושבוק לנא לחובנא
כד נשבוק לחיבנא

The play on words and the internal parallelism render any other division unlikely.

Verse 5

ולא איתינא לנסיון
אלהין שידבנא מבישא

Apparently 'lead us not into' balances 'deliver us', just as 'temptation' is parallel to 'evil' or 'the evil one'.

---

70 The two are often found in collocation, see Gen. 11:4; Deut. 7:24; 9:14; 29:19; 2 Kgs. 14:27; Ps. 8:2; 124:8; 148:13.

71 Cf. W.G.E. Watson, *Classical Hebrew Poetry* (Sheffield, 1984) 328–332.

Doxology

אלי דילך מלכותא
וגבורתא ויקרא לעלמין

There is no way to separate the cola of this verse, the internal
parallelism of which is guaranteed by 1 Chron. 29:11.

3.9.2 Division into Strophes

Strophe 1

אבונא דבשמיא
יתקדש שמך
תיתי מלכותך
תעביד רעותך
כדבשמיא ובארעא

Separation up: vocative; jussive.
Separation down: jussives; tricolon.
External parallelism: an impressive inclusion embraces the
strophe, דבשמיא//דבשמיא; the inner three cola all end in ך—.

Strophe 2

לחמנא פתגם יום
הב לנא ביומיה
ושבוק לנא לחובנא
כד נשבוק לחיבנא

Separation up: emphatic position of the object; imperative;
tautological parallelism.
Separation down: imperative; כד; tautological parallelism.
External parallelism: although the following cola also contain
נא—, the concatenation between לנא//לנא is doubtlessly
stronger. Moreover, the separating force of the imperatives
cannot be glossed over.

Strophe 3

ולא איתינא לנסיון
אלהין שידבנא מבישא
[אלי דילך מלכותא
וגבורתא ויקרא לעלמין]

Separation up: imperatives; אלהין.

Separation down: idem if no doxology followed; otherwise: ‏ארי;‏
‏לעלמין‏.

External parallelism: It appears that the final strophe was deliberately left incomplete to accommodate the optional doxology. Note that *any* affirmation of the supreme power of God in the closing verse automatically creates an antithetical external parallelism with the Seventh Entreaty.

3.9.3 The Canticle

It appears that the Prayer was composed as a canticle of three strophes of two verses each. If the expected doxology was added, a powerful inclusion embraced the whole poem. The hallowing of the name of God (‏יתקדש שמך‏) balances the eternal glory of God (‏ויקרא לעלמין‏), in accordance with the Targum on Ps. 72:19 ‏בריך שום יקריה לעלמא‏ (*berēk šum yeqārēh leʿālemā*) 'bless the name of his glory forever.' The link between the first strophe and the optional doxology is further underlined by the suffix ‏ך–‏ (*−āk*, not in the second strophe) and the responsion ‏מלכותא‏ (*malkūtā*, 'kingdom/kingship').

However, since the doxology was optional, the first verse of the final strophe had to provide an independent connection with the first strophe. This was achieved by a second inclusion involving the personal pronoun ‏נא–‏ and the verb ‏אתא‏, and the implicit parallelism between 'thy will be done' and 'deliver us from evil/the evil one.'

We finally point to a few responsions between the three strophes: ‏כד//כד‏, ‏חובא//נסיונא‏, ‏חיבא//בישא‏.

3.9.4 Luke's Version

We now print the long version of Matthew and the shorter one of Luke side by side:

Matthew	Luke
‏אבונא דבשמיא‏	‏אבא‏
‏יתקדש שמך‏	‏יתקדש שמך‏
‏תיתי מלכותך‏	‏תיתי מלכותך‏
‏תתעביד רעותך‏	
‏כדבשמיא ובארעא‏	
‏לחמנא פתגם יום‏	‏לחמנא פתגם יום‏

הב לנא בימיה
ושבוק לנא לחובנא
כד נשבוק לכל־חיבנא

ולא איתינא לנסיון

הב לנא בימיה
ושבוק לנא לחובנא
כד נשבוק לחיבנא

ולא איתינא לנסיון
אלהין שידבנא מבישא

It appears that nothing essential is missing from Luke's version, because every *verse* is represented in it. A colon of two words is reduced to a colon of one word, a tricolon is replaced by a unicolon, colon 9 is slightly expanded by כל, and finally, a bicolon is contracted to a unicolon. *All this is perfectly normal in North-West Semitic poetry!*[72] This kind of poetry was a breathing universe, it left those who recited it a certain freedom to elaborate or to compress the text according to the occasion. Although the fuller text as transmitted by Matthew is doubtlessly a better balanced whole, it was not an outrageous act to recite the Lord's Prayer in a somewhat shortened version. Actually it is almost certain that Luke was acquainted with the fuller version too, because in Luke 22:42 he makes Jesus pray πάτερ ... πλὴν μὴ τὸ θέλημά μου ἀλλὰ τὸ σὸν γινέσθω which clearly recalls the Third Entreaty.

The structural analysis teaches us to abandon our typically Western, historicizing approach which asks first of all which of the two versions is the original. Usually we follow this up with a fleetingly motivated verdict to the effect that of course the shortest is the older version.[73] Could this be a relic of evolutionism? We have to learn that in the Oriental world

---

72 For examples of cola reduced to only one word, see Korpel—De Moor: 1986:177f., and for expansion and contraction on the level of the verse, 186—189.

73 A typical case is Jeremias: 1966:158. Others, however, defend the authenticity of the Matthaean version, e.g. Carmignac: 1969:18—28.

Equally wrong is the statement that variations in the transmission of the Prayer 'tell strongly against any theory that the words of Jesus were committed to memory and that there was any great concern to preserve them exactly.' (F.W. Beare, *The Gospel According to Matthew* [Oxford, 1981] 171). Preserving them in *this* fluctuating form was exactly the way in which poetry was transmitted, orally or in written form, in the ancient Oriental world.

poems could exist in several, non—competing forms. It is the wrong question, then, to ask which one is the most 'original'. What is true of the *Qaddīš*, is true of the Lord's Prayer: 'originally the prayer may have had no fixed wording, it may have depended on the preference of the speaker.'[74]

4. Conclusions

We have attempted to reconstruct the Aramaic original of the Lord's Prayer with the help of the techniques developed in connection with our work on the structural analysis of North—West Semitic poetry. In the end a poem of singular, well—balanced beauty emerged:

אבונא דבשמיא	*'ᵃbūnā dᵉbišmayyā*
יתקדש שמך	*yitqaddaš šᵉmāk*
חיתי מלכותך	*tētē malkūtāk*
תחעביד רעותך	*tit'ᵃbēd rᵉ'ūtāk*
כדבשמיא ובארעא	*kidbišmayyā ūbᵉ'ar'ā*
לחמנא פחגם יום	*laḥmannā pitgām yōm*
הב לנא בימיה	*hab lannā bᵉyōmēh*
ושבוק לנא לחובנא	*ūšᵉbōq lannā lᵉḥōbannā*
כד נשבוק לחיבנא	*kad nišbōq lᵉḥayyābannā*
ולא איתינא לנסיון	*wᵉlā 'aytēnā bᵉnisyōn*
אלהין שידבנא מבישא	*'ᵃlāhēn šēzēbnā mibbīšā*
[ארי דילך מלכותא	*'ᵃrī dīlāk malkūtā*
וגבורתא ויקרא לעלמן	*ūgᵉbūrtā wiqārā lᵉ'ālᵉmīn]*

Rhythm, rhyme, inclusions and responsions are as skillfully applied as in the most beautiful Psalms of Israel. In the course of our investigation it became increasingly clear that this is what must be expected from a teacher who was so completely versed in the Holy Scriptures. It appeared that to a much larger extent than is generally realized Jesus was borrowing from the Old Testament, often quoting from the Aramaic Targums.

---

74 Elbogen: 1931:93: 'Das Gebet mag anfangs keinen bestimmten Wortlaut gehabt, vom Belieben des Redners abgehangen haben.'

For the exegete it would seem important to take this Semitic background into account. Only a few interesting facts may be pointed out here. The Aramaic wording of the Third Entreaty proves that γενηθήτω may never be interpreted as justifying a wait—and—see attitude. The will of God has to be *done*. The Aramaic of the Fourth Entreaty appears to contain an explicit reference to the manna—tradition[75] which helps us to see that Mt. 6:11 does not contradict Mt. 6:25—34 in any sense. And only an Aramaic original can explain the ambiguity of the Fifth Entreaty in a satisfactory way.

Also the structure that emerged must be taken into account. It is not without theological consequence that the coming of the kingdom appears to be on a par with the doing of the will of God (one verse!). It is indicative of the kind of sin Jesus had in mind when He combined the Fourth and the Fifth Entreaty in one strophe. The concatenation between חובנא and נסיון proves that the responsibility for the outcome of the temptation cannot be laid with God, whereas the concatenation in the same verses between חייבנא and בישא provides us with an argument in favour of a personal interpretation of the latter.

It is clear that our approach may yield interesting results. One of our findings was that we Westerners are apt to frame the wrong questions. The differences between Matthew's and Luke's version of the Lord's Prayer, for example, can be fully explained on the basis of the characteristics of Semitic poetry. They do not warrant any conclusion as to which one was the more authentic.

---

75 Cf. Th.C. de Kruijff—M.J.H.M. Poorthuis, *Abinoe*. Onze Vader (Utrecht, 1985) 95—101.

Contributors

1. HARM W.M. VAN GROL is Lecturer, Department of Biblical Studies, Catholic Theological University, Amsterdam, The Netherlands.

2. RAYMOND DE HOOP is Student Assistent, Semitic Section of the Department of Biblical Studies, Theological University of the Reformed Churches in the Netherlands, Kampen, The Netherlands.

3. WILLIAM T. KOOPMANS is Research Student, Semitic Section of the Department of Biblical Studies, Theological University of the Reformed Churches in the Netherlands, Kampen, The Netherlands.

4. MARJO C.A. KORPEL is Research Student, Semitic Section of the Department of Biblical Studies, Theological University of the Reformed Churches in the Netherlands, Kampen, The Netherlands.

5. PIETER VAN DER LUGT is Teacher of Religion, College Oostergo, Dokkum, The Netherlands.

6. WILLEM VAN DER MEER is Lecturer, Old Testament Section of the Department of Biblical Studies, Theological University of the Reformed Churches in the Netherlands, Kampen, The Netherlands.

7. JOHANNES C. DE MOOR is Professor of Semitic Languages, Semitic Section of the Department of Biblical Studies, Theological University of the Reformed Churches in the Netherlands, Kampen, The Netherlands.

8. JOHAN RENKEMA is Lecturer, Old Testament Section of the Department of Biblical Studies, Theological University of the Reformed Churches in the Netherlands, Kampen, The Netherlands.

9. KLAAS SPRONK is Minister, Reformed Church, Monnickendam, The Netherlands.

JOURNAL FOR THE STUDY OF THE OLD TESTAMENT
Supplement Series